FOR Dummies

BESTSELLING
BOOK SERIES

Insurance For Dumm...

W9-CBD-830

Reference Card

Buying home insurance

- Insure your building for 100 percent of its replacement cost new.

- Buy a Home Replacement Guarantee that will rebuild your home even if the cost exceeds your insurance amount. Buy the guarantee without a percentage cap.

- Buy liability limits equal to your automobile liability limits.

- Choose the highest deductible for which you receive adequate premium credit.

- Buy Special Perils coverage for building and contents, which covers any accidental loss not caused by a handful of excluded causes.

- Don't just accept the standard coverages for detached structures and contents that come with the policy. Make sure that the dollar amount for those two coverages will fully replace what you own.

- Read your policy. Discover what kinds of personal property are excluded or subject to dollar limits. Buy the optional coverages you need to eliminate those restrictions.

- Read your policy liability exclusions. Buy the optional coverages you need to cover anything you're doing that is excluded.

- If you bring work home, buy the optional business liability endorsement to cover injuries to the occasional delivery person.

- If you have a home-based business, don't buy the restrictive home-business endorsement. Buy the Businessowner's policy instead.

- Buy the optional sewer backup coverage. And buy federal flood insurance if you're exposed to flood or heavy rains.

- Buy earthquake coverage if the risk exists in your area.

Buying car insurance

- Buy more liability insurance than you think you need — $500,000 or more. It's cheap stuff.

- Choose the highest deductibles you can comfortably afford for damage to your car. This strategy not only saves you money but also helps to pay for the extra liability coverage you need.

- Buy Uninsured and Underinsured Motorist coverage in limits equal to your liability coverage limits.

Buying umbrella insurance

- Strongly consider an umbrella liability policy of $1 million or more that will protect you against major lawsuits.

- Make sure that this is a true umbrella policy that will cover many lawsuits not covered by your automobile or Homeowner's liability coverage.

- Consider $1 million more coverage than you think you need. The annual cost is typically $50 to $75.

- Do not automatically buy the umbrella policy offered by your automobile and Homeowner's insurance company. It often doesn't cover all the activities of your personal life.

- Always read the exclusions before buying. Don't buy an umbrella policy that excludes anything you're doing now or may do in the future.

Insurance For Dummies®

Quick Reference Card

Buying life insurance

- ✔ Cover both incomes.
- ✔ Cover the homemaker for the amount you would need to hire an outside service to perform the homemaker's functions.
- ✔ Buy coverage of at least 6 to 7.5 times your current income. Add to this amount for final expenses and college costs.
- ✔ Buy term life insurance, in most cases. Buy cash-value permanent insurance only if your need is permanent.

Insuring townhouses and condominiums

- ✔ Read your association agreement, called the *Declarations*. Find out how much of the interior of your building unit you're responsible for insuring. Then buy the optional building coverage you need. And buy the optional Special Perils endorsement for the broadest possible coverage.
- ✔ Buy $25,000 to $50,000 optional Loss Assessment coverage that can cover some of the assessments made by the association for uninsured insurance claims.

Buying health insurance

- ✔ Buy at least a $2 million policy limit, covering all illnesses and injuries. Avoid dread disease insurance.
- ✔ Don't buy any policy with internal limits such as limits on room and board charges, surgical charges, and so on.
- ✔ Avoid plans that deny you the freedom to choose your own doctor for serious medical conditions.
- ✔ If your group coverage at work is weak, consider buying a major medical policy with high deductibles to plug the gaps.
- ✔ If you're medically uninsurable, see if your state offers guaranteed health insurance.
- ✔ If you're eligible for Medicare, absolutely buy a Medicare supplement policy. Make sure that it covers at least 80 percent of the gap between what doctors actually charge and what Medicare allows.

Buying disability insurance

- ✔ If you're married, cover both incomes.
- ✔ Consider a supplemental policy if your group disability coverage at work is weak. Many are.
- ✔ Buy coverage, ideally, to age 65, or for no less than five years if you're financially strapped.
- ✔ Choose the longest waiting period you can comfortably afford before coverage begins, such as 60 or 90 days. You'll save 30 percent or more on your costs.
- ✔ If you expect your future income to increase, add a Guaranteed Purchase Option that guarantees your right to buy more coverage in the future, regardless of your health.
- ✔ Don't buy a policy that won't cover partial disabilities on a long-term basis.

The IDG Books Worldwide logo is a registered trademark under exclusive license to IDG Books Worldwide, Inc., from International Data Group, Inc. The For Dummies logo and For Dummies are trademarks of IDG Books Worldwide, Inc. All other trademarks are the property of their respective owners.

For Dummies™: Bestselling Book Series for Beginners

Praise for Insurance For Dummies

"If you ever vacation with family, friends, or have ever rented a vehicle, you will want to read this book. Jack has done it again. He's given us the information in plain and easy-to-read-and-understand language. You will do yourself a great favor and enjoy peace of mind by taking the right actions, before you experience any financial loss or ruin. Jack has included many great tips and techniques. You can't afford not to read this now!"

> — Carmen Ellingson, Education Director, Minnesota Society of CPCU

"A great book for people who want to know what their insurance needs really are and that they are properly covered. Every chapter is loaded with tips that can save buyers money, both when purchasing insurance and at claim time. Jack's insights concerning rental-car insurance alone are more than worth the book's purchase price. *Insurance For Dummies* is written in jargon-free language by a professional whom I have known and admired for years — both for his command of insurance and for his deep concern for his clients."

> — George Williams, CPCU, Editor in Chief, *American Agent & Broker* magazine

"While I understand the importance of having insurance coverage, reading an insurance policy makes my eyes glaze over. Jack Hungelmann actually manages to make insurance interesting. He uses stories (some of them scary) and anecdotes to show risks and then clearly explains the best and most cost-effective way to protect yourself. This book is like having your own personal risk manager."

> — Janet Eian, Chief Administrative Officer, Endurant Business Solutions.

"Jack has been my go-to guy for many years whenever I've had insurance questions or concerns. I rely on his depth of knowledge in every facet of insurance culled from his many years in the business. I know he will have the answers and will suggest what's best for me."

> — Peter D. Zimpelman, P. J. Zimpelman & Sons, Inc.

"I have the privilege and advantage of having Jack Hungelmann as my insurance consultant. For all of you who do not have this advantage, I highly recommend *Insurance For Dummies* as an excellent way to prevent anguish and save money."

— Ron Strand, Owner, Resource Connections

"*Insurance For Dummies* is an indispensable walk through the insurance maze with your hand firmly in Jack's. The book's true value lies in the prevention of heartaches, headaches, and potential insolvency. *Insurance For Dummies* is your lifeline to risk management — business and personal — clearly identifying potential problems, and providing straightforward solutions for your peace of mind. An invaluable resource."

— Danelle J. Wolf, Owner, Wolf's Wayzata Pharmacy, Inc.

"This book is a gem of a resource. The author is knowledgeable about insurance. He gives you the nitty-gritty information you need and never have before purchasing insurance. Follow his advice and you'll end up buying protection as opposed to paying premiums. The next time you make that call to ask if your insurance covers a loss, the answer will be *yes* rather than the customary *no!*"

— Alice Randall, School System Administrator

"If you think insurance is about as confusing as it gets, but consider it a necessary evil, then this is the book to read. Jack Hungelmann has the ability to transform insurance jargon into clear, concise, and readable terms. Jack has examined special circumstances surrounding different types of coverage, for example, condominium/townhouse insurance, car rentals, and automobiles provided by an employer. Jack clarifies the unusual and sometimes confusing areas of insurance that the average consumer does not understand. He definitely knows this business, especially after twenty-five years of consumer consulting and advice."

— Angela Althoff, Staffing Avenue Partners, Inc.

TM

References for the Rest of Us!™

BESTSELLING BOOK SERIES

Do you find that traditional reference books are overloaded with technical details and advice you'll never use? Do you postpone important life decisions because you just don't want to deal with them? Then our *...For Dummies*® business and general reference book series is for you.

...For Dummies business and general reference books are written for those frustrated and hard-working souls who know they aren't dumb, but find that the myriad of personal and business issues and the accompanying horror stories make them feel helpless. *...For Dummies* books use a lighthearted approach, a down-to-earth style, and even cartoons and humorous icons to dispel fears and build confidence. Lighthearted but not lightweight, these books are perfect survival guides to solve your everyday personal and business problems.

Already, millions of satisfied readers agree. They have made *...For Dummies* the #1 introductory level computer book series and a best-selling business book series. They have written asking for more. So, if you're looking for the best and easiest way to learn about business and other general reference topics, look to *...For Dummies* to give you a helping hand.

1/99

Insurance
FOR
DUMMIES®

by Jack Hungelmann

IDG Books Worldwide, Inc.
An International Data Group Company

Foster City, CA ◆ Chicago, IL ◆ Indianapolis, IN ◆ New York, NY

Insurance For Dummies®

Published by
IDG Books Worldwide, Inc.
An International Data Group Company
919 E. Hillsdale Blvd.
Suite 300
Foster City, CA 94404
www.idgbooks.com (IDG Books Worldwide Web site)
www.dummies.com (Dummies Press Web site)

Library of Congress Control Number: 00-109283

ISBN: 0-7645-5294-5

Printed in the United States of America

10 9 8 7 6 5 4 3 2 1

1O/RQ/QR/QR/IN

Distributed in the United States by IDG Books Worldwide, Inc.

Distributed by CDG Books Canada Inc. for Canada; by Transworld Publishers Limited in the United Kingdom; by IDG Norge Books for Norway; by IDG Sweden Books for Sweden; by IDG Books Australia Publishing Corporation Pty. Ltd. for Australia and New Zealand; by TransQuest Publishers Pte Ltd. for Singapore, Malaysia, Thailand, Indonesia, and Hong Kong; by Gotop Information Inc. for Taiwan; by ICG Muse, Inc. for Japan; by Intersoft for South Africa; by Eyrolles for France; by International Thomson Publishing for Germany, Austria and Switzerland; by Distribuidora Cuspide for Argentina; by LR International for Brazil; by Galileo Libros for Chile; by Ediciones ZETA S.C.R. Ltda. for Peru; by WS Computer Publishing Corporation, Inc., for the Philippines; by Contemporanea de Ediciones for Venezuela; by Express Computer Distributors for the Caribbean and West Indies; by Micronesia Media Distributor, Inc. for Micronesia; by Chips Computadoras S.A. de C.V. for Mexico; by Editorial Norma de Panama S.A. for Panama; by American Bookshops for Finland.

For general information on IDG Books Worldwide's books in the U.S., please call our Consumer Customer Service department at 800-762-2974. For reseller information, including discounts and premium sales, please call our Reseller Customer Service department at 800-434-3422.

For information on where to purchase IDG Books Worldwide's books outside the U.S., please contact our International Sales department at 317-572-3993 or fax 317-572-4002.

For consumer information on foreign language translations, please contact our Customer Service department at 1-800-434-3422, fax 317-572-4002, or e-mail rights@idgbooks.com.

For information on licensing foreign or domestic rights, please phone +1-650-653-7098.

For sales inquiries and special prices for bulk quantities, please contact our Order Services department at 800-434-4322 or write to the address above.

For information on using IDG Books Worldwide's books in the classroom or for ordering examination copies, please contact our Educational Sales department at 800-434-2086 or fax 317-572-4005.

For press review copies, author interviews, or other publicity information, please contact our Public Relations department at 650-653-7000 or fax 650-653-7500.

For authorization to photocopy items for corporate, personal, or educational use, please contact Copyright Clearance Center, 222 Rosewood Drive, Danvers, MA 01923, or fax 978-750-4470.

About the Author

Jack Hungelmann's policy knowledge, problem solving expertise, and coverage analysis was gained through more than 25 years in the insurance business as a claims adjuster, agent, and consultant. He has advised individuals and commercial enterprises on their insurance needs and has earned several distinguished designations. Among these are the Certified Insurance Counselor (CIC), the Chartered Property and Casualty Underwriter (CPCU), and the Associate in Reinsurance (ARe).

Jack graduated from the University of Minnesota in 1969 and has taught professional continuing education classes for both the CPCU and CIC societies. He has been published numerous times in *American Agent & Broker* magazine. He lives in Chanhassen, Minnesota with his wife Judy.

ABOUT IDG BOOKS WORLDWIDE

Welcome to the world of IDG Books Worldwide.

IDG Books Worldwide, Inc., is a subsidiary of International Data Group, the world's largest publisher of computer-related information and the leading global provider of information services on information technology. IDG was founded more than 30 years ago by Patrick J. McGovern and now employs more than 9,000 people worldwide. IDG publishes more than 290 computer publications in over 75 countries. More than 90 million people read one or more IDG publications each month.

Launched in 1990, IDG Books Worldwide is today the #1 publisher of best-selling computer books in the United States. We are proud to have received eight awards from the Computer Press Association in recognition of editorial excellence and three from Computer Currents' First Annual Readers' Choice Awards. Our best-selling ...*For Dummies*® series has more than 50 million copies in print with translations in 31 languages. IDG Books Worldwide, through a joint venture with IDG's Hi-Tech Beijing, became the first U.S. publisher to publish a computer book in the People's Republic of China. In record time, IDG Books Worldwide has become the first choice for millions of readers around the world who want to learn how to better manage their businesses.

Our mission is simple: Every one of our books is designed to bring extra value and skill-building instructions to the reader. Our books are written by experts who understand and care about our readers. The knowledge base of our editorial staff comes from years of experience in publishing, education, and journalism — experience we use to produce books to carry us into the new millennium. In short, we care about books, so we attract the best people. We devote special attention to details such as audience, interior design, use of icons, and illustrations. And because we use an efficient process of authoring, editing, and desktop publishing our books electronically, we can spend more time ensuring superior content and less time on the technicalities of making books.

You can count on our commitment to deliver high-quality books at competitive prices on topics you want to read about. At IDG Books Worldwide, we continue in the IDG tradition of delivering quality for more than 30 years. You'll find no better book on a subject than one from IDG Books Worldwide.

John J. Kilcullen

John Kilcullen
Chairman and CEO
IDG Books Worldwide, Inc.

Eighth Annual
Computer Press
Awards ≥1992

Ninth Annual
Computer Press
Awards ≥1993

Tenth Annual
Computer Press
Awards ≥1994

Eleventh Annual
Computer Press
Awards ≥1995

IDG is the world's leading IT media, research and exposition company. Founded in 1964, IDG had 1997 revenues of $2.05 billion and has more than 9,000 employees worldwide. IDG offers the widest range of media options that reach IT buyers in 75 countries representing 95% of worldwide IT spending. IDG's diverse product and services portfolio spans six key areas including print publishing, online publishing, expositions and conferences, market research, education and training, and global marketing services. More than 90 million people read one or more of IDG's 290 magazines and newspapers, including IDG's leading global brands — Computerworld, PC World, Network World, Macworld and the Channel World family of publications. IDG Books Worldwide is one of the fastest-growing computer book publishers in the world, with more than 700 titles in 36 languages. The "...For Dummies®" series alone has more than 50 million copies in print. IDG offers online users the largest network of technology-specific Web sites around the world through IDG.net (http://www.idg.net), which comprises more than 225 targeted Web sites in 55 countries worldwide. International Data Corporation (IDC) is the world's largest provider of information technology data, analysis and consulting, with research centers in over 41 countries and more than 400 research analysts worldwide. IDG World Expo is a leading producer of more than 168 globally branded conferences and expositions in 35 countries including E3 (Electronic Entertainment Expo), Macworld Expo, ComNet, Windows World Expo, ICE (Internet Commerce Expo), Agenda, DEMO, and Spotlight. IDG's training subsidiary, ExecuTrain, is the world's largest computer training company, with more than 230 locations worldwide and 785 training courses. IDG Marketing Services helps industry-leading IT companies build international brand recognition by developing global integrated marketing programs via IDG's print, online and exposition products worldwide. Further information about the company can be found at www.idg.com.   1/26/00

Dedication

To Jewels, the love of my life for 31 years, for her support of this year-long project, for sacrificing much of our time together, and for her unbridled, enthusiastic response to the book offer — "Show me the money!"

And to the One from whom all inspiration flows, who gave me the vision for this book, the passion for the subject, and the help along the way that made it all possible.

Author's Acknowledgments

This book would never have been possible without the help of many people. I'd like to especially thank my wonderful assistant, Kelley Lawrence, who appeared in my life just as the book offer arrived, and who has professionally handled my clients' needs while I was busy penning this manuscript over most of a year. Thank you, Kelley, for being so wonderful — professionally and personally. Also, thanks to Linda Peterson, for all the countless hours spent entering my microscopic handwriting into Word documents and *For Dummies* format. (And for the magnifying glass you had to buy to read it!)

Thanks to all the people who worked on this project and made it happen. A special thanks to my project editor, Keith Peterson, for his kindness, patience, and quirky sense of humor in walking with me through the many challenges of my first book experience. And thanks to Ben Nussbaum for his rigorous editing of my writing. If you find this book easy to understand, Ben (and Keith) get the credit. Thanks to Jon Malysiak for his help getting this project off the ground and overseeing it to its completion. Thanks to Erica Bernhelm for all her help arranging the book's testimonials.

Thanks to my niece, Molly Joseph, and my brother, Jim Hungelmann, attorneys, for their help with the book contract. And to Jeanne Hansen, my agent, for all the effort in first believing my book had potential, for all the effort in finding a publisher, and for her help in negotiating the deal. Thanks to those people at Corporate 4 Insurance Agency in Edina, MN, for covering for me and servicing my clients. Thanks in particular go to Dwight Lewis and Shaun Kuffel. And to customer service reps Pam, Sharon, Dawn, Margaret, and Terri. Thanks to these insurance folks for their technical assistance: Michael Sir (long-term disability), Sonia Kieffer (flood), and Ivey Jackson (medical evacuation). Thanks to Maxine Coldren for her calligraphy talents on the Perils of the Sea in the Introduction.

A special thanks to those many clients who have believed enough in my efforts to offer value-added agent services to support the concept financially. I am only still offering those services almost 30 years later because of them. Thanks to those of you whose stories I have anonymously shared in this book to help make for better understanding by readers. Thanks to the North Shore of Lake Superior and its winds and crashing waves for providing inspiration and energy for the drafting of the first 200 pages of book notes. Thanks to Kinko's of Chanhassen for the zany idea of being open 24 hours, where authors with weird schedules could get their rush copying and FedEx needs met. And finally, thanks to a fine gentleman, Mr. E. W. Blanch, Sr., a staunch supporter of insurance education and professionalism, who provided me with my first job in the insurance business 30 years ago and who, unknowingly, became a source of inspiration and resolve on my part to pursue those same ideals.

Publisher's Acknowledgments

We're proud of this book; please register your comments through our IDG Books Worldwide Online Registration Form located at http://my2cents.dummies.com.

Some of the people who helped bring this book to market include the following:

Acquisitions, Editorial, and Media Development

Project Editor: Keith Peterson

Acquisitions Editor: Mark Butler

Associate Acquisitions Editor: Jonathan Malysiak

Copy Editor: Ben Nussbaum

Acquisitions Coordinator: Lauren Cundiff

Technical Editors: Jennifer Martin, Matthew McClure, Dexter Means

Senior Permissions Editor: Carmen Krikorian

Editorial Manager: Pamela Mourouzis

Media Development Manager: Laura Carpenter

Editorial Assistant: Carol Strickland

Special Help: Suzanna R. Thompson

Production

Project Coordinator: Maridee Ennis

Layout and Graphics: Sean Decker, Kristin Pickett, Jacque Schneider, Julie Trippetti, Erin Zeltner

Proofreader: David Faust, Dwight Ramsey, York Production Services, Inc.

Indexer: York Production Services, Inc.

General and Administrative

IDG Books Worldwide, Inc.: John Kilcullen, CEO; Bill Barry, President and COO; John Ball, Executive VP, Operations & Administration; John Harris, CFO

IDG Books Consumer Reference Group

Business: Kathleen A. Welton, Vice President and Publisher; Kevin Thornton, Acquisitions Manager

Cooking/Gardening: Jennifer Feldman, Associate Vice President and Publisher

Education/Reference: Diane Graves Steele, Vice President and Publisher; Greg Tubach, Publishing Director

Lifestyles: Kathleen Nebenhaus, Vice President and Publisher; Tracy Boggier, Managing Editor

Pets: Dominique De Vito, Associate Vice President and Publisher; Tracy Boggier, Managing Editor

Travel: Michael Spring, Vice President and Publisher; Suzanne Jannetta, Editorial Director; Brice Gosnell, Managing Editor

IDG Books Consumer Editorial Services: Kathleen Nebenhaus, Vice President and Publisher; Kristin A. Cocks, Editorial Director; Cindy Kitchel, Editorial Director

IDG Books Consumer Production: Debbie Stailey, Production Director

IDG Books Packaging: Marc J. Mikulich, Vice President, Brand Strategy and Research

◆

The publisher would like to give special thanks to Patrick J. McGovern, without whom this book would not have been possible.

◆

Contents at a Glance

Table of Contents

Introduction

· ·

"It takes rough seas to make good captains."

So says a plaque on my desk, given to me by a good friend who knows that I loved to sail for many years. As I grow older, I sail much less. But if I never sail again, I will always remember the lessons sailing taught me about personal empowerment in managing my own life.

Storms *do* come up. In all shapes, sizes, and colors. Fires. Tornadoes. Hurricanes. Earthquakes. Floods. Premature death. Disability. Catastrophic health problems. Lawsuits. The list goes on and on. You can't always prevent these storms from occurring. But you can take many constructive actions before the storms occur that greatly reduce the damage they cause in your life. You're already familiar with many of these actions, such as controlling your diet and exercising; wearing seatbelts and driving a car with an airbag; and installing a home alarm system. And you are at least a little familiar with the device that allows you to share the impact of any losses you have with others — insurance.

Insurance. A dreaded word for most people. It's cringe factor ranks right up there with such joys as filling out your income tax return. Or balancing your checkbook when the bank says you're $500 overdrawn. Or perhaps shopping for your own cemetery plot. My beloved wife, Judy, has a favorite saying when having to deal with such dreaded tasks: "I'd rather eat glass!"

If you're a cringer when it comes to insurance, I wrote *Insurance For Dummies* for you. To demystify the complexity of insurance policies for you. To enlighten you regarding where the traps and pitfalls are and how you can best protect yourself from getting hurt by them. I wrote this book so that when you need help understanding any insurance topic, you can pull the book down from the shelf and quickly find out what you need to know to protect yourself properly.

If you cause serious injury in a car accident, I show you how to have the right coverage to fully compensate the person you hurt, with no cost out of your own pocket. I show you how to insure your home properly so that when storms blow through and cause some serious damage, you get paid the full cost to rebuild without experiencing any of the penalties that are hidden in a Homeowners policy. If you have a home business, I introduce you to some of the potential lawsuits or property damage you may be facing and what types of insurance are best for you.

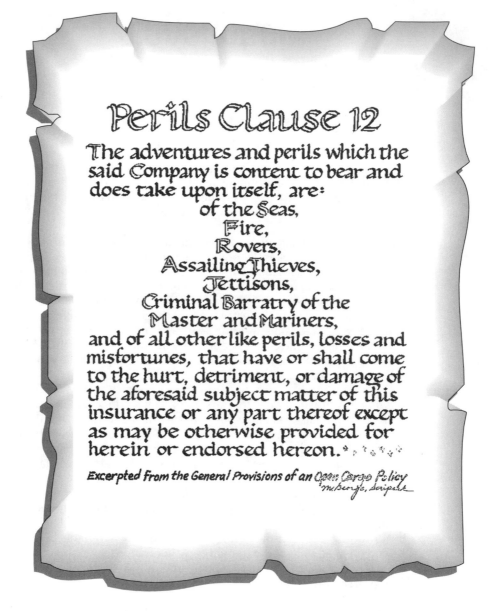

Perils Clause 12

The adventures and perils which the said Company is content to bear and does take upon itself, are:
of the Seas,
Fire,
Rovers,
Assailing Thieves,
Jettisons,
Criminal Barratry of the Master and Mariners,
and of all other like perils, losses and misfortunes, that have or shall come to the hurt, detriment, or damage of the aforesaid subject matter of this insurance or any part thereof except as may be otherwise provided for herein or endorsed hereon.

Excerpted from the General Provisions of an Open Cargo Policy

If you have concerns about life insurance, I show you how to calculate the amount of insurance that you need to provide for your survivors. You discover all about health insurance and how to select a good individual policy. You discover how to avoid some of the dangers of employer-provided health insurance. Plus, I throw in some tips on what to do regarding health insurance when you're between jobs.

For seniors, I write about some of the pitfalls of Medicare and how to distinguish a good Medicare supplement from some of the mediocre supplements available.

How This Book Is Different

This book is different than other insurance books in several important ways.

First, this book is written by someone who has actually worked in the trenches, directly with consumers, helping them creatively manage and insure the risks in their lives. So the book is full of practical, hands-on advice that really works — not academic stuff.

Second, this book is different because it emphasizes solutions to problems other than just buying insurance. In fact, there's a whole chapter on creative noninsurance strategies that not only help prevent or reduce the chances of a loss happening, but can also lower your insurance costs. Strategies like putting jewelry you don't wear in a safe-deposit box rather than insuring it. Or carrying higher deductibles than normal on your health insurance, if you're fit and healthy.

Third, this book is different because it has a Forms Directory in the Appendix — forms created for your personal use from my experience coaching clients. Forms that help you estimate the most cost-effective deductible for car, home, and health insurance policies. I include forms to help you compare health insurance policies, even a special form for seniors to compare Medicare supplements. And I created a questionnaire form to help you interview and pick a good agent.

Fourth, this book includes two full chapters on getting what you deserve at claim time — for both claims for damage to your car as well as to your home and belongings. The chapters contain tips I've gathered from my experience as a claims adjuster and an agent, helping clients get what they deserve for 30 years. You find out tips on how to get paid top dollar for your car when it's stolen or totaled in a collision. You find out tips on how to be in the driver's seat and minimize hassles when dealing with insurance adjusters. And you find out tips on creating an inventory of your belongings, after they're stolen, so that you can collect the full value of what you lost.

Fifth, this book is different than others because it addresses *all* areas of personal insurance. Most insurance books are more limited, such as life insurance only, health insurance only, or maybe auto and home insurance together. But this books covers just about every type of insurance you could ever need help with.

How This Book Is Organized

Insurance For Dummies is organized into seven parts. You're welcome to start at the beginning. I've written so that you can. But I've also written the book so that you can use it as a reference guide. So you can skip around and pull out just the information you need

Here's a thumbnail sketch of the seven parts:

Part 1: Getting Started

How much is enough coverage for lawsuits? How big a deductible should I choose? Should I buy earthquake insurance if I live in Nebraska? In this part you discover seven principles that help you make good insurance decisions You also learn four noninsurance strategies for reducing the chances of a loss in your life — they also can help lower your insurance costs.

Part 11: Understanding Automobile Insurance

How much coverage should I buy for lawsuit protection? How large a deductible makes good sense for me? How do I get top dollar for my 1965 Mustang, fully restored? How can I avoid being uninsured when I rent cars? The answers are in this part.

Part 111: Understanding Home Insurance

In this part I show you how to insure your home and your belongings. I show you what kinds of personal property aren't covered by a typical home policy and how you can get them covered. I show you how to cover personal lawsuits. I even show you some of the basics when it comes to insuring a home business.

Part 1V: Buying an Umbrella Policy

What is an umbrella policy, and how does it protect me from catastrophic lawsuits? The answers are in this part. I also show you how to choose an Umbrella policy that covers you for lawsuits not covered by your other policies.

Part V: Dealing with Insurance Companies

Most insurance programs are full of coverage gaps, because insurance is bought the wrong way. Discover here the right way to buy insurance. And discover tips on how to collect top dollar on your auto and property claims.

Part VI: Managing Life, Health, and Disability Risks

Life, health, and disability insurance aren't fun to think about. This part shows you the common mistakes people make. In this part, I show you how to calculate how much life insurance to buy and what type is best. I give tips on buying individual health policies and Medicare supplements. I also give advice on buying disability insurance.

Part VII: The Part of Tens

In this part, I list some useful Web sites. I give tips on managing the changes to your insurance program when your life changes. And I give some suggestions to insurance companies on how they can make your life a lot easier.

Icons Used in This Book

Maybe you want to know a little more on *why* some insurance strategies work better than others. This icon is the place to look to find that sort of information. If you just want to catch the basic concepts, give this icon a pass.

This icon flags things that are especially useful for making the most of your insurance program.

This icon reminds you of information so important that you should read it more than once, just to make sure it stays with you.

This icon alerts you to areas of potential danger. Read any paragraphs that are flagged with this icon and take a close look at your life and your insurance situation.

My ironclad rules are tips that are very strong — this icon denotes a serious rule that you should always follow to avoid serious consequences.

My wish for you is that your sail through life be a mostly peaceful one, full of gentle breezes. But if storms do come up, I hope the information and tips I've shared with you helps get whatever claim you have fully covered and arms you with the tools you need to get paid promptly and fairly.

Good luck,
Jack Hunglemann

Part I
Getting Started

The 5th Wave   By Rich Tennant

"Let's see if we can determine your capacity for assuming risk. Now, how familiar are you with snake handling?"

In this part . . .

Being well insured gives you peace of mind. A hazard that many people face is thinking that they're well insured, only to find out otherwise at claim time. Your risks are best insured well in advance of the need for insurance. By organizing your life such that you minimize some risks and insure for others, you can strategically sculpt your insurance program to cover your assets for any eventuality. The chapters in this part provide an overview on how to blend your life and your need for adequate insurance coverage.

Chapter 1

Covering the Basics

1'm writing this book to help people take responsibility for their lives. I'm writing for people who don't wish to be victims — people who want the tools and information to be empowered when they make decisions.

This book is designed to arm you with the information you need, not only to make good insurance purchases, but also to be alert to where the potential gaps are in each policy and how best to avoid the nasty problems those gaps may cause. I also give you some tips on noninsurance strategies to help you reduce both risks and premiums. (*Risk* is used in this book to mean the chance of a loss happening.)

I've been coaching consumers for over 25 years as a claims adjuster, an insurance agent, and a consultant. In that time, I've worked with over 2,000 people and I've concluded that:

✓ Insurance is mistakenly bought and sold *primarily on price,* ignoring the fact that insurance policies are complex legal contracts full of exclusions and limitations.

✓ Alarmingly, the vast majority of consumers have at least one, and usually several, major gaps in their coverage — leading to potentially disastrous results at claim time.

✓ Many of those gaps can be plugged without significantly increasing insurance costs, just by transferring premium dollars from relatively unimportant coverages to pay for the missing coverages.

In this book, I show you all the major personal-insurance policies, familiarize you with the major coverages available under each policy, and give you my buying advice for each coverage. More importantly, I show you the major pitfalls and traps of each policy and coach you on what you can do now to avoid being burned at claim time.

I also arm you with what you need to know when you do have a claim to get every dollar you're entitled to from your policy, with the least amount of hassle.

Here are the guiding principles of this book.

- Keep it simple.
- Don't risk more than you can afford to lose.
- Don't risk a lot for a little.
- Consider the odds.
- Risk a little for a lot.
- Avoid Las Vegas insurance.
- Buy insurance only as a last resort.

Follow these seven principles when making decisions about your insurance program, and your decisions will be good ones. Before getting started, here are some definitions of insurance terms I use in this section. Insurance-ese is a difficult language — I promise to keep the jargon to a minimum.

- **Coverage:** A promise to pay a certain type of claim if it occurs (examples include automobile liability coverage, theft coverage, and so on).
- **Deductible:** The amount of a loss that you pay out of your own pocket before insurance kicks in.
- **Liability:** Your financial obligation to another person for injuries or property damage you cause.
- **Liability coverage:** A promise in an insurance policy to defend you in court and pay what you owe another person for injuries or property damage you cause.
- **Peril:** A cause of a loss (examples include windstorm peril and flood peril).
- **Policy:** The legal contract between you and an insurance company in which the company agrees to pay covered claims when you have them in exchange for a monthly (or some other periodic) payment from you. Any given policy contains many coverages.
- **Premium:** The price you pay for the insurance policy covering a defined time period — six months or one year.

Keeping It Simple

Managing risk and buying insurance is tough enough without making it any more complicated than it has to be. For every risk I show you, generally more than one strategy exists that effectively minimizes the risk. Using the keep it simple (KISS) principle, we'll take the simple path. Simple means more likely to be implemented and easier — not less effective.

Here is an example of how this principle can be used. One of the requirements in a Homeowners policy following a major fire or burglary is to create an inventory of what was lost or destroyed. Including, if possible, any receipts and canceled checks. Does that sound like a nightmare to you? It is! Even harder than *documenting* what you had is *remembering* what you had! Imagine coming home from a hard day at the office and finding either charred remains of what once was your dream home or finding your front door broken and your home torn apart by a burglar. The emotional trauma is bad enough. But in addition, you have to remember what's missing, because you only get paid for what you can remember.

Conventional insurance wisdom has always held that the solution to this dilemma is to fill out a household inventory booklet prior to any loss, listing descriptions and values for every piece of personal property you own in every room of the house. Talk about a fun way to spend an evening. Or, more realistically, your two-week vacation. Some people have fun with it though:

"Hi, sweetie! When are you coming home? Have I got a fun evening planned! A couple of nice, juicy steaks on the grill. A nice bottle of wine. And your favorite dessert. Then we can slip into something more comfortable and . . . do the household inventory for the insurance company."

A written inventory isn't such a bad idea, but it violates the KISS principle. It's complex. It takes far too much time. And as a result it's rarely accomplished.

A far simpler strategy for handling this documentation is a video or photographic inventory. It's easy, you can film the whole house in an hour and a half, and it's even fun. Especially when you add a verbal description: "This vase here that looks like a garage sale reject is really an antique from the Ming Dynasty worth $2.5 million."

I particularly like the video camera strategy because everything you own can be on one tape, it's easily stored, and best of all, can be easily added to when you buy new belongings. All without ever paying for film developing. Even if you don't own a video camera, one can be easily rented or borrowed. An extra benefit of having film at claim time is a reduced need for receipts. Most adjusters will waive that requirement if they can see the item in your home prior to the loss, on film. All in all, the film strategy is superior in every way to the written inventory strategy. Of course, if the house burns down, so will all your records. Be sure to store the photos or videotape safely off-premises.

Risking Only What You Can Afford to Lose

I'm all for taking risks if it makes economic sense. Carrying large deductibles to lower insurance costs is a smart gamble if you save enough on your premiums. Not buying Collision insurance on older cars that you could afford to replace is another smart gamble. But be sure to insure any risk that is a part of your life if the risk could cause you major financial — if it's more than you can afford to lose.

For example, the financial hardship of your paycheck stopping as a result of a long-term illness or injury is substantial. About one-third of all workers, at some point in their career, have a long-term disability. Yet, many people who totally depend on their paycheck don't have disability insurance. Big mistake — it's a clear violation of the principle to only risk what you can afford to lose. Disability insurance is the most underpurchased major insurance coverage in this country. If the loss of your income would cause major financial problems in your household, and your employer doesn't provide disability insurance for you, make sure you carry a good disability policy. (I explain the difference between a good disability policy and a bad disability policy in Chapter 17.)

Not Risking a Lot for a Little

Spending a little now (for coverage) makes more sense than spending a lot of your own money later when something happens you're not covered for.

Most people who buy insurance can't afford to buy unlimited quantities; you probably don't have millions of dollars of liability coverage, for example. So you tend to buy a limit that feels comfortable and doesn't blow your budget. But too many people are considerably underinsured, and, tragically, seldom are aware that better insurance would cost them very little.

Using car insurance as an example, the most commonly purchased liability insurance limit in the United States today is $100,000 per person for injuries you cause to others. Is that enough to pay for a seriously injured person's medical bills, lost wages, and compensation for that person's pain and suffering? Just the medical bills alone could easily use up the entire coverage limit, leaving you to personally pay all other costs, plus some of your own defense costs. Your personal, uninsured financial loss could easily reach several hundred thousand dollars. Table 1-1 shows some typical annual costs for additional liability coverage for two cars in a metropolitan area.

Table 1-1	Typical Annual Liability Costs for Two Cars	
Liability Limit	Additional Annual Costs Beyond the Cost for $100,000	The Amount of Additional Coverage beyond $100,000
$300,000	$ 50	$200,000
$500,000	$ 80	$400,000
$1.5 Million	$150	$1.4 Million
$2.5 Million	$225	$2.4 Million

Following the rule to not risk a lot for a little means don't buy only $100,000 of coverage when each additional $100,000 of coverage costs so little. In fact, you can usually pay for the extra cost simply by boosting your policy deductibles to the next level. Increasing your deductible by $250 to $500 often saves you enough on your insurance bill to pay for most or all of the added cost of additional liability coverage.

Considering the Odds

This rule says that when the odds of a claim happening are virtually zero, and the insurance costs are inappropriately high, don't buy the insurance. Considering the odds also means buying insurance when the possibility exists that a serious claim could occur.

Homeowners policies exclude earthquake losses. But they do offer an option to buy the coverage for an additional charge. Here are two examples of how the principle of considering the odds applies. It's estimated that only about 20 percent of California homeowners had earthquake coverage to protect themselves against the devastating California earthquake of 1989, despite the high odds of an earthquake occurring. The 80 percent who were uninsured were in clear violation of both this rule, to consider the odds, and the rule not to risk more than you can afford to lose. As a result, many homeowners suffered ruinous, uninsured earthquake losses that could have easily been avoided with the purchase of insurance.

But, if you live in an area that has no prior history of earthquakes and is located nowhere near any known faults, the probability of an earthquake may be near zero. Considering the odds, in this instance, means maybe not buying earthquake insurance if it costs more than a few dollars a year.

Like earthquake damage, flood and surface-water losses are excluded under the traditional Homeowners policy. Considering the odds means that if your home is located high on the pinnacle of a hill overlooking a valley and your basement is unfinished, you probably don't need to spend your money on flood insurance. On the other hand, if your home is located in a low-lying flood plain or near a river, you probably should consider buying flood insurance, since the odds of a large loss are good. (Flood insurance is available from the Federal Government — more on that later in this book.)

Risking a Little for a Lot

This principle encourages you to avoid insurance when the risk is small in relation to the amount of the premium. Say, for example, you own a 1986 Honda worth $1,000. You just had a DWI and are facing premiums of two to three times what you had been paying. Not just this year, but for each of the next three to five years. The Collision insurance premium with a $500 deductible has just increased from $100 to $300 a year. If you keep this coverage, the maximum risk to the insurance company is shown in Table 1-2.

Table 1-2	Net Risk to the Insurance Company
(A) The value of the car	$1,000
(B) Less deductible	$500
(C) Less salvage value	$50
Net risk to the insurer (A minus B and C) if the car is totaled	$450

This rule advises you not to buy what turns out to be $450 of insurance for a $300 annual premium. Under these circumstances, the smart move is to drop the Collision coverage.

Avoiding Las Vegas Insurance

Avoid any insurance that transfers only part of the risk to the insurance company, leaving you unprotected for the rest. Accidental Death insurance purchased from an airport vending machine is a good example. It often only pays if you die in a plane crash in the next few days! What you really may need is more life insurance, protecting you all the time and from any cause.

With Las Vegas insurance, you are, in effect, betting that if the claim occurs, it will be the result of a limited cause-of-loss you bet on. Not smart. Table 1-3 shows some examples of Las Vegas insurance and a better alternative that gets rid of the gamble:

Table 1-3	Types of Insurance and the Associated Risks	
Type of Insurance	*Terms*	*Better Solution*
Accidental death	Pays only if you die accidentally	Life insurance
Travel accident	Pays medical bills only if incurred on a trip	Major medical health insurance
Cancer or dread disease coverage	Pays only medical bills caused by a specific calamity	Major medical insurance
Rush-hour liability insurance	Doubles your lawsuit protection if the accident occurs between 7:00 and 8:30 a.m. or between 4:30 and 6:00 p.m.	Adequately high auto liability limits

Yes, the last item in Table 1-3 is tongue-in-cheek (no insurance company has come out with rush-hour insurance yet), but it hopefully makes the point. The bottom line? If you buy any insurance that transfers only part of the risk as these examples of Las Vegas coverage do, you leave yourself vulnerable. Spend a little more money, and get much better insurance.

Buying Insurance Only as a Last Resort

This principle advises to buy insurance only when it's the best and most cost-effective solution. You have many options in treating any given risk. Insurance is only one. Treat your risks with noninsurance strategies first. See Chapter 2 for all kinds of information on how to do that. But here is one example of how this principle works.

Say you've inherited Grandmama's heirloom sterling silver. It's precious to you, so naturally you want the best coverage possible. Your agent has you get an appraisal that costs you $100. You buy a special rider to your Homeowners policy covering the silver's appraised value of $10,000 at a premium of $90 a year.

One year later, burglars break into your home and steal your precious heirloom. In the meantime, the silver has increased in value to $15,000. You collect the $10,000 insurance proceeds from the policy, but you've suffered three disappointments:

- ✔ The $5,000 difference between the value of the stolen silver and the amount that insurance covered.

- ✔ Grandmama's pattern has been discontinued and it's difficult to find an identical match.

- ✔ Even if you find the same pattern, it doesn't have the sentimental value that Grandmama's *exact* set had.

Insurance is not the best solution for managing this risk. Not only because cash is a poor substitute for treasures, but also because of the hassle and cost of the appraisal, as well as the insurance premium that's due every year.

A better, noninsurance, method for handling Grandmama's silver risk and at the same time following the KISS (keep it simple) strategy of an earlier principle is to store the silver in an off-premises safe-deposit box, thus preventing the loss almost entirely. Or, if that isn't practical because you want to use the silver for special occasions, hide it well, reducing by about 90 percent the chance of a loss through theft. You can further reduce the risk by adding a central burglar alarm.

When it comes to irreplaceable treasures, preventing the loss altogether is a far better strategy than insurance, without the costs or the pitfalls.

Chapter 2

The ARRT of Risk Management

The goal of this book is to provide you with tools to help you effectively manage the personal risks in your life. One of the focuses is enabling you to first identify and then treat those risks with creative noninsurance strategies whenever possible, rather than limiting your choices just to insurance purchases. Noninsurance strategies reduce insurance costs and are often more effective than their insurance counterparts.

Many people throw insurance at every problem. Their child turns 16, and they rush out to buy insurance. They inherit a stamp collection worth $50,000, and they buy more insurance. When in need of temporary transportation during a repair, they rent and insure a replacement car.

In this chapter, I want to familiarize you with a different, and I think better, way of doing things: *risk management.* The essence of risk management is to treat risks with noninsurance methods first and to buy insurance second.

Using noninsurance strategies means you perhaps delay letting your 16-year old get her license until she has more practice and until you can find a safer car than the 1982 subcompact with no seatbelts. You don't insure the stamps that you wouldn't replace anyway but protect their sentimental value by buying a fireproof, waterproof home safe. You don't rent a car because where you're going is right on a bus line.

Discovering Effective Noninsurance Strategies

I cover four noninsurance strategies in this chapter. A good way to remember them is with the acronym *ARRT.*

A = Avoid

R = Reduce

R = Retain

T = Transfer

Here is a more in-depth look at each of these so you can see how you can apply them to your own life.

Avoiding risk

Avoid means exactly what it says. When none of the other strategies for treating a risk seems suitable, sometimes the wisest decision is to simply avoid the risk. I avoid risks like skydiving, hang gliding, and auto racing. I'm sure I would enjoy the activities if I ever took them up. It's just that for me the rewards aren't worth the risks. Other examples where avoiding the risk may be the best strategy:

✔ Not licensing a teenager driver who clearly is still immature and irresponsible

✔ Not buying an expensive sports car while your driving record is poor and insurance costs are sky-high

✔ Canceling your vacation plans to a war-ravaged part of the world

✔ Not buying a backyard trampoline for your kids because of the impossibility of preventing unsupervised use by other neighborhood children

Reducing risk

Reduce means taking actions that lower the probability of either the loss happening at all, or if it does occur, lowering its possible severity. The person inheriting Grandmama's sterling silver could reduce the theft risk with a central alarm and/or by hiding the silver well. Collectors of valuable stamps can greatly reduce the water damage risk by mounting and sealing the stamps in waterproof plastic album pages. (Just as my son, JP, did with my 1950s baseball card collection for Father's Day one year.) Other examples:

✔ Regularly checking prongs on a valuable diamond ring to reduce the risk of loss of the stones

✔ Eating healthy foods and working out regularly, not smoking, and getting plenty of rest

✔ Not drinking and driving

✔ Buying cars with safety features like air bags and antilock brakes and that test well in crash tests

Reducing risk has the advantage of being the one treatment strategy you can do the most with and have the most personal control over. It has other advantages too. If you significantly reduce the risk:

✔ The risk may be small enough that you feel safe avoiding insurance altogether (for example, if you've stored valuables in a safe-deposit box).

✔ You may feel comfortable carrying higher deductibles. You may be able to save 50 percent on your health insurance costs by buying a $1,000 deductible, and know that a high deductible is a smart choice because your healthy lifestyle results in few claims.

✔ You may be able to get insurance at a better cost.

In each of the succeeding chapters, I talk a lot about reducing risk — and recommend it as at least a part of the solution to managing many of the risks in your life.

Retaining risk

Retain refers to the strategy of paying losses out of your own pocket. This can be *voluntary,* such as carrying higher deductibles in order to lower premiums. Retaining may mean taking the entire risk on less valuable items, like the risk of theft to a $300 canoe. It may mean not carrying insurance to cover low frequency catastrophic losses with almost no chance of happening, such as an earthquake in Minnesota.

Retaining can also be *involuntary* — bad news. These are the surprises you get at claim time, the risks you take every day without even knowing it. For example:

✔ Not having any coverage to protect against a lawsuit from the person who delivers a package to your home-based business and falls on your icy sidewalk

✔ Not being protected against the lawsuit from your coworker who was injured while riding with you in your company car

✔ Receiving only $30,000 for your $50,000 kitchen fire because of depreciation deductions under your Homeowners policy

✔ Being sued by a car rental company for $10,000 in damages to a rental car — damages caused by a friend or coworker — for which you naively agreed to be responsible when you scribbled your signature on the rental agreement

Much of the focus of this book is on uncovering these involuntary retentions — the many pitfalls of personal policies. I show you steps you can take to protect yourself that effectively deal with these hidden risks.

Transferring risk

Transfer refers to shifting the risk in whole or in part from yourself to another party. The most common form of transfer is the insurance mechanism whereby, in exchange for a predetermined premium payment, an insurance company will assume losses that you would have otherwise had to absorb yourself. An example:

You transfer the risk of fire damage to your home to an insurer for $300 a year. Your home is destroyed by fire. The insurance company pays the entire cost to rebuild, the cost to replace all your destroyed belongings, and even the additional costs you incur to live elsewhere while your new home is being rebuilt.

The other type of transfer (the bad kind) occurs in just about every contract you sign in your daily life. "But I *never* sign contracts," you protest! Really? I'll bet you do — we all do. In any given year, you likely sign contracts for an apartment lease, a boat rental, a vacation condo, a rental car, a credit card, a real estate purchase, or a home repair proposal.

These are just some examples of the contracts you sign in your daily life. I could give you many more. It's almost impossible to be alive and not sign contracts in today's busy world. In just about every one of the above contracts, someone is attempting to transfer some kind of risk to you, often without your knowledge. If there is a problem, you're simply out of luck. Courts don't accept failure to read what you've signed as an excuse.

Take a closer look at two types of everyday contracts in which you assume responsibility unknowingly, and the surprises that can be waiting for you.

✔ **Hardware store rental of a chainsaw.** You assume absolute liability for damage to the saw, even if it's not your fault and all liability for injuries to another person (for example, a friend using the saw), even if the injury was caused by a defect in the saw. You also release the store from responsibility for your injuries, even if they're caused by a defect in the saw.

> ✓ **Wedding reception catering.** You assume all liability for injuries to guests, even when they're caused by the negligence of the restaurant (for example, food poisoning). You agree to pay all defense costs of the restaurant in such injury lawsuits and to pay any judgment against the restaurant out of your pocket.

Can you imagine how upset you would be if some dear friends at your daughter's wedding reception suffered serious illness or even death from contaminated food, and you were forced to pay to defend the restaurant? And you had to pay all judgments against the restaurant, just because you innocently signed a contract to do so?

Does this scare you? I hope so. Fear is a good thing when it keeps you from hurting yourself. And if you don't start paying attention to the routine contracts of your daily life, you could easily assume a risk that can ruin you financially!

Practicing the Art of ARRT

The four risk treatment strategies of avoid, reduce, retain and transfer work together in the following examples that illustrate why the strategies are often combined, instead of used individually.

Managing the risk of teenage driving

You can obviously **avoid** the risks associated with a 16-year-old driver by not allowing him or her to get a driver's license. Other methods of avoiding this risk include chaining your teenager in the cellar or giving your child up for adoption.

You can **reduce** the risks of injuries, property damage, and lawsuits through:

> ✓ Thirty or forty hours of practice for your teen behind the wheel, alongside you, while facing all different driving scenarios and weather conditions
>
> ✓ A structurally solid and mechanically safe car to minimize injuries, with working seat belts and air bags
>
> ✓ A contract such as the Students against Driving Drunk (SADD) contract where your child agrees not to drive after using drugs or alcohol, and you agree to a hassle-free pick up

You can **retain** some or all of the risk of damage to the car itself (collision, fire, theft) by either not buying damage insurance on the car at all, or if the car is worth too much, at least choosing large deductibles. This strategy will save you a bundle on your insurance costs.

You can **transfer** the risk of personal lawsuits related to vehicle maintenance by transferring the vehicle title and maintenance responsibility to your teenager. This won't absolve you of responsibility for your teenager's behavior, but it can avoid lawsuits against you related to not maintaining the vehicle in a reasonable manner. It is important to check your state law as to what the minimum age is that your teen can legally own a vehicle. Your teen has considerably fewer assets and income than you, is much less a target for lawsuits than you, and therefore will need far less liability insurance coverage than you.

Keep the ARRT acronym in your memory bank for future use. Try to get in the habit of first considering noninsurance alternatives before slapping insurance on every risk you face.

Super Bowl insurance

We had the Super Bowl in Minneapolis in 1992, which created an unexpected windfall for a few of my clients with nice homes. The hoopla of the Super Bowl attracts many more people than will ever attend the game itself, and there is a severe shortage of hotel rooms and other types of housing. About a month before the game, I started receiving calls from clients who were being offered incredible sums of money ($10,000 for 2 weeks) to rent their homes to wealthy groups of international visitors wanting a nice environment for sleeping and entertaining. Understandably, the offers were incredibly tempting. But they were dangerous too, because the standard Homeowners insurance policy is normally suspended during such a significant increase in exposure. Which means my clients would have been totally uninsured for fires, injury lawsuits, and many other claims occurring during the rental.

The safest strategy was obviously to avoid the risk and not do the rental. But for those who succumbed to the lure of the large cash offer, I suggested the following strategies:

✔ We *reduced* the risk by collecting sizable damage deposits and checking references.

✔ We *transferred* risks contractually to the renters through a short-term rental contract making them absolutely liable for all damages to building and contents as well as all injuries, regardless of fault. And we required them to provide proof, prior to occupancy, of both property and liability insurance which named my client as an Additional Insured for the duration of the rental.

✔ Just in case the contractual transfer didn't hold up, we *transferred* property and liability risks to insurance by successfully negotiating with my clients' home and umbrella liability insurers to waive any coverage suspensions on grounds of the short duration of the rental. **Note:** The only time this negotiation is possible is *before* the loss. All the insurers reluctantly agreed. To make certain that there would be no misunderstandings with the insurance companies, we got written confirmation.

By paying close attention to all the risks and applying creative insurance and noninsurance strategies, the potential financial ruin was averted, and my clients were $10,000 richer. I wish I'd been working on a percentage!

Part II

Understanding Automobile Insurance

The 5th Wave   By Rich Tennant

"Frankly sir, issuing you reasonably priced auto insurance isn't going to be easy given the number of crashes you've been involved in."

In this part . . .

I drive, therefore I am. For most of us, our vehicle is as indispensable as oxygen. When you drive, you career about at amazing speeds in multi-ton containers of metal, glass, and explosive liquid. You expose yourself (and others) to incredible liability simply by driving. Insurance on your vehicle is as indispensable as the vehicle itself. Without insurance on your vehicle, you could lose everything. These chapters show you how to protect yourself and others from the driving risks you face each day.

Chapter 3

Managing Your Personal Automobile Risks

Americans have a love affair with cars, and since Americans own more cars per capita than any country in the world, a good place to begin examining insurance risks is to look at those associated with the ownership, maintenance, and use of our beloved *PTU* (personal transportation unit). Unless you walk around with a loaded gun in your pocket, an automobile represents the most dangerous device you own. In one split second, you can experience lawsuits, death, long-term disability, major medical expenses, and major property damage! Pretty scary stuff!

That's why it is so important to spend time setting up a solid car insurance program which will keep you from suffering heavy financial losses following a serious car accident. I show you how to create a solid car insurance program in this chapter.

Managing Your Lawsuit Risks

Your personal automobile represents the single largest possible source of catastrophic lawsuits and legal judgments against you for major injuries, death, and property damage. Because of that, you need to be especially diligent as to the strategies you adopt to manage this risk.

Reviewing noninsurance strategies

Before I show you how to best choose necessary insurance coverages, here are some proven noninsurance strategies that lower your risks — and often lower your insurance costs as well.

- Obey traffic laws, including the speed limit — laws designed to reduce both the frequency and severity of automobile accidents.

- Perform regular safety maintenance of your vehicle (brakes, tires, steering, lights).

- Purchase a safer vehicle that is highly rated for low damageability and passenger safety.

- Pay extra for added safety features like air bags or antilock brakes.

- Always wear your seat belt and insist your passengers do too.

- Buy the highest-rated child safety seats and always use them.

- Take behind-the-wheel defensive driving classes.

- Require your teenager to have at least 30 hours practice behind the wheel on his permit under all sorts of driving conditions before allowing him to get a driver's license. No one can ever develop the skills needed to be a safe driver in just a few hours of mandatory driver's education.

- Allow your teenager to drive based upon your determination of his or her ability to responsibly operate a car — *regardless* of when your state says your teenager can drive. The teen who behaves immaturely and irresponsibly out of a vehicle usually behaves in similar fashion in a vehicle.

These are just a few examples of how to reduce your personal automobile risks. For more information, see the section on preventing and reducing loss in Chapter 4.

Buying liability insurance

People who buy liability insurance that provides for their defense and pays legal judgments on their behalf frequently make two mistakes:

- They buy far too little coverage, not realizing the substantial amount of money involved in a death or an injury suit — both in the cost of a judgment and the costs to defend the case.

- They buy inconsistent limits ($100,000 on their car, $300,000 on their home, $50,000 on their boat, and so on), even though they are protecting the same income and monetary assets, not realizing the danger of inconsistent coverage.

In the above example, suppose you injure someone seriously with your car. You have only $100,000 of coverage, yet had the same injury occurred at home, you would have $300,000 of coverage. See how illogical that is? Your only hope for enough coverage in this scenario is to drag the victim's bleeding, unconscious body home, throw them down the stairs, and hope they don't remember the car accident!

"How much is enough liability insurance?" you may be asking. It depends on who the victim is. It also depends on how sueable you are. I call this your *sueability factor.* See the section titled "Knowing your sueability factor" later in this chapter.

Understanding why who you hit matters

You're on your way to work. You're running behind schedule. You decide to run a yellow light. But just before the intersection it turns red. You slam on your brakes but it's too late. You broadside another vehicle, right in the driver's door, seriously injuring the driver. The driver is taken to emergency care, undergoes surgery, and spends a month in the hospital. Following his release, the driver spends two years in rehabilitation, in and out of physical therapy, missing two years of work. Table 3-1 shows hypothetical claim values for four different situations.

Table 3-1	Your Potential Liability			
Occupation	*Medical Bills*	*Lost Wages*	*Pain/Suffering*	*Total Claim*
Teacher	$100,000	$60,000	$300,000	$460,000
Banker	$100,000	$120,000	$400,000	$620,000
Doctor	$100,000	$300,000	$500,000	$900,000
Baseball player	$100,000	$12 million	$10 million	$22,100,000

Pretty eye-opening, isn't it? Can you imagine what the numbers would be if the driver were killed, or had a permanent disability with a lifetime loss of income? Believe me, I'm not trying to scare you, but I am trying to show you how vastly underinsured you may be for lawsuits. The most common liability limit I see when I review a prospective client's insurance is $100,000! That's ridiculously low.

I'm not suggesting that everyone rush out and buy $22 million or more in liability insurance. More than $5 to 10 million is generally not even available. I *am* suggesting that you reevaluate your coverage limit based on a combination of this new awareness, the cost and availability of higher insurance limits, and how sueable you are. See the section titled "Knowing your sueability factor" to help you determine how sueable you are. I suggest that you help pay for the increased insurance costs for higher liability limits by shifting premium dollars away from less important coverages, like higher deductibles on coverage for damage to your own vehicle.

Knowing your sueability factor

I define sueability factor (SF) as the probability of an injured party suing you for large sums — often for more than the amount of insurance you're carrying. For that to happen, you must be worth something, either currently or in the future. Why? Because if there's nothing to go after, no pot of gold at the end of the rainbow, many attorneys won't take the case and help an injured party sue you. Your SF is influenced by several elements. Table 3-2 shows four of those.

Table 3-2	Your Sueability Factor
SF Elements	*Examples of People with a High Sueability Factor*
Current income	Athlete, doctor, investment banker, lawyer, executive
Current assets	Successful retiree with high net worth
Future income	Medical intern, law student, MBA student
Future assets	Anyone with a potential inheritance

People with high current incomes or assets usually are aware of their sueability. But people with little current income or assets often overlook their future income or asset potential and the effect it has on their current sueability.

The bottom line is that if you have one or more of these four elements contributing to a high SF, you are more apt to be sued for amounts greater than your insurance coverage and you need higher liability limits on all your insurance policies. An added advantage of higher liability limits is that the closer your liability limit comes to the economic value of the injury you cause, the greater the likelihood that the injured party will settle for your insurance policy limit and not pursue you — personally — beyond that. Another variable in choosing a liability limit for many people is their sense of moral responsibility. For example, a person who is not very sueable may buy a higher liability limit than they would otherwise need, to make sure that any fellow human being they injure is provided for financially. If you are one of these people, my hat goes off to you in admiration.

You may be wondering how much it costs to raise your liability coverage — well, it costs very little. I invite you to call your agent and find out for yourself. You'll be amazed! (Don't forget to raise all your liability limits on your other personal policies to the same limit as your car insurance.) Table 3-3 shows an example of fairly typical costs involved in raising liability coverage from $100,000 for two cars, a home, a cabin, and a boat. The numbers may vary depending on the insurance company and the circumstances of the insured.

Table 3-3	Cost of Raising Liability Limits from $100,000
New Liability Limit	**Additional Annual Premium**
$300,000	$70
$500,000	$120
$1.5 million	$220
$2.5 million	$280
Each additional $ million	$60

It is important to note that coverage beyond $500,000 is sold in $1 million increments under a catastrophic excess policy commonly referred to as an *Umbrella* policy. See Chapter 10 for more on Umbrella policies.

When you look at what you're spending for the first $100,000 of coverage, you see that you can tremendously increase your catastrophic lawsuit coverage (not to mention your peace of mind) for just a small additional amount. Additional liability coverage is the best value in the insurance business.

Avoiding the danger of split liability limits

Most liability coverage for homes, boats, recreational vehicles, and other personal policies is sold by insurance companies as a single limit (such as $300,000) that applies to all injuries and property damage you cause in a single accident, no matter how many persons are injured or how much property is damaged. In other words, if you're in an accident, you have one pool of money to pay for all your liability. Liability coverage for car accidents is also available as a single limit, but just as commonly it's sold with *split limits*.

With split limits automobile liability coverage, you select three limits. You select one *limit* — the maximum your policy pays — for injuries you cause to a single person. You select another limit for all injuries you cause in a single accident involving two or more people. And you select a third limit for all damage to property you cause in a single accident.

See Table 3-4 for examples of three of the most typical combinations of split limits.

Table 3-4	Typical Split Limits Policies Sold		
	Example 1	Example 2	Example 3
Injury limit per person	$ 50,000	$100,000	$250,000
Injury limit per accident	$100,000	$300,000	$500,000
Property damage limit per accident	$ 25,000	$ 50,000	$100,000

If you buy a single liability limit of $300,000 on your home, cabin, and boat policies, you should get the same $300,000 limit on your car insurance. If you request that limit from an agent selling only split limits, instead of a single limit of $300,000, here are the split limits the agent may suggest as an alternative:

- ✔ $100,000 per person for injuries you cause

- ✔ $300,000 per accident for injuries (two or more people injured)

- ✔ $50,000 per accident for all property damage you cause

The danger of buying split limits coverage is a false sense of security given to you by the injury limit *per accident*. The limit you are actually most likely to exhaust in a car accident is the injury limit *per person*.

Suppose you buy the limits shown in the second column in Table 3-4. Your policy limits you to $100,000 per person and $300,000 per accident for injuries you cause. Here are some hypothetical injury claims, what a jury may award, and what your policy pays with those split limits.

- ✔ You rear-end a car ahead of you with only one occupant, resulting in injuries to the driver's neck and back. Jury award: $250,000. You have a $300,000 limit per accident for injuries, so you're fine, right? Well, your limit per person that you injure is $100,000, so you're out $150,000.

- ✔ You rear-end the same car, but with two occupants. Both have neck and back injuries, one more serious than the other. Jury awards: $200,000 to one, $50,000 to the other. You guessed it. The policy pays the full $50,000 for the less-seriously injured person but only $100,000 for the more-seriously injured person, and you're out $100,000 ($200,000 less the $100,000 per person limit).

None of the scenarios involve catastrophic lawsuits, permanent serious injuries, or death. They are, in short, relatively ordinary. But look at what you would owe with split limits coverage!

In both accident examples, the total amount of jury awards is within the $300,000 per accident limit. But because the policy also has a per person limit, the judgment costs you astronomical sums of money that you would not have owed if you had a $300,000 single limit coverage.

Don't forget about legal fees. Legal fees in an accident defense case can run $50,000, $100,000, or more! Once you've used up your liability limit per accident, those legal costs come from your pocket. Every time you are sued for more than your policy limits, you will receive a friendly letter from your insurance company (certified mail, of course) that tells you once their policy limits have been reached, you are on your own.

So, how can you avoid the per person pitfall of split limits coverage? Since the vast majority of car accidents involve cars occupied by only one person, I recommend one of three strategies:

- ✔ Select a per person limit high enough to meet your lawsuit coverage needs for one person's injuries. In the two accident examples I just gave, for example, $250,000 to $500,000 of liability coverage per person would have saved you hundreds of thousands of dollars out of pocket for as little as $100 a year in additional insurance costs, if you're insuring two cars.

- ✔ Buy *single limit coverage* — one pool of money large enough to cover all injuries and property damage without a limit on the amount paid to any one person. Since this includes property damage, and any amount spent to pay for property damage reduces the amount left to pay for injuries, be sure to buy a little extra coverage. $300,000 to $500,000 is the least amount of coverage you should consider.

- ✔ Buy a second layer of liability insurance, called an *umbrella* policy, of $1 million or more. (See Chapter 10 on the Personal Umbrella policy.)

Insuring Your Personal Injuries

Injuries, often quite serious ones, happen in car accidents far more than in any other type of accident — plane, train, industrial, and so on. If you are injured in a car accident, you usually have more than one source from which to collect your medical bills and lost wages. One source may be your own health and disability insurance. Another source may be the personal liability coverage of the other driver, if the accident was his fault and if he has any insurance. But the process of collecting from the other driver can take months or even years. A third source is your car insurance.

You've got two types of coverage in a Personal Auto policy for your injuries in a car accident:

- ✔ Coverage for compensatory damages (what your injuries would be worth in a court, including compensation for pain and suffering) for your injuries caused by uninsured or underinsured motorists.
- ✔ Coverage for your medical bills (and lost wages in some states) regardless of fault.

I address them separately, since I have different recommendations for each.

Understanding how Uninsured and Underinsured Motorist coverage works

When you're injured in a car accident caused by the other driver, you can legally sue the other driver in most states to collect the fair value of your injury. If that driver has auto liability coverage, his policy pays you on his behalf, up to the liability policy limit he purchased. The economic value of your injury equals your out-of-pocket expenses plus compensation for your pain and suffering. But what if the other driver has no insurance at all? Or what if the insurance limit he has is less than the value of your injury? You can get a legal judgment against him and try to collect from him personally. But that can be an expensive, long, drawn-out process. Plus if he's not worth very much and has a limited income, you may not collect very much at all.

Fortunately, your own car insurance policy can solve the problem, if you buy *Uninsured Motorists* and *Underinsured Motorists* coverage:

- ✔ **Uninsured Motorists:** When the other driver is unidentified (hit and run) or has no liability insurance at all
- ✔ **Underinsured Motorists:** When the other driver has less auto liability coverage than you and the economic value of your injury exceeds the other driver's liability limit

I see these two coverages as a form of *reverse liability* in that you collect some or all of the economic value of your injuries caused by another driver from your own insurance company, almost as if they were the other driver's insurer. In short, Uninsured and Underinsured coverage make up the gap between the other driver's liability coverage and the amount of liability coverage he would have needed to pay your claim in full.

How do the two coverages work? Say you're injured in a car accident by another driver who runs a stop sign. The economic value of your injury is $450,000. Further, assume that you bought $500,000 of both Uninsured and Underinsured Motorists coverage under your own auto policy. For an underinsured motorist, first, you collect for your injury from the other driver's insurance in the amount of the other driver's liability limit, say $100,000. Then, you collect the balance of $350,000 from your own insurance company under your *Under*insured Motorists coverage. Had the other driver been without *any* insurance, you would have collected all $450,000 under your *Un*insured Motorists coverage.

Debunking some common myths

People often ask me why they should have to pay extra premiums because other drivers either buy inadequate insurance coverage or have no insurance at all. It's not fair, I agree. However, if you buy the higher liability limits recommended in this book, the vast majority of other drivers are underinsured compared to your fine coverage. And since the process of collecting any amounts over the other driver's insurance limits is laborious and expensive, the combination of Uninsured and Underinsured Motorists coverage is the most effective way to make sure you have adequate funds available to properly compensate you for your injury — an injury you did not cause.

You may object to the idea that the other driver (the underinsured) benefits from your good Uninsured and Underinsured Motorists coverage by avoiding action against him for damages.

Even though it may seem like the other driver gets away without having to carry insurance, that's simply not true. The other driver is still held accountable. These two coverages just assure you that a pool of money is available to you that's easily accessible and provided by your own insurance company. However, once you have been paid, you transfer your rights to sue the other party to your insurance company. The insurance company will then have the right to pursue the other party's assets and income until it's fully reimbursed. By buying these two coverages, you are compensated much more easily and quickly and you avoid the hassle and expense of chasing down the other driver for payment. You also avoid the risk that the other party may not have the resources to compensate you adequately for the damages caused in the accident.

You may think that by carrying Uninsured and Underinsured coverage, you're duplicating coverage that you have elsewhere, such as in your personal health and disability insurance — or even the medical coverage of a car insurance policy. To some degree this is true. If you are injured by another driver, you *can* collect for your medical bills and lost wages from some of the other policies you personally own. However, none of your other coverages compensate you for the economic value of your pain and suffering the other driver caused. You've got only three sources for that compensation:

- The other driver's automobile liability insurance
- The other driver's personal assets and income
- Your own Uninsured and Underinsured Motorists coverage

Therefore, if you want to make certain that you have adequate coverage to compensate you for your potential pain and suffering, the *only* sure way is by buying these two coverages. This, of course, begs the question: "How much coverage should I buy?

My recommendation is to buy as much protection for your own injuries (as caused by another) as you buy to cover the injuries you yourself cause to someone else. In other words, buy the same Uninsured and Underinsured Motorists coverage limits as you buy liability insurance limits to the extent those coverages are available in your state. Why? Because you are worth every bit as much as a complete stranger whom you might injure. Cover yourself accordingly.

Preventing some dangerous mistakes

One of the most common mistakes people make when buying insurance is in the areas of Uninsured and Underinsured Motorists coverage. They either buy one coverage without the other, buy lower limits than their auto liability limits, or buy inconsistent limits (a higher limit for one coverage than the other). The following list gives each of these pitfalls and what you're, in effect, saying if you make the mistake.

- Buying Uninsured and not Underinsured coverage. "I'm willing to bet that the other driver will have zero insurance. If I am injured by a driver with less insurance than he needs to pay for my injuries and no sueable assets, I'm willing to not be compensated fully."

- Buying less Uninsured and Underinsured coverage than you buy in liability coverage for injuries you cause to others. "I sincerely believe my injuries and suffering are worth less than those of someone I may hit."

- Buying inconsistent Uninsured and Underinsured limits (for example, $300,000 Uninsured and $50,000 Underinsured). "I'm willing to accept less compensation when injured by an underinsured driver than when I'm injured by an uninsured driver."

Clearly none of these assumptions make any logical sense. It's worth repeating: Buy Uninsured and Underinsured Motorist coverage limits in equal amounts, and equal to the liability limits you buy.

Saving money on medical coverage

I've stressed the importance of buying high protection limits for injuries you cause as well as for injuries caused to you. Both of these strategies increase your insurance costs. In this section and the next, "Dealing with Damage to Your Vehicle," I show you strategies that lower your costs and help you afford better coverage for the big stuff, like higher liability coverage. Coverage for your medical bills (and sometimes lost wages and *replacement services* — help around the home you have to hire) is generally offered by car insurance companies. Depending on your state's laws, this medical coverage generally comes in two flavors:

✔ **Medical Payments** (Med Pay) coverage (Plain Vanilla)

✔ **Personal Injury Protection** (PIP) coverage (Banana Fudge Supreme)

Both coverages are similar in the sense that they pay your medical bills suffered in a car accident, regardless of fault, up to the limit you purchased. Personal Injury Protection has the added advantage (at a considerably greater cost) of also reimbursing you for some of your lost wages or replacement services. Some states even allow you (for an additional premium) to add together the medical coverage limits per car (called *stacking*) to cover a single injury. ($5,000 coverage per car × 3 cars on the policy = $15,000 total medical coverage for a single injury.)

I don't attempt to cover all the different requirements or costs relating to these coverages. Keep in mind three things when buying either coverage: First, check the law in your particular state. State laws on Med Pay or PIP coverages vary dramatically. Second, buy only as much medical-related coverage as the law requires. Medical and disability costs should be covered under other policies you have; and therefore, having additional car insurance coverage is redundant. Third, buying additional coverage for your medical bills and/or lost wages from car accidents only is betting that those particular kinds of expenses will happen just from an auto accident and is a clear violation of the Chapter 1 principle: Don't buy Las Vegas insurance.

Not buying more than minimum coverage limits for either Med Pay or PIP is an area where you can save money on your insurance. To fully transfer the risks of medical payments and personal injury, not just those arising from car accidents but from any illness or injury, you need major medical insurance and long term disability insurance — both of which cover financial losses no matter how the losses are caused, rendering special insurance to cover the damages caused only by car accidents superfluous.

If you do not already have major medical and long-term disability coverage in your insurance portfolio, I urge you to consider adding both immediately. See Chapter 16 on buying health insurance and Chapter 17 on disability insurance.

Dealing with Damage to Your Vehicle

In this section, I discuss how to manage the risks of damage to your vehicle — risks such as fire, theft, collision, vandalism, glass breakage, and so on. The AART noninsurance strategies from Chapter 2, particularly reducing and retaining, apply to managing vehicle damage risks. Here are just a few examples of how to use noninsurance strategies to reduce risks:

- ✔ Carrying an onboard fire extinguisher to reduce the risk of a serious fire

- ✔ Always locking your car and installing a burglar alarm to reduce the theft risk

- ✔ Parking in a locked garage at home and always parking in well-lit, nonisolated areas when away from home to reduce both theft and vandalism risks

- ✔ Keeping a safe distance behind the vehicle ahead of you to reduce the risks of both glass breakage and collisions. You can use the retaining strategy by either choosing higher deductibles or by not buying damage insurance at all and paying all claims out of your own pocket

Insurance for vehicle damage is usually offered in two parts:

- ✔ **Collision** coverage, covering damage from colliding with another object (for example, a vehicle, post, or curb), regardless of fault

- ✔ **Comprehensive** (also known as *Other Than Collision*) coverage, covering most other kinds of accidental damage to the vehicle, such as fire, theft, vandalism, glass breakage, hitting a deer, wind, or hail

Deductible psychology

Make sure that you can emotionally afford a high deductible before changing your policy. I've had a number of clients who chose higher deductibles, but when the loss occurred shed tears when actually parting with the money. I have one well-to-do client who could easily replace her new Jaguar out of petty cash but who opts for the lowest deductibles the insurance company offers. She knows herself well enough to be aware that that parting with *any* money at claim time would be emotionally traumatic.

Both of these coverages are subject to a front-end copayment on your part, called a *deductible*. When buying either or both of these coverages, it is wise to assume as much risk as you can afford, financially and emotionally, through higher deductibles — or possibly not purchasing these coverages at all. A couple of things to keep in mind here:

✓ Make sure that the insurance company gives you enough of a price discount for taking the additional risk. I offer some guidelines for choosing the most cost-effective deductibles, as well as for determining the point where dropping these coverages on an older car makes sense, later in this chapter.

✓ If you're on a tight budget but still need higher liability insurance limits to protect future assets or income (like if you're a student in medical school), it may make sense to carry higher deductibles even if the money to cover them isn't currently available. The savings will often pay for most or all of the cost of the additional liability coverage you need.

Incredibly, the savings for raising your Collision coverage deductible by just $250 (from $250 to $500) is often enough to pay for an extra $200,000 of liability insurance. No matter how tight things are, coming up with another $250 to fix dents is far easier than coming up with $200,000 to cover lawsuits!

If your driving record has deteriorated and your premiums are in danger of rising significantly with one more claim, I recommend very high deductibles, such as $1,000. In all likelihood you won't file a small claim — and risk higher rates — so why pay for something you're not going to use?

Choosing cost-effective deductibles

I estimate that the average client has a claim for damage to their vehicle every four or five years. I therefore advise clients to choose a higher deductible if the *extra risk* (the difference in deductibles) can be recouped via premium savings within a reasonable time (in other words, four to five years). The number of years it takes to recoup that added risk is called the *payback period*. The formula looks like this:

Payback period = the difference in deductibles ÷ the difference in annual premiums

If you're trying to figure out the most economical deductible, look at the hypothetical examples (Tables 3-5 through 3-8) to better understand how to determine the best deductible for you.

Table 3-5	A Three-Year-Old Lexus Coupe, Driven by a 47-Year-Old Female for Business	
	Collision	*Comprehensive*
Deductible	$250/$500/$1,000	$100/$250/$500
Extra risk (difference)	$250/$500	$150/$250
Annual premiums	$500/$400/$300	$250/$200/$150
Annual savings	$100/$100	$50/$50
Payback period (extra risk ÷ savings)	2.5 years/5 years	3 years/5 years

Here's an example of how to use a table:

Table 3-5 is an example of insurance costs for Collision and Comprehensive coverage for a three-year-old Lexus driven by a 47-year-old female and used for business. Reading across from left to right, the first row, *Deductible,* shows the different deductible choices for both damage coverages. The second row, *Extra risk,* shows the dollar amount of difference between each deductible (the extra dollar amount you will be at risk for if you choose a higher deductible). The third row, *Annual premiums,* shows the annual insurance cost for each deductible. The fourth row, *Annual savings,* shows the annual insurance cost savings if you choose the next higher deductible. And the fifth row, *Payback period,* represents the number of years it would take without a claim to save, through your reduced premiums, the amount of extra risk you would assume by opting for higher deductibles. The payback period is determined by dividing the extra deductible risk in row two by the annual insurance premium savings in row four. If the payback period is less than four or five years, choosing the higher deductible makes good sense.

In Table 3-5, the extra risk, from the second row, to increase your Collision coverage deductible from $250 to $500 is $250. The annual premium savings, from row four, to make that change is $100. Dividing the $250 extra risk by the $100 annual savings gives you 2.5 years. That means if you go 2.5 years without any claims, you save $250 on your insurance costs — the amount of the added risk you took by raising your deductible. Using the rule of choosing a higher deductible if the payback period is less than four or five years, it's clear that raising the deductible makes sense.

The payback period from the example in Table 3-5 — even for the highest deductibles — is only five years for Collision and Comprehensive coverages, making it logical to take the added risk for both coverages.

Table 3-6	A Five-Year-Old Honda Accord, Driven by a 35-Year-Old Male, 10 Miles Each Way to Work	
	Collision	*Comprehensive*
Deductible	$250/$500/$1,000	$100/$250/$500
Extra risk (difference)	$250/$500	$150/$250
Annual premiums	$300/$200/$100	$150/$100/$50
Annual savings	$100/$100	$50/$50
Payback period (extra risk ÷ savings)	2.5 years/5 years	3 years/5 years

Table 3-6 shows a five-year-old Honda used to commute to work by a 35-year-old male. Although the premiums are less than they are for the more expensive Lexus in Table 3-5, the extra risk of the higher deductibles can still be recaptured in five years and is still worth taking.

Table 3-7	A 12-Year-Old Chevy Cavalier, Driven by a 19-Year-Old Male with Three Speeding Tickets	
	Collision	*Comprehensive*
Deductible	$250/$500/$1,000	$100/$250/$500
Extra risk (difference)	$250/$500	$150/$250
Annual premiums	$1,200/$1,000/$800	$600/$450/$300
Annual savings	$200/$200	$150/$150
Payback period (extra risk ÷ savings)	1.3 years/2.5 years	1 year/1.7 years

Table 3-7 shows an older Chevy driven by a 19-year-old with three recent speeding tickets whose rates are much higher due to both his age and his driving record.

Clearly, with payback periods of 2.5 years or less for each deductible, this high-risk driver is better off with the highest deductibles possible. Not to mention that, with three tickets, he won't be turning in small claims anyway as they may result in his being dropped by the insurance company. Would he be better off not carrying the coverages at all? See the section "Knowing when to drop Collision and Comprehensive coverage" for tips on making that call.

Table 3-8	The Same 12-Year-Old Chevy Cavalier, Driven by a 74-Year-Old Widow with a Clear Record	
	Collision	**Comprehensive**
Deductible	$250/$500/$1,000	$100/$250/$500
Extra risk (difference)	$250/$500	$150/$250
Annual premiums	$150/$100/$50	$75/$50/$30
Annual savings	$50/$50	$25/$20
Payback period (extra risk ÷ savings)	5 years/10 years	6 years/12.5 years

In Table 3-8, check out what happens to the insurance costs for this same Chevy if the 19-year-old sells the car to his 74-year-old granny who has never had a ticket in her life. The payback period for the highest deductibles far exceeds the four to five year guideline. This driver would clearly be better off with low to midrange deductibles.

Knowing when to drop Collision and Comprehensive coverage

When deciding whether a vehicle's value has decreased enough to drop one or both of these vehicle damage coverages altogether, you apply the same four to five year payback guideline. The only difference is that the extra risk you're assuming is the full value of the vehicle (less any salvage value collectible from a junkyard).

Assuming an old Chevy has a junk value of $300 and would cost $2,500 to replace with an equivalent automobile, the net risk is $2,200 (the $2,500 value less the $300 salvage value). Dividing the $2,200 risk by the Collision and Comprehensive premium will give you the payback period. Drop the coverage if the payback period is five years or less.

Evaluating Road Service and Car Rental Coverages

Other coverages offered by most insurers are towing/road service coverage and loss of use/car rental coverage. I believe road service coverage, though inexpensive, is better suited to automobile clubs, like AAA, Amoco, and others. They are good at it, claims are paperless, and they offer a number of other vehicle services — all for a flat fee. On the other hand, the coverage under car insurance is not paperless — you must pay the claim first yourself (usually), then file a formal claim report and wait two to three weeks for reimbursement. Coverage also is often limited to a dollar amount ($25, $50, $75, and so on). And a large number of these claims combined with other tickets and accidents can impair your relationship with your car insurance company. I've seen it happen several times.

Loss of use/car rental coverage is quite important. Everyone depends on their vehicle. If a collision or other covered loss deprives you of your car, you probably need a substitute. If your car is badly damaged, or there is a parts delay, that car rental bill could be several hundred dollars out-of-pocket. Loss of use covers the daily cost to rent a vehicle while yours is out of commission due to a covered loss. Costs covered typically range from $10 to $50 per day for up to 30 days. I recommend buying at least a $30 per day benefit.

Chapter 4

Dealing with Special Auto Insurance Situations

Some vehicle risks have their own special set of problems, beyond the usual issues addressed in Chapter 3. Here, I address the special risks associated with renting cars when the typical Personal Auto policy covers those risks, and when it doesn't. I address the two uninsured risks you face when you're given a company car. I show you the unfair pitfall found in insurance coverage for antique and classic cars. And I even share a few pointers on motorcycle insurance.

Insuring Rental Cars

Renting a car, whether for business or for pleasure, puts you face-to-face with risks that your Personal Auto policy sometimes does not cover. Here are the four main sources of liability you face when renting a car:

✔ You have direct liability for injuries or property damage that you cause to others while operating the rental car. If you run a red light and injure others or damage their vehicle, for example, you're at fault and responsible. No surprises here.

✔ You are directly liable for damage to the rental car that you cause by your negligent driving. If you run a red light and damage the rental car, for example, you're responsible for the repair costs.

✔ You are responsible for damage to the rental car — damage that *you* did not cause but for which you agreed to be responsible when you signed the rental contract. Every rental contract I have ever looked at makes the renter absolutely liable for all damage *regardless of fault!* This clause has always been non-negotiable.

This means that you are responsible for damages such as hail damage, someone else running a red light and hitting you, someone vandalizing the car by keying it, or someone hot-wiring the car and stealing it. In short, if you return the car with any damage at all, you owe. With the cost of new cars today, that could mean more than $25,000 if the car is totaled or stolen.

✔ You are liable for the loss of revenues the car rental agency suffers as a result of the car being unavailable to rent while being repaired. Again, you will owe this loss-of-revenue regardless of whether you actually caused the damage. You agree to be responsible when you sign the contract.

Here's a tip for the car rental industry: If you want to attract new customers, offer more reasonable contracts.

Uncovering how your auto policy covers car rentals

How well do you think your auto policy would cover the four types of claims I just listed? Because Personal Auto policies vary somewhat, it's always best to check with your agent or insurer prior to renting, but here's the norm:

✔ **Injuries and property damage that you cause as a driver.** Usually you're covered up to your liability policy limit.

✔ **Damage to the rental car that you cause.** You are covered only if you have Collision and Comprehensive coverage on at least one of the vehicles on your policy, subject to your deductible. You are not covered otherwise; in this case, you may need to buy the collision-damage waiver coverage from the car rental company.

✔ **Damage to the rental car that you didn't cause.** You have contractually agreed to be responsible for all damage whether you caused it or not. Again, you are covered only if you have Collision and Comprehensive coverage on at least one of the vehicles on your policy, subject to your deductible. You are not covered otherwise.

Be sure to check with your insurance provider prior to renting a car to see exactly how your policy will apply, as policy language varies from company to company. Also, ask your agent to advise you about any state laws that might affect your coverage. Minnesota, for example, has a state law requiring that, in most cases, Personal Auto policies sold in Minnesota must cover 100 percent of all damage to a rental car. The rental car can be rented anywhere in the United States or Canada, and the policy must cover any damage the rental contract makes you responsible for, whether you cause the damage or not.

✓ **Rental company's lost income while a damaged car is being repaired.** You may be covered only if you have loss-of-use coverage on at least one vehicle on your policy, and then only up to your loss of use policy limit (usually $10 to $50 per day). Your coverage depends on your insurance company. You are covered only up to a limit — for example, $20 a day. If you buy the optional collision-damage waiver coverage from the rental company, loss-of-use may be covered in full. Courts have ruled that rental companies can only charge you for their lost income on a car you return with damage if they had no other vehicles available to rent.

Evaluating coverage from the rental agency

If you don't have automatic coverage under your Personal Auto policy for any damage to a car you are renting, regardless of cause, you normally buy the optional *collision-damage waiver (CDW)* from the rental agency. It's not true insurance, and the coverage has some holes.

Exposing the flaws

The CDW coverage supplied by rental car companies usually has two problems:

✓ **Cost:** Usually about $10 a day. If that amount doesn't sound like much to you, consider that the bill comes to $3,650 over the course of a year. Compare that to perhaps $500 a year for Collision and Comprehensive coverage to insure the same car on your Personal Auto policy. Ouch!

✓ **Restricted coverage:** The average collision-damage waiver coverage is full of restrictions that you would not tolerate if you were buying personal auto insurance. Often excluded are unlisted drivers, such as a spouse or friend who is sharing the driving with you. Other exclusions include driving outside the permitted geographic area, driving in a careless manner, or driving after drinking anything alcoholic — even a single drink. *Read the fine print before you sign!*

One for the road

I once had a client who took a business trip with a friend and coworker to California. My client signed the rental contract and listed his friend as a permitted driver. He bought the collision-damage waiver coverage from the rental agency. Later, he and his friend went to dinner. Both had a glass of wine with their meal. The friend drove the rental car back to the hotel parking lot where, in the dark, he drove over one of the concrete meridians, causing significant damage to the underside of the car — $3,500 in damage, to be exact.

Although the friend was a permitted driver, the rental agency declined to pay for the damage because of the alcohol-use exclusion and a careless-driving exclusion. If that wasn't bad enough, guess who the rental agency came after for the $3,500? It was not the friend who caused the accident. It was my client, who signed a contract in which he agreed to be absolutely responsible for all damage no matter what the cause.

The moral of the story? Avoid buying the collision-damage waiver coverage from the rental agency unless you have no other alternative. And if you are sharing the rented car with a second person other than a family member, have the rental agreement listed jointly in both names and have the other person cosign the rental agreement, so that you share the damage responsibility.

When buying CDW coverage makes sense

Even if you have insurance coverage for damage to a rental car under your Personal Auto policy, buying the collision-damage waiver coverage from the rental agency may be advantageous in two circumstances — when protecting your auto insurance rates and when renting for business.

One disadvantage of relying on your personal auto-insurance policy to pay for damage to a rental car is that if you file a claim for which you are responsible, your rates will usually increase from 20 percent to 25 percent for three years (the period of time most insurers surcharge rates for tickets and accidents). This is not so if you purchase coverage from the rental agency. In addition, if your driving record is already borderline, filing another claim against your insurance may even lead to your company dropping your policy. If either of those is an issue for you, you may want to consider buying the coverage from the rental agency and saving your Personal Auto coverage as a backup.

Buying the rental agency's coverage is also a good idea when you are renting for business purposes and your employer reimburses your expenses. Because you're using the rental car for your employer's benefit, it seems reasonable that your employer should pay for the insurance and any claim costs.

Covering your car with a credit card

Your fancy, new, super-shiny credit card has promised you insurance coverage if you use it to rent a car. How safe should you feel knowing that your card is protecting you and your rental car? Well, some cards offer very broad coverages; some are very restrictive. Some have a dollar limit; some don't.

Most credit card coverages don't pay for damage to a rental car until you prove in writing that your Personal Auto policy doesn't provide coverage. That can be a major disadvantage, as the entire cost of the rental-car damage will be charged to your credit card until you get that proof.

I wouldn't rely on coverage from your credit card unless it both provides *primary coverage* (as does Diners Club), which means it pays first and ignores your Personal Auto coverage; and has no exclusions that could hurt you, such as careless driving, driving after even a single drink, and so on. Best advice? Order a sample policy ahead of time. Read (or ask your agent to read) the policy and all its exclusions, and to make sure it pays first before any other insurance you have. If it does that, with no exclusions of any concern, use the card and decline the watered-down coverage from the rental agency.

As for the four risks associated with renting a car, your Personal Auto policy covers the first one — injuries and property damage you cause. The credit card coverage should cover the other three.

Getting the necessary coverage

If you don't have automatic coverage under a Personal Auto policy and you do not want to purchase the very limited insurance that the rental agency or credit card company offers, you can protect yourself in other ways.

In advance, contact your insurance provider with a description of the vehicle you are renting, the name of the rental agency, and the length of the trip. Request that Collision and Comprehensive coverage apply on the car you are renting for the duration of the rental period. Some insurance agents are unaware that they can do this, so you may need to do a little arm-twisting. Over the years, I have arranged this type of coverage for clients on numerous occasions. Your insurance company has the right to charge you, although they seldom do for a short-term rental because the cost would be insignificant.

Another strategy is to check with the agent or company writing your Personal Umbrella policy, if you have one. (See Chapter 10 for more on Umbrella policies.) It's a little-known fact that many — but not all — Umbrella policies pay 100 percent of the damage to a car you rent, whether you cause the damage yourself or because you agreed in the rental contract to pay for it no matter how the damage was caused. The umbrella coverage is usually subject to a small deductible, typically $250 or $500.

If a rental contract requires you to actually *insure* the vehicle — not just to be responsible for the damage — in most cases your Umbrella policy will not protect you; you will need to buy collision-damage waiver coverage from the rental agency or insure the rental car under your Personal Auto policy.

If you decide to rely on your Umbrella policy to cover damage to a car you rent, it is critical you:

- ✔ Confirm with your agent beforehand that your Umbrella policy covers all damage to a rental car, no matter how the damage is caused.

- ✔ Check that the umbrella deductible does not exceed your comfort level.

- ✔ Read the fine print of the rental contract to make sure you are only agreeing to pay for any damage and are not required to insure the car.

If any of these three are not true, don't rely on your umbrella to cover your responsibility for rental car damage.

Relying on this umbrella strategy has a disadvantage — possible claims settlement delays. Most claims departments handling umbrella-policy losses aren't set up to provide you with the immediate claim service you may need when you return a damaged rental car. If you are willing to charge the entire amount of the damage to your credit card and accept slow claim service, you're probably safe relying on the coverage that your Umbrella policy provides. If you're not comfortable using your credit card to pay the rental company up front, you may want to buy collision-damage waiver coverage from the rental agency. Your Umbrella policy is still a nice backup to cover those claims not covered by the collision-damage waiver coverage.

Renting abroad

When you are renting an automobile abroad, the rental agency offers you two optional insurance coverages:

- ✔ Liability coverage, covering your responsibility for injuries and property damage you cause to others

- ✔ Vehicle damage coverage, covering your responsibility for any damage to the rental car (this coverage is very similar to the domestic CDW coverage)

Virtually all automobile policies sold in the United States do not provide coverage outside the United States, its possessions, and Canada. Therefore, I'd advise you to buy all the coverage you can from the rental agency when you're abroad, including liability coverage for injuries and property damage, as well as vehicle damage coverage for damage to the vehicle being rented.

However, an exception exists. If you have a Personal Umbrella policy, you're probably protected worldwide for liability. I've never seen an Umbrella policy that did not provide worldwide coverage. To be safe, have your Umbrella policy agent confirm this fact before you decline other types of international coverage. I do, however, recommend that you buy the vehicle damage coverage from the rental agency. Even if your Umbrella policy covers the damage, as many do, this additional protection can help you avoid unnecessary hassles and delays in your trip.

Vacationing with friends, family, and expensive vehicles

This type of share the expense, share the driving arrangement happens fairly frequently among friends and family members taking trips together. Usually, it involves renting something expensive like a deluxe van or a motor home. Anytime you are responsible for a $150,000 motor home, you better be sure about the insurance arrangements *before* you get started!

Now that's on the hook

I had a client, Gilligan, who rented a motor home with several fishing buddies. They were heading into Canada on a dream fishing trip. They were, as usual, sharing the driving and expenses. There were only two problems with the arrangement. First, Gilligan didn't check beforehand with his agent (me) to see how to protect himself. And second, Gilligan was the only one who signed the rental contract, and therefore Gilligan and no one else was responsible for all damages to the motor home, regardless of the cause! If one of his buddies was driving and carelessly rolled the motor home, Gilligan and not his buddies would be legally responsible for the *entire* amount. If the motor home were stolen in the middle of the night, Gilligan alone would owe the $150,000.

Fortunately for Gilligan, they came home with just a broken windshield, which they all chipped in on, and a few fish stories. Gilligan was very lucky. I advised him, for next year's trip, that everyone sign the rental agreement and to buy the CDW coverage from the rental agency.

When you rent a vehicle in this type of situation, always do three things:

- ✔ Have all parties sign the contract so that everyone is jointly liable.
- ✔ Buy the optional CDW coverage from the car rental agency to avoid possible hassles if the vehicle is damaged.
- ✔ Most importantly, check with your insurance agent in advance. Ask if your automobile and umbrella coverage will protect you (as a backup).

Before renting a vehicle, whether it be for a vacation or a business trip, call your insurance provider to make sure that your policy covers all four of the liability risks associated with rental cars (injuries and property damages caused by you to others; damages caused by you to the rental car; damages to the rental car *not* caused by you; and loss of revenue while the car is being repaired). Don't be afraid to get it in writing if you're not comfortable with your agent's response. If you don't have automatic coverage, your insurance company may arrange coverage for you for the length of your trip and make whatever charge is necessary. The majority of the time, insurance companies waive the charge if the trip is for only a few days. The only disadvantage is that you have a deductible to pay for damage to the rented vehicle for which you are responsible, but that's a bargain for far better coverage at a much lower cost.

So, You've Got a Company Car — Be Careful

If you're fortunate enough to have your employer provide you with a company car, you've got a tremendous perk. These days, it's probably worth at least $400 per month to you. Like the rental car situation, it has a few pitfalls; employers are seldom aware of these pitfalls and may not be able to warn you about them.

What I'd like you to draw from this section is a healthy fear — just enough so that if you're ever furnished a company car, you'll know that insurance limitations exist. Fully informed, you can avoid those types of uses for which you are uninsured, or you can provide supplemental insurance for the company car through one of the two insurance strategies I lay out for you in this section.

When you're furnished a company car, you're insured while driving it for your liability for injuries and property damage you cause to others by your employer's Business Auto policy (BAP). You're covered when driving other company vehicles as well, and even when driving borrowed or rented vehicles on company business.

There are, however, two driving situations that the company BAP usually won't provide liability coverage for: When you borrow or rent vehicles for personal use, and when you injure a coworker riding with you in the company car.

Getting coverage if you have a Personal Auto policy

If you own and insure another car, the solution to both liability coverage gaps is simple and cheap. For driving borrowed or rented cars, your Personal Auto policy includes liability coverage automatically. Problem solved!

To protect yourself from the risk of injuring coworkers while driving your company car, call your insurance agent to add an *Extended Non-Owned Auto* endorsement. The annual cost for this optional coverage — about $10 per year.

Getting coverage if you don't have a Personal Auto policy

If you don't own a personal vehicle and the only car in your household is the company car, you've got three possible strategies to choose from.

- The best (but also the most expensive) and safest is to cover both uninsured liability coverage gaps by buying a *Named Non-Owner Personal Auto* policy. Because it is a Personal Auto policy, you have automatic liability coverage for driving other cars you borrow or rent. And because you're specifically insuring your use of the company car, your liability for coworker injuries is also covered automatically.

- A second strategy for managing the company car coverage gap has two parts:

  - Have your employer add a *Broad Form Drive Other Cars* endorsement to his BAP, which covers your liability while driving borrowed or rented vehicles. Make sure you also add all licensed family members to this endorsement or they aren't covered.

  - Buy a Personal Umbrella policy of $1 million or more to cover injuries you cause to coworkers while using the company car. (See Chapter 10 for more on Umbrella policies.) Be careful. Not all Umbrella policies cover this risk. Be sure you include the company car on the application for the policy. And be sure the insurance company makes a premium charge for the car.

✔ A third strategy is one of the ARRT noninsurance strategies from Chapter 2 — avoidance. You can avoid both risks by never driving cars other than the company car and never driving with coworker passengers.

The avoidance strategy works only if you follow it perfectly. If you cheat even once, you risk incurring a catastrophic amount of liability. Because of the difficulty of following the avoidance strategy, I recommend you use one of the first two strategies. I mention the strategy only because I've had clients choose it — although their choice made me extremely nervous.

Insuring Corporate Cars Personally

Some owners of small, family-owned corporations choose to insure a vehicle they use personally (but that is titled in the corporate name for tax purposes) under a personal rather than a corporate auto policy. Personal auto insurance is, on the average, about 30 percent less expensive than corporate auto insurance, so this does save money on the front end. But it can also lead to large uninsured claims on the back end. (See the sidebar, "Third party pooper.")

Third party pooper

Yvonne, the owner of a small company, Terrific Consultants, Inc. (TCI), is driving her new sport utility vehicle, owned corporately and insured personally. She drops her cell phone and, while she bends to pick it up, traffic ahead comes to an abrupt stop. She slams her new SUV into the back of another vehicle, causing serious injuries and property damage.

The attorney for the injured party in the other vehicle sues both the driver (Yvonne) and the owner of the vehicle (TCI) for $650,000. Yvonne carries insurance liability limits on her Personal Auto policy of $100,000. She also has an extra $1 million of coverage under a Personal Umbrella policy. Both personal policies are in the name of Yvonne and her husband jointly. The good news is that, for the injuries and property damage that Yvonne caused as the driver, she is personally protected under her two personal policies with total limits of $1.1 million. That's where the good news ends.

Because TCI is not protected under her Personal Auto policy or her Personal Umbrella policy, Yvonne will need to drain corporate dollars to defend TCI. That is not small change — usually at least $50,000. Further, if there's a judgment against TCI, she has to pay that out of TCI coffers as well!

But wait, the bad news isn't over. When the claims adjuster arrives with a $40,000 check payable to Yvonne to make up for the destruction of her SUV, he requests that Yvonne sign over the title. When he sees that the car is owned by TCI, whose interest is not listed on the policy, he expresses his regrets, tears up the check, and leaves. Yvonne and her corporation are out $40,000! Why? Because a Personal Auto policy covering Yvonne and her husband does not cover the ownership or liability interest of unlisted vehicle owners even if premiums were paid for the coverage.

If you have a corporately-owned auto insured personally, here is how you can protect yourself. You have three choices:

✔ An expensive, but easy and safe, solution is to insure the car under a Business Auto policy for the same liability limits as the rest of your business insurance.

✔ Using a risk management strategy, you can avoid the risk to your corporation completely when you initially buy the car by titling and insuring the car personally. Then the corporation won't have any ownership risks and the entire problem is solved.

✔ A more dangerous approach is to insure the corporately owned or leased vehicle under your Personal Auto policy. Do this only if you can name the corporation jointly with you as a Named Insured on the cover page (also known as the *Declarations* page) and only if your liability limits are equal to the limits of the other insurance policies the corporation carries. Otherwise, don't use this alternative.

When it comes to large risks, safe is better than cheap. When buying a car that you use for business, the safest approach is to insure the vehicle the same way you title it. Business title? Get a business policy. Personal title? Get a personal policy.

Insuring Your Car if You're Married

One of the most common mistakes I have seen, and continue to see, agents make when insuring a married couple is to list the policy in the name of only one of the spouses — usually the husband. Besides the obvious sexism, this practice creates a coverage concern. An unnamed spouse has automatic insurance only while she lives in the household. If she moves out, her automatic coverage ends — even if she's named on the policy. "But a spouse is covered equally with the partner who's named on the policy. The policy says so!" goes the rebuttal argument. True, but only if the spouse is a resident of the household. Under many policies, if you, the unlisted spouse, are not a resident of the listed spouse's household (for example, if you separate for a long period), you may have coverage only if you have your spouse's permission. It's important to know that this exclusionary language is fairly universal, not just in auto policies but in virtually every personal policy (covering homes, boats, and so on).

What this means for you if you are, say, the wife who has moved out during a separation, is that you must have your husband's permission to drive *your* car! Do you think it's possible that during a bitter divorce proceeding and following an accident you caused while on a date with another person, your soon-to-be ex may angrily tell the adjuster, "There's no way I would have given permission to her to drive this car!" Is it likely that an adjuster may ask that question? No. Is it possible? Yes. If you're the person not listed on the policy, do you want to take this chance?

And to rub salt in the wound, the spouse who isn't listed on the policy doesn't receive notice if the policy is canceled for nonpayment. Also, if one partner's car is damaged, the claims check is made out to the spouse whose name is on the policy, regardless of who the car belongs to.

When you get married, get every insurance policy listed in both names, on page one. If you are either married or separated, check your policies before you read any further — every one of them. If any are not in both names, call your agent or insurance company as soon as possible and get this omission corrected.

The insurance industry is introducing new policy forms with language that tries to solve this problem. In my opinion, some succeed and others do not. I'm not comfortable with any policy insuring a married couple unless the names of *both* the husband and the wife appear on page one. You shouldn't be comfortable, either. Also, if you are separated, do not assume that you are still covered under your old auto policy. When separated, both partners should immediately get their own policies at their current addresses in their own names. There are no other options here and neither partner should delay.

Insuring Specialized Vehicles

The Personal Auto policy covers stock vehicles, as they come from the factory, pretty well. But it doesn't cover nearly as well vehicles that stand out from the crowd, vehicles whose values are greater than the norm because either expensive additional equipment has been added or because they have a higher value as a collectible. Here are some of the insurance pitfalls to beware of and my suggestions on how best to protect yourself.

Vehicles with custom equipment

Buying vehicles that are highly customized is fairly common today. This could cover anything from custom paint jobs to captain's chairs, carpeting, high-end stereos, refrigerators, and so on. It can also include sliding campers and pickup toppers. And don't forget the specialized equipment installed in vehicles designed to assist the handicapped, such as wheelchair lifts. If the equipment is anything beyond that which comes standard from the factory, the majority of auto policies do not insure that extra equipment for damage (for example, loss through theft, fire, vandalism, or collision).

You can, however, insure the custom equipment if you declare it to the insurance company and pay an extra premium. Compare the price against the benefits and make a good decision. That way there won't be any surprises if you opt not to cover your customizations.

Antiques and classics

The biggest concern that owners of classic cars have when insuring them is getting back the full collector value of the car — not just the book value. For example, the book value on a 1965 Ford Mustang convertible may be $500 for an unrestored car. However, the car may be worth $10,000 in restored condition. So how does a classic car owner get an insurance company to pay out the $10,000 instead of the $500?

The insurance industry's solution to this problem is an optional coverage they call *stated-amount coverage*. Here's how it works, assuming that you are the owner of the Mustang: You collect and send to your insurance company both interior and exterior photos of the car and a market value appraisal from a competent appraiser. The Mustang is then listed on the policy for $10,000 and you pay a premium based on that $10,000.

If the car is stolen, how much do you expect to collect? $10,000? Not necessarily likely. Stated amount coverage pays the market value of the car at the time of the loss, not to exceed the stated amount (in this case, $10,000). People who buy stated-amount coverage mistakenly expect to receive the appraised value of the car if it is stolen or totaled. In the case of the Mustang, however, if the market has recently soured and the market value of the car is $6,000, you receive $6,000 — not the $10,000 that your premiums have been based on. Now assume that the market for the Mustang has improved, and the car's value is now $13,000. How much will you receive? Unfortunately, $10,000 — not the $13,000. This does not make for a happy camper!

Obviously, an inequity exists here. The major pitfall of stated-amount coverage is that it pays the *lesser* of the stated amount and the actual value of the car at the time of the loss. It does not pay any increases in the car's value.

Until the insurance industry comes up with a better solution, I recommend that you adopt the following strategy when insuring antique or classic cars:

1. Do *not* buy the optional stated-amount coverage. Instead, opt for the usual actual cash value coverage that comes standard with the policy.

2. Gather the same photos of both the interior and exterior and appraisals and keep them in a secure place outside the vehicle to prove what you had if the car is ever stolen.

If the car is ever totaled or stolen, the insurance company owes you the actual cash value (most commonly the actual market value) of your vehicle on the date of loss. That is where the photos and appraisal come in. You simply bring that documentation to a competent appraiser at claim time, have them give you a new current value appraisal, and submit the photos and the new appraisal to the adjuster for payment. In the case of the two examples involving the Mustang, you would receive its actual value at the time of the loss — $6,000 in the first example and $13,000 in the second.

In sum, if you adopt this strategy, you get paid properly. Plus, you save the added premium that you would be charged for stated-amount coverage.

A Swing and a Myth: Automatic Coverage for New Cars

I often get phone calls from clients wanting to add coverage for a newly purchased automobile that they've been driving casually for a couple of weeks. When I tell them that they've been driving without car insurance, they reply with a shocked, "But I thought I had 30-days automatic coverage!" That is often not the case. Yes, you do have automatic coverage for newly acquired vehicles under certain circumstances (for example, if it's the first Tuesday of the month following a full moon). But *assuming* that you have automatic coverage is a huge mistake. I won't bore you to tears describing all the scenarios in which you don't have coverage. Let me give you the bottom-line instead.

When adding a newly purchased vehicle to your auto policy, *always* arrange for the insurance on the vehicle to commence prior to the day you transfer the title or the day you start driving the new car regularly, whichever comes first. If you don't, you may be uninsured at claim time.

All Personal Auto policies provide automatic liability coverage when test-driving a vehicle. That coverage, however, often stops the day you acquire possession. Follow this ironclad rule and never be caught with your insurance pants down.

If you're selling a car, don't rely on the buyer to complete the title transfer for you, or you may get a phone call in the middle of the night from the police wondering about your abandoned car that was in an accident involving some serious injuries. Whether you are a buyer or a seller, always accompany the other person to the title-transfer office and request proof of the transfer. Then, if you are the seller, remove the insurance from the car.

Motorcycles

Because most of Chapter 3 on the subject of automobiles also applies to motorcycles, this section is brief. Here are my insurance tips for two-wheelers:

- Buy the same liability insurance limits for injuries and property damage to others that you buy for all your other insurance coverage (home, boat, cabin).

- Likewise, buy the same liability limits for guest passengers riding with you, if those limits are available. If they're not, don't carry passengers!

- Avoid lay-up periods, during which all coverage except Comprehensive is suspended for a small premium credit. It's simply not worth the risk of you forgetting and accidentally driving during the lay-up period, such as on an unseasonably nice day in February, with no insurance.

- Avoid buying more medical coverage than state law requires. It simply duplicates the health insurance you already should be carrying. Following this tip will save you quite a bit of money on your cycle insurance. (If you do not carry health insurance, you're breaking one of my Chapter 1 rules and gambling with more than you can afford to lose!)

- If it's available in your state, carry Uninsured and Underinsured Motorists coverage in limits equal to your liability limits.

- If you've customized your cycle, make sure to list the additions on your application. You may have to pay an extra premium if you want that equipment covered.

- If your cycle is worth enough that you carry Collision and Comprehensive coverage, follow the guidelines in Chapter 3 regarding how to choose the most cost-effective deductibles.

I close this motorcycle section with the two best risk management tips I know of. They reduce both the chance of — and the seriousness of — injury claims to yourself and others.

- Prevent serious head injuries. Everyone on the cycle should wear a helmet. No exceptions.

- Minimize the amount of time you carry passengers, as passenger injuries are the number one source of lawsuits against motorcycle operators.

Preventing and Reducing Automobile Loss

One of the ARRT noninsurance techniques discussed in Chapter 2 of managing the risks that you face is loss reduction. Some of the following tips reduce your insurance premiums. Some save lives. Some simply reduce the chance of claims happening.

General tips

If you're really serious about being the captain of your own ship and managing the personal risks in your life, give some serious thought to this advice. Insurance only pays cash after the loss. It cannot undo or prevent accidents, reverse injuries, or bring back the dead.

- Take a defensive driving course. Even if you don't get a premium credit, you will be a better driver and have less chance of being involved in a serious accident, either one that is not your fault or one that you cause. And fewer accidents means better rates (and maybe longer lives).

- Drive within the speed limit. People who speed have a lot more accidents. (See the statistics later in the chapter.)

- If you have teenage drivers, give them many more hours of behind-the-wheel practice than they get in a driver's education class. Experts recommend at least an additional 40 hours.

- Don't drink and drive. Use a designated driver. If you have teenager, mutually sign a SADD contract agreeing with your teenager not to drink and drive. *SADD* stands for *Students Against Driving Drunk*. More information and their contract can be obtained from their Web site at www.saddonline.com. It's a wonderful contract.

- Always wear a seatbelt, and insist that your passengers do too. My own son was the passenger at age 16 in a friend's car. There was a head-on collision on a curve. Both cars were traveling at 40 mph. The front end of his friend's Monte Carlo was crushed like an accordion. My son, fortunately, walked away unharmed, except for a few scrapes to his knees. When I saw the car later, I couldn't believe that anyone had lived, let alone walked away. Thankfully, my son wore his seatbelt!

- Equip your car with all the optional safety equipment — antilock brakes, air bags, safety tires, and so on. Most of these safety features result in a premium credit, too.

✔ Get into the habit of locking your car. Doing so not only reduces the risk of your car being stolen but also prevents loss of personal belongings that are in the car. (And don't forget to put those unattended valuables in the trunk with the trunk release disabled. My wife and I learned that one the hard way!)

✔ Consider a security system (also a premium credit) or at least a theft deterrent like those devices that lock over your steering wheel. An alarm system is especially important if your car contains an expensive stereo system or has a rag convertible-top.

Most of these tips are pretty simple to implement and cost little or no money. But implementing them definitely reduces the likelihood of injuries and property damage to you and those you love. Some may result in immediate insurance premium savings. The rest save you premiums in the long run because of much lower than average claims activity.

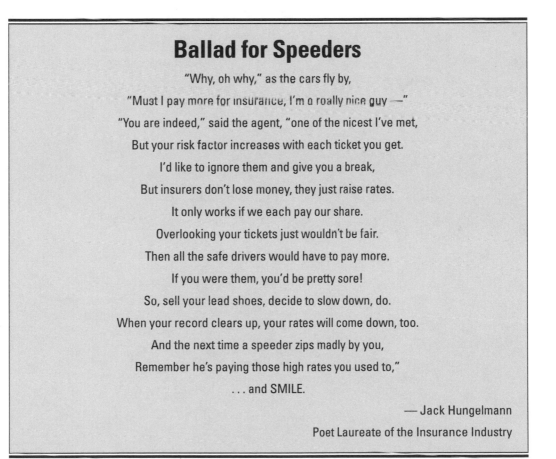

Ballad for Speeders

"Why, oh why," as the cars fly by,

"Must I pay more for insurance, I'm a really nice guy —"

"You are indeed," said the agent, "one of the nicest I've met,

But your risk factor increases with each ticket you get.

I'd like to ignore them and give you a break,

But insurers don't lose money, they just raise rates.

It only works if we each pay our share.

Overlooking your tickets just wouldn't be fair.

Then all the safe drivers would have to pay more.

If you were them, you'd be pretty sore!

So, sell your lead shoes, decide to slow down, do.

When your record clears up, your rates will come down, too.

And the next time a speeder zips madly by you,

Remember he's paying those high rates you used to,"

. . . and SMILE.

— Jack Hungelmann

Poet Laureate of the Insurance Industry

Especially for speeders

I would like to close this chapter with a section for those who like to speed. A recent study indicated that, with one speeding ticket in the last two years, your probability of having an at-fault accident increased 95 percent. With two tickets, your probability increased 170 percent. If you received three speeding tickets, you were 254 percent more likely to have an accident. If you have four speeding tickets, you are almost 300 percent more likely to have an accident. This should help you understand why insurance companies bump your rate up when you get speeding tickets.

Part III

Understanding Home Insurance

The 5th Wave   By Rich Tennant

Neither one of us wanted a silo on the new master suite, but things like this can happen when you don't clean the coffee rings off your building plans.

In this part . . .

Most of us live a significant portion of our lives in and around our homes, whether those homes are single-family residences, condominiums, town houses, or apartments. We fill these places with the necessary and unnecessary stuff of our lives. Losing the home and/or the stuff would be catastrophic. These chapters show you ways to insure against a loss, how to expose gaps in your current coverage, and how to minimize the risk of a loss ever occurring.

Chapter 5

Understanding the Basics of Homeowners Insurance

1 consider Homeowners insurance policies to be outstanding values. They offer tremendous amounts of coverage for very few dollars. I also consider them to be the most dangerous personal policies you can buy because they contain the largest number of exclusions and limitations.

Therefore, it's critical when buying Homeowners insurance to identify what you're exposed to that falls outside the basic box of coverages. Then, you can develop a strategy for avoiding, reducing, retaining, or transferring (via insurance) those exposures prior to a serious uninsured loss. See Chapter 2 for more information on these various strategies.

In auditing hundreds of insurance plans over my career for prospective clients, I've seen that the vast majority of those people had at least one, and often several, parts of their life that were uninsured. Luckily, we worked out better coverage that plugged those coverage gaps. But when do most people find out that they have inadequate insurance? At claim time, when the loss isn't covered!

Most people make the mistake of shopping their insurance on price alone. What they usually end up with is a cheaper price for the wrong coverage! (See Chapter 12 on the right way to buy insurance.)

To buy Homeowners insurance right, one must first understand something about the basic policy. In this chapter I show you the fundamentals of Homeowners insurance.

Introducing the Six Parts of a Homeowners Policy

All Homeowners policies have six major coverage parts (except renters policies, which have four). They're presented in Table 5-1.

Table 5-1	The Six Major Coverage Parts of a Typical Homeowner's Policy
Type of Coverage	**What It Covers**
Coverage A	Damage to or destruction of your residence
Coverage B	Damage to or destruction of detached structures
Coverage C	Damage to, destruction of, or theft of personal property anywhere in the world
Coverage D	The added living costs you incur as a result of a loss covered by A, B, or C (lodging, meals, and utilities)
Coverage E	Personal liability (non-automobile) for injuries and property damage at home and anywhere else worldwide
Coverage F	Medical payments to guests injured on your premises, regardless of any fault

Coverages A and B don't apply to renters. Find out about each of the six coverages, including some of the pitfalls to be careful of, in the rest of this chapter.

Insuring your residence (Coverage A)

If you arrange the coverage on your residence properly, the insurance company fully repairs or replaces your home if it is damaged or destroyed by a covered cause-of-loss — fire, tornado, or whatever your policy happens to cover. Be aware of two possible claims penalties for insuring your home for less than its full replacement cost.

The first penalty occurs if you are underinsured for a *total loss* — for the complete destruction of your home. Say your home that you bought and insured for $275,000 burns to the ground. The cost to rebuild that house in today's market is $350,000. Since you insured the house for $275,000, you suffer an out-of-pocket loss of $75,000.

The second penalty for underinsurance occurs when your home is partially damaged. Say you purchase a beautiful, turn-of-the-century, two-story home. You insure it for the $250,000 you paid for it. (The purchase price of $300,000 less the $50,000 lot value). Were you to build this home new today, it would cost you $500,000. Let's assume that you have a kitchen fire with extensive smoke and water damage. And that the total cost to repair your home is $150,000. Your insurance company pays you $100,000. You're out $50,000! Why?

The vast majority of Homeowners policies will only pay the full cost to replace partial damage to your home if you insure your home for at least 80 percent or more of the cost to rebuild new. If you insure your home for less than 80 percent of the home's full replacement cost, your claim settlement will be depreciated. On older homes, that may reduce your claim settlement by 35 percent or more. In the earlier example, the cost to completely rebuild your 100-year-old home isn't the $250,000 you insured your home for, but $500,000. Since $250,000 is far less than 80 percent of $500,000, your settlement will be depreciated.

Translated into English from insurance-ese, the policy essentially says that if you insure your home for its depreciated market value (in this case, $250,000), the insurance company settles with you on a depreciated basis at claim time. The $50,000 penalty in the example above represents the amount of depreciation deducted from the repair costs.

If, on the other hand, you insure your home for its cost to build new (or at least 80 percent of that value, according to the formula in the policy), the insurance company settles your claim for the full replacement cost of the damage — up to your policy limit.

In short, if you insure for depreciated values, at claim time the insurance company deducts depreciation from repair costs. If you insure for the cost to rebuild, the insurance company pays the full repair costs at claim time.

Always insure for 100 percent of the estimated new replacement cost. Paying the extra premium is far easier than facing thousands of dollars in losses out-of-pocket at claim time from either not having enough insurance to rebuild if your home is destroyed or having your repair costs substantially depreciated on partial losses. And add a Home Replacement Guarantee, if it's available — more on these later.

Insuring detached structures (Coverage B)

Virtually all Homeowners policies extend ten percent of Coverage A — the residence coverage — to detached structures. In other words, if your home is insured for $200,000, you've got up to $20,000 worth of coverage for any detached structure. There is no added charge for this feature. Examples of structures would include garages, pole barns, and in-ground swimming pools. Always check your particular policy. This book is written with the average or typical policy in mind, but your policy may be different.

This coverage has two pitfalls including the possibility of underinsurance if the structure can't be replaced for the ten percent automatic coverage. The second pitfall is that any structure used even partially for business is excluded. Here's an example from my own files that illustrates both pitfalls.

Bob and Bobbie have a home insured for $150,000. They have a four-car, detached garage with an upstairs loft. If they were to build this garage new today, it would cost them $35,000. They have automatic coverage from the policy that covers their house in the amount of $15,000 (ten percent of $150,000). To be properly insured, they have to buy an additional $20,000 of detached structure coverage to bring their total coverage to $35,000.

Make sure your detached structure limit equals the total replacement value of all detached structures on your premises.

Continuing on with their story, Bob is self-employed. He owns and manages several rental properties. His detached garage, besides storing vehicles, also houses business equipment like lawn mowers, snowblowers, and so on. In addition, his business office is located upstairs in the loft portion of the detached garage. Now, assume a tornado comes through destroying his $35,000 garage. Since he bought the extra $20,000 coverage, he does have $35,000 of insurance. His adjuster shows up with a $35,000 check the next day, right? Wrong. Because Bob stored business equipment in that garage, the insurance company could deny his entire claim.

It certainly doesn't seem fair, but this is how the coverage works. The equipment had nothing to do with causing the destruction of the garage. Yet, all the insurance company has to prove to deny the claim is that the garage was even partially used for business purposes. There is no requirement at all that the business in the garage had anything to do with the loss.

If you have a detached structure on your home premises that is even remotely used for business other than for storing business vehicles, you *must* request an endorsement to your Homeowners policy that permits that business use.

Excusing the exclusions

I'm often asked why are there so many property exclusions and limitations in Homeowners policies. One reason is *fairness*. Remember, insurance is just a mechanism where people facing similar risks pool resources (pay premiums) into a large pot (the insurance company). It's from that pot that compensation for damages from fires, thefts, lawsuits, and so on is paid. Insurance companies don't pay claims, really. We do with our premiums. The insurer is simply a middleman. The company collects money from those of us who don't have losses and redistributes it to those who do.

It's important that people who share losses be similar in the risks they face. That way, people with greater risks than the norm aren't being subsidized by those with normal residential risks. For example, people with vast amounts of jewelry have considerably more jewelry claims than the usual homeowner. If jewelry coverage were unrestricted in the policy, the rates for non-jewelry owners would go up every time the jewelry owner lost or had another piece stolen.

Contrary to public perception, then, these exclusions and limitations are not in the policy to be nasty. They are there primarily to make sure that the premiums will be fair to all payers. Most of what is limited or excluded in the basic policy can be insured for an extra charge.

Read your policy to know what is limited or excluded, before a serious loss happens, so that you can properly modify the policy to cover those things that otherwise would not be covered.

Insuring your belongings (Coverage C)

Even renters need the next four coverages, starting with coverage on belongings. Two ways exist to value personal belongings for insurance purposes — used, referred to in the policy as *actual cash value,* or new, referred to as *replacement cost.*

Buy the replacement cost option! It's generally only about ten percent more expensive but you'll receive 30 to 40 percent more at claim time. If the total cost of replacing your belongings after a major loss is $100,000, with replacement value coverage, you will receive $100,000 less your deductible. With actual cash value coverage, you will probably receive from $60,000 to $70,000, after deducting depreciation. Believe me, at claim time you'll be glad you bought the better coverage.

It is a requirement of the replacement value coverage that you actually do replace the damaged or stolen property. Until you do replace it, the insurance company only pays you the depreciated or used value.

For residence owners, the basic Homeowners policy comes standard with personal property coverage of 50 to 75 percent of your Coverage A building limit. The exact percentage varies, depending on the insurance company. If you have a lot of high-end personal property, the automatic coverage provided under the Homeowners policy may not be enough. Later in this chapter, I show you some tools to help estimate what your belongings are worth.

Continuing with the Bob and Bobbie example from earlier in the section, in addition to the usual personal belongings, Bob owns $30,000 of mechanic's tools. (He's a former auto mechanic.) He maintains only his own vehicles with the tools, so they're not excluded under business-use provisions. Bob and Bobbie insure their home for $150,000, with the Home Replacement Guarantee and replacement cost contents coverage. Their automatic contents limit is 70 percent of the $150,000, or $105,000. They feel they need the entire $105,000 to replace their normal household property. So, to customize their policy to their unique needs, they purchase an additional $30,000 coverage for the tools, or a total of $135,000.

Be sure you evaluate the contents-coverage limit on your policy and customize it to your needs. Don't just take what comes automatically with your policy. It may not be enough.

Insuring additional living expenses (Coverage D)

Your house is blown away by a tornado. Even your kitchen sink is in the next county. You check into a motel and call your insurance agent. You will need a place to live until you rebuild. You'll need to eat your meals out. You'll need a daily massage to soothe your shattered nerves. But you won't have much in the way of utility bills. And you won't be buying any groceries. Some of your living expenses will go way up. Others will shrink. The difference between the two expenses — the *additional living expense* — is covered by Coverage D — additional living expense coverage.

This helpful coverage pays the additional — not the total — expenses you have to incur for lodging, meals, utilities, and so on as a result of a covered loss, such as a fire, smoke, or windstorm, that causes you to vacate your home. It usually will pay these costs for up to the policy limit, if any, or 12 months, whichever is exhausted first. With some insurers, the benefit is unlimited (always a plus). With others, the benefit is a percentage of the Coverage A building limit. Though higher limits are available, the odds of exhausting the base benefit are quite slim and therefore almost no one buys more. After all, can't Aunt Matilda put you up for a few weeks in her basement?

Insuring your personal liability (Coverage E)

Though the cost of coverage for your personal liability for injuries and property damage you cause represents a small part of your total Homeowners bill, in my opinion, this is just about the most important coverage in the policy. Why? Because it covers lawsuits — and the cost of defending against lawsuits. And because it's so comprehensive, covering most of your nonvehicle personal liability worldwide. Here are some examples of claims Coverage E would cover, including some from my own files.

- ✔ Your six-year-old spills red punch on the neighbor's white carpet, which requires a $3000 carpet replacement.

- ✔ You get sued by a neighbor who, in spite of your repeated warnings, has allowed his child to climb your fence and harass your German shepherd. The child gets mauled, and you get sued.

- ✔ Your riding lawnmower kicks up a rock — into a neighbor — and injures her.

- ✔ A child is hurt while you are babysitting her.

- ✔ In a baseball game, your teenage son throws errantly to home plate and hits another player in the face, causing a loss of vision. That player grows older, still suffers from a loss of vision, and sues five years later for $100,000.

- ✔ You hit someone in the face playing racquetball.

- ✔ You are snowboarding and collide accidentally with a skier who sues for injuries.

- ✔ Playing golf, your errant tee shot hits a bystander in the head. (Happens to me all the time.)

The bottom line? It's great coverage! Most Homeowners policies usually include the first $100,000 of coverage at no extra charge.

The two biggest mistakes I see people make in with this personal liability coverage are not buying more than the $100,000 free coverage, and not setting their liability limit to match their other liability policy limits (on cars, a cabin, boats).

To illustrate the latter, I often see people buy $100,000 Homeowners liability coverage, $300,000 automobile liability coverage, and $50,000 boat liability coverage. You don't know where the lawsuit may come from and therefore you want the same pool of money protecting you no matter where it does come from. You wouldn't want different liability limits for different policies any more than you'd want different liability limits for different days of the week!

How much liability coverage should you buy? Here are some considerations:

- ✔ **Your sueability factor.** Defined in Chapter 3, how sueable you are is affected by the size of your bank account, your income, your future income, and your asset prospects (in other words, inheritances). In short, it represents how likely it is that an attorney for the person you injure will come after you personally if you don't have enough insurance.

- ✔ **Your comfort zone.** How high do you need the limits to go for your own peace of mind? Remember a guideline from Chapter 1 — Don't risk more than you can afford to lose.

- ✔ **Your sense of moral responsibility.** Many people with a modest income and few assets buy high liability limits to be sure anyone they may hurt gets provided for. If you are one of these thoughtful people, I tip my hat in admiration and respect.

- ✔ **The insurance cost of higher limits is minimal.** Additional liability insurance is truly one of the best values in the insurance business. An extra $200,000 costs only about $15 a year! And an extra $400,000 costs only about $25 a year. Follow another Chapter 1 guideline — Don't risk a lot for a little. Accepting the $100,000 basic limit and not having an extra $200,000 to $400,000 of lawsuit coverage, when the cost is $15 to $25 a year, clearly violates this principle. If you need to scrimp, do it where the potential pain is much less, such as an extra $250 added to your deductible; your life won't be ruined if you have a higher homeowners property damage deductible, but it may be if you owe hundreds of thousands of dollars due to losing a personal liability lawsuit.

Another consideration in setting your liability limit is the economic value of the injury you cause. How much would you sue for if you were the one injured? Imagine yourself with a serious back injury caused by someone else. Let's say you're at their house, and you fall through a floorboard that they'd forgotten to nail back into place. You're hospitalized for a while, and undergo a couple of surgeries. Then you need several years of medical care and rehabilitation. You are off work two or more years. Table 5-2 illustrates is the economic value of your injury.

Table 5-2	Economic Value of an Injury
Type of Expense	*Expense*
Total medical bills	$125,000
Lost wages	$100,000
Years of pain and suffering	$250,000
Total	**$475,000**

Assume this is the judge's ruling: "I hereby award you the amount of your own Homeowners liability limit!" Now, pull out your policy. Look at your liability limit. Could you live with that? Could you live with it if your injury resulted in your paralysis?

So, how much liability coverage should you buy? Here is my bottom line advice regarding liability limits. Choose a liability limit that considers your current and future assets and income, feels emotionally comfortable, satisfies your sense of moral responsibility to others, and matches what you would expect if you were the one suing.

Don't dismiss the last point as trivial. There *is* a strong correlation between the amount you would sue for, based on your own financial position and expectations, and the amount someone else may sue you for, also based on your financial position. The bottom line? In my opinion, anyone with less than $500,000 liability coverage is underinsured. Most of us should have limits of $1 million or more.

Whatever limit you decide on, be sure to adjust your auto, boat, and personal liability limits to match.

Insuring guests' medical bills (Coverage F)

This is the sixth and final (and least important) Homeowners coverage part. Let's start with what this is not. It is not health insurance for you or your family. Rather, it's what I call *good neighbor* coverage. If a guest gets hurt on your premises, even if the injury is caused by their own carelessness, this coverage pays her medical bills up to the coverage limit, usually $1,000.

You can increase the limit for an extra premium, but I would save your money. Most guests have health insurance already. If they are seriously hurt and may sue, your liability coverage responds. Just be aware that you have this coverage if you have an injured guest. Like I said — good neighbor coverage.

Choosing the Right Homeowners Property Coverages

Coverages A, B, C, and D of Homeowners policies cover property damage to your dwelling, detached structures and their contents, and any increase in living expenses related to property damage. That's how Homeowners policies

are similar. How they differ is in the kinds of losses they cover. All Homeowners policies cover damage from fire or a windstorm, for example. But
only some policies cover water damage from cracked plumbing or toilet overflows. And none automatically cover damage from a flood or an earthquake,
though both coverages can be purchased. In order to make a good decision
when choosing the Homeowners policy best suited to your needs, understanding your choices as to which causes-of-loss are covered and which are
not is important.

Understanding the causes-of-loss option

When you have a Homeowners claim for damage to your property, the first
question is "Was the cause of the damage covered by the policy?" If "yes,"
your claim is paid. If "no," your claim is denied. Most insurance companies
offer three choices for the types of losses covered — Basic Form, Broad
Form, and Special Form.

- **Basic Form causes-of-loss.** Very limited coverage. Limited to a handful of
  covered causes-of-loss, including fire, wind, vandalism, and very limited
  theft. Rarely sold or purchased anymore.

- **Broad Form causes-of-loss.** Covers about 15 causes-of-loss. From my
  experience, the vast majority of the kinds of loss that damage a home or
  contents are covered. If you have a loss that's on the list, you're probably covered. If the cause of the loss isn't on the list, you're probably not
  covered.

- **Special Form causes-of-loss.** The best. Covers any accidental cause-of-
  loss unless that cause-of-loss is specifically excluded. (Damage from
  floods, ground water, sewer backup, earthquakes, and a few others
  causes-of-loss aren't covered.)

I flat out suggest that you not buy the Basic Form coverage. The coverage is
way too restrictive. I like any of the choices that include the Broad Form coverage because the majority of your losses will be covered. But my favorite is
the Special Form. It puts you in the driver's seat. No matter how bizarre the
cause, from Martian invasions to some kind of damage from new cybertech-
nology, your loss is covered.

Here are some examples, many from my own experience, of losses not
included in the Broad Form list that are covered by the Special Form:

✔ Massive interior water damage from roof leaks to a townhouse. $30,000 paid.

✔ Interior damage to ceilings and walls caused by melting ice and snow that backed up under the shingles. Claims have averaged $2,000 to $5,000.

✔ Scorched counters or floors from hot pans dropped onto them. Claims to replace counters and floors run $5,000 or more.

✔ Paint spills on furniture. The average claim runs $2,000.

✔ Spills of any liquids on oriental rugs. Claims to replace the rug range from $600 to $20,000.

Probably the most unusual example I've heard of involved someone who took a month-long winter vacation in Florida. To keep their pipes from freezing back home in the cold North, they set their thermostat at 50 degrees. Shortly after they left home, the thermostat malfunctioned and never shut off. The combination of 90-degree heat and winter dryness warped all the floorboards in the house, requiring the entire flooring to be torn up and replaced. Most of the floor coverings — tile, carpet, and so on — which had to be removed to get at the floor, also had to be replaced. The claim cost was in excess of $20,000.

Neither "thermostat malfunction" nor "excessive heat" is on the list of covered losses on the Broad Form. But the Special Form covered the loss in full because "thermostat malfunction" is not on the list of exclusions. The annual extra insurance cost for the Special Form over the Broad Form? Probably $50 a year. (I'd say the homeowner with the faulty thermostat got his money's worth!)

Introducing the six most common Homeowners policies

If you looked at a typical menu of Homeowners policies available from most insurance companies, you would see six entrees. From light fare to a full course meal. One is designed specifically for renters, one specifically for townhouse or condominium owners, and the rest for owners of private residences.

Table 5-3 shows the six Homeowners forms most commonly used in the industry, the type of buyer they are designed for, and the causes-of-loss covered under each (Basic, Broad, or Special).

Table 5-3		The Six Homeowners Policy Forms	
Type of Buyer	*Form #*	*Building Coverage*	*Contents Coverage*
Homeowner	1	Basic	Basic
Homeowner	2	Broad	Broad
Homeowner	3	Special	Broad*
Renter	4	N/A	Broad*
Homeowner	5	Special	Special
Townhouse or condo owner	6	Broad*	Broad*

*The Special Form is available as an option at additional cost.

To choose the Homeowners form best for you, first determine what type of buyer you are — homeowner, renter, or townhouse/condominium owner. Second, determine the causes-of-loss you want covered — Basic, Broad, or Special — for the building and again for the contents.

For example, if you rent, you would choose Homeowners Form 4. It comes automatically with Broad Form coverages. You can buy the Special Form for an extra charge. If you're a homeowner and you want Special Form coverage on your structures but are comfortable with Broad Form coverage on belongings, you would choose Homeowners Form 3.

Which form do most insurers sell and 90 percent of homeowners buy? The Form 3, covering buildings with the Special Form and contents with the Broad Form. The logic behind this is that the structure is the biggest property risk, and totally exposed to the elements, whereas most contents are more protected by being inside. It's a reasonable argument. I think Form 3 is a reasonable choice for most people.

If you have expensive personal belongings, fine arts, expensive rugs, paintings, or antiques, or if you simply like having the best, Special Form contents coverage is the best choice for you. It's only about 10 percent more expensive than Broad Form coverage.

Here's how to get Special Form coverage for both your home and contents:

✔ **If You Own A Home,** you have two choices: Buy a Homeowners Form 5, if available, or buy a Form 3 and add a Special Perils contents endorsement.

✔ **If You Own A Townhouse or Condo,** add a Special Perils endorsement to Coverage A (building coverage), and add a Special Perils contents endorsement.

✔ **If You Rent,** add a Special Perils contents endorsement.

Establishing Property Coverage Limits

Insuring your home and contents properly to get the very best payout at claim time means insuring both for their full replacement cost. You have a pretty good idea of the market value of your home. But where do you find the replacement value? And how in the world do you compute the cost now of all your furniture, clothing, appliances, and other belongings without taking six months off from work and consuming a drawer full of pain-reliever for all the headaches you will have?

Here are some tools that can help you establish the approximate replacement cost of your building and contents.

Determining the replacement cost of your home

Most insurance companies and/or their agents will estimate the replacement cost of your home using a computer program designed for that purpose. But how can you be sure their estimate is accurate?

Insuring your home for its replacement cost is important, to avoid serious penalties at claim time. But not spending more than you need to by over-insuring your home is important too.

Perhaps the most accurate way to estimate your home's replacement cost is to spend $200 to $500 (or more) and have a professional appraisal done. But that strategy is tough on the budget. And it violates the KISS rule of Chapter 1 — to keep it simple.

You have four alternatives to a professional appraisal that are quicker and far less costly and that still yield a pretty accurate replacement cost estimate. I recommend you use at least one to double-check your insurance company's estimate.

Double check the agent's worksheet

Have the agent send you her worksheet. Make sure all the features and square footage are correct. Many times the information is not correct because of the difficulty of the computation process.

Use your home mortgage appraisal

If you've financed or refinanced your home recently, you paid for an appraisal. You're entitled to a copy. If you don't have a copy already, call your mortgage company and have them send you one. True, the appraisal is for market value, not cost new. But in almost all appraisals, the appraiser also lists the replacement cost. Their numbers are typically conservative, so be sure your building insurance equals or exceeds the mortgage appraisal's replacement cost estimate.

For example, if the insurance agent calculates the cost, new, of your home at $278,000 and your bank appraisal estimated it at $262,000, I'd be comfortable with the agent's number. But if your bank appraisal estimated the cost, new, at $175,000, I'd make an issue out of that big difference. If you send the agent your bank appraisal, I'll bet you can get her to adjust her number downward. Even if the agent has all the correct features and square footage, she still can err. Why? Because in the agent's replacement-cost computer program, there's a major criteria that is judgment-based — the quality of construction. A huge gap between your bank appraisal and the agent's estimate could mean that the agent misjudged the class or quality of construction of your home.

For what it's worth, I use my clients' bank appraisals constantly to check my numbers and judgment. I'm human and so is your agent.

Deducting the lot value from the market value

If your home is newer and you have a good idea as to its current value, subtract from that amount the value of the lot and detached structures. You can get those values from your bank appraisal or from a good realtor.

Assume the home was built four years ago at $245,000. Now, four years later, the cost new would be somewhat larger. If the agent's replacement cost is $258,000, new, that would be reasonable. But if the agent's calculation is $205,000, it would have to be in error since the cost to rebuild the home is never going to be less than the cost spent to build it four years ago.

If the agent's calculation is $378,000, and considering your four-year-old value of $245,000, the agent has to have made an error. That $100,000 plus error, if you don't contest it, will cost you $400 a year — $4,000 if you keep your home for ten years!

Using a builder

A builder who knows your neighborhood (or your builder if you had your home built) can give you a rebuilding estimate on a cost per square foot basis. Multiplying that cost per square foot times the number of square feet gives you an estimated cost to rebuild.

None of these four methods is precise, but any of them will give you some leverage in negotiations with the insurer. I've found that the larger and/or more customized your home is, especially if it's an older home, the more likely it is that the insurance company's estimate is wrong. Determining the replacement cost of your home is a difficult process, but definitely worth your time.

Guaranteeing you'll have enough insurance to rebuild

You've done your homework. You've double-checked your agent's replacement cost estimate and made appropriate coverage corrections. Suddenly, your home burns to the ground. You've insured your home for $258,000, but after the fire, the true cost to haul all the debris and rebuild is $292,000. You tried your best to buy the right coverage but your out-of-pocket loss is $34,000! ($292,000 minus $258,000.) Good news! This problem has a great solution — an optional coverage called Home Replacement Guarantee.

As a result of the lessons of Hurricane Andrew, many insurers have capped their Home Replacement Guarantee (usually 125 percent of your building coverage). Unlimited coverage, though, is still very available. I like the unlimited, especially if you have an older home where the exact replacement cost is difficult to determine.

Not all Homeowners insurance companies offer this guarantee on older homes. I recommend you only consider insurance companies that do offer it.

When insuring your home, always double-check the insurance agent's replacement cost estimate so you don't overinsure your home and thus pay too much for your insurance. And always buy the optional Home Replacement Guarantee, without a cap if possible.

Estimating the cost to replace belongings

The most accurate way to determine the cost of replacing all your belongings, of course, is to take a full inventory of *everything* that you own. No one does that. But three methods get you close enough, whether you own or rent.

The 200 percent method

I like this method and use it a lot because you can do it in 30 minutes or less (remember the KISS principle from Chapter 1).

1. **Total the estimated new cost for all the major items in your home —** **furniture, stereo, TVs, appliances, computers, and so on.**

2. **Double the total.** This will insure that you not only have enough coverage to replace all the major items you own, but that you have an equal amount available for all the smaller items — clothing, dishes, linens, athletic equipment, seasonal and stored items, and so on.

3. **Add to that the values of any exceptional property or collections, artwork, tools, home workshops, and so on.**

Keep it fast and simple. Use your best guess on values. No catalogs or phone calls to stores, or it won't get done.

Remember Bob and Bobbie from earlier in the chapter? When they used this method to estimate the value of their belongings, they came up with a total of $43,000 for their major items (stereo, TV, furniture, and appliances). Doubled, that came to $86,000. Then, they added Bob's auto-mechanic tools, with a replacement cost of $35,000, for a total of $121,000. That's how much they have their possessions insured for.

The square-footage method

A leading property-appraisal firm furnishes the insurance industry with guides they developed by actually going to people's homes and apartments and physically adding up the replacement values of people's personal property, then relating those results to either the number of rooms or the total square feet.

If your agent has this guide, he can help you estimate the average value of the belongings for a home or apartment your size. You can use your judgment to increase or decrease that average value.

The percent of building-value method (for home-owners only)

Oddly, the vast majority of Homeowners insurance buyers accept the amount of contents coverage that comes with their Homeowners policy (usually 70 percent of the building-coverage value). Why? Partly because it's easy, and partly because many agents don't ask the client if the automatic coverage is enough to fully replace all her belongings.

If you accept the percent of building-value method as a means of determining the amount of content coverage you have, make one modification. Inflate your contents limit by the value of any exceptional property: fine arts, collectibles, antiques, tools, and so on.

Don't accept as gospel the estimates of others when they value your property, and don't automatically accept the stock coverage that comes with your policy.

Choosing your deductible

The usual deductible that comes with a Homeowners policy is $250 per claim. Most insurers allow you to increase the deductible to $500, $1,000, or more, in exchange for a lower premium. When deciding how big a deductible to carry, use three criteria:

> ✔ How much can you comfortably afford, financially, out of cash reserves?
>
> ✔ How much can you emotionally afford? (If parting with that much of a deductible would bring on tears, it's too high!)
>
> ✔ How much premium credit are you receiving for taking the extra risk?

It's been my experience that the average home property claim occurs once every seven to ten years. My advice is to pick the deductible that has a seven- or eight-year *payback period*. You determine that by dividing the extra risk of a higher deductible by the annual savings. If you can recoup, in premium savings, the added risk in eight years or less, pick the higher deductible. Remember the payback period is the result of dividing the difference in deductibles by the difference in premiums.

Documenting Your Claim

Suppose your house burns to the ground. Along with every shred of your belongings. Or suppose you come home to an empty house after that cheap "moving company" steals most of your furniture. What do you do?

"No problem" you say. "I read *Insurance For Dummies* and I bought all the right coverages. The Replacement Cost on building and contents. The Home Replacement Guarantee. The Special Causes-of-loss Form. I'm set."

The insurance adjuster comes to your door and the first thing she does is compliment you on the brilliant design of your insurance coverage: "My, you have a wonderful insurance plan! How did you learn how to plug all those gaps in our insurance policy?" You grin and share your ...*For Dummies* secret. (She quickly calls her supervisor and urges the insurance company to buy up the remaining supply of books so that this can't happen again!)

Her day is ruined. For once, she's cornered and has to pay the entire claim without penalty. Then, a smile comes over her face as she remembers her secret weapon — hidden in the fine print of the policy is the requirement that you have to prove what you lost, and that any property you forget to claim, she won't have to pay you for. "You don't happen to have records of everything that you own, do you?" she asks. How would you respond, right now, as you read this? Don't feel bad. Few people have adequate documentation of their loss at the time of a major claim.

Here are some easy ways of documenting your home and its contents. Keep these records off-premises so they aren't lost in a fire.

- Have photos of the exterior of the house and any detached structures.

- Have photos of any special structural features in the interior, like stone fireplaces, built-in buffets, custom woodwork, and so on.

- Have a photographic inventory of all your personal property. Take pictures of every cupboard and closet with the drawers open. Don't forget storage areas, the basement, and property in garages and other structures. (Photos can be video or still. The video is simpler, cheaper, and easier to update.)

- Keep your home blueprints, if you have any. They are wonderful for making sure you get exactly the house you had. (It wouldn't hurt to put a copy of your home appraisal with the blueprints.)

Without documentation, even great coverage won't get you an easy — or full — claim settlement.

Loss-reduction tips

Here is a list of things you can do to reduce risk, to reduce the chances of having a claim at all, and to reduce the severity of any claim you do have. You can save on your insurance premiums by putting some of these tips into effect.

- Install a UL approved smoke detector on each floor. Replace the batteries yearly (doing it on your birthday is an easy way to remember).

- Install a UL approved dry-chemical fire extinguisher in the kitchen for grease fires. Check it periodically to make sure it's fully charged.

- Install dead-bolt locks on all access doors.

- Install a motion detector alarm.

- Install a central burglar-and-fire alarm (the premium savings are huge for this one — 10 to 20 percent).

- Have your fireplace, flues, and chimney cleaned regularly to prevent chimney fires (and all the horrible interior smoke damage that results).

- If you want a wood stove, buy a UL approved one and have it professionally installed. Don't leave it unattended. Have it professionally cleaned annually.

- Change your locks immediately if your purse or keys are ever stolen.

- Install a sump pump system to prevent damage from ground water, which is excluded by virtually every Homeowner's policy. (Be sure to buy optional sump pump failure coverage.)

- Keep trees trimmed so they are safely away from the house.

- Keep walkways clear and safe.

- If you have a swimming pool, have an approved fence. Take out the diving board (where most injuries occur). Add a locking pool cover to prevent unauthorized use.

- Buy your kids membership to a health club offering a supervised trampoline instead of buying a trampoline yourself, to avoid all the potential liability for injuries to the neighbor kids.

- Install a carbon monoxide detector.

Chapter 6

Avoiding Homeowners Personal Property Pitfalls

In This Chapter

▶ Identifying the three types of Homeowners coverage gaps

▶ Arming yourself with gap management strategies

▶ Examining the coverage restrictions on a case-by-case basis

▶ Applying the gap management strategies to each restriction

One of the coverages provided by all Homeowners insurance policies is coverage for personal property. Pricing for the coverage has two components. The base premium, designed to provide coverage for the types of low-hazard property common to us all — furniture, clothing, appliances, electronics, and so on. The second component is supplemental premiums, designed to make coverage available for higher-hazard property not covered much or at all by the base policy — such as jewelry, silver, boats, and business equipment.

The good news is that this dual pricing is fair. People with only low-hazard property don't pay extra to subsidize those with high-hazard property. The bad news is that consumers with high-hazard property often just buy the basic Homeowners policy, off-the-shelf, with minimal customizing of the coverage. Thus, their high-hazard property is either poorly insured or is completely uninsured. My goal in this chapter is to make you aware of the types of personal property not well-covered by the basic Homeowners insurance policy, and to show you creative ways of getting the best coverage for your money.

I must caution you that most of my comments are based on the coverages and limitations found in the vast majority of policies, but there are differences from one company to another. Please read your particular Homeowners insurance policy — and, ideally, discuss it with a professional.

Exposing the Three Major Coverage Gaps

Your higher-hazard personal property can have little or no Homeowners coverage for three reasons:

- ✔ The basic policy sets a dollar limit on that property type.
- ✔ Certain causes-of-loss are excluded.
- ✔ The property is unique and difficult to put a value on.

Here's a personal example that illustrates all three problems.

My bride of 30 years, Judith Marie, owns a top-quality, half-carat, solitaire diamond engagement ring, worth — today — about $4,000. Our Homeowners policy, without customizing, has a $1,000 limit on jewelry theft (the *dollar limit*). In addition, it has an exclusion for any loss of the stone from its setting (the *excluded cause-of-loss*). Finally, even if $4,000 of coverage were available, the burden of proof rests with my wife and me to prove the quality and value of the ring in order to be paid that value *(unique and difficult to value)*. Can you imagine how difficult that would be? Depending on quality, a half-carat diamond is worth from $1,000 to $10,000. How would you prove to an adjuster your diamond's quality if the ring or the diamond is gone? A photo can't. A bill of sale can't. (See "Applying noninsurance strategies" later in this chapter for more on the ring.)

Identifying dollar limits

In the Coverage C section of your Homeowners policy — the section covering personal property — you find a list of property subject to limitations. It should look something like this partial list:

- ✔ Theft of jewelry: $1,000
- ✔ Theft of silver: $2,500
- ✔ Theft of guns: $2,000
- ✔ Damage to or theft of coins: $250
- ✔ Damage to or theft of stamps: $500
- ✔ Damage to or theft of boats, motors, and trailers: $1,000

If you don't want to be a victim at claim time of the personal property coverage limitations of your Homeowners policy, reading the list in your particular Homeowners policy is imperative. Almost all the limitations can be eliminated for an extra premium charge.

Examining excluded causes-of-loss

Two reasons exist that the cause of damage or a loss to your personal property won't be covered.

✔ The cause is specifically excluded from coverage in the policy language.

✔ The cause is not in the list of covered causes-of-loss if your policy contains a *Broad or basic cause-of-loss* form (See Chapter 5 for more information.)

An example of the first is the loss-of-stone exclusion mentioned earlier, excluding coverage for a stone that slips from its setting. An example of the second exclusion is a paint spill that ruins a valuable Persian rug. Under the Basic or Broad Form, any loss not appearing on the list won't be covered. Since "paint spills" isn't one of the listed, covered causes, the loss would not be covered.

Read your policy to find out which items of your personal property are not covered for certain causes-of-loss so you can use insurance or noninsurance strategies to close the gap.

Tracing valuation problems

Even if no dollar limit exists on an item of personal property, and even if the cause of your loss is fully covered, a third obstacle to collecting full value for your property is the difficulty in proving the value of certain types of property. Antiques, original art, and collectibles are examples of items that have this problem. How do you prove to the adjuster that your stolen painting was an original and not a copy? How do you prove its value after it's gone? The next sections show you how to protect yourself against this problem and other coverage problems.

Arming Yourself: Four Successful Strategies

So how do you protect yourself from being burned by one of the personal-property coverage problems common under Homeowners insurance? Here are three insurance strategies and one noninsurance strategy to help you.

Raising the dollar limit

For some of the property with dollar limits, insurers offer you the option, for a price, to increase that limit to a limit better suited to your needs. It's quite common, for example, to be able to raise your typical jewelry theft limit of $1,000 to $2,500 or $5,000, or to raise silver theft limits from $2,500 to $10,000 or $15,000.

If the limit you buy adequately covers what you own, this strategy solves the dollar-limit problem. It won't help with the cause-of-loss or valuation problems, however. Raising dollar limits is not usually an expensive proposition. A $5,000 jewelry theft limit, for example, typically costs $25 a year. A $10,000 theft limit might cost you $50 a year.

Scheduling valuables

A strategy that addresses all three problems of dollar limit, cause-of-loss, and valuation is to specifically list or *schedule* certain valuables as an amendment to the basic policy. A value for each item is declared and a premium is paid.

- ✔ The dollar-limit problem is solved by insuring the scheduled valuable for its full value.

- ✔ The causes-of-loss problem is solved because almost any cause of accidental loss, no matter how bizarre, is covered (other than a handful of exclusions).

- ✔ The valuation problem at claim time for hard-to-value items, such as jewelry and fine art, is solved by providing the insurance company with credible appraisals at the time the insurance is arranged.

Because scheduling addresses all three problems so well, it's usually the best strategy for many types of valuables — but not always.

The two advantages of scheduling valuables are, first, having the broadest possible causes-of-loss coverage and, second, having no deductible. The disadvantage of scheduling is that you lose inflation coverage if the item increases in value. For example, if the particular style of your scheduled antique table becomes quite fashionable, and the table's value skyrockets, you only collect the scheduled amount.

To solve the inflation problem, yes, you can get your items reappraised every year, if you're willing to go through the hassle and the expense. No one — absolutely no one — does so. Nor will you.

"Honey, it's been a whole year since we had our jewelry, artwork, antiques, and sterling appraised. Remember what our agent said last year about how we need to update our values every year or we'll be underinsured? Instead of going to dinner and the movies this weekend, what do you say we spend $500 and about eight hours and get our stuff reappraised? You do? Great! Sounds like fun to me too!" You'll be exceptional if you even did a reappraisal every five years.

Buying Special Perils coverage

A strategy for partially dealing with the problem of excluded causes-of-loss is to buy an optional coverage called *Special Perils contents coverage.* See Chapter 5 for further discussion. It broadens the coverage so that anything that accidentally happens to your belongings, no matter how bizarre, is covered unless the cause of the loss is one of those specifically excluded (a flood, an earthquake, breakage of fragile items, and a few others).

If you have a lot of treasures, I recommend Special Perils for its better coverage and also because it usually adds only about 10 percent to your Homeowners insurance bill. See Table 6-1 for some examples of how you could benefit at claim time with this better coverage (ignoring the deductible).

Table 6-1	The Benefits of Special Perils Coverage			
Loss Description	*Amount of Claim*	*Amount Paid under Typical Homeowners Policy*	*Amount Paid under the Special Perils Endorsement*	*Remarks*
Red wine spilled onto Oriental rug.	$1,500	$0	$1,500	No exclusion for red wine stains.
Free-standing shelving unit topples, destroying TV and stereo system.	$7,500	$0	$7,500	Breakage exclusion applies only to glassware and fragile items.
Loss of the diamond from engagement ring.	$4,000	$0	$1,000 or whatever the jewelry dollar limit is	The Special Form covers the loss but still has a dollar-limit problem.
Roof leak ruins stamp collection.	$2,800	$500 dollar limit	$500 dollar limit	There is a dollar limit on stamps. Must be scheduled to cover the full dollar loss.

(continued)

Table 6-1 (continued)

Loss Description	Amount of Claim	Amount Paid under Typical Homeowners Policy	Amount Paid under the Special Perils Endorsement	Remarks
Rain soaks almost all personal property while the roof is being replaced.	$35,000	$0	$35,000	No exclusion for rain damage.
Dry cleaner ruins wardrobe by shrinking it during cleaning.	$20,000	$0	$20,000	"Shrinking from dry cleaning" is not an exclusion.

The Special Perils endorsement, as you can see, won't solve all your claims problems, such as the dollar limit problem. But it surely puts a dent in them.

Applying noninsurance strategies

In Chapter 2, you find out about the four noninsurance methods of handling the risks of loss to your personal property. Avoiding, reducing, retaining, and transferring: otherwise known as ARRT. See the list for an example of how I could apply each of these noninsurance strategies to managing the risk of my wife's $4,000 diamond engagement ring.

- ✔ **Avoiding.** Remaining a bachelor. (I plan to take this page out of the copy of the book I give my wife, but in case she ever sees it, Honey, I'm a *very* lucky man, and I know it!)

- ✔ **Reducing.** Secretly buying a cubic zirconium — a man-made diamond worth about $35 — and passing it off as a diamond to my sweetie, thus reducing my risk from $4,000 to $35. (Of course, yours is real honey. I'd never do that to you!) Storing it in the safe deposit box when she doesn't wear it anymore, after reading this page.

- ✔ **Retaining.** Self-insuring out of my own pocket. (As in, "If anything happens to the ring, I can buy another ring by liquidating some of my vast Microsoft holdings.")

- ✔ **Transferring.** My wife wants nothing more to do with me and gives the ring to our daughter. (If it's lost, it's no longer my problem.)

What did my wife and I actually do? She definitely wants to wear the ring. The only realistic options are retaining the $4,000 risk of loss or insuring it. Since I don't really have any Microsoft stock (drat), insuring is a better option than retaining the risk, so we chose to schedule the ring.

In the following sections, find out about the many types of personal property that either have restricted coverage under a basic Homeowners policy or face unique risks that require special handling. I show you how to use these insurance and noninsurance strategies to protect yourself.

Covering Portable Items

The Homeowners policy does a pretty good job of protecting stationary personal property when it's contained safely within the walls of your home. The most common causes-of-loss — fire, wind, vandalism, and theft — are covered even under the most basic of policies. But the Homeowners coverage falls short when it comes to certain types of belongings that you carry with you, such as cameras, jewelry, musical instruments, guns, and furs.

Cameras

A good example of a type of property more vulnerable away from home: cameras, including gear and accessories. Because people take them wherever they go, cameras are subject to breakage or loss, water damage, and other unusual risks not covered by your basic Homeowners policy. In addition, there is almost no coverage for business use — a problem for those who occasionally make money from their gear, by filming weddings, for example. Some good news — Homeowners policies usually have no dollar limit for camera gear.

My advice for managing the risk of photographic equipment is as follows:

✔ If your investment is modest, retain (self-insure) losses.

✔ If you own expensive gear but either no longer use it or wouldn't replace it if it's lost, retain any losses yourself.

✔ If you own expensive gear and you do want insurance to replace it if it's lost or damaged, buy better coverage than the primary Homeowners policy offers in one of two ways:

  • Specifically insure the camera gear, called *scheduling* it.

  • Buy the Special Perils endorsement which covers all your personal property — not just cameras — for more causes-of-loss than the basic Homeowners coverage.

Both of these strategies cover camera gear for any accidental damage, unless the cause-of-loss is one of just a handful of excluded causes. Scheduling offers the advantage of having no deductible on claims. See the section on scheduling earlier in this chapter for more information. If you do schedule, be sure that the values you declare are replacement costs *new* — not used values. Also be sure to add sales tax to the value you declare, if applicable where you live.

If you use your equipment, even occasionally, to make money, the only way to cover it is to schedule it. Make sure that you add an endorsement for business use.

Jewelry

Besides being portable, personal jewelry has two other unique problems: items are usually small and easily lost, and jewelry often can only be valued under a microscope. Jewelry is also subject to two policy limitations.

- ✔ A dollar limit for theft — usually $1,000 per claim — not a limit per item
- ✔ No coverage for the loss of a stone from its setting (a very common claim)

For managing the dollar limit on theft problem, the strategy of raising the dollar limit on jewelry coverage is available from most insurers, usually to a limit of $5,000 to $10,000. All insurers vary, but common pitfalls of this strategy include no broader causes-of-loss being covered, a per piece limit of $1,000 to $1,500, and that you have to prove the value of what you lost — very difficult to do with unique jewelry. If you can't prove what you lost, you're vulnerable to the insurance company replacing what you lost with a lesser quality item or gem. Note: The insurance company normally replaces your gem with another gem, instead of cash. It reduces the number of fraudulent claims for "stolen" jewelry.

The strategy of scheduling jewelry items works better because almost every accidental claim, including the loss of the stone or even the loss of the entire piece, is covered, there's no deductible, and, because an appraisal is required to schedule an item, there's no dispute over what you lost. You simply take the most recent appraisal to the jeweler who is doing the replacing. She uses the appraisal to closely match what you lost. The only negative of scheduling, besides the cost and hassle of getting an appraisal, is the danger of being underinsured if the value of your jewelry increases. You can protect yourself by getting new appraisals and raising your coverage limit every three to five years.

Out of hundreds of jewelry claims, I've only had two clients get paid less than the replacement cost. In both cases, their appraisals were over ten years old.

The strategy of buying the Special Perils causes-of-loss coverage option is only partially effective for jewelry. Though it broadens the kinds of loss covered, it doesn't help with the dollar limit problem.

I find noninsurance strategies — avoid, reduce, or retain — very helpful with regard to personal jewelry risks. Avoid the risk for seldom-worn jewelry you eventually want to pass on to your kids. Pass it on now, while you're still here to enjoy them enjoying it — and the risk now belongs to someone else. You can retain, meaning self-insure, smaller jewelry items — especially those you won't bother replacing should anything happen to them. Reduce the risk to your jewelry by putting expensive, seldom-worn pieces in a safe-deposit box. Reduce the risk of the loss of stones from their settings by regularly having the prongs checked. The burglary risk is reduced significantly when you install a central burglar alarm. Hide expensive pieces to further reduce the risk — the first place the burglar looks is in your jewelry box. (Longtime client Mary — God bless her — showed me her favorite hiding place: her freezer! Did she microwave her jewelry when she wanted to wear it?) If you hide it, don't forget where you hide it. (I'm guilty of that one!) There usually is no way to transfer the risk to someone other than through insurance.

My recommendations for managing your jewelry risks are:

- ✔ Retain the small stuff — especially items you wouldn't replace.

- ✔ Schedule items worth $1,000 or more — especially those you would replace. Don't forget to add sales tax to the value of the item.

- ✔ Add up the values of the items under $1,000 you would replace, if you want them insured. Then raise the jewelry dollar-limit high enough to cover those items, or to the maximum available from the insurance company. (When you talk to the agent, impress her with the technical name for this: *blanket unscheduled coverage.*)

  Still get appraisals for the unscheduled jewelry items you're covering under the blanket coverage and store the appraisals off-premises. The insurance company won't require an appraisal of you like they will for scheduled items, but being able to prove what you lost will greatly enhance your claim settlement.

- ✔ Store pieces you seldom wear — especially heirlooms — in a safe-deposit box. Insurance can only pay cash. It won't begin to replace the sentimental value of your treasures.

- ✔ If you have a lot of jewelry, reduce the burglary risk by hiding it and/or adding a central burglar alarm.

What you should know about jewelry claims

You've done all the right things. You obtained a quality appraisal from a certified gemologist on your diamond wedding ring for $4,200, which feels good because you only paid $3,200. You scheduled it for $4,200. You even added the sales tax to the value. Six months later, the ring is stolen. You're very happy you bought *Insurance For Dummies* and followed its advice. Until, that is, you discover that the cost to the insurance company, through their wholesale connections, to replace this ring is only $2,100. You're outraged! You insured your ring for $4,200. You want a $4,200 ring. They refuse. Then you demand $4,200 cash. They offer $2,100 cash. More outrage!

What can you do? Nothing. Jewelry is appraised at retail and settled at wholesale. That's how the system works. Pricing for scheduled jewelry is discounted because of this fact.

There are a few insurance companies who sell *agreed amount* jewelry coverage and would pay you the $4,200. But those jewelry policies are much more expensive.

I actually like the current system. You benefit in three ways:

✔ Reduced insurance premiums

✔ Reduced fraud, preventing people from profiting from a claim (collecting $4,200 cash for a ring that cost $3,200 six months earlier)

✔ Some inflation protection. Your $4,200 ring will increase in value each year. But you won't get updated appraisals each year — human nature and cost. Your appraisal won't need updating more than every five years until the $2,100 wholesale price has increased in value to match the $4,200 insured amount. (If five years from now the retail value of the ring is $8,400 and wholesale value is $4,200, you still have enough insurance at $4,200.)

I want you to know and understand how the system works so you won't be disappointed at claim time. What's really important is that insurance replaces what you lost. And it will, up to the scheduled amount.

Musical instruments

The good news with musical instruments is that Homeowners policies neither contain any dollar limits nor have any added causes-of-loss excluded. But if you own an expensive instrument, it is subject to two pitfalls:

✔ No damage or breakage coverage in the basic Homeowners policy.

✔ Limited coverage at home and virtually no coverage away from home if the instrument is used even partially for business.

You can get damage or breakage coverage by either scheduling the item or buying the Special Perils option for all your belongings. Coverage is similar under either choice. Scheduling has the advantage of no deductible, a particularly popular feature with parents of eight-year olds.

If you use your instrument even occasionally for business, the only way to avoid the Homeowners policy dollar-limits on business property is to schedule it *and* add the business-use endorsement.

It's quite common for parents to rent instruments rather than buy them, especially for the child's first instrument. The rental agency requires you to insure the rental and offers you insurance on the $800 guitar you're renting — typically $4 to $8 a month added to your rental fee. That's $48 to $96 a year. You can schedule the $800 guitar under your Homeowners policy for $4 to $8 a year! That's the way to go — always. Be sure to include the rental agency as Loss Payee on the schedule so its interest is properly covered.

Guns

If all you own is a handgun or a standard shotgun or a hunting rifle, you can probably skip this section. The basic Homeowners policy has a dollar limit on theft of guns — usually $1,000 to $2,000 — and no added exclusions. Business-use restrictions exist that won't be addressed here (for detectives, bounty hunters, and Mafia hit men), but you can find out about them in *Hired-Gun Insurance For Dummies*.

You've got two reasons to buy better gun coverage. First, you might need to raise the basic dollar limit for theft, and second, you may need broader coverage, especially for guns used recreationally, like if you hunt and you may lose a gun overboard while sitting in a duckboat.

If you have both needs, scheduling the gun is the best choice. If you don't need broader coverage, just raise the theft limit. If the insurance company's optional limit isn't high enough, you need to schedule. I have 400 clients, with almost no gun schedules, and very few increased gun limits. Why? Because gun claims rarely occur. And because preventing the loss, with a high-quality gun safe, is so effective. By the way, locking guns in a safe not only reduces the risk of theft but, more importantly, keeps your children, or grandchildren, or anyone else from accessing the guns and hurting themselves or others.

Many people do have elaborate gun collections, often including vintage guns. For those readers, here are my recommendations to help improve future claim settlements, whether you schedule the guns or just increase the limit in your policy: Take good photos and store a set off-premises to document what you had at claim time, and get appraisals on the collectible guns and also store these appraisals off-premises.

Furs

If you have valuable furs you should know that your policy probably has a dollar limit for theft of furs *included in the jewelry dollar limit* of, usually, $1,000. That's a problem if a burglar takes your jewelry and furs in the same burglary. (Most considerate burglars know better and don't do that.)

Since most fur theft occurs away from home, preventing the theft risk by keeping the fur with you at all times is probably the best strategy. If you do still want insurance, I recommend you schedule the item for its full value. Besides the increased dollar limit, you also will broaden coverage for nearly every accidental loss, including tears, stains, dry cleaner damage, and so on. To schedule a fur, you will need a furrier appraisal. If you want your claim settled for the cost, new, and have purchased Replacement Cost coverage on contents with your basic policy, make sure that the appraisal is for the new (not used) value.

Covering Artwork and Antiques

In this section, you find out about the special problems and pitfalls related to the ownership and insurance of historical property and art of all kinds, including tips on how to protect yourself if you own property like original paintings and antiques.

Problems

Since the value of these items is based both on authenticity and condition, good documentation is essential. Can you imagine owning an original Picasso worth $2 million, having no documentation, and trying to get that amount from the insurance adjuster after it's stolen? Impossible, of course.

Another problem common to fine arts and antiques is valuation. Replacing this type of property — much of it one of a kind — with new isn't even possible, usually. What is the replacement cost of a Picasso? (First, there's the cost of bringing him back from the dead — not as cheap as it used to be!) What's the replacement cost of your antique, hand-carved table? Even if it can be replaced with a new, identical table, doesn't its historical value often exceed — sometimes far exceed — the value of a new table?

As a result of the inappropriateness of Replacement Cost coverage for these types of items, most insurance policies now settle these losses for the market value at the time of the loss. That's good news for you. The bad news is that the burden of documenting what you have falls entirely on your shoulders. Yet another difficulty with insuring this kind of property is that the value can increase while your coverage remains static, especially if you schedule the items. With each passing year, your coverage becomes more and more inadequate.

Two insurance strategies

How can you solve the problems of documentation and valuing your fine arts and antiques, and still protect against underinsurance due to inflation? You can choose between two methods of insurance, neither perfect, both with advantages and drawbacks.

Scheduling

The first strategy for insuring this type of property is the one used and recommended exclusively by the insurance industry — scheduling. It requires you to document what you have at the time you insure it by providing a credible appraisal, and often a photograph. The item is then scheduled for the appraised amount and an extra premium is charged. The advantages? First, the documentation problem is solved in advance of any claim. Items in the schedule are valued at their market value. Second, most insurers — for fine arts only — include *agreed amount* coverage, meaning they pay you the scheduled amount for a theft or total loss with no value argument. Another advantage is the option to add breakage of glass and other fragile items to the schedule. If breakage is a big concern, then scheduling the item with breakage coverage is the best course of action. But, again, scheduling leaves you vulnerable to the inflation problem, unless you're willing to incur the time, expense, and hassle of new appraisals almost every year. Virtually no one is willing to appraise their items yearly — and it completely violates one of our rules of the road in Chapter 1— to keep it simple.

Annual appraisals done easy

I had a client once who, instead of investing in real estate or the stock market, invested hundreds of thousands of dollars in original art. When I asked him why, he replied that art values more than keep up with inflation, virtually never decline, and, unlike stock certificates, can be a source of visual warmth and pleasure every day. What a great idea! He scheduled all his paintings and also solved the annual appraisal problem. He simply bought every single painting from one art dealer who, as part of the deal, annually provided me, with no prompting, an entire list of all the paintings including up-to-date values. If you collect art and can do the same thing, then scheduling is the perfect strategy!

Creative nonscheduling: The three-part plan

The second insurance strategy is one I devised for my clients in order to solve the inflation problem without the hassle and expense of new appraisals. It has three parts and works only if your Homeowners policy has no dollar limits on paintings, collectibles, and antiques. Almost all Homeowners policies don't have a dollar limit on these items, but be sure to check yours.

1. **Buy the optional Special Perils coverage endorsement for your personal property.** It raises your total Homeowners cost about 10 to 15 percent. Special Perils gives you coverage for any accidental loss, not including a few exclusions. It covers losses not covered by a basic Homeowners policy, like paint spills on the antique rug or piano, water damage to your paintings or antiques from a roof leak, and so on. It has very broad coverages — not only on fine arts and antiques, but for all your other belongings as well.

2. **Increase your total Homeowners limit for Coverage C — personal property — high enough to cover all these valuables as well as all your other personal property.** Most Homeowners policies, in a total loss, don't have enough contents coverage to pay for all these treasures and all your other belongings.

3. **Get photos of everything and appraisals on all items where authenticity is vital to a claim settlement.** Store the photos away from home, at work or in a safe-deposit box. If you don't follow through on storing this critical documentation off-premises, this strategy will fail you and you'll be extremely disappointed at claim time.

With this method, you don't need to get regular appraisals. When you do have a claim and need a current appraisal to document the claim value, you bring your original appraisals with the photos to a dealer or appraiser. A hidden benefit of this method: The cost of the valuation is completely paid for by the insurance company as a claims-adjusting expense!

My recommendations

Here are my bottom-line insurance recommendations for insuring artwork, collectibles, and antiques:

✔ For high-end pieces (for example, expensive paintings), especially if you can get your appraiser to agree to send you annual value updates, I recommend scheduling. Scheduling fine arts makes for a far easier claim settlement, with no arguments about value, as opposed to not scheduling, where you must prove the authenticity and value of what you lost.

✔ For glassware or other highly-fragile items, including antique glass, I recommend scheduling if you want breakage coverage. Remember to add optional breakage coverage to the policy when you schedule.

✔ For most other treasures, I recommend the three-part plan — *but only if you faithfully keep the necessary documentation away from home.*

Creatively managing an inherited art collection

Suppose you inherit such a high-value art collection that you don't want to deal with the hassle and expense of protecting it, yet you want to maintain ownership for posterity. Transferring (see Chapter 2) is an excellent risk-management technique for this type of situation. Here's how it works:

✔ Contact places such as art museums, historical societies, and the like.

✔ Tell them they can display your artwork in exchange for assuming the risk for any loss or damage.

✔ If some place agrees, get the deal in writing.

If you're successful, you avoid the insurance problem — hundreds of dollars in premiums — and the expense of the high-end security you would need to properly protect your collection. You gain peace of mind by not having all those expensive items in your home. You maintain the ownership of the items to pass on to future generations. And, finally, you can still enjoy your art by visiting the museum anytime during normal business hours. In fact, they may even give you a key to the place!

Reducing the risk of loss with an alarm system

If you have any kind of property that's quite valuable and could be stolen, like jewelry or fine paintings, install a central burglar-and-fire alarm. Installation costs are often $200 or less. The monthly cost to monitor the alarm is about $20. You reduce the risk of losing an irreplaceable treasure, and you receive 10 to 20 percent off your Homeowners rates.

Covering Collectibles

Collecting — anything from baseball cards to bottle caps, from coins to comic books, from stamps to sterling silver — is all the rage and has been for years. But this type of property has insurance pitfalls. In this section, I show you how to protect yourself from the pitfalls, case-by-case.

Money, coins, and the like

We all desire to collect money — the more of it, the merrier! What you need to know is that your Homeowners policy wants nothing to do with your money. Or almost nothing. The policy has a dollar limit on money, typically $200. That's $200 for everything — not just what's in your wallet. It's $200, total, if it even looks, tastes, or smells like money — banknotes, bullion, gold, silver, platinum, coins (including coin collections), and medals.

Yes, you can increase the $200 policy limit, or, in some cases, schedule collections — for a fortune in premiums. I never recommend either strategy. How do you prove your loss? Imagine losing that wonderful coin collection. Now imagine proving to the adjuster the exact coins you had, what their condition was, and the current value of each. If you insist on keeping any money collectibles at home, then hide your collection very well, and strongly consider a central burglar alarm — or a home safe. Otherwise, put the money items in a safe-deposit box, where they aren't insured but where the theft risk is extremely remote.

Stamps and valuable papers

Another item insurers don't want to cover is anything valuable contained on a piece of paper. They'll cover the blank paper. They just don't want to cover what's on the paper. So the Homeowners policy has another dollar limit, usually about $1,000 for this type of property. Stamp collections are a good example. Some other examples include manuscripts (like the one this book used to be), passports, tickets, letters of credit, and deeds.

Yes, you can raise the dollar limit on this type of property. You can even schedule stamps, but I don't recommend it. Prevention is better. Getting a safe-deposit box is a good option. Some of my clients have even installed in-home fireproof safes.

The Wares — Silver, Gold, or Pewter

All Homeowners policies have a dollar limit on theft — usually $2,500 to $5,000 — of silverware, gold ware and pewter ware, including plated ware. It applies not just to flatware, but accessory pieces like tea sets. It even applies to trophies.

The policy limit is usually adequate if your pieces are plated. But the limit is inadequate if you have solid sterling, solid gold, or solid pewter. Here are some insurance solutions, their pitfalls, and tips on avoiding the pitfalls for sterling silver risks. The examples also apply to gold and pewter.

Examining the pitfalls of scheduling

The most common insurance-industry solution for insuring sterling silver is to get it appraised and then schedule it on the policy like you do jewelry. The problem I have with this solution is that silver is a commodity, and goes up and down in value. If you schedule each of your silver pieces, when silver prices go up, you are immediately underinsured on every piece. And when silver prices drop, you're overinsured.

Silverware isn't like jewelry — it doesn't need to be examined under a microscope. It more closely resembles camera gear. It usually has a manufacturer and pattern name. You can generally look up prices in a book.

Even if you decide to schedule silver, don't spend money for an appraisal. Just contact a dealer for a current price list, or bring a couple of pieces down to the store for a ballpark estimate. Since the values fluctuate daily, an exact price isn't necessary. Sterling silver has a low chance of loss. What can happen to solid silver? Fire and theft. Fire is fully covered, without limit. Theft is your only insurance concern.

Two alternatives to scheduling

I don't recommend scheduling your sterling. You have better options. If you don't use your silver every day, hide it. Hiding works. If you want more security, add a central burglar alarm. In the past ten years, not one client of mine has had a silver theft claim. Silver prices have dropped a lot and burglars just aren't stealing silver anymore. Especially if they can't find it.

But if you do use silver regularly or prefer to keep it displayed, you probably need to insure it. Check with a dealer first to see what it's worth. Then, since theft is the only cause-of-loss with a dollar limit, raise your silver theft limit from the basic limit ($2,500) to the true, current value of your silver. Round up a bit so that you're covered if prices rise.

The one exception where you don't hide the silver but insurance isn't needed is when the sterling silver was a gift and you either wouldn't replace it or are comfortable replacing it with silver plate. In this case, you can skip the extra insurance and live with the $2,500 policy limit.

Documenting your silver

If you increase the silver limit and don't schedule your silver, the burden of proof, as usual, is on your shoulders at claim time to prove what you had. Here's how to protect yourself:

> ✔ Take photos and write the name of the manufacturer and the pattern on the back of the photos.
>
> ✔ Get appraisals just once for any pieces that don't have that information, not to prove value but to prove that the piece is solid silver.
>
> ✔ Store the photos and appraisals off-premises along with a single piece of flatware to prove what you had.

Failure to maintain documentation will cause you, at the least, claims hassles — and probably lead to your claim payment being inadequate. Remember, don't store the documentation in your home where a fire can destroy both your silver and your documentation.

Don't feel like you have to follow just one strategy. Maybe some silver you're comfortable hiding, some you want to display and would replace if it were stolen, and some you display but wouldn't bother replacing. If so, combine strategies.

Cards, comics, and other collections

People used to collect just stamps, or coins, or art. These days, anything goes: CDs, books, antique toy trains, soldiers, Barbie dolls, baseball cards, comic books, miniature Christmas villages, porcelain dolls, teddy bears, and now Beanie Babies. Some people even collect old insurance policies. I'm absolutely amazed by our interest in collecting things.

Until recently, virtually every kind of collection was fully covered for its market value. But now, some insurers are inserting dollar limits on some of these items. A major insurer I represent just added dollar limits on trading cards and comic books, much to my dismay. I'm hoping it's not a trend. Personally, I don't see the need. Most of these collections aren't carried around, and they're not a target of burglars. But they are a huge problem to establish a value for at claim time.

Examining the problem

The biggest problems with collections are documentation and valuation: proving what you had and putting a value on it. If you have a claim, every policy has a requirement that you make a detailed inventory of what you lost. It's a nightmarish task. Suppose you own hundreds of books — some collectibles. If you don't have photos or other documentation and the books are destroyed by fire, how could you possibly make up a list of what you lost?

Singing a different tune, now

My client's home was burglarized. One of the things the thieves stole was her entire collection of about 300 CDs. The claim was a nightmare for her. She had to remember and list each CD. Any she forgot she wouldn't get paid for. She had to spend about 60 unpaid hours shopping CD racks and mail-order catalogs to put together her list.

If you have a collection yourself — of anything — you already have the job of making an inventory should your collection be stolen. Protect yourself — after my client replaced her CDs, she kept a CD inventory on her computer. A good idea.

Assume a fire destroyed your 2,000-card baseball card collection and you're asked for an inventory from the claims adjuster. You finally put together your list. Now, how do you value it? The value of each card will fluctuate wildly, depending on condition. Since your collection is destroyed, how do you prove to the adjuster that your 1952 Mickey Mantle rookie card was the mint one worth $12,500 and not the bent, folded, crinkled one worth $75? The burden of proof is on you. If you can't prove condition, you'll probably end up getting paid for average cards when many of yours were mint.

Solving the problem

To get what you deserve for your collections at claim time, you need to document every item to prove its existence for the claims inventory and to prove its condition for the valuation. You need to authenticate the originality of items whose value depends on their originality. You need to make sure your policy limit on belongings is high enough to cover all your collectibles and all other, normal, personal property. And, finally, you need to make sure that the kinds of losses that can damage your collections (breakage for porcelain dolls, water damage for baseball cards) are covered.

Here are suggestions that will allow you to do all of the above and still keep it simple:

- Check your Homeowners policy under Coverage C — personal property. Are your collections subject to any dollar limitations that could hurt you? If so, either raise the limit or, better yet, switch your insurance to an insurer whose policy does not have these dollar limits.

- Generally, don't schedule collections and spend big bucks for appraisals if the values can change quickly, making your schedule obsolete overnight. The two exceptions would be (a) if you need breakage coverage or (b) when the values are high-end and dependent on proof of authenticity. If you do schedule, insist on the fine arts form so at claim time the insurer must pay out the scheduled amount regardless of current value.

✔ Take a close-up photographic inventory. A video camera works best for extensive collections like books, comic books, or sports cards. You can probably film your whole collection in one or two tapes. (It's also easy — and cheap — to add to as your collection grows.) Then at claim time, you can make up your inventory of what you lost from the photos. The photos will also document the condition. Be sure to store photos away from home!

✔ If any or all of your collection's value depends on proving authenticity or mint condition, get an appraisal just once that does so. Store the appraisal off premises with the photos. A signed statement from a credible dealer works fine. To enhance the appraisal, consider attaching an individual photo.

✔ Buy the optional Special Perils contents coverage for the broadest possible coverage on your collection (if you don't schedule).

✔ Determine the approximate value of your collection, add it to the estimated value of your belongings, and raise your Coverage C personal property limit as needed. (See Chapter 5 for how to estimate the value of your contents.)

✔ Do whatever you can to reduce the risk of loss to your collections. For example:

  • Don't store moisture-sensitive collections, like old record collections, in a damp basement where they can warp (like I'm currently doing) or be subject to water damage. Instead, seal them in airtight, plastic zipper bags. (This works well for comic books, too.)

  • Put breakables out of the flow of traffic and, ideally, in protective storage — cabinets or trunks.

If you follow these suggestions, especially the one about having a photographic inventory, your satisfaction on any claim involving a collection will improve substantially. If you do nothing at all, you'll have a major hassle and get paid less than you deserve. Enough said.

Covering Business Property at Home

The Homeowners policy is designed for residential — not business — risks. As such, it's no surprise that coverage for business personal property is minimal — typically $2,500 at home and $250 away. Also, there is usually a complete exclusion for business data — both on paper and electronic media. This section deals with how to protect yourself from being hurt by those limits.

(For a more in-depth look at managing risks associated with a full-fledged, home-based business you operate from your home, see Chapter 9.) This section addresses insuring business property you have at your home if you don't own the business.

Defining "business"

The definition of *business* in most Homeowners policies clearly includes your regular job. But does it include part-time jobs, home babysitting, or summer lawn jobs? Unfortunately, that's subject to interpretation. Because the policy is vague, the courts have gotten involved.

The courts have defined *business,* as used in Homeowners policies, to mean an activity that both earns revenue and is continuous. A once-a-year garage sale would not be a business. But my friend Bobbie's garage sales, which she's conducted out of her garage for the whole neighborhood, once a month for 20 years, may be a business, and the $2,500 limit would apply.

Similarly, your 12-year-old son's use of your $600 Toro mower to do a few summer lawn jobs probably isn't a business because it's not continuous. But your 18-year-old son's $10,000 investment in landscaping equipment, pulled on a utility trailer and used year round, may be a business.

Finally, if you have an incidental home office where you telecommute or bring work home to with a desk, filing cabinet, computer, fax, and so on, you are subject to the business-property limitations of the policy.

Getting business property covered

For starters, if the $2,500 in business property coverage that comes with your Homeowners policy is enough to replace all you own or use at home and you never take for-business items off-premises, you're set. Remember, though, to read your policy and be sure that the limit is the typical limit of $2,500, and not a smaller limit.

If some of the business property at your home is owned by your employer and furnished for your use, see if your employer is covering it already or can cover it. You won't need supplemental insurance if the items are already covered.

If you own substantially more than $2,500 worth of business property, or take more than $250 worth of business property away from home, or have a lot of business data at risk, here are some things you can do:

✔ If you have more than $2,500 at risk at home, increase your business property on-premises coverage high enough to cover your exposure.

✔ If you take more than $250 worth of business property out of your home, try to reduce the risk by taking less. Home insurers seldom offer an option to buy a higher limit. If they do, it's pretty pricey. Exception — laptop computers. If you own a laptop, you can avoid the $250 limit by scheduling the laptop. Be sure to include a business-use endorsement and get Special Perils coverage, as computers can be easily damaged through a variety of causes. The cost is only about $5 per $1,000 of coverage. I strongly recommend scheduling to every laptop owner. A $3,000 laptop costs about $15 a year to insure, with no deductible.

✔ If you have business data at risk, you can buy optional data coverage when you schedule a computer. But what a hassle to recreate lost data! A better strategy is avoiding the risk with daily backups of data. Store a copy of the backup away from home. See Chapter 7 for more on business liability risks not covered by Homeowners insurance.

Covering "toys"

Minnesota — my home state. The "toy" capital of the world. We've got it all — 10,000 lakes for boats and jet skis. Lots of snow and open terrain for snowmobiles and ATVs. And more golf courses per capita than any other state, with plenty of golf carts. Needless to say, I've had a lot of practice arranging insurance for these things.

The average Homeowners policy limits coverage on recreational items. For example, boats, boat motors, trailers, and related equipment are typically excluded for wind losses in the open and for theft when away from home. Other trailers typically have no coverage when stolen away from home. Often, snowmobiles and all-terrain vehicles won't be covered at all. And golf carts are typically not covered with a few limited exceptions for use around home. Your policy will be slightly different. Be sure to read the "toy" section of Chapter 7 for information on pertinent Homeowners liability insurance exclusions.

Watercraft

Boats, including their motors, trailers, and other equipment, are usually limited in most Homeowners policies to $1,000 of coverage, plus no wind coverage unless they are stored inside a building and no theft coverage away from home. In addition, a lot of the hazards related to boating are not covered at all, such as collisions, sinking, and hitting submerged rocks. If your entire watercraft setup is worth less than $1,000 and you can live with those limitations, then retention is a good management tool. (See the section on ARRT in Chapter 2 for more on retention.) Always make sure that you store the boat in an enclosed building to prevent wind problems. While using the boat, prevent theft by securing it well if you leave it unattended.

If you want broader coverage, including coverage for normal boating hazards, buy Special Perils coverage. Annual premiums are about two percent of the value of the boat and equipment. The deductible is at least $100, however. Choose a higher deductible if you save enough on the premium to justify taking the extra risk.

You can buy this Special Perils coverage for your boat and boat equipment either as a scheduled item on your Homeowners policy, if that option is available, or under a separate boat insurance policy. Coverage is equally good under either option.

Don't forget to include watercraft liability coverage for injuries and property damage, in the same dollar amount as the rest of your personal liability insurance. Some noninsurance strategies you can use to decrease the risks involved in owning a boat include:

- Don't mix drinking and boating. This one doesn't need any explanation.

- If you have a motorized boat, have all users take a boating safety class that's been approved by the U.S. Coast Guard. In addition to being safer boaters, you usually get a nifty discount (10 to 15 percent) on your boat insurance premiums, for the rest of your life.

- If young people drive the boat, make sure that they're well-trained and know exactly what they are and are not allowed to do. A large amount of boating accidents start with kids goofing off behind the wheel.

Recreational vehicles, snowmobiles, and golf carts

By *recreational vehicles,* I mean motorized vehicles not licensed for road use, such as all-terrain vehicles, go-carts, golf carts, minibikes, mopeds, and so on. All motorized vehicles are excluded from Homeowners property coverage except those used for service to the home premises. The reason for the exclusion is that these vehicles present a greater-than-average risk Special policies are available for these recreational vehicles.

Applying noninsurance strategies

You can really make good use of the noninsurance techniques of avoid, reduce, retain, and transfer (ARRT) in managing these risks. You can avoid the risk, particularly for three-wheelers and four-wheelers. A lot of kids go to the emergency room who have been hurt on these vehicles. Don't own one. You can reduce the risk by using your "toys" responsibly, storing them in a safe place, making sure that they're always locked when not in use, and being careful about who you let use the vehicles. Make sure that the guy driving *your* go-cart is a safe driver. Just because he's your wife's sister's neighbor, doesn't mean he should be allowed behind the wheel. Retaining is another good strategy: If the items are older, their damage may not be worth insuring. Transferring works too, but mainly through insurance.

Buying insurance

If any of your toys set you back the big bucks, you'll need insurance. Be aware that the insurance for damage to these vehicles is often quite expensive. Self-insure the physical-damage risk if you can afford to.

Most insurers offer property and liability coverage for these motorized toys. Some offer the coverage under a Homeowners policy endorsement. Others offer a stand-alone recreational vehicle policy. The coverage is usually equally good under either choice.

Even if you decide not to insure your "toy" for damage or theft, always buy liability coverage. And always for the same coverage amounts as your auto, home, and other personal liability coverage.

Trailers (Those not used with watercraft)

Trailers (camping, utility, and such) are typically covered only up to a $1,000 limit. Like watercraft, there is usually no windstorm coverage if they are outside a building and no theft coverage away from home. If your trailer is worth under $1,000, if you can protect it against wind damage in the open and theft away from home, and if you can live with paying your Homeowners deductible if it's damaged or stolen, don't buy additional insurance.

If you own an expensive house- or camping-trailer, you can insure it best and most economically by adding the trailer to your car insurance policy. Use a five to seven year payback period with the formula from Chapter 3 to determine the deductibles that are most cost effective for you. And because car insurance covers only the trailer, add Special Perils contents coverage to your Homeowners policy to get better coverage for the belongings in your trailer in case of damage from a collision or overturn.

Don't forget about liability coverage. You need coverage for when you're towing it and when it's parked. Normally the coverage is free. Your Personal Auto policy covers your trailer when you're towing it. And your Homeowners covers it while parked.

Your Homeowners liability coverage extends to your trailer when it's parked for a short period of time, like if you're camping. But sometimes, people semi-permanently park their deluxe camping trailer on a choice vacation site they either own or lease long-term and use it like a cabin or vacation residence. In Minnesota, for example, it is frequently done along our many lakes and rivers. If you're using your trailer as a residence on a long-term leased lot, your liability for injuries and property damage is probably uninsured. The best solution? Call your Homeowners agent to extend liability coverage to this "vacation residence." The annual cost is $20 or less.

Policies differ from one insurance company to the next. Always read your policy and consult with a good agent. Most of the information in this book will apply to your particular policy; some of it may not, or it may apply with slight variations.

Chapter 7

Protecting Yourself from Major Homeowners Exclusions

In This Chapter

▶ Managing excluded property losses

▶ Protecting yourself from Homeowners liability exclusions

▶ Understanding the National Flood Insurance Program

*T*he Homeowners insurance policy is extremely comprehensive in coverage. It covers the majority of property and liability claims related to a residence. (See Chapter 5 for Homeowners policy fundamentals.) But it does have limits on what it covers. Unfortunately, most people don't discover these limits — called *exclusions* — until it's too late, when the adjuster denies their claim. In this chapter, I show you what the major excluded causes-of-loss are, and how to protect yourself from being victimized by them.

Even the broadest Homeowners property coverage — Special Perils coverage — has a handful of excluded causes-of-loss, including:

✔ Any kind of earth movement, such as earthquake, tremors, landslides, mudflows, and sinking or shifting.

✔ Water that enters the house at or below ground level, such as a flood, runoff from heavy rains, sewer backup, and foundation seepage.

✔ Ordinance or law requirements that either increase the cost of repairs or require demolition.

✔ War or nuclear risks of any kind.

✔ Others, including intentional damage, failure to protect the property after a loss, and off-premises power failures.

This book does not address the last two groups of exclusions because either the coverage is not available (you can't get insurance to protect yourself from war) or the cause-of-loss is one that you cause (intentional damage, such as arson).

Understanding the exclusion for failure to protect your property

An insurance policy is a legal contract. To be a valid contract, both parties agree to do certain things for the other. The obvious obligations are for you to pay all premiums by the due date and for your insurer to pay your covered claims when they occur.

But your obligations don't end with the premium payment. You can find them in the back of every insurance policy. They're called *conditions.* You're required to comply with each of them. If you don't, you jeopardize your claim settlement if your noncompliance affects the claim. Here are a couple of examples.

One condition in every policy is a requirement to report claims promptly. Suppose you injure someone in a car accident but you don't report the claim for fear your rates will increase. Six months later, you're sued for $200,000. If the insurance company investigates and discovers they could have settled the injury claim for $25,000 five months earlier, it will probably refuse to defend you or pay any part of the claim. Your failure to report the claim seriously affected the settlement amount.

Another condition is to cooperate fully with your insurance company. If you refuse, it can refuse to pay your claim.

A third condition (and one that most people are unaware of) is the obligation to protect the property from further loss once a claim has occurred. If you don't, any resulting damage won't be covered. Examples:

- Not acting to put a tarp over the hole in your roof caused by a storm, leading to an additional $20,000 interior water damage.

- Not moving high-valued items to a safe place after a fire on one side of the house has made easy access to the interior possible, leading to a theft of six major jewelry pieces valued at $52,000.

- Not changing the locks on your house after someone stole your purse with your keys inside, leading to a major burglary of $35,000 of stereos, TVs, and other property after the burglar entered using the stolen keys.

Following any kind of property claim, you *must* take immediate, reasonable action to prevent further damage to your property, or you likely won't be covered for the additional damage. If you incur expenses in the process, the insurance company should always reimburse you, as long as you promptly notify them, the costs are reasonable, and you get their approval.

As for the risk stemming from war or nuclear activity, one of the ARRT strategies from Chapter 2 of avoiding the risk works best. Don't build next to a nuclear power plant or a missile facility. If a war is about to begin that may affect your property, sell quickly and move to Switzerland, or accept the possibility of uninsured damage.

Earthquake insurance when it's not your fault

If you live nowhere near any known fault, should you buy earthquake insurance? I live in Minnesota — far from any known fault. As a result, earthquake insurance here is extremely cheap — about $20 per $100,000 of coverage.

So, does one buy insurance for a potentially catastrophic event that has never occurred nor is ever expected to occur? Especially when the insurance cost is so low? It's a very difficult call.

The decision to carry catastrophic insurance when the catastrophe is highly unlikely creates a conflict of three guiding principles from Chapter 1:

- ✓ Consider the odds. (Extremely remote.)

- ✓ Don't risk more than you can afford to lose. (In this example, a lot — your home.)

- ✓ Don't risk a lot for a little. (In this example, it's $100,000 coverage for only $20 a year.)

I recommend that if there is even the remote possibility the loss could occur, buy the insurance. If there is no possibility, don't buy coverage.

Managing the Earth Movement Risk

You have three strategies to choose from to protect yourself from earth movement, a normally uninsured cause-of-loss.

- ✓ My favorite strategy — don't mess with Mother Nature. In other words, avoid the risk completely. Don't live near a fault, don't live on or near an active volcano, and don't buy or build a home on a steep hill vulnerable to mud slides. If you do, you have to be willing to live with the consequences.

- ✓ My second favorite strategy, for new construction only, is to reduce the risk in construction design. Like the people who live near the ocean and build houses on stilts to avoid the risk of high tides, spend what you need to spend so that when nature brings its wrath, your house is built to take it.

- ✓ The third strategy is to buy earthquake insurance. I heard a startling statistic — that less than 20 percent of Californians living near a fault carry this insurance!

- ✓ Buy earthquake insurance if you live in these high-risk areas, in the same way someone on the east coast of Florida buys hurricane insurance. Yes, it's expensive. But not carrying the insurance violates one of our major guiding principles in Chapter 1 — don't risk more than you can afford to lose.

One of the added dangers of choosing to live in an area with more exposure to natural disasters is that if the disasters occur too often, insurance for them may become unavailable. Insurance companies are businesses. They can't operate if losses continually exceed income. After Hurricane Andrew, Homeowners insurance in the southeastern United States became nearly impossible to find.

In another example, I have a client who owned a beautiful home in the U.S. Virgin Islands. After a few hurricanes devastated that area, virtually every standard insurance company not only quit writing new policies, they completely pulled out, canceling every existing policy. I subsequently found my client home insurance through Lloyds of London after an exhaustive international search, but the annual cost went from $800 to $2,500 for less coverage. The same fate could happen to you if your home is located in an area that is vulnerable to earthquakes, if huge losses force insurers to pull out.

Managing the Excluded Ground Water Risk

Water can enter your home at or below ground level by a true flood — where a nearby body of water, usually a river, overflows its banks, heavy surface runoff, foundation seepage, or sewer backup.

Noninsurance strategies

You can avoid the true-flood risk by living nowhere near a body of water. Or by living on top of a mountain. You can significantly reduce the basement water risk from runoff or seepage with landscaping, gutters, and so on. You can also use my personal favorite — a sump pump system. You can also reduce the sewer backup risk by installing a one-way valve that allows sewage to flow out, but not in.

Insurance strategies

There are only two types of insurance available today to cover ground water risks — neither covers the entire risk. The first is a sump pump failure/sewer backup endorsement you can add to your Homeowners policy. The other is participating in the National Flood Insurance Program.

Sump pump failure/sewer backup endorsement

This coverage varies significantly from insurer to insurer, so I'll just give you an indication of how the coverage typically works. These endorsements cover water damage, including cleanup. The sump pump coverage applies (a) only if you have a sump pump, and (b) only if it fails to handle the intruding water. It usually even covers failure caused by power outages. The sewer backup coverage covers damage and cleanup anytime the sewer backs up. The basic limit for these two coverages, usually sold together, is $2,000 to $5,000 with limits available to $25,000 or more in some insurance companies.

This endorsement addresses the seepage and surface runoff problem. *This insurance coverage is not intended to apply to true floods.* Avoid insurers who offer watered-down versions of this coverage. Some of these endorsements exclude any failures caused by you or exclude situations where the unit fails to work properly without your knowledge. An example of the first is where you accidentally overload a circuit, cutting power to the pump. An example of the second is where the motor is burned out and you have no way of knowing the pump is fried. (The motor could be burned out on my own pump as I write this.)

The National Flood Insurance Program (NFIP)

Homeowners policies don't cover flooding or ground water damage from heavy rains.

With the private insurance industry unwilling, for a number of reasons, to offer flood insurance, Uncle Sam stepped in to offer coverage to homeowners, either directly, or indirectly through a select list of participating insurance companies who act as the government's agent. Premiums start as low as $106 per year. The program is incredibly complex to price and to explain, although it is significantly easier to use than it was 10 years ago. The only requirement to be eligible is that you must live in a community that participates in the program. Some communities don't. All should.

The Feds offer two programs — the *Emergency program* for homes in communities that are applying for participation in National Flood program but have not yet been accepted and the *Regular program* for homes in communities that are active NFIP participants. The Emergency program's sole purpose is to allow homeowners in those waiting communities to at least get some flood coverage until the community is officially NFIP-approved. As you might expect, in the Emergency program prices are higher and less coverage is available. The maximum available coverage through the Emergency program is $35,000 for dwellings and $10,000 for contents. If your home is located in the Emergency Program, those maximums might pretty inadequate. Change them as soon as your community gets NFIP approved. The maximum coverage limits in the Regular program are more reasonable: $250,000 for dwellings and $100,000 for contents.

Flood insurance covers dwellings and/or contents above grade very well. However, coverage for basements (defined as all four sides below grade) is quite limited. The NFIP Flood policy covers only basement structures including equipment, such as furnaces, water heaters, and air conditioners. It does not provide coverage for finished walls, floors, and ceilings. Belongings in the basement are completely excluded, except for large appliances (washers, dryers, freezers). This is bad news to basement owners. The below grade part of your home is your biggest flood risk, yet there is very little coverage available.

To be a basement, the floors of all four sides have to be below grade. So, if your basement is a *walkout,* meaning the floor of one side is at grade level, you'll be fully covered because the Flood insurance policy would not consider your basement a true basement. On the other hand, if you own a split-level where a lower level is half in the ground and half above ground, the Flood policy would consider that level a basement because the floors of all four sides are below grade.

The NFIP Flood policy doesn't cover just any ground water entering your home. To be considered a flood and thus be eligible for coverage, the water damage must be substantial enough to damage either two adjacent properties or cover two or more acres. So, if you get flooded from heavy rains but none of your adjacent neighbors do, the Flood policy you purchase won't cover the damage. The NFIP Flood policy has $500 deductibles that apply separately to building and contents losses.

There is a 30-day waiting period between the date you apply for Flood insurance and the effective date of coverage, so it's important you apply early. Don't wait to apply from your cell phone while you're laying sandbags around your house to keep out the river that just overflowed.

If your home is located in an area considered very low risk by the NFIP folks and if you meet other requirements, you might qualify for the low-priced Preferred Risk Flood Policy.

For more information on the National Flood Insurance Program, go to NFIP's excellent Web site, www.fema.gov/nfip. If you prefer the phone, dial 888-CALL-FLOOD for answers to general questions. You can buy Flood insurance directly from the NFIP, *but don't!* It's a huge hassle. You've got enough stressors in your life. Don't add this one to your list.

Instead, buy it from your Homeowners agent. If he doesn't handle Flood insurance, either change agents or buy it direct without an agent. The easiest place I know of where you can get a quote and buy direct is a private company, America's Flood Insurance Services. You can reach this company by phone at 800-333-0883. I've talked to the folks at AFIS about the possibility of your calling. They'll be happy to assist you. (America's Flood Insurance Services also takes agent calls.)

If you're seeking a new agent and you need Flood insurance, put "experience dealing with Flood insurance" on your list of required qualifications. See Chapter 12 for more information on shopping for an agent.

Comparing Flood insurance to disaster assistance

Many people wonder why they should purchase flood insurance when Uncle Sam provides disaster assistance through low-interest loans. The important thing to know is that having Flood insurance is a much better idea than relying on federal disaster assistance. Check out the list of reasons below.

- ✔ Flood insurance provides immediate help. Using disaster assistance involves hours of waiting in line, tremendous paperwork, and a wait of many months before you see any money.

- ✔ Flood insurance provides coverage even for local rains or runoffs. Disaster assistance requires a presidential decree before it goes into effect.

- ✔ You don't have to pay back Flood insurance, once you get your settlement. Most disaster assistance is in the form of a loan that must be paid back.

- ✔ Coverage limits are much higher with flood insurance.

- ✔ Need one more reason? The usual cost of a Flood insurance policy that pays you a maximum of $50,000 is $166 per year. The cost to repay a $50,000 disaster loan is $3,840 per year for over 20 years.

My ground water risk management recommendation

Here are my recommendations for managing ground water risks in your life:

- ✔ If your home is at risk for serious ground water damage from flood or heavy rains, buy federal Flood insurance. Buy a policy limit at least high enough to cover your maximum probable loss. Then reduce that amount by the value of all furnishings, carpet, wall coverings, and so on, below ground if you have no walkout, since those items won't be covered. Be sure to buy coverage well in advance of any potential flood, because the NFIP policy has a 30-day waiting period.

- ✔ For almost everyone else with any potential risk from rain runoff or seepage, install a sump pump system with a guarantee from a reputable firm with good references. It's far less expensive than you'd guess. And it costs considerably less than uninsured water damage claims. Buy optional sump pump failure Homeowners coverage for the lesser of the maximum probable loss or the maximum coverage available.

- ✔ Buy at least some sewer backup coverage unless you can prevent a backup with a one-way valve in your sewer pipe, or unless your lowest level is unfinished. Buy enough to cover the maximum probable loss or the maximum available, whichever is less.

Managing Ordinance Risks

Municipalities have building codes. Those codes often change between the time a house is built and the time a structural loss occurs. Then, when the structure is damaged, the homeowner is often required to upgrade the damaged area to satisfy current codes. The good news is that the code improvements usually mean a safer, better-quality home. The bad news is that much of the extra costs are often out of your pocket, because most Homeowners policies cover only the added costs of municipally required upgrades up to 10 percent of your Homeowners coverage limit for your residence. And some insurers completely exclude coverage altogether.

The picture gets even worse if there is a demolition requirement. A demolition ordinance requires that, if more than a specified percentage of the home is damaged, the house can't be repaired. It has to be completely demolished and rebuilt.

I had a client who had a home in a city that required the home be demolished and rebuilt if 25 percent or more of the home was damaged. It was an older home with a replacement value of $240,000. Assume you are this homeowner. You're unaware of this law. You diligently insure your beautiful Cape Cod home for its full replacement cost of $240,000. You have a kitchen fire that damages one-third of the house. Your insurance company happily sends a check for the $80,000, the cost to repair the damage. They add 10 percent of the building limit for ordinance coverage. Check out Table 7-1 to see how happy you are. Here are the total costs, assuming the replacement cost is actually $300,000 after all the mandatory building code improvements:

Table 7-1	Costs to Rebuild
Expense	*Amount*
Cost to demolish and haul away	$35,000
Cost to rebuild per code	$300,000
Total costs	$335,000
Amount of damage	− $ 80,000
10% of bldg. coverage	− $ 24,000
Total Insurance coverage	$104,000
Your out-of-pocket loss	$231,000

Protecting yourself

The good news is that you can get supplemental coverage from most insurance companies under an Ordinance and Law endorsement to your Homeowners policy. This endorsement usually allows you to raise the automatic coverage that comes with your Homeowners policy from 10 percent of the building coverage to 25, 50, 75, or even 100 percent.

So, for example, if you're insuring your home for $200,000, your automatic Ordinance and Law coverage will be $20,000 (10 percent). If you estimate that it will take $50,000 to rebuild your home according to new building codes, you will need an Ordinance and Law endorsement of 25 percent. (25 percent of $200,000 building coverage equals $50,000.)

My recommendations to help you avoid getting burned big time by this ordinance exclusion are:

- ✔ Don't be too concerned if your home is less than five-years old. Make sure you get a policy that provides the extra 10 percent extension. That should be enough.

- ✔ If your home is older than five years, I don't recommend you try to estimate how much extra ordinance coverage to buy — it violates the KISS (keep it simple) principle from Chapter 1. Instead, check with your State Insurance Department to see if there's a State law requiring insurers to pay all costs associated with an ordinance, as there is in Minnesota. If so, just add a Home Replacement Guarantee to your building coverage and you should be all set.

- ✔ If your state has no such law, switch your Homeowners insurance to an insurer that has no ordinance exclusion. If that's not practical, then consider buying some additional ordinance coverage, especially when you know newer building codes would significantly increase your rebuilding costs.

Protecting Yourself from Homeowners Liability Exclusions

The goal of this section is to make you aware of the major Homeowners liability exclusions, show you how they can hurt you, and teach you strategies to minimize the possibility of your being uninsured in a personal lawsuit.

My comments are based on a typical Homeowners policy. Every insurer differs slightly from this norm. Therefore, reading and understanding *your* Homeowners policy is quite important, especially regarding any unique exposures you have related to any of the areas I'm addressing here.

Every policy has a few exclusions that you should know about, but there's not much you can do about them. Exclusions like war and nuclear-related liability, intentional acts, communicable diseases like herpes, abuse (sexual, physical, mental), and anything related to the buying or selling of illegal drugs. All you can do is avoid these activities. Optional insurance just isn't available for something like a nuclear blast you set off.

The business exclusion

Homeowners policies exclude coverage for injuries or property damage you cause in any way related to business — your own or someone else's. (See Chapter 9 for a more detailed analysis if you actually operate your own business from your home.)

The courts have defined *business,* as used in the Homeowners policy, as any activity for which there is both revenue and continuity. Naturally, anything arising from your job or occupation fills that definition. But so can income you earn on the side. If you have a single garage sale, it's not a business. If you have one once a month for ten years, it probably *is* a business. If you baby sit occasionally, it's not a business. If you're a nanny for another family's children, it is a business. If you're part of a babysitting co-op where you take turns watching each other's children and no money is exchanged, it's not a business. But, if you decide to quit your job and have a home day care, you have a business.

The problem with having your activity defined as a business is that if you're sued for injuries or property damage arising from those activities, your Homeowners policy won't cover you. It won't even pay for your defense. You would have coverage for none of the following:

- ✔ Injuries to children you're caring for as a nanny or day care provider.
- ✔ Someone getting electrocuted from a used iron she bought from your weekly garage sale.
- ✔ The courier who your boss sends to deliver work to you while you are sick and working from home slips on your icy driveway and is injured.
- ✔ A burn to a coworker at work, whom you spill hot coffee on.

As the last two examples show, this exclusion applies to not only self-employed people but also to injuries or damage you cause as someone else's employee, whether at home or at work!

Here are some examples of insurance and noninsurance strategies that help prevent the business exclusion from hurting you:

✔ If you're an employee and want coverage for injuries you cause to someone while on the job, buy the business pursuits Homeowners endorsement for about $5 a year. I think every employee should buy this. Remember: Don't risk a lot for a little.

✔ If you telecommute or have an incidental office at home, buy an incidental office liability endorsement for $10 to $25 a year (many of these endorsements include extra coverage on your business furniture and equipment).

✔ If you host weekly neighborhood garage sales, consider avoiding the risk of uninsured injuries by stopping. The few dollars aren't worth the potential uninsured lawsuit. You can either give the items to a worthy cause and play golf on Saturdays instead, or sell your stuff only occasionally, maybe at someone else's neighborhood garage sale instead. By no longer doing it regularly, it won't be a business.

If you won't give it up, then either buy a small business policy for at least $300 a year, or — in writing — have your agent or insurance company state that they won't exclude coverage for your garage sales.

✔ If you're caring for other people's children regularly, either at your home or their home, you flat-out need to buy childcare liability insurance. It's available from one or more of these four sources:

• An endorsement to your Homeowners policy. Check here first. If available, it's normally the least expensive.

• Small business policies from insurance agents.

• A state office that licenses childcare.

• An association of childcare providers.

✔ If your children earn money from home doing something that has a regular pattern (babysitting, lawn care, and so on), I recommend you be safe and get a statement from your insurer — in writing — that your kid's activities won't be excluded as a business. If your insurer won't do it, change insurance companies. Some insurers have customized and broadened their policies so that children's business activities are not excluded.

Whatever it is you're doing that produces income, whether you're an owner or an employee, deal with the business exclusion now, even if it means stopping your activity if you can't get affordable insurance. The cost of an uninsured lawsuit can be ruinous.

The exclusion for renting part of your home

The Homeowners policy excludes coverage for injuries to any roomers or boarders anytime more than two of them live in your home. A good example is a duplex owner who rents the large upstairs unit to six college kids. If any of them get injured at your home and sue you, you have no coverage. If you are the duplex owner, you only have two choices to protect yourself: (a) cancel your Homeowners policy and get a more expensive, commercial policy for rooming houses, or (b) don't rent to more than two individuals or families in any one unit. Note that the exclusion doesn't apply if you rent occasionally — like renting out your home for a week during a Super Bowl when hotel rooms are scarce. And it doesn't apply if you rent part of your home as an office, school, studio, or garage.

The exclusion for any other premises you own or rent

The Homeowners policy covers your primary home but not other locations you rent long-term or own, such as vacation homes or rental properties. The easy solution is to include liability coverage with the policy you buy on the other location. Or you can extend your primary Homeowners liability coverage to the other location with an endorsement costing about $15 a year, if you occupy the house, and about $25 if you're renting it to others.

Vacation time share units

Buying a week or two in a vacation condo co-owned with others has become quite popular in recent years. You can either use the unit during your allotted time, swap for another time in the same complex, swap it for another unit anywhere else in the world, or even rent your unit out. The condominium association manages and insures the whole complex, including liability. Most association policies cover your liability for community injuries such as a drowning at the swimming pool, but they usually don't cover your liability for injuries or property damage you cause arising out of your personal use (for example, your guest is burned in a kitchen fire).

Your Homeowners policy won't cover your personal liability if you have deeded ownership, and most ownerships are deeded.

How do you cover your liability for your two weeks?

- Your primary Home Liability coverage covers you automatically at those places you swap for. No charge.

- To cover yourself using your unit during your allotted time, the safest thing to do is to endorse your Homeowners policy to extend to this time share unit, for about $15.

- If you rent the unit to others, I'd advise you to endorse your Homeowners policy to cover that rental, for about $25 a year.

Remember: Don't risk a lot for a little.

The motorized vehicle exclusion

No surprises here — you certainly didn't expect your cars to be covered by Homeowners insurance. That's what car insurance is for. And, I don't think you're overly surprised to learn that other motorized vehicles are excluded too — like all-terrain vehicles (ATVs), go-carts, trail bikes, snowmobiles, and even golf carts. There are Recreational Vehicle policies you should buy to cover your liability using these items.

What is surprising are the exceptions, when you are insured for motorized vehicles use under your Homeowners policy. See Table 7-2 for more information on these pleasant surprises. Just to be safe, if you own or rent one of these vehicles and think it may be covered under your Homeowners policy, send your company a letter requesting confirmation.

Table 7-2	Exceptions: When Homeowners Policies Cover Motorized Vehicles
The Exception	*An Example of How You Benefit*
ATVs, snowmobiles, and golf carts not owned by you	You're covered for liability when you rent or borrow these toys anywhere — like on vacation.
ATVs, snowmobiles, and golf carts owned by you when used on your insured premises (home, cabin, 300-acre vacant land in the woods)	You keep snowmobiles at your 300-acre parcel up North. If you've extended your Home Liability insurance to the parcel, you're covered for injuries you cause operating the snowmobile on your land. (But you've got zero coverage off your land!)
Golf carts — owned or non-owned — when playing golf on a course only (not while driving your owned golf cart to and from the course)	I rent golf carts. My Homeowners policy automatically covers me for injuries or damage to property I cause.
ATVs, golf carts, and so on, used to service your home	If you regularly use your ATV to help at home, such as attaching a trailer for yard cleanup, or a plow to clean the driveway, you probably have free liability coverage to drive it anywhere else! (Be safe. Get that confirmed in writing by your insurer to avoid claim fights.)
A nonlicensed motorized vehicle designed to assist the handicapped (The key word here is *designed*)	Free liability coverage for a motorized wheelchair — even when used to play basketball.

The boat exclusion

Like the vehicle exclusion, the boat exclusion under a typical Homeowners policy isn't all bad news. This exclusion includes some exceptions too that actually provide some coverage. The references to boat lengths and horsepowers in Table 7-3 are for illustration only. Read your policy to find out the specifics for your situation — Homeowners policies vary widely when it comes to the boat exclusion.

The boat exclusion addresses eight different scenarios. This is a confusing section of the Homeowners policy, even for insurance agents. I attempt to simplify it in Table 7-3.

Table 7-3	Automatic Homeowners Liability Coverage for Boats					
	Boats With Inboard or Inboard/Outboard Motors		**Boats With Outboard Motors**		**Sailboats**	
	50 HP or less	**More than 50 HP**	**25 HP or less**	**Over 25 HP**	**Less than 26 Ft.**	**26 Ft. or more**
Owned	No	No	Yes	No	Yes	No
Borrowed	Yes	Yes	Yes	Sometimes	Yes	Yes
Rented	Yes	No	Yes	Sometimes	Yes	No

Sometimes in the table means yes, if you don't own the outboard motor. Otherwise, no.

Your Homeowners policy watercraft coverage may be different than that indicated in Table 7-3.

Here are some tips for managing your boat liability risks under your Homeowners policy. Remember, check with your agent or carefully read your policy to determine exactly what your policy covers. The following tips assume coverage identical to that in Table 7-3.

- ✔ If you own a boat with an outboard motor of 25 HP or less, or a sailboat less than 26-feet long, you won't need to buy separate boat liability coverage because coverage is included — free — in your Homeowners policy. If you own any other typeof boat or motor, you don't have automatic coverage and need to buy boat liability coverage, either as a Homeowners endorsement or in a separate boat policy.

- ✔ If you operate almost any boat of any size that is borrowed (meaning neither owned nor rented), you have automatic liability coverage. Here are two examples of when this most likely would occur:

- Your friend invites your family to go water skiing with his boat. He does the driving at first, but now he wants to ski so he asks you to drive. If you carelessly drive the boat in a way that injures him or you hit a swimmer and are sued, where would you get your coverage? Right here — in your wonderful Homeowners policy.

- If you go sailing with a friend on her boat and she lets you take the helm, where do you get liability coverage if you cause injuries or collide with another boat? Again, your Homeowners policy.

✔ If you rent a boat, say on vacation, you have automatic coverage for your liability for injuries or property damage in each case but two:

   - Boats with inboard or inboard/outboard motors of more than 50 HP.

   - Sailboats 26 feet long or greater.

To get liability coverage for the two excluded types of rented watercraft at the end of the list:

✔ Buy coverage it from the boat rental agency, if it offers the coverage. Many don't.

✔ If you own a boat at home for which you have a boat liability policy, it may include coverage for when you rent most other boats. Again, many don't.

✔ You may get the coverage from a supplemental personal-liability policy called an *Umbrella* policy. See Chapter 10 and 11 for more information on Umbrella policies. Be sure to read your policy or check with your agent. Not all umbrellas cover boat rentals. If yours doesn't, shop for a better policy.

If you are unable to get coverage when renting boats that are excluded under your Homeowners policy from some other source, then the ARRT strategy to practice is to avoid the risk. Either don't rent at all, or rent something else for which you will be insured. (See Chapter 2 for more on ARRT.)

Avoiding the hidden danger of recreational rentals

Even when you have automatic liability coverage for injuries and property damage you cause to the public while renting boats, snowmobiles, ATVs, go-carts, and golf carts, you don't have liability coverage for damage to the rented item itself. (See the exclusion in the Homeowners policy for property that is in your custody.)

When most people see a fun boat that they want to rent, they scribble their signature on a contract they don't read. They pay a damage deposit, usually about $500, and they assume that if they damage the boat, they will lose their deposit. Then they're off, operating a boat that they're unfamiliar with, usually on a body of water that they're also unfamiliar with.

Your uninsured liability for damage to the boat itself is exposed in two ways:

- ✔ Your legal liability for damage you actually cause to the boat
- ✔ Your contractual liability in which you agreed to be responsible for anything that happens to the boat, even when the damage is not your fault

"Okay, but the worst that can happen is that I'm out the damage deposit," you say. Not true, unless the damage is less than the damage deposit. The damage deposit is just a deposit. If the boat is destroyed in a tornado, or if you hit some submerged rocks, causing an engine fire that burns the boat, you're liable for the cost of the repairs or the cost to replace the boat.

Now, assume you're sharing the rental with a friend. You're both driving the boat, and you're splitting the cost. But you signed the contract. He didn't. Your friend drives recklessly and seriously damages the boat. Who does the rental agency go after? You — you agreed to be responsible for anything that happens! Ouch!

How can you protect yourself? Read the contract before you sign it or have it faxed to your agent. If the contract makes you responsible (most rental contracts do), there are two ways to protect yourself:

- ✔ Buy the optional insurance from the rental agency, but only if it covers all the damage you're responsible for. Often, it does not.
- ✔ Rely on coverage in your Umbrella policy. If it doesn't cover damage to any boat you rent, find an Umbrella policy that does. The good ones do.

The aircraft exclusion

This will be short and sweet. Homeowners policies do not cover any kind of aircraft risks. They don't cover injuries. They don't cover damage to other property. They don't even cover damage to the aircraft itself.

If you own an aircraft, buy an aircraft policy. If you borrow one and fly it yourself, make sure that you are insured under the owner's policy. If you rent one to fly, buy complete coverage from the rental agent.

If you charter an aircraft with a hired pilot or crew, you can be sued personally for injuries or damage the pilot causes to others, since he is flying the plane for your benefit. Make sure that your charter contract includes what's called an *indemnity agreement* in which the rental agency, in the event you're sued for pilot errors, agrees to defend you and pay for any judgment against you.

Up the creek without a policy

I rented a 28-foot sailboat, worth $30,000, on Lake Pepin in Southern Minnesota. I paid the $500 damage deposit and was told that amount would be all I owed if I damaged the boat. When I read the contract, I pointed out to the gruff character behind the desk that his contract made me responsible for the entire $30,000 — not just for the $500 — if any serious damage should occur. He scoffed, "Don't worry about that! The owner has the boat insured. All you'd owe is the $500 deductible. She'd collect the rest from her insurance company." He's correct. But what he doesn't know is how quickly the insurance company would send me a registered letter and a copy of the rental contract I signed, demanding that I reimburse them for all repair costs, or even for the cost of buying a new boat.

And I would owe them every penny! That is exactly what would happen (not a pretty picture!).

Read rental contracts. See if you're responsible for just your deposit or for the entire boat. If for the entire boat, you need to arrange insurance. *Do not rely on verbal statements from rental agents.* And don't assume the optional insurance the rental agent offers is comprehensive — that it covers all damage you're responsible for. Make sure there's no dollar limit on the coverage (such as a $2,000 limit on a $30,000 boat). Read the policy exclusions. Make sure the policy doesn't exclude something important. If the policy has either a dollar limit less than the boat's value or if it excludes anything you're doing, don't buy it.

The loss assessment exclusion

This exclusion denies coverage for assessments for either injuries or property damage made against you by a community of townhouse or condominium owners of which you are a member. If you own a townhouse or condominium, you can buy optional Loss Assessment coverage as an endorsement to your unit owner Homeowners policy that covers some but not all of these assessments. See Chapter 8 for the details, and be warned that these assessments can be very substantial!

The contracts exclusion

The Homeowners policy excludes liability coverage for all contracts, oral or written, but then has two nice *coverage givebacks*. A coverage giveback means that the exclusion in your policy is nullified — or the insurance company's excuse for not paying you in a given circumstance is taken away. These givebacks apply to written — not oral — contracts that:

✔ Involve the ownership, maintenance, or use of a location you have insured, such as your home.

✔ Involve your assuming the liability of others *prior to* any claim (for example, you rent a chainsaw and in the rental agreement you agree to protect the hardware store if they get sued for any injury that occurs while you're using the saw).

I have a wheelchair-bound client, Betty, who owns a beautiful two-story home on the Mississippi River. The house has an elevator to help her navigate between floors. In her contract with the elevator maintenance company, she unknowingly agreed to defend them and pay any judgment against them for any lawsuit arising from an elevator injury. The first coverage giveback for written contracts will do exactly that for her because the contract has to do with the maintenance of her home. So, if someone is injured in the elevator when a cable snaps, the Homeowners liability coverage will defend and pay any judgment against Betty and, because of the elevator contract, will do the same for the elevator maintenance company.

Be careful. These two givebacks won't cover all your written contracts. But a good Personal Umbrella policy will cover most of the liability you assume when you sign a contract. See Chapter 10 to learn more about the contractual coverage of Umbrella policies for all types of personal contracts.

Damage to Property of Others coverage

Every Homeowners policy includes a very useful supplemental coverage called *Damage to Property of Others*. It's a wonderful little coverage that hardly anyone knows about and under which very few claims are filed.

It covers up to $500 or $1,000, depending on the insurer, for damage you cause to other people's property, including property in your custody. There's no deductible. It's meant to be good neighbor coverage. It even covers intentional damage (pranks) by your children if they are under a certain age, such as the age of 13. The good neighbor coverage applies if your ten-year-old throws a rock through the neighbor's window, or if you cut down a tree limb and it crashes through your neighbor's sun room, or if your dog chews apart the neighbor's new couch.

You can be a recipient of this coverage too. Switch places with your neighbor in the examples. If your neighbor or his family does any of this damage to your property, remember he has this coverage too, if he has a Homeowners policy. Just ask him to report the claim. That's all there is to it.

This coverage can pay even when the damage isn't your fault, such as when a windstorm blows your tree onto your neighbor's roof. I've seen insurance adjusters deny payment for this type of claim because the damage isn't your fault. Don't let an adjuster do that. This coverage is true no-fault insurance.

The property in your custody exclusion

Homeowners policies exclude coverage for damage to the property of others in your possession (See one small exception in the sidebar, "Damage to Property of Others coverage."), whether you rent it (a boat), occupy it (a friend's cabin she lets you use for the weekend), or use it (your employer's laptop computer). There is one coverage giveback — coverage for fire, smoke, or explosions you cause, such as for a kitchen fire you cause in your rented apartment.

Once you know this pitfall exists, you can protect yourself, at least partially. Here's how:

✔ Buy a Personal Umbrella policy that plugs this gap by covering damage to property you don't own that is in your care. See Chapter 11 for more details.

✔ When renting equipment, boats, and so on, if the value of what you're renting exceeds what you're willing to pay for out-of-pocket, see about buying coverage from the rental company, if you don't have an Umbrella policy that covers it.

✔ When renting hotel rooms or borrowing cabins, you do have coverage for fire damage — probably your biggest risk.

✔ When using other people's property on a long-term basis, like a laptop computer, you can specifically insure it on your Homeowners policy (called *scheduling*). Be sure to list the owner as a *loss payee* on the policy to protect the owner's interest.

The Workers' Compensation exclusion

Workers' Compensation is an insurance program of state-mandated benefits that employers provide employees, usually covering the employee's medical bills and lost wages from a job-related injury or illness. Workers' Compensation is no-fault coverage. To collect benefits, an injured person must only meet two requirements: he was your employee and he was hurt on the job. If an employer fails to buy a Workers' Comp policy, he has to pay, out of his own pocket, the same benefits to the injured worker that the policy would have paid.

Homeowners liability coverage excludes liability coverage for Workers' Compensation benefits. If you are exposed (in other words, if you have even one employee), you must buy Workers' Compensation coverage. You may need Workers' Compensation coverage even if you don't have any employees but often use independent contractors. See the sidebar, "You may need Workers' Comp coverage — even if you have no employees."

You may need Workers' Comp coverage — even if you have no employees

A very unhappy consumer, Allen, hired me to review his whole insurance program. He was upset with his insurance company. He was paying it several thousand dollars a year for auto, home, and Umbrella policies. But the insurer was completely denying coverage for his first ever claim! It wouldn't even defend him in court.

Allen had no actual employees. But he was affluent and hired a lot of contractors to maintain his property. One of the contractors, Joe, a one-man lawn-care service, fell off a ladder and injured his back. Joe's attorney advised him to sue Allen for Workers' Compensation benefits on the grounds that Joe should have been Allen's employee. Because Allen had no employees, he didn't carry Workers' Compensation coverage. Therefore, he had to pay for his own defense and pay the claim out of his own pocket.

If you do have an employee, pay them as such, and buy any required Workers' Compensation policy. When you hire independent contractors to help you with home projects, I recommend you do one of the following to reduce the chances of the contractor later trying to sue you for Workers' Compensation benefits as your employee if he is injured on your job:

✔ At a minimum, always gather proof of the contractor's independence — a business card, an estimate with the business name on it, and a State or Federal tax ID number given to the contractor for registering a business.

✔ Ideally, request evidence that the contractor has a Workers' Compensation policy in his business name, especially if he has any people helping him on the job. *Note:* Many st ates don't require one-person businesses to have Workers' Compensation insurance. A fail-safe solution is to hire only contractors who prove they have the coverage. Why? Because the only time you're completely exempt from Workers' Compensation liability is if the injured worker has his or her own Workers' Compensation policy or is employed by a contractor who does.

If you have no employees but do hire contractors or laborers who do not have their own Workers' Compensation policy, I recommend a third strategy — especially if you are affluent and very sueable — *Contingent Workers' Compensation* (CWC) coverage. A very small number of Homeowners insurers offer CWC coverage as a policy endorsement for a nominal charge. If your Homeowners insurer doesn't offer Contingent Workers' Compensation coverage, find one who does. Or else buy a Contingent Workers' Compensation policy from your state Workers' Compensation insurance pool, if it is available.

CWC works like this. If any injured contractor ever sues for Workers' Compensation benefits, this optional coverage completely defends you and, if you lose, pays the state-required benefits.

Not all agents are aware of this Workers' Compensation potential danger. There are, however, plenty of good agents who are aware of your potential liability and would be happy to help you. Add "knowledge of Contingent Workers' Compensation coverage" to your shopping list for your agent (see Chapter 12 for tips on finding a good agent and making up an agent shopping list). Note that it's possible your state has a law exempting homeowners from this risk. Check with your state insurance department if in doubt.

If you want to be completely insulated from any claims for Workers' Compensation benefits for injuries to contractors or laborers you hire to work at your home, you must either *always* get proof they have their own Workers' Compensation insurance before they start working, or you must buy Contingent Workers' Compensation coverage.

Chapter 8

Managing the Special Risks of Condominium and Town House Owners

....

....

*T*he single biggest change in the housing market in the past 20 years has been the movement away from single-family homes toward town houses and condominiums. A new type of Homeowners policy, called a *unit-owner policy* (often referred to as the *Homeowners Form 6*), has been created to meet the special needs of town house or condominium owners.

The good news is that there's now a special policy for those who own town houses or condos. The bad news is that this policy is the single most difficult Homeowners policy to set up correctly — without serious gaps.

Defining the Problem

People who buy townhouses or condominiums *(unit owners)* band together to form homeowner associations. One of the functions of the association is to arrange insurance coverage — both property and liability — for the entire complex of buildings (the insurance is called the *master policy*). The master policy insures all structures, including the majority of the structure owned by each unit owner. Each unit owner is responsible for insuring her own belongings, plus any part of her unit structure not covered by the association master policy. The board of directors of the association determines exactly which part of each unit is insured by the master policy and which part is the unit owner's responsibility. That information is contained in the association documents (the Bylaws, Declarations, or Operating Policies).

There are really two problems for unit owners. The first is identifying exactly what part of the unit structure is the unit owner's responsibility and is not insured by the master policy. The second is finding the expert advice you need to help you modify your unit owner policy to plug the coverage gaps that exist between the two policies.

Distinguishing between condominiums and town houses

Town houses and condominiums are individually owned, residential units, similar to apartments, that are part of a complex of similar units attached together in one or more buildings. The usual distinction between the two is that town houses have their entry doors open to the outside, have other adjacent units only on either side but not above or below, and are often multilevel; condominiums, like most apartments, open to a common hall, are usually one level, and normally have adjacent units on either side, as well as above and/or below. From the outside, town houses look like single homes attached at the sides; condominiums look like apartments in an apartment building.

Similarities between condos and town houses are that:

- ✔ In addition to the ownership of their individual units, owners also own a proportionate interest in common areas like lawns, community structures, swimming pools, and so on.

- ✔ A board of directors of elected unit owners acts on behalf of the association of all unit owners.

- ✔ Several association documents exist that define rights, obligations, and operating policies.

Exposing the coverage gap

In the vast majority of associations, a significant structural coverage gap between the association's master building insurance policy and the unit owner's personal Homeowners policy exists. This gap is normally the result of a misperception on the part of the unit owner.

The unit owner believes — usually mistakenly — that he is responsible for insuring his personal belongings only, and that the association's master policy pays for everything structural in the unit, after a policy deductible of typically $1,000. This misperception is reinforced by the basic unit-owner Homeowners policy, which covers the contents of the unit and usually only has $1,000 of building coverage — enough to cover the master policy deductible.

But the reality, most of the time, is that the association master policy covers, at a minimum, the bare exterior walls of your unit and the bare floors, but then makes you responsible for some or all of the rest of your unit. This could be a *big* coverage gap — I've seen it be as large as $100,000! Can you imagine discovering this gap only after a fire destroys most of your unit? Sadly, that's when most people find out.

Discovering where the gap is defined

The gap is not, as you may expect, spelled out in the master policy. Rather you will find it in one of your association documents, usually the Declarations. The Declarations define which part of your unit the association will insure. Here are some typical examples of items that the unit owner may be responsible for replacing — things excluded by the association master policy:

- ✔ Drapes, carpets, and wallcoverings

- ✔ Any structural improvements you make

- ✔ Any improvements made by any unit owner since the unit was built (a fun one! How do you ever determine that?)

- ✔ Everything but exterior bare walls and floor — you're responsible for carpet, wall coverings, built-in appliances, all interior walls, cabinets, plumbing appliances like tubs and toilets, lighting fixtures, and even unit-specific wiring! Ouch!

The price of a commission

I suggest that you have your agent review your Declarations for you or with you. Often this may be difficult to do. Why? Because of how agents are paid. It's the American way that people take jobs where they get paid well for their talents. Agents usually do the same. Because the premium is small on a unit-owner policy, the average commission to the agent is about $50 a year. As a result, these policies tend to get sold by relatively inexperienced agents and tend to be mass-produced, neither of which helps you find the expertise you need. See Chapter 12 on buying insurance the right way for tips on hiring a good agent. The expertise and care you need are out there. You may have to dig a little deeper to find them.

It is imperative if you own a condo or town house that you and your insurance agent read the Declarations to find out the extent of your obligations and modify your unit-owner Homeowners policy before you have a serious uninsured loss.

Preventing Problems with Proper Homeowners Insurance

The Homeowners policy created specifically to meet the unique property and liability risks of town house and condominium owners has six types of coverage — four are reviewed here:

- Coverage for damage to the unit structure (Coverage A)
- Coverage for any detached buildings, like sheds or garages (Coverage B)
- Coverage for belongings (Coverage C)
- Coverage for injuries and property damage you cause (Coverage E)

See Chapter 5 for a review of the six coverage parts of Homeowners insurance and the two causes-of-loss forms I recommend — Broad Form and Special Form. Coverage for additional living expenses when your home is impossible to live in (Coverage D) and coverage for paying the medical bills of injured guests (Coverage F) are addressed fully in Chapter 5 and are not affected by town house or condo ownership.

Now find out how to set coverage limits for yourself as a unit owner when buying a unit-owner Homeowners policy.

Coverage A — building

There are two components you must consider when buying building coverage on your unit-owner policy:

- The amount of building coverage you need to cover what is not covered by the association master policy
- The kinds of claims, or causes-of-loss, you want covered

Measuring the gap

Once you've read your Declarations, the next step is estimating the dollar amount of your potential obligations. Not easy! Just make two columns — the left listing item by item everything structural you are responsible for, and the right listing your estimated cost to replace each item. Whatever your right column totals is the amount of structural coverage you need. Round that number up by about 20 percent to cover guestimation errors. See Table 8-1 for an example.

Table 8-1	Estimating Building Coverage
Structural Item	*Replacement Cost*
Carpet	$4,000
Wallpaper	$3,500
Lighting fixtures	$6,000
Plumbing fixtures	$7,500
Floor tile, hardwood	$8,000
Cabinets	$8,000
Total	$37,000
Plus 20%	$45,000

The coverage that comes automatically with the vast majority of unit-owner policies is the *Broad causes-of-loss Form,* covering your claims only if they appear on a list of about 15 covered losses. Anything not on the list isn't covered. I don't recommend this as an option for insuring a structure.

For insuring a condominium or townhouse unit structure, request the optional *Special Form* (also known as *Special Perils*) that covers any accidental cause-of-loss if the cause is not on a small list of exclusions (flood, earthquake, and so on). It's very inexpensive, too, only about $1 per $1,000 worth of coverage. See Chapter 6 for more on Special Perils.

Coverage B — detached structures

Some garages that you buy with town houses are attached to the first level of your unit. Many are in a separate, detached structure. To determine your insurance responsibility for garages, read the Declarations. If you are required to insure the garage, increase Coverage A — building coverage — if the garage is attached. And, if the garage is not attached, buy the appropriate amount of Coverage B. You would also include in the Coverage B limit all other detached structures, like sheds, permanent docks, dog houses for elitist dogs, and so forth.

Coverage C — belongings

One thing common to every association's Declarations is the unit owner's sole responsibility for their personal belongings. My bottom line recommendations for insuring your belongings are:

- Buy a limit high enough to replace what you own.

- Buy the optional Replacement Cost coverage so claims will be paid on a new cost basis rather than a depreciated value.

- Upgrade the covered causes-of-loss from Broad Form to Special Form so that any cause-of-loss, other than a few that are specifically excluded, is covered.

Do these three and you'll have enough to replace everything you own following a major loss. You also will have more causes-of-loss covered. As the song says: "Who could ask for anything more?"

When it rains, it pours

Here's an example of why having the right coverage is so important.

Sarah owned a condominium and hired me as a consultant to review her insurance program and to suggest changes to plug any gaps. She had had three recent water-damage claims to her unit — two from a worn, leaky roof and the third from the negligence of a roofer who failed to cover the roof while replacing it. She had been out of her unit for months when I met her because the mold and mildew were so bad she couldn't breathe.

Neither Sarah nor her agent had ever read her Declarations. She had the worst kind — the bare walls, bare floor type that puts coverage responsibility almost entirely on the unit owner. When we added up the values of everything between the bare exterior walls that she was responsible for, including carpet, interior walls, lighting, and plumbing fixtures, it came to about $100,000! Her agent sold her a policy (without reading the Declarations) that only covered $10,000. The mold, mildew, and water damage was $30,000 — almost none of which was covered by the association's master policy. Her coverage was $20,000 short — just on the building loss.

Further, her entire wardrobe was ruined because of the mold and mildew. She did not have the Special Perils contents coverage I recommend, which covers aboveground water damage, so she was out another $35,000 for clothing. Her total out-of-pocket loss was $55,000. It would have cost her an extra $400 per year to have had the right kind of coverage.

Coverage E — liability

When it comes to your personal liability for injuries or property damage, be consistent. Buy the same limit that you buy for other policies you own. You are protecting the same assets and the same income — yours! You would not want different liability limits on different policies any more than you would want different car insurance liability on weekends than what you have for the rest of the week.

So, for example, if $500,000 is the liability insurance limit you buy for your car insurance, buy the same $500,000 for Homeowners liability too. See Chapter 5 for tips on choosing a liability limit that's appropriate for you.

Reducing Your Exposure to Association Loss Assessments

One of the things common to associations is dues and assessments. Assessments are allowed in the Bylaws. They occur when there is not enough money in the association bank account to pay the bills — usually when the bills exceed expectations. One of the reasons associations have unexpected bills is inadequate insurance coverage. When the association suffers a loss beyond the limits of its property or liability insurance coverage, it assesses you, the unit owner, with a bill to help pay for that loss. Therefore the term *loss assessment.*

Understanding why loss assessments happen

Suppose you are a unit owner and that there are 100 units in your association. When an insurance claim is not fully covered, Table 8-2 shows examples of how you could be assessed.

Table 8-2	Possible Association Assessments			
Claim	*Claim Amount*	*Insurance Pays*	*Assessment*	*Your Share*
Guest drowns in pool	$2 million	$1 million	$1 million	$10,000
Injured worker sues for Workers' Comp	$700,000	None — not covered	$700,000	$7,000
Complex destroyed by tornado	$20 million	$14 million	$6 million	$60,000

The bad news is that this all sounds pretty scary. And it is. The good news is that it doesn't occur often. Homeowners policies offer partial coverage inexpensively, and you can use one of the ARRT risk management strategies in Chapter 2 — loss reduction — to lower the chances of an assessment ever occurring for an insurance claim.

Protecting yourself

Two problems can arrive in your mailbox, in the form of a bill, if you ignore the risk of loss assessments in your insurance coverage. The first problem is that the usual unit-owner policy has only $1,000 Loss Assessment coverage. This means that if the association sends you a big, ugly assessment, say for $50,000, your personal unit-owner policy will pay only $1,000 of that — not much help. In the three examples in Table 8-2, you could have needed up to $60,000 coverage.

The second problem is that the insurance company only pays that puny $1,000 if the cause of the loss is covered by your unit-owner policy. In the three examples in Table 8-2, your policy covers lawsuits and tornadoes but not Workers' Compensation. Even if you bought extra loss-assessment coverage, it wouldn't cover your assessment for the injured worker.

Reducing your risk by changing the association insurance program

The better your association coverage is, the better your chances of avoiding an uninsured assessment. If you sit on the board, your impact is strong and you can, perhaps, play a direct role in improving association insurance coverages by getting the board to hire an outside insurance consultant. In every association insurance plan I have reviewed, there has been at least one, and usually several, major coverage gaps. Board members aren't insurance experts and they often don't hire an expert to design their insurance specifications.

Even as a unit owner not on the board, you can still have an impact. You can write to your board representative and request the board hire an independent insurance consultant to audit the association insurance program. If the board balks, pay your Homeowners agent yourself to review the association insurance, using the checklist in the sidebar "An association insurance checklist." I have done that scores of times for clients. If that sounds like a lot of work, just remember the alternative is a possible substantial, out-of-pocket, uninsured loss assessment to you

If there are coverage gaps, you can send a letter to the board warning it of your concerns about uninsured risks and advising that, if it doesn't buy the missing insurance coverages, you won't be responsible for any loss assessments resulting from those missing coverages. If you can have your attorney send the letter, even better. The letter gives you a leg to stand on if you refuse to pay an assessment resulting from an uninsured claim, but it's not a guarantee that you can avoid the bill. Insurance is still, by far, your best bet.

An association insurance checklist

Here is a list of coverages and/or policies that I think every homeowner's association should have, as a minimum. Each association is different, so remember that your association may have insurance needs in addition to these:

✔ Building insurance for the full replacement cost of all buildings required to be insured by the association, including Replacement Cost coverage (an *Agreed Amount* coverage which waives any penalties for underinsurance on partial losses) and, if available, a building replacement guarantee if rebuilding costs exceed the insurance amount. Also, flood and/or earthquake coverage if there is the danger of either one happening

✔ Public liability insurance of $1 million, or whatever limits are required for an umbrella policy

✔ An umbrella liability policy with at least $1 million limits

✔ Workers' Compensation insurance, even if there are no association employees, to cover claims brought by uninsured independent contractors, covering all defense costs and judgments

✔ Non-owned automobile liability coverage which protects the association from lawsuits arising out of car accidents caused by people running errands on behalf of the association in their own personal car

✔ Directors and Officers liability coverage, for two reasons. First, people nice enough to volunteer their time to serve on the board should be given this coverage so they have insurance in case they make an honest mistake and are sued for it. Second, if the director does make an error that could lead to a possible loss assessment, this coverage may cover the error and keep the loss assessment from being passed to you

✔ A Fidelity bond — to protect the association from the dishonesty of anyone handling money

As the unit owner, you have every right to ask for proof from the board that it has every one of these policies. If it does not, I encourage you to write the board and express your concerns in order to reduce your chances of a possible loss assessment.

Measuring how much Loss Assessment coverage to buy

Here is a quick and dirty formula to easily determine how much Loss Assessment coverage to buy. Start by estimating the maximum probable uninsured loss that could happen (say, a $5 million uninsured lawsuit). Then, divide that number by the number of units in the complex (in the example earlier, 100 units). $5 million divided by 100 units equals a possible maximum loss assessment of $50,000 each. If this is your situation, I recommend that you buy $50,000 of Loss Assessment coverage. The really good news? The $50,000 of coverage costs only about $20 a year with most insurance companies!

A good rule is to buy at least enough Loss Assessment coverage to pay your assessment to replace the entire complex if it's destroyed without insurance coverage (such as if the Treasurer forgot to pay the premium on the master policy, coverage runs out, and a fire breaks out two days later). So if the replacement value of the association buildings is $2 million and there are

80 units, buy at least $25,000 of Loss Assessment coverage. It's cheap stuff, so buy a little more than you think you need.

Improving your assessment coverage through better building coverage

It is imperative that you buy the broadest possible unit-owner building coverage — Special Perils coverage — in order to have the most possible types of claims covered by Loss Assessment coverage. Even buy optional earthquake coverage if there is the slightest chance of an earthquake. Your Loss Assessment coverage only pays for those assessments where the cause of the loss is a cause covered by your building coverage (Coverage A).

For example, suppose an earthquake crumbles the entire complex you live in and causes $4 million in damages. The association failed to buy earthquake coverage. There are 100 unit owners in the association: $4 million divided by 100 units equals an assessment of $40,000 to you and all other owners. If you've purchased the optional earthquake damage coverage on your unit-owner Homeowners policy and at least $40,000 of Loss Assessment coverage, your policy pays the full assessment.

If you own a condominium or town house, always add extra Loss Assessment coverage to the Homeowners policy covering your unit. And always buy the Special Perils endorsement, including earthquake coverage if you're exposed.

Preventing Problems on Building Damage Claims

Suppose that your association's Declarations require the association to insure the majority of your unit and for you to be responsible for insuring carpets, drapes, wallcoverings, and improvements you made to the unit. Now suppose a fire damages both the property that the association is responsible for and the property that you are responsible for. Can you imagine the frustration of sorting out, between two different insurance companies, which company pays for how much damage? This is especially vexing after you've already gone through the trauma of significant loss to your property.

Getting the insurance companies to work together

If you want your claim to go smoothly, you'll have to be a little assertive. Here is how you do it. If at all possible, since you have the strongest personal relationship with your unit-owner insurance company, request that they act as "front man" on your claim, meaning that they will handle their own claim as well as act as an agent for you in dealings with the insurance company insuring the association, so that you'll only have to deal with one insurance company — yours. It also means that your insurance company will take the responsibility to dicker with the association insurance company regarding any disputed areas and that they will agree to resolve any differences between them, without involving you.

You may get some resistance to this request at first. However, I urge you to persist. It's a perfectly reasonable request. You and your association have paid for the services of insurance professionals. They're the experts, and they should be willing to do their job.

Getting a hassle-free full claim settlement

The best way to improve your odds of getting a hassle-free, full settlement is to buy the best possible coverage. No matter how nice your insurance company is, no matter how caring your adjuster is, they will not pay you for coverage you don't have!

I see and hear a lot of people criticizing their insurance company when their claim is either denied or underpaid. Trust me when I tell you that in nearly every instance, the coverage was lacking — not the insurance company. If you do not want to be a victim at claim time, you must take personal responsibility for making sure that you have the right coverage in advance of the claim. Helping you get that coverage is one of the objectives of this book. See Chapter 12 for more information on buying insurance the right way.

Managing the Special Risks of Vacation Condominiums

Another trend I've witnessed in recent years is an increasing number of people buying seasonal vacation condominiums, usually either near beaches or trendy ski areas. Someone else manages the property and all the regular maintenance is taken care of, so you can have fun when you're at the condo rather than do chores. The strategies I recommend for managing these risks are the same as for primary condominium residences, with two exceptions that require special handling:

 ✔ When your condominium is co-owned with friends and/or

 ✔ When your condominium is rented to others when you're not there

Avoiding the insurance gaps of co-ownership

Because of the substantial cost savings, people buying these vacation condominiums often co-own them with close friends. A lot of advantages exist, true, but one major disadvantage also exists — the insurance is often set up in correctly. Here's an example from my own files.

Clients Desi and Lucy purchased a Colorado condominium with their ski-buff friends, Fred and Ethyl. They didn't call me at the time because their friends said that they would take care of all the insurance. However, in an annual review of Desi and Lucy's program, the subject came up. At my urging, they got me a copy of the policy from their friends. The pertinent coverages, as arranged by Fred and Ethyl:

- ✔ The Named Insured listed only Fred and Ethyl. Desi and Lucy's 50 percent ownership in the building and contents was uninsured.

- ✔ The unit-owner building coverage limit was only $1,000, with no Special Perils endorsement.

- ✔ The liability limit was $100,000 and again, Desi and Lucy were uninsured.

- ✔ There was only $1,000 of Loss Assessment coverage — far too little.

- ✔ The personal property limit was $45,000. The replacement cost was $80,000.

Assume a hypothetical claim. Suppose the microwave shorts out, causing a fire that seriously injures a guest and destroys the condominium. See Table 8-3 for what the unit-owner policy would pay on behalf of each couple.

Table 8-3	Desi and Lucy's Ski Condominium			
Loss Description	*Total Claim*	*Each Party's 50 percent share*	*Amounts Paid for Fred and Ethyl*	*Amounts Paid for Desi and Lucy*
Jury award to burn victim	$450,000	$225,000	$100,000	$0
Defense costs	$80,000	$40,000	$20,000	$0
Jointly owned belongings	$80,000	$40,000	$40,000	$0
Structural damage responsibility per Declarations	$30,000	$15,000	$1000	$0
Totals	$640,000	$320,000	$161,000	$0

Fred and Ethyl were seriously underinsured, and Desi and Lucy had no insurance whatsoever. Their total out-of-pocket loss would have been $320,000 — all of which could've been avoided with a couple of simple policy changes.

Three mistakes were made:

✔ Desi and Lucy's 50 percent ownership interest was unprotected. Because Fred and Ethyl only own one-half the unit and half the contents, the insurance company only had to pay for half the contents loss.

✔ The $100,000 liability limits — $50,000 per couple — was grossly inadequate.

✔ No one had read the association Declarations to discover that the unit owners were responsible for insuring about $30,000 of the structure.

The annual cost to repair all three problems was about $100 per couple. It's so often the case that the extra premium to do the job well can save potential out-of-pocket losses of hundreds of thousands of dollars. The added premium is peanuts in relation to the risk being protected.

Avoiding coverage gaps when renting to others

Vacation condominiums are often rented by the association management during the times the owners aren't using them. If you allow your unit to be rented, your insurance coverage may be suspended due to rental exclusions in the policy. Had the burn victim in our hypothetical story above been a renter, there very likely would have been no property or liability coverage that would have applied. The bottom line?

If you're renting your vacation town house or condominium even occasionally, check with your agent or insurance company and buy the optional rental coverage.

Protecting the property when you're gone

If you are not renting the property to others and you only occasionally use it, a good strategy to reduce the chance of both burglary and fire is a central burglar-and-fire-alarm system that, after installation, costs only about $20 a month to monitor. You can even add an option for temperature monitoring if the condominium is in a cold weather climate — the alarm company will be alerted if your temperature drops below a certain temperature, so that if the furnace has failed, your pipes won't freeze and cause massive water damage.

Chapter 9

Managing the Risks of Your Home Business

In This Chapter

▶ Identifying the risks of a home business

▶ Reducing business risks with noninsurance strategies

▶ Making up a home-business insurance checklist

▶ Identifying sources of home-business insurance

*H*ome businesses have been around for a long time — mostly in the form of moonlighting situations, like tax accounting, or part-time businesses, like piano lessons, day care, ceramics classes, and all the various franchises like Mary Kay.

I have, personally, worked with scores of home businesses over the years. Most have one thing in common — little or no business insurance. And yet these businesses have uninsured risks that are often serious enough to cause financial ruin if they occur. How sad that the dream of one's own business, if not properly protected, could lead to a tragic result.

So many home businesses are inadequately insured for two reasons:

✔ The Homeowners policy, even with the optional business endorsements, falls far short of meeting the coverage needs of most home-business owners.

✔ Many home-business owners are unaware of all the risks arising from their business and that their Homeowners policy doesn't cover many of the risks that they do know about.

This chapter is designed to help the home-business owner, as well as those contemplating starting a home business, identify the many different property and liability risks you face and determine how best to protect yourself, using both insurance and noninsurance strategies.

If you don't own and operate a business your home, but you do work from home (even occasionally) as someone else's employee, see Chapter 7 to find out how to avoid the property and liability coverage gaps in your Homeowners policy.

Identifying the Risks of a Home Business

Perhaps the most important part of managing home business risks is, first and foremost, knowing what those risks are. You can't manage what you don't know about. If you currently own, or are even considering owning, a home business of your own, I encourage you to make a list as you read through this section, identifying the unique risks your business faces.

Keep in mind the business restrictions of the typical Homeowners policy as you review the various types of risks identified here:

- Zero business liability coverage of any kind — no premises liability, no products liability, no professional liability, no Workers' Compensation, and so on.

- Minimal coverage on business personal property — typically $2,500 on-premises and only $250 off-premises

- Zero coverage on any detached structures used even in part for business purposes, other than garaging cars.

Property risks

Home businesses almost always involve some property risks, either *structural* (a building) or *personal* (stuff). Maybe both. Consultants have offices complete with office furniture. Wholesalers and retailers have inventory. Even piano teachers have a piano. To properly cover your home-based business assets, you need to consider replacement cost totals for five types of business property:

- The rebuilding costs of the home office or work area that is located in your residence

- The rebuilding costs of any detached structures used even partially for business

- The cost to replace your business personal property at home

- The cost to replace your business personal property away from home

- The labor costs to reproduce valuable papers, like customer files, maps, and so on

When determining your business property values in this chapter, use the current replacement cost for a new item. You will be consistent with how most small-business policies value property.

Assessing structural property risks

Sometimes, having a home business requires the owner to build a structural environment to operate from. Sometimes, this new environment is part of the residence itself, like a finished office. Other times, it is located in all or part of a separate, detached structure.

- ✔ **If built into your home structure:** If the business space is built into your residence, you need only to raise your Homeowners coverage (Coverage A) on your home high enough to rebuild a new structure, including the cost to rebuild the business environment. Why? Because the Homeowners policy has no restrictions or limitations for any part of your primary residence structure used for business purposes. There are limitations on business personal property but not on the building itself.

- ✔ **If built into a detached structure:** If your business operates from a detached structure, the entire structure — not just the part used for business — is excluded from Homeowners coverage. Discover some ways to avoid this exclusion later in the chapter. Do two things for proper coverage:

    - Buy an endorsement allowing the business use

    - Raise detached structure coverage (Coverage B) high enough to rebuild all detached structures on your lot.

Assessing business personal property risks

Consultants have offices full of computers and equipment. Franchisees have garages or basements full of inventory. Attorneys have client files that contain vital information. What kinds of business property does your business have? I encourage you to make up an inventory of your equipment as we go through the following checklist. Next to each item, list your best guess as to its current replacement cost, if bought new today.

- ✔ **Office furniture & equipment.** The majority of home businesses have at least some office equipment. Besides the usual desk and filing cabinet, you probably have a telephone, copier, fax machine, and possibly a scanner. Add these and other furniture and equipment and their values to your list.

- ✔ **Computers.** You have at least one — it's a given in the 21st century. Include on your list not just the computer itself but also all peripherals — cabling, labor, printers, and other hardware. Include a separate item for software if you don't keep off-site duplicates. You can also include a labor value to recreate lost data, but I don't recommend it. I recommend instead keeping daily backups and storing them offsite. Far better than insuring them. Insurance won't pay you for your mental anguish suffered in recreating lost information. (What a nightmare!)

✔ **Inventory — owned and non-owned.** If you keep inventory on your premises — either in the house or in a detached structure — you need to add it to your list of risks. Set the value on your list at your peak inventory limit. Even if you do not own the inventory but are holding it on consignment, you still may be responsible for it. Check your supplier contract to see whose responsibility it is. If it's yours, add the peak values to your list under non-owned inventory.

✔ **Supplies.** Supplies such as business cards, letterhead, staplers, computer paper, and, of course, the caffeine tablets you take to help you stay conscious during your 80-hour workweek are often overlooked. I recommend setting this value, at least, at $2,000.

✔ **Valuable papers.** No, this doesn't refer to that pile of computer paper you've got in a corner. Rather, valuable papers include client files, promotional brochures, appraisals, and so on. For example, I have 400 client files. If these files are destroyed, I can pay someone to go to insurance companies and clients and get the information I need to recreate the files. If I pay someone $15 per hour, and he averages 2.5 hours per file, my exposure (400 files x 2.5 hours x $15/hour) is $15,000. Establish your own number for how much labor cost would be involved in recreating your valuable papers. (For clarification, *Business Property* coverage pays only for the blank paper. *Valuable Papers* coverage pays for the labor to reproduce what's on the paper.)

✔ **Accounts receivable.** This risk represents the estimated lost revenue from your inability to collect old receivables when your records are destroyed. Put this on your list only if you aren't willing to store backups, made at least weekly, off-premises.

✔ **Away from home — transit, storage, shipping.** Because Homeowners policies cover business property away from home for much less (typically a $250 limit) than they cover items when the items are at your home, having a separate category on your list for property away from home is important.

- **In transit** means items you take with you, such as laptop computers, attaché cases, or sales samples.

- **In storage** means stuff like the dead files and excess equipment I keep in offsite storage. You may keep inventory or other items.

- **Shipping** can be incoming, outgoing, or both. If both, have a separate value for each on your list. Even if you are currently arranging insurance through the shipper, put a value here anyway. You may be able to reduce your shipping insurance costs by arranging the insurance on a bulk basis if you do a lot of shipping.

Liability risks

Recall one of the guiding principles of Chapter 1: Don't risk more than you can afford to lose. Most lawsuits cost $40,000 to $100,000 — or more — to defend, and judgements or jury awards can add, potentially, hundreds of thousands of dollars to that amount. Being uninsured for any potential business liability is probably risking more than you can afford to lose, and puts your personal assets in jeopardy.

If you cannot afford to either buy the liability insurance your business needs to protect itself or find a way to avoid uninsured risks, close the business.

Injuries at home

If you have a home business, you're sueable for injuries that occur in your home if they're business related. "But," you protest, "I never have clients or customers come to my home!" Maybe so. But almost any business gets an occasional package delivered. If that delivery person falls and is injured, your Homeowners policy has zero coverage for you or the business. I recommend you include this risk on your list. The cost to insure it can be as little as $15 a year.

Injuries and property damage away from home

If you venture outside your home for business purposes, you could injure someone or damage their property. Sometimes the risk is great, such as a personal trainer who works at clubs as an independent contractor, or a sales-person for personal-care products who sells through home parties. Large or small, the risk is real.

Products liability

Add this risk to your list if you sell any kind of product. Also add it if you perform any kind of service, such as the building trades, computer or equipment repair, and so on.

The essence of the risk is that it involves your liability for injuries or property damage after the product or completed service is being used by the customer, such as a customer's carpet being ruined by cleaning products that you sold, or a serious eye injury resulting from an eyeliner that you sold. Or maybe a computer starts crashing a day after you performed a tune-up, or a deck you built collapses, resulting in people being seriously injured.

Independent contractors

Whether you like it or not, when you, as a small-business owner, subcontract some of your work to others, you are sueable for their alleged mistakes. You can avoid that risk by having the customer buy direct from the contractor. If you act as the front person with the customer, add this risk to your list.

For example, I'm an insurance agent. If I recommend a roofer to a client to fix storm damage and two months later the roof leaks, I have no liability — just a customer not too happy with the quality of my referrals. If, however, I tell the customer that I'll send someone out to fix the roof and subcontract a roofer to do it, the client pays me, and I take a cut and pay the roofer, I'm then liable, along with the roofer, for the water damage caused by the roofer's defective work.

Employee risks

If your business requires that you hire one or more employees, your business faces some additional risks — most of which can be insured. Risks such as those related to state-mandated Workers' Compensation benefits. Less-obvious employee-related risks include the possibility of being sued for discrimination when you don't hire someone. Or do hire a person and later terminate him. Take a close look at some of these employee-related risks and my recommendations on handling each.

Workers' Compensation

In most jurisdictions, if you have an employee, you're required by law to provide Workers' Compensation insurance to cover medical bills and lost wages for your employee if she suffers an occupational injury or certain occupation-related diseases. If your business has even one employee, add this risk to your list. (Check with your agent or state department of labor to find out if you can exempt yourself, and family members who are employees, from coverage.)

Treating employees as independent contractors

I see a lot of small-business owners — especially building-trade contractors and one-person shops — try to reduce their employee costs by treating workers who should be employees (because they work almost exclusively for the business owner, often on the business premises) as independent contractors. By employing these people as independent contractors, the business avoids paying Workers' Compensation premiums, the employer's share of Social Security taxes, unemployment compensation taxes, group benefits, retirement plan contributions, and so on. All together, this is a substantial savings — usually from 25 to 50 percent of the total compensation. That's a ton of money saved for a small-business owner. But some real downsides to this exist besides ethical issues — primarily with the risk you take by not buying Workers' Compensation insurance and then having to pay Worker's Comp benefits out of your own pocket if your worker gets injured on the job. The Internal Revenue Service has really been cracking down on this practice.

If your independent-contractor-who-should-be-an-employee is injured on the job and you have no Workers' Compensation insurance, you may be required by a court to pay the injured worker's medical bills and lost wages, often for life, out of your own pocket. *Often for life.* If the IRS audits you and determines your contractor should have been an employee, you'll be required to pay all back payroll taxes that you avoided. In some states you may also be subject to substantial fines and penalties.

If an independent contractor is really your employee, don't play games. Hire them as an employee and absorb the costs of doing so. However, if you want to avoid the employee risk and are willing to surrender a lot of your control, you can continue to hire them as an independent contractor. Have a good attorney draw up an independent contractor agreement incorporating all the standards the IRS uses for determining whether a person is an employee or a contractor, so the agreement will stand up to IRS scrutiny. Be sure to.

- ✔ Comply with those IRS standards when working with your contractors.

- ✔ Include in the contractor agreement language in which the contractor agrees to defend you and pay any judgment against you arising from the contractor's errors and to name you as an additional insured on their liability policies.

- ✔ Require the contractors to register their business with the federal and state governments and provide you with federal and state tax ID numbers. By doing so, they officially declare to the government their status as an independent business.

- ✔ Include in the contractor agreement that the contractor is responsible for all his own insurance, including, but not limited to, property, liability, Workers' Compensation, professional liability, health, life, and disability insurances. I'd further recommend they furnish you proof of public liability and maybe professional liability in their business name, naming your business as an additional insured if you get sued for their errors.

Employment practices liability

Employment practices liability refers to your risks for alleged employee mistreatment — specifically alleged sexual harassment, job discrimination, and wrongful termination.

I recommend that you reduce this risk with an employee manual. You can buy a computer program for $50 that helps you create such a manual. But a safer approach is to hire, or at least consult with, a good attorney who specializes in this area.

An employee manual reduces the chances of an employment-related lawsuit because it can include protective language explaining your firm's opposition to any employee mistreatment; it should state, for example, that sexual harassment is not tolerated and require immediate reporting if there's any such behavior. An employee manual has two advantages. It reduces the likelihood of suits ever being filed and it gives you something in writing to help your defense if you do get sued. An employee manual written or revised by an attorney is stronger and holds up better in court.

Insurance for this exposure has recently become available to small-business owners, with premiums starting at $1,000 a year. I especially recommend this insurance if you are a lawsuit target — in other words, if your business is successful, or if you, personally, have wealth. Whether you buy the insurance or not, add the risk to your list if you have one or more employees.

Employee benefit liability

The employee practices liability risk is applicable to you if you both employ someone and provide him or her any kind of group benefits — health, disability, or life. It represents your risk from errors in administering the group insurance program, such as not adding newly hired employees properly to the coverage, or not notifying terminated employees properly of government-mandated continuation rights that they have when they leave. If you have a group program covering your employees, add Employee Benefit Liability coverage to your risk list and to your business insurance coverage. The annual cost is as little as $150 a year! Remember, don't risk a lot for a little.

Professional errors

If you sell a professional service, add this risk to your list. Some of the professionals who should be concerned are insurance agents, accountants, lawyers, virtually every kind of consultant, architects, engineers, beauty consultants, doctors, dentists, veterinarians, realtors, real estate appraisers, and morticians.

A professional liability policy covers you if a mistake you make on the job hurts your client. Examples include:

- The surgeon who leaves the scalpel in her patient
- The insurance agent who forgets to add a client's car to an auto policy prior to an accident
- The lawyer who loses a client's case because he forgot to file the suit on time

Buying a separate professional liability policy is important because, without it, you have no coverage elsewhere. Business liability policies almost always exclude coverage for professional errors. And Homeowners policies exclude liability coverage for anything business-related.

Be sure when you buy professional liability coverage, also known as *Errors and Omissions* insurance, that it does two things:

- ✔ It covers what you do. I recently had a very successful business client, who did management consulting, buy a less expensive Errors and Omissions policy from another agent. When I reviewed the new policy, it covered computer consulting but specifically did not cover — guess what — management consulting!

- ✔ It covers your defense costs and any legal judgment stemming from your responsibility for the errors of independent contractors who do work for you. Be careful: *Many policies do not cover defense costs or your liability for errors involving your independent contractors.*

Contractual risks

Here I'm referring to contracts you sign that include provisions where you agree to protect someone else from your mistakes. Examples include:

- ✔ Working as an independent contractor for someone and agreeing in writing to protect them from your errors under your Errors and Omissions policy

- ✔ Renting warehouse space and agreeing to protect the landlord under your general liability policy

- ✔ Leasing a vehicle in the business name and agreeing to protect the leasing company under your auto policy

- ✔ Leasing computers or other business equipment and contractually agreeing to insure the lessor if someone is injured by the equipment you're using

The reality is that few small-business owners who sign contracts ever read them. They rarely are aware of what they have agreed to from an insurance standpoint. If you don't have expertise yourself, you'd better seek help from a professional insurance agent with expertise in identifying risks in contracts, or hire a small-business insurance consultant or an attorney. And it's best to seek help before you sign a contract, while you still have a chance to negotiate the language. Of course, anytime you change language in a business contract, it's safer to contact an attorney. What's important here is to add contractual risks to your list if you have signed *any* business contracts at all that were given to you by someone else.

Vehicle risks

Don't skip this section, even if you have no business vehicles! There are several ways you and your business can be at risk regarding vehicles:

- ✔ If the business owns or leases vehicles
- ✔ If your personal auto is used on behalf of the business
- ✔ If you occasionally borrow or rent vehicles for the benefit of the business
- ✔ If you have any employees or independent contractors who even occasionally run an errand for your business with their vehicle

It's pretty hard to be in business and not have at least one of those exposures. Add the ones to your list that apply to your business, and read on for more info on each.

Owned or leased vehicle risks

For specific information on auto insurance coverages, see Chapter 3. For more information on avoiding the pitfalls of insuring a corporately owned vehicle on a Personal Auto policy, see the section in Chapter 4 on the subject.

Why you should only have one agent

I've been the business insurance agent for a small company for about eight years. The owner, Elmer, and I review the program every year. Elmer has his personal insurance through a different agent. One year in our review, I discovered he had purchased two company-owned vehicles for his and his wife's use, but he never informed me because he chose to insure them through his personal insurance agent. This created some serious gaps in his coverage.

The corporation, who, as owner, would be named in every lawsuit involving the vehicles, had *no* liability coverage under Elmer's Personal Auto policy. The corporation, who was the sole owner of both cars, had *no* Collision and Comprehensive coverage. Worse yet, because Elmer had no personal ownership interest, his Personal Auto policy would have owed nothing at all if either car had been damaged, totaled out, or stolen! Unbelievable, but true.

Even if Elmer had properly added the corporation to the coverage, the corporation would have had only $100,000 injury liability coverage per person whereas it carried $1 million coverage for all its other corporate liability. Why? Because Elmer's Personal Auto policy liability limit was only $100,000 per person. Carrying different liability limits violates one of the ironclad rules of this book, to always buy the same liability limits for all your insurance because you are protecting the same assets. If Elmer's personal and business insurance were through the same agent, these gaps would have probably not existed.

The tricky part of this risk is to make sure that both you as an individual and your corporation as owner or lessee are *both* properly protected. Coverage of owned or leased vehicles used by small businesses is often arranged incorrectly, especially when the business insurance agent is different than the personal agent and no one is acting as overseer. If not done correctly, you and your business can be hung out to dry.

Non-owned vehicle risks

If your business is incorporated and occasionally borrows or rents vehicles, even it has no owned or leased vehicles, the business will need *Hired Auto Liability Coverage.* If not incorporated, you're covered automatically for this risk under the built-in Drive-Other-Cars coverage of your Personal Auto policy.

If your business, whether incorporated or not, has even one employee or independent contractor, the employee will at least occasionally run an errand and your business will need *Non-Owned Auto Liability Coverage.* Both are inexpensive — only $30 to $50 each per year. This coverage should be added to your list.

Managing Human Risks

Here we're dealing with your life, health, and disability risks. All three of these risks can be substantial. Major medical bills. Your loss of income from a long disability. The impact on your loved ones of your early death. You would normally get some coverage if you worked for someone else. These risks are your responsibility in your home business. Add them to your list. See Chapters 15, 16, 17, and 18 for specific coverage information and recommendations on life, health, and disability insurance.

From a business risk perspective, don't overlook business-overhead disability coverage that can help pay fixed business expenses when you're not able to generate income. And life insurance in addition to your personal life insurance to pay off business debt when you die. One of my beliefs is that whatever benefits you'd receive as an employee from someone else should be at least matched, if not better, when working for yourself. This includes an equally good retirement plan and vacation package. If you can't provide these things for yourself, are you doing what is best for yourself by being self-employed?

You can buy life, health, and disability coverages privately if you qualify medically, or under a company group plan if you have employees. It doesn't matter where or how you get these vital coverages. Just get them, and add them to your list of risks.

Using Noninsurance Methods to Protect Home-Business Risks

Avoiding, reducing, retaining, and transferring (ARRT) are the four noninsurance methods of treating risk. (For more information, see Chapter 2.)

Avoiding

When it comes to risks related to a home business, you can either completely avoid the risk by not starting the business or by closing down the business if it's already started. Or you can avoid part of the risk by making prudent business decisions. For example, you may decide, if you're a manufacturer's representative, to stop offering a line of home trampolines because your projected annual profit on the line is $3,000 and the cost of the products liability premium is $10,000.

Reducing

A home-business owner can use several strategies to reduce risk to both himself and his company:

- ✔ You can reduce the risk of lawsuits threatening your personal assets by incorporating your company. It's not for everyone but I do recommend every home business consider it — with the help of a good small-business attorney.

- ✔ Most states allow a company to organize as an LLC, a Limited Liability Company. Such business structures allow the owners to limit their liability without corporate double taxation penalties. Consult an attorney experienced in business organizations to see how an LLC might work for you.

- ✔ If you have a single line of products from one manufacturer or franchiser, you can reduce your product liability insurance cost significantly or possibly even eliminate it by requesting that the manufacturer or franchiser who already carries product liability insurance add you as an Additional Insured to its policy.

Retaining

Retention amounts to paying the loss yourself. It works well in two situations. One is a good use of deductibles, such as saving 40 percent on your health insurance bill by adding a $1,000 deductible. The other occurs when you reduce the risk as much as you can and self-insure what remains, such as backing up your accounts receivable weekly and self-insuring any losses that occur between the two backups.

There are also two ways to retain losses that I do not recommend. One is declining critical insurance. One of my former clients declined long-term disability on himself. Two years later, he was seriously injured and out of work for two years. But with no income and no insurance, he lost both his home and his business. Not a good decision. Another bad use of retention is accidental retention, where you have a major uninsured gap in your coverage that you don't know about and a serious loss happens with no coverage. That's the worst kind of retention. It can easily occur if you don't work with an insurance expert. (See Chapter 12 for tips on how to find an expert.)

Transferring

Transferring occurs when someone else agrees to pay your claims so you don't have to. The most common use of this is buying insurance. But transferring can also be used in noninsurance ways. A good example of a noninsurance use of this strategy is a client who designed high-end bicycle pedals, sold them on the Internet, assembled them himself, and bought an expensive product liability policy. As orders grew for the pedals, he subcontracted the production and assembly to a local manufacturer who agreed to do 100 percent of the assembly and packaging and, in writing, agreed to add my client as an additional insured on the manufacturer's product liability policy. The client thus transferred the risk and insurance to a third party successfully and significantly reduced his insurance costs in the process.

Insuring Your Home Business

Assuming that you have identified your home business risks as you've read this chapter, it's now time to create a custom insurance plan for yourself. You do not have to insure every risk you've identified. Understanding the risks that your business faces is what's so important, so that you don't have surprises later. Nothing is worse than a serious claim that is uninsured unknowingly.

Examining the sources of home business insurance

You can choose from several sources for home-business insurance. Usually, business owners mix and match. You may be getting your property, liability, and Workers' Compensation insurance from an insurance agent. Your professional liability insurance may come from your association. Your product liability may come from your franchiser. And your life, health, and disability may come from a second insurance agent. The pros and cons of each source are listed below.

Homeowners business endorsements

As a general rule, Homeowners policy endorsements are inadequate for most home businesses. They typically cover only sole proprietorships and often can't cover your incorporated business. They can provide on-premises liability coverages but few provide off-premises liability, products liability, or several other kinds of business liability included in the risk identification section of this chapter. They can cover business property at home but most don't offer much coverage away from home. Because the extent of coverage varies so dramatically from one company to another, I won't comment specifically on the exact nature of these endorsements other than that they usually leave the home-business owner with several coverage gaps. In my opinion, most Homeowners home-business endorsements provide coverage that is a lot like having car insurance Monday through Friday and being uninsured weekends.

A home-business endorsement is often a great idea for employees of companies who do a lot of their work at home. The home-business endorsements generally do a good job of covering the two major concerns of these people — liability coverage for people getting injured on their premises making deliveries and property coverage on their home office furniture and equipment. (See Chapter 7 for more information on how to protect yourself if you're someone else's employee but do some work from home.)

Businessowners policies

A Businessowners policy is my recommended insurance policy for the majority of home businesses. They are reasonably priced at about $300 a year to start, though there are a few, as of this writing, that were available in the market for as little is $150 a year.

The great thing about Businessowners policies is that they're designed for small businesses. Most of the property and liability coverages you'll need as a home-business owner (check your risk identification list from earlier in the chapter) are either included automatically or are available for a nominal extra charge. I hands-down prefer Businessowners policies to Homeowners home-business endorsements. Far better coverage for not much more money.

Not all home businesses, however, qualify for a Businessowners policy. Insurance companies differ greatly as to what kinds of home businesses they will insure under a Businessowners policy. Some insurers restrict eligibility to offices and small retail stores. Others are willing to insure nearly every type of home business, including building contractors, software developers, Web site designers, and franchises like Amway or Mary Kay.

If you are told your business won't qualify for a Businessowners policy, you can still get your business insured under a more expensive commercial insurance policy. But before you shell out the extra cash, check around with other insurance companies. Your business may easily qualify for a Businessowners policy somewhere else.

Insurance from franchisers

Whether your home franchise is in cleaning products, environmental products, cosmetics, or is any other kind of home business, franchisers offer franchisees two major advantages with the insurance programs they make available — a great price for what they do offer and access to specialty coverages that would be hard for you to find elsewhere. But they also have two major disadvantages, and there's one huge misperception on the part of the buyer.

The first disadvantage is that the coverage is often not comprehensive for the franchisee — usually a number of holes exist in the coverage. I have found large coverage gaps in each of these policies that I've reviewed. The second disadvantage is the lack of professional advice in helping you set up the right coverage for your particular needs. Some good advice is extremely important when buying any insurance, especially business insurance.

The huge misperception by the franchisee buying the coverage is that, if the franchiser is offering them the coverage, it must be wonderful. I've never found that to be completely true. For the coverages that you are offered, the price is great. I can also say that, if you work with a good insurance adviser locally, you can get the expert help you need to overcome both disadvantages and supplement the franchise insurance program with the other insurance coverages you will need that are available in the market. You can end up with both a comprehensive plan and a very good price, if you have good professional help.

The strategy I recommend to every single client who is considering getting involved in a franchise is to gather all of the contracts you will be required to sign, as well as a detailed summary of the different insurances available from the franchiser, and bring them to a qualified insurance professional. She will help you identify the hidden risks of the contracts and the insurance gaps and help you design strategies to avoid both. See the section later in this chapter on hiring a risk manager for more on this idea.

Association programs

Professionals in a particular trade often band together to form associations. Benefits of belonging include access to information, the ability to build relationships, on-going education, lobbying power, and the availability of various types of insurance that are discounted due to mass purchasing power. Associations are often a good place to buy professional liability at up to 50 percent off market rates. They are also a good place to buy specialty coverages unique to a particular industry that are unavailable or quite expensive in the open market, such as insurance protection against unintentional alleged sexual or physical abuse of children (necessary if you operate a day care, for example).

Chambers of commerce

For a home-business owner who doesn't have the leverage to get great pricing on her own, chambers of commerce sometimes are a good source for small-business group insurance — life, health, and disability products in particular. Often the annual cost of chamber membership is returned many times over in premium savings on chamber insurance programs.

Getting the professional advice you need

If, at this point, you feel that either you have enough to lose or have a complex enough home business that you want professional advice to help you do it right, here are my suggestions. Also, see Chapter 12 on buying insurance the right way.

Hiring an agent

Insurance agents, like all professionals, come in lots of colors and flavors. Some are novices with one week of schooling. Others are experts with hundreds of hours of education and years of experience. Most fall somewhere between those two extremes. Many specialize in one or more aspects of the insurance market.

If your needs are complex, choose an agent who is an insurance expert in the area of home-business insurance as well as personal insurance. How much more will an expert cost? In most states, not a penny! Why? Because they work on the same commission percentage as the non-expert — by law. Use the best, it doesn't cost anything extra.

If possible, buy both your personal and home-business insurance from one agent and, ideally, one company. Having one agent reduces the chance of gaps between your home and business policies because he oversees both programs. Be sure you choose someone with both personal and business insurance expertise. Having one company insure both your home and your home business also improves your chances of not having a major gap between the two programs and helps you to avoid the fights over which company pays what if you have damage to both business and personal property in the same loss (such as what might occur were there a fire).

The ultimate strategy — hiring a risk manager

What I'm about to recommend to you comes from over 25 years in the trenches, working with individuals and small-business owners. What I'm about to recommend is a philosophy I deeply believe in that has been very successful with my business clients over the years. (My definition of *success* is that a client has no major unexpected uninsured losses.)

If you have read this chapter, you know by now how complex small-business insurance can be. And, therefore, how dangerous it can be. If you want expert help with everything covered in this chapter — insurance plan design, advice on noninsurance strategies, advice on business contracts, and even help with insurance you buy elsewhere such as through professional associations — then this is the very best advice I can give you:

Promote the best agent you can find to *risk manager.* If your state law allows, pay a negotiated annual fee — probably ranging from $200 to $600 a year — to provide the following value-added services to better manage and coordinate your business and personal risks. Most of these services aren't paid for by sales commissions — hence, the need for an added fee. Your risk manager will help you:

- ✔ Place whatever insurance he is able to place for you *competitively* through the insurance company or companies he represents (your personal insurance, home-business insurance, and your health, life, and disability insurance). Why? Because he has more leverage to help you get the coverages you need with insurers he already has relationships with. Also, the insurers send him copies of your policies to more easily monitor your program. And as an agent, he is empowered to make the changes to your insurance program directly so you won't have to.

- ✔ Help you come up with creative noninsurance strategies for avoiding, reducing, retaining, and transferring risks to help you minimize your insurance purchases. Insurance companies don't pay agents anything to help you lower your insurance costs. The fee makes it possible for him to do this for you.

- ✔ Design coverage specifications for your entire personal and businesses insurance program and help oversee the policies you buy elsewhere and coordinate them and reduce gaps between them.

- ✔ Help you read your business contracts and make recommendations that your attorney can use to reduce risks in the language before you sign them. Also, modify your insurance program as needed to keep your insurance coverage in full compliance with what you have agreed to do contractually.

- ✔ Do a complete review of the entire insurance and noninsurance program about once a year. Then help you implement any changes.

Part IV
Buying an Umbrella Policy

The 5th Wave   By Rich Tennant

"Does our insurance cover a visit from Mike Wallace?"

In this part . . .

Just as an umbrella covers you against the weather, an umbrella policy protects you from some unforeseen insurance risks. What is an umbrella policy, and how does it protect me from catastrophic lawsuits? They're all different, so how do I choose the right one for me?

Chapter 10

Introducing the Personal Umbrella Policy

· ·

In This Chapter

▶ Discovering the three major coverage advantages of an Umbrella policy

▶ Understanding how an Umbrella policy integrates with your other insurance

▶ Determining how much coverage to buy

· ·

A New York jury awarded a paralyzed woman $163.9 million in damages from a car accident.

From a July 22, 1993, news item in *The New York Times*

You don't have enough liability insurance. Period. No one does. Certainly not anywhere near enough to cover a $164 million jury award.

In over 2,000 insurance reviews I've done for prospective clients, I've seen that at least 80 to 90 percent were grossly underinsured for injury lawsuits. The most common liability limits on auto and home policies I see are either $100,000 per person or $300,000 per accident. That's not much for a human life. Not enough to pay for all the medical expenses of the person you severely injure, plus a possible lifetime of lost wages, and compensation for pain and suffering. (See Chapter 3 for examples of various types of car accidents and the economic value of injuries, if you need more examples.)

If you don't have nearly enough protection, what can you do? Here's some really good news. You can buy a second layer of liability coverage, called a *Personal Umbrella* policy, that sits on top of your other personal liability coverages for your car, home, boat, and so on. It defends you and pays legal judgments against you when a covered lawsuit exceeds your primary liability insurance limits.

Best of all, an Umbrella policy is amazingly inexpensive — usually about $100 to $200 per year for $1 million of coverage. And about $60 to $100 per year for each additional $1 million of coverage. *Note:* This is not a typo. These costs are truly per *year* — not per month!

Buying an Umbrella liability policy is flat-out the best value in the insurance business. It includes some of the broadest coverage in the insurance business at an incredibly low price. Buying an Umbrella policy also satisfies two guiding principles from Chapter 1: not risking more than you can afford to lose and not risking a lot for a little.

Affording an Umbrella is easy. You don't even have to increase your insurance bill — just shift dollars away from less important coverages. For example, you can save a few hundred dollars by raising the deductible on your car insurance and Homeowners insurance by $250, or by dropping Collision coverage on an older car. Use that savings to more than pay for an Umbrella policy.

Discovering the Umbrella Policy's Major Coverage Advantages

If you decide to buy an Umbrella policy, you gain more than just higher coverage limits for injuries and property damage you cause — although the higher limits are a great advantage. You also receive:

- ✔ Additional coverage for defense costs when the defense coverage under your primary policies runs out
- ✔ Coverage for many types of lawsuits not covered by your other policies (those famous coverage gaps everyone complains about)

Gaining higher defense costs

What actually happens when you're sued for a dollar amount greater than your primary liability insurance limits? You receive, from your insurance company, a piece of mail — probably registered mail — that looks something like this:

We Care About You Mutual Insurance Company
Re: Your June 19, 20XX Accident
Dear Mr.SoonToBeVeryPoor:

You are being sued by Mr. James Johnson, the injured party in the above-referenced accident, for $650,000. Your automobile liability insurance limit with us is only $250,000. We will pay your defense costs for the first $250,000 of this lawsuit. You will be responsible for your own defense costs beyond that amount.

We strongly suggest you hire your own attorney right now to protect you for that part of the lawsuit not covered by our policy.

Yours truly,
Grumpy Corporate Attorney
We Care About You Mutual Insurance Company

Why do they send you this letter? Because each of your primary insurance policies defends you only for lawsuit amounts up to your liability policy limit. If you are sued for more than your liability limit, you are personally responsible for the amount of any lawsuit that exceeds your primary liability limit, including the cost of defense for that difference as well. Those added defense costs often run $50,000 or more. One huge advantage of an Umbrella policy is that it pays for those added defense costs.

Gaining gap coverage

Client Mike and several of his friends were all turning 50 at about the same time. So they decided it would be fun to have a jumbo group 50th birthday party. They rented a big barn at an empty local fairground. And they decided to make beer and wine available, at no charge, which added to their list of risks their potential liability for alcohol-related car accidents.

Mike called me because the fairgrounds required the friends to carry $1 million of liability insurance for the one-day event that also had to include the fairgrounds as an insured party. I asked him if he was signing the rental contract personally. He said no, it was in the name of two of his friends. I advised Mike that a one-day, special-event policy would cost about $500. But I also advised him that if either of his friends had an Umbrella policy the friend might be covered automatically. Neither one of them did. Mike signed the contract because he had an Umbrella policy that fully covered him for $2 million for liability for this type of rental contract. His Umbrella also was broad enough to automatically protect the fairgrounds too, as he had contractually agreed to do. It also was broad enough to cover the risk of liability for alcohol-related car accidents.

To briefly explore the insurance issues involved in a little more detail, the exposures that Mike faced were:

- ✔ Liability for his own actions that caused injuries
- ✔ Liability he assumed in the contract, agreeing to be responsible for the actions of everyone else at the event
- ✔ Liability if any partygoer drank too much and caused an auto accident, resulting in a lawsuit — a lawsuit that any provider of alcoholic beverages at a social event may face
- ✔ The costs to defend and protect the fairgrounds for any lawsuit brought against it
- ✔ Liability for damage caused by anyone to the rented barn, such as a fire caused by a guest's carelessly thrown-away cigarette

Many of these risks were not covered by any other policy, at least not for the amount required by the fairgrounds. Mike's Umbrella covered every single risk, automatically. His group saved the $500 cost of a one-day policy that may not have even covered all five of the risks I just listed. I sent the fairgrounds proof of insurance. Everybody was happy!

One little problem remained. In the remote chance that a lawsuit exceeded Mike's $2 million Umbrella policy limit, by contract, Mike would have been solely responsible for that excess amount. Therefore, each of his fellow birthday celebrants separately signed a legal agreement to share equally in all losses not covered by the Umbrella. By the way, the party was a great success.

What's the point of the story? To illustrate a little-known, major advantage of a good Umbrella policy. It not only provides a second layer of liability coverage on top of your other liability policies, but it also fills a lot of the gaps — the gaps between the policies.

A really good Umbrella policy covers many of the lawsuits against you that aren't covered by your auto, home, or other personal policies. (See Chapter 11 for more information on how to determine what your coverage gaps are and how to find a good Umbrella policy that covers them.)

In fact, the only real difference between a poor Umbrella policy and a great one is how well it covers the cracks.

Coordinating an Umbrella With Your Other Insurance

The coverage under an Umbrella policy can be triggered when you're sued for more than your primary liability limits. It also can be triggered when you are sued for something covered only by your Umbrella and not by your primary policies (in other words, the gaps). When the latter happens, the Umbrella "steps down" and defends and protects you as if it were primary coverage, subject only to a modest deductible called a *self-insured retention* (SIR) — typically $250 or $500.

In the earlier fairgrounds story, four of the five risks Mike assumed were gaps and were covered only by the Umbrella policy. If any of those four risks occurred, Mike would have paid only the $500 Umbrella deductible or *self-insured retention*.

There are four parts of a liability insurance program that includes an Umbrella:

✔ Your primary liability insurance program for your cars, home, cabin, boat, or other

✔ An Umbrella deductible or self-insured retention payable only for claims covered by the umbrella policy and not covered by your other primary insurance policies.

✔ The Umbrella policy

✔ Defense costs

Changing your primary insurance program to meet Umbrella requirements

One reason Umbrella policies are so inexpensive is that they don't cover small lawsuits. Therefore, an Umbrella policy requires that your Personal Automobile, Homeowners, and other personal policy liability limits (also known as *primary* liability limits) meet certain minimum requirements. Depending on the insurance company, the minimums vary from about $100,000 to $500,000. To get an Umbrella, you must first raise your primary liability limits to these minimums and guarantee that you will always maintain them. If you violate this guarantee and fail to meet these minimum requirements, you will be personally liable for the difference between what you've guaranteed your coverages will be and what they actually are. For example, say that the minimum auto liability coverage needed to obtain the Umbrella that you have is $100,000, but you've allowed your coverage to slip to $50,000. If you're found liable for $200,000 in damages, the Umbrella policy still kicks in after the first $100,000 has been paid — $50,000 by your insurance company, and $50,000 by you. (You promised to maintain $100,000 of coverage. You broke that promise by carrying only $50,000. You owe out of your own pocket the $50,000 shortfall.)

Insurance companies offering Umbrella policies are not consistent in the amount of primary liability coverage that they require. See Table 10-1 for two examples of these differences for two hypothetical insurance companies.

Table 10-1	Underlying Liability Insurance Requirements for an Umbrella Policy	
Type of Policy	**Insurance Company A Minimum**	**Insurance Company B Minimum**
Automobile: bodily injuries per person	$100,000	$500,000 for all auto liabilities, combined
Automobile: bodily injuries per accident	$300,000	----
Automobile: property damage per accident	$50,000	----
Homeowners: per accident	$100,000	$300,000
Rental Property: per accident	$300,000	$500,000
Boat: per accident (under 100 hp or under 26 ft)	$100,000	$300,000
Boat: per accident (over 100 hp or over 25 ft)	Won't insure	$500,000
Three-wheelers: per accident	Won't insure	Won't insure
Four-wheel ATVs, golf carts, and so on: per accident	$300,000	$500,000

Because Company A's requirements for the amount that other insurances must pay are lower, its Umbrella coverage is used more frequently, so the cost of its Umbrella is higher. Company B's Umbrella, used less frequently, is lower in cost. A $1 million Umbrella policy from Company A starts at around $200 a year. From Company B, the policy costs about $100.

Avoiding gaps between primary and Umbrella coverage

Because an Umbrella policy requires you to maintain specific primary liability insurance limits, you must be aware of very serious dangers.

- ✔ Be very careful not to let any primary policy cancel for nonpayment or, if you are sued, you will have to pay the loss out of your own pocket, a loss that would have otherwise been covered.

- ✔ Be very attentive to all notices that come from your Umbrella insurer. They often require you to raise one or more of your primary coverage limits as a condition of keeping the Umbrella. If you don't see or don't read the notice and don't raise your limits as required, you'll be personally responsible for the gap.

Illustrating the dangers

Assume that you cause an accident that injures the other driver, and that the case settles for $650,000. Assume that you have Company B's Umbrella with the required underlying car insurance limit of $500,000. Further assume that, two days prior to the accident, your car insurance ran out because you overlooked paying the bill. You are personally responsible for the full $500,000 that the Umbrella requires you to have. (Plus a sizable amount of legal costs.) The Umbrella only chips in $150,000 — the difference between the $650,000 settlement and the $500,000 you now owe.

Assume that you have Company A's Umbrella. The required underlying car insurance limit for injuries was $100,000 per person when you bought the policy. But six months ago, Company A informed you that it was increasing its primary automobile limits to $300,000 per person. You didn't see the notice. You're required to carry $300,000 in coverage. You only have $100,000 in coverage. You are personally responsible for the $200,000 gap between the required amount of primary coverage and the amount that you actually had. Of the $650,000 you owe the person you injured, your car insurance pays $100,000, your Umbrella pays $350,000, and you pay the remaining $200,000.

Protecting yourself

Simple, but oh-so-expensive, oversights created both of the scenarios I just explained. Here's how you can protect yourself from each:

To avoid unintentional cancellation of a primary policy for nonpayment, I recommend two strategies. First, if your insurer offers this payment choice, set up all your insurance on automatic, electronic, monthly payments from your checking account. This avoids the cancellation risk by transferring the payment responsibility to the insurance company. Second, if your insurer doesn't offer electronic payment, work with an agent who will commit to phoning or writing you on every one of those notices so that you can pay the premium and immediately reinstate the lost coverage. Most agents will. If this service is important to you, add this to your agent checklist in Chapter 12.

I also have two strategies for avoiding the unintentional coverage gap caused when an Umbrella insurer sends you a notice requiring increased primary coverage limits and you miss seeing the notice. First, buy your Umbrella policy — if possible — from the same insurance company as your primary policies. Since it also has your underlying insurance, it has some added responsibility, beyond just sending you a single notice, to make sure your primary liability limits get increased when the Umbrella requirements change. Second, buy all your personal insurance, including Umbrella, through the same agent. When the Umbrella requirements change, the agent gets notified as well as you. A good agent will immediately contact you for permission to raise your primary limits to the higher level required by the Umbrella insurer. If you have the same agent and the same insurance company for all your personal liability policies, you've eliminated, almost entirely, the chance that this gap could occur. Plus, if the gap does occur and you get burned by it, you have some recourse against the agent or insurance company.

Determining How Many Millions to Buy

Here's my bottom-line recommendation (for those of you who read the ending of a novel first): Buy $1 million more Umbrella coverage than you think you need. If you think you don't need an Umbrella at all, buy a policy with $1 million of coverage. If $1 million sounds right, buy a $2 million policy. And so on.

Most people underestimate the economic value of a serious injury, as determined by a court of law. Also, an extra million of coverage costs so little — around $75 a year. When it comes to catastrophic lawsuits, better to err on the high side. No one ever went bankrupt over a $75 premium.

Reviewing available limits

Personal Umbrella policies are sold in million dollar increments. Most insurers offer a maximum available coverage limit from $2 million to $5 million — several up to $10 million. Beyond $10 million, the choices are limited and the cost per million escalates because those buying more than $10 million of Umbrella coverage are generally quite wealthy and highly vulnerable to lawsuits.

For those seeking high Umbrella policy limits, such as $10 million, it is possible to buy part of the limit from one insurer and the rest from a second insurer, but I don't recommend doing so. To avoid potential coverage gaps, try to get all the Umbrella limits you need from one insurance company and ideally one policy. No two Umbrella policies are alike. With two, it's possible to have a lawsuit covered by one and not the other.

Assessing how sueable you are

In addition to the seriousness of an injury, there are several factors that influence not only the likelihood of your being sued for more than the amount your policy covers you for but also the dollar amount of the lawsuit.

Your current financial status factor

The size of your current income and/or current assets, particularly liquid assets like investments, affects the probability of your being sued for an amount that's greater than your Automobile or Homeowners liability limits. If you have a high income and/or a high net worth, congratulations. You're very sueable.

I often see people who have only one of the two — a high income or a high net worth — overlooking how sueable they really are. People like new doctors or lawyers in their first year of practice, making almost six figures, but with no money in the bank — yet. Or seniors on a modest retirement income but with a large, mostly liquid, portfolio. Both types of people are highly sueable, and definitely should have an Umbrella policy — probably with limits of $2 million or more.

Your future financial status factor

If you get a large judgment against you today, for more than your liability insurance limits, it sits out there in limbo waiting for your financial situation to improve. The lawsuit may even be delayed until you start acquiring assets or have a decent income.

Future sueability is the area most easily overlooked in assessing today's need for an Umbrella policy. Keep this in mind for medical students, law students, or computer engineers — anyone who is training for a high-paying career. If you think you may have a lot more money in the future than you've got today, you need an Umbrella policy to cover your liability risks.

The exceptional risk factor

Lawsuits can occur from either activities (hunting, fishing, playing sports) or exposures (cars, homes, boats, animals). The exceptional risk factor recognizes that one or more of the activities or exposures in your life has a greater potential of causing serious injuries or death and thus more substantial law-suits. Examples include owning a pit bull, operating a day care center, having a swimming pool — especially one with a diving board — and having a tram-poline in your yard.

If you have these or other exceptional risks in your life that have large lawsuit potential, you're a candidate for an Umbrella, even if you're only of modest means.

Of course, a better choice, if possible, is to avoid or at least reduce the danger. Try:

- ✔ Building a dog kennel so that your dog is safely behind walls when it's outside and exposed to the public
- ✔ Working in a day care center to avoid the huge liability exposure of running a home day care
- ✔ Removing the diving board from the swimming pool
- ✔ Buying your kids a membership in a club that offers safe, supervised trampoline use instead of buying a trampoline
- ✔ Refusing to haul kids to functions, as a teacher or coach, in your vehicle, thus avoiding any liability you would have for the students' injuries in a car accident (unless the school agreed to defend you and pay all the claims against you.)

The legal environment factor

The legal climate in your geographic area is definitely a factor in the size of legal judgments and jury awards.

In California, where there are a zillion lawsuits for substantial amounts of money, you need a larger Umbrella policy limit. In rural Siloam Springs, Arkansas, where the pace is slow, people don't lock their doors, and lawsuits are rare, you may still need an Umbrella, but the legal environment is proba-bly not a factor in how large it needs to be.

Your personal comfort factor

Insurance is all about peace of mind. Once you decide on an Umbrella policy limit, do a gut check. If you still feel fearful of possibly not having enough insurance, spend an extra $75 and buy another $1 million.

I'm a good example of this recommendation. I'm your typical middle-class American. My income, assets, and other factors suggest that a $1 million Umbrella policy is about right. But my gut disagrees. I feel a lot better, espe-cially when the extra million only cost me $5 a month.

The walking time-bomb family

Max and Josephine own five acres on the edge of town. Their children are the happiest kids — and the most popular kids — in the neighborhood. They have two goats, two dogs (both Dobermans), a swimming pool with a diving board, and, of course, a trampoline. (Oh, and let's not forget the potbellied pig.) The question isn't whether they need an Umbrella. The question is, what insurance company in its right mind would possibly sell them an Umbrella?

No — I couldn't convince them to give up any of these risks (much to their kids' joy!). Yes — I did find them an Umbrella in a high-risk market for mucho bucks. And yes, I do wish that I could be their kid.

Your moral responsibility factor

Every once is a while, a client reminds me of that golden rule about caring for your fellow men and women. They will often be of modest means and not necessarily very sueable. They may not really need an Umbrella. I'll suggest a liability limit on their Automobile, Homeowners and other policies, say $300,000, and they'll say, "Oh, no, I want more than that. If I seriously hurt someone, I want to make sure they're fully cared for — that I can provide for them by paying all their medical bills, all their lost wages, and pay them something extra for all the pain and suffering I put them through. I can't undo the hurt I've caused in their life. But at least I can help take care of their financial burden." Such people are rare and wonderful.

Here are my recommendations for Umbrella policies:

- ✔ Buy a personal Umbrella policy of at least $1 million.

- ✔ Buy at least $2 million in coverage if you have some affluence.

- ✔ Buy at least $5 to $10 million in coverage, or more, if you're very affluent.

- ✔ Buy $1 million more than you think you need.

- ✔ Buy a policy that covers the major liability gaps in your primary insurance program.

Chapter 11

Choosing the Right Umbrella for Your Lifestyle

*L*et me share a true story that helps to illustrate the dominant message of this chapter. A few years ago, clients Jon and Mimi did something I've often fantasized about. They rented a houseboat with some friends and their kids for about 10 days on gigantic Rainy Lake on the Minnesota-Canada border. It was a 40-foot floating luxury cabin, propelled by two 125 horse-power outboard motors, and worth about $300,000.

Jon signed the rental agreement on behalf of the group and was offered insurance for $10 a day from the rental agency, Happy Houseboats. He called to see if he needed to buy the optional insurance. I assured him he did not. His auto policy, however, didn't cover boats (no surprise there). And although Homeowners policies do provide some liability coverage for small, rented boats (see Chapter 7), they definitely don't provide coverage for 40-foot houseboats with 250 horsepower motors. Nor do they provide coverage for damage to the boat itself, regardless of the boat's size. Jon and Mimi did not have a Personal Umbrella policy at the time.

Jon faxed me a copy of the rental contract and a copy of Happy Houseboat's optional insurance coverage. The risks that Jon and Mimi were facing that were *completely uninsured anywhere* were:

✔ Injuries they caused to others (including drownings — expensive!)

✔ Damage they caused to the houseboat itself (up to the $300,000 replacement cost)

✔ Damage they caused to all the houseboat furnishings, valued at $50,000 to $100,000

✔ Lost rental income while the damage they caused to the houseboat was being repaired

In addition, the contract they signed with Happy Houseboats made them responsible for:

✔ Injuries, property damage, damage to the boat, damage to the furnishings and loss of rental income caused by their *friends'* careless driving. Scary, isn't it?

✔ All other damage to the houseboat no matter *how* caused, even Acts of God. (Meaning that if a tornado tore the boat to shreds, Jon and Mimi needed to ante up over $300,000!)

As horrible and unfair as this contract is, similar language and obligations are found in almost every rental contract you sign. Read your rental agreements and make sure you've arranged full insurance somehow. Otherwise, avoid the risk and don't rent. Don't risk more than you can afford to lose (a guiding principle from Chapter 1).

Just how good is Happy Houseboat's insurance coverage? The good news is that it covers any damage to the boat, no matter how caused, subject to a $500 deductible. The really bad news is that the most the policy pays is $2,500. (No, that's not a typo — it's a $2,500 coverage limit on a $300,000 boat!) Even the guy behind the counter selling the insurance didn't know it had a $2,500 limit.

Even if the insurance covered damage to the boat without any dollar limit, I wouldn't have advised Jon and Mimi to buy the insurance — because it covers only the damage to the houseboat. It provides zero coverage for all the other liability risks for injuries and property damage to the public. Besides, my clients had a far better option — the right Personal Umbrella policy.

The rotten insurance coverage from Happy Houseboats would have cost Jon and Mimi $100 ($10 a day for 10 days.) I found them a $2 million Umbrella policy covering all the otherwise uninsured risks for an annual cost of $150. Then I did what I recommend you or your agent do in this type of high-risk circumstance — get the interpretation confirmed by the claims department of the insurance company. All the risks were indeed covered, subject to a $1,000 deductible.

It's important to know that many umbrellas wouldn't cover all the risks my clients assumed in renting the houseboat. Some, in fact, wouldn't cover any. Helping you identify an umbrella policy that covers the special risks in *your* life is the goal of this chapter.

Covering the Gaps

A Personal Umbrella policy has three advantages: higher liability limits, extended coverage for defense costs, and gap coverage — coverage for many of the lawsuits excluded by primary policies (like the gaps in coverage in the houseboat example).

Virtually all umbrella policies are identical in providing higher limits and extended defense costs. Where they differ — hugely — is how well they cover the gaps in your primary coverage.

The worst umbrella policies don't cover any gaps. I've looked at umbrella policies from about 30 insurance companies. Two major insurance companies — both household names — offer umbrellas that have no gap coverage at all. Selling an umbrella without any gap coverage is like selling a car with three wheels.

On the flip side, some of the best umbrella policies, with the highest ratings, cover all kinds of gaps but may not cover your unique coverage gap. For example, you may have a pilot's license and occasionally rent planes. Because you don't own a plane, you don't have aircraft liability coverage. This is a big gap. You also have no liability for damage you cause to the rented planes. With the price of planes, that is a second huge gap. When you select your umbrella policy then, you should be looking for an umbrella that covers both of those gaps. Only a few do.

Again, by *gaps* I mean the liability risks in your life that are not covered by your primary insurance policies. Here are just a few possible examples of activities you may engage in that aren't often covered by auto or home policies.

- Renting "toys" of all kinds — snowmobiles, boats, all-terrain vehicles
- Renting cars outside the United States and Canada
- Racing sailboats
- Employing a nurse or nanny
- Assuming liability when you sign a contract
- Serving on nonprofit boards of directors
- Having underground fuel tanks and septic systems (your liability would be for pollution from leaks or spills)

A closer look at a few of these gaps follows, along with the reasons why it's so important to get an umbrella that covers them.

The renting "toys" gap

When you rent "toys" — boats, snowmobiles, ATVs — you're liable for any injuries and property damage you cause to other people and their possessions. You're also responsible for damage you cause to the rental item, sometimes even when the damage wasn't caused by you, if the rental contract requires it. If you occasionally rent these items, you want to make sure that your umbrella policy covers all of these risks.

Watch out for umbrella coverage on rented boats. Many have length or horsepower limitations and don't cover the type of boat you may rent.

For example, I occasionally rent sailboats that are up to 30 feet in length. My Homeowners policy covers boats I rent only if they're under 26 feet, for liability, and completely excludes all damage to the boats in my care. I have an umbrella policy, therefore, without any length restrictions. If I rent the Queen Mary for the afternoon, I am fully covered — up to my umbrella policy limit, that is.

The car rental gap

Like rented "toys," when you rent a car, you're liable for injuries and property damage you cause to others, and all damage to the rental car, whether you caused it or not.

In the United States and Canada

Your Personal Auto policy covers you for the first risk, your liability for injuries and damage to the public, and sometimes the second risk, damage to the rental car, depending on whether you have Collision and Comprehensive coverage on at least one of your cars. If you rent cars even rarely, don't consider an umbrella that doesn't cover both of these risks (see Chapter 4 for more information on managing car rental risks). Most umbrellas do.

In Mexico and abroad

When you rent a car in Mexico or abroad, you have the same two liability risks as you do in the United States and Canada. The difference is that 99 percent of Personal Auto policies don't cover any automobile usage outside the United States and Canada. If you will ever rent a car outside the United States and Canada, make sure that your Umbrella policy covers both of these risks worldwide.

Even if your umbrella covers you, I do recommend that when you're outside the United States or Canada you buy the optional coverage for damage to the rental car from the rental agency and keep your umbrella as a backup. Why? So you're not tied up with claim hassles when you return a damaged car. Domestic insurance companies are not set up to provide immediate claim service in foreign countries.

The wedding reception contract

My client, Kathleen, was getting married and was busy with the planning. She negotiated with a restaurant to host the wedding reception. Once they agreed to the terms, the restaurant asked her to sign their standard contract, which she faxed to me to see if her home and umbrella policies covered her. The contract had the usual terms that you can expect: She would agree to be responsible for injuries or property damage she caused, as well as those caused by guests. In addition, she would agree, in the event of the restaurant being sued, to protect, defend, and pay any judgment against the restaurant, *no matter what the cause!*

In short, by signing the contract, she would be agreeing to be responsible for injuries caused by the restaurant or its employees. If several guests got sick or died, caused entirely by food poisoning from the restaurant's contaminated food, she would be agreeing to "take the fall" for the whole thing. Even if her umbrella would cover this unjust provision, her $1 million limit wouldn't be enough for that type of multiple-injury claim. I advised her to remove that requirement from the contract or withdraw from the deal. The restaurant's reaction? It refused to alter the contract. It scoffed and said, "People have been signing this same contract for years and *no one has ever* complained before." (Very scary!) My client wisely withdrew from the deal, much to the restaurant's amazement. Two days later, the restaurant called her and agreed to add the phrase, "except for the negligence of the restaurant and its employees," which solved the problem. This true story has two points:

- Don't sign a contract — especially for something with as much risk as a wedding reception — without reading the contract. Preventing the claim is far better than being liable for it, even if the claim is covered by insurance.

- Own a Personal Umbrella policy. Most of them cover a lot of obligations people take on through the everyday contracts they sign.

Make sure you have true worldwide coverage. I recently reviewed a "worldwide" umbrella that excluded lawsuits not filed in the United States! If you need worldwide coverage, make sure that's what your policy gives you.

The contracts gap

Are you aware of how many times you've signed a personal contract? Sure, car rentals are fairly common, and you may have signed a contract for a vacation residence. But what about all the others?

- The rental of tools and equipment for household projects (like the chainsaw you rented to cut up the dead tree in your yard) in which you agree not only to be responsible for damage to the tool but to pay for an attorney and pay any judgment against the rental company for injuries caused while you're using the tool.

> ✔ The rental of facilities for special occasions, like the wedding reception hall you rented, agreeing to be responsible for anything that happened, even injuries or damage caused by one of the guests, even if you had to defend and pay any judgment against the facility owner.

I wouldn't even consider an umbrella that doesn't cover the liability you take on when you sign a car rental contract.

The nonprofit board gap

Suppose you're caring enough to serve on the board of directors for your son or daughter's youth hockey association. Further suppose that, with the potential for head injuries in that sport, the board took on the responsibility of the selection of the hockey helmet to be worn by the kids. If a child using the helmet suffers a head injury because the helmet has a design flaw, everyone would be sued. Certainly the helmet manufacturer. And most likely you, personally, and the entire board. Even if you win, you'd be responsible for legal fees, which could run into the tens of thousands of dollars. And if you lose, you'll also be responsible for your share of the judgment. Your Automobile, Homeowners, and other primary liability policies won't pay a dime. But many umbrella policies would completely defend you and, if you lose, pay the full judgment against you, subject only to a small deductible.

If you serve without compensation on a nonprofit board, one of your criteria in selecting an umbrella should be coverage for your board activities. It is not comprehensive coverage. It covers primarily injuries or property damage stemming from your activities or decisions. It won't cover other types of lawsuits such as failure to buy the right insurance coverage, sexual harassment, wrongful termination, discrimination, and so on. But at least you have partial coverage.

If you receive any compensation or serve on a for-profit board, the umbrella won't apply. The only way I'd serve on these boards is if the organization had in place adequate amounts of *Directors' and Officers' (D&O)* liability coverage and if, in writing, the company agreed to defend me in court and pay any judgment against me for any of my activities stemming from my involvement with the board and not covered by the D&O insurance.

The company-furnished car gap

If your employer furnishes you with a company car, be aware of two possible gaps in your liability insurance protection. One has to do with coworkers who are injured riding with you; the other has to do with Drive-Other-Cars coverage.

Coworker injuries

The majority of Business Auto Policies covering your company car exclude coverage for you if you injure a coworker riding with you. The coworker, who was injured on the job, in most cases receives Workers' Compensation benefits for medical bills and lost wages. But, unless local laws prohibit such suits, in addition to the Workers' Comp benefits, the coworker can also sue you. The really bad news is that most of the time you have no insurance protection. If you have a company car, make sure the umbrella you buy provides coverage for this serious risk in order to close the gap. (**Note:** you may also need to add *extended non-owned* coverage to your Personal Auto policy. Check with your agent.)

Drive-Other-Cars gap

When you're furnished a company car by your employer, you're covered to drive the car by the employer's Business Auto policy. But you're not covered under the Business Auto policy for cars you borrow or rent personally.

If you have a personal automobile in addition to the company car, skip this section. Your Personal Auto policy already provides coverage for you driving borrowed or rental vehicles. If, however, you have no personal vehicles and thus no Personal Auto policy, you will have no Drive-Other-Cars coverage. Have your employer add the coverage for all family members to his Business Auto Policy, if he's agreeable. Most employers will. The small additional cost may be your responsibility, however. But even if your employer won't add the coverage, the right umbrella policy will cover you for two risks you face driving borrowed or rented cars:

- ✔ Your liability for injuries and property damage you cause to the public
- ✔ Your liability for damaging the car itself

If you have a company car, make very sure that your umbrella covers both of these risks.

The Employee Liability gap

Workers' Compensation insurance pays an employee who is injured on the job her medical bills and lost wages in such amounts as required by your state law, regardless of fault. A second coverage in a Workers' Compensation policy is *Employer's Liability* coverage. Employer's Liability coverage defends and pays any judgements against the employer if the employer is sued for a work-related injury by others, such as the employee's husband who is suing for his loss of his wife's companionship.

The underground heating oil disappearing act

Clients Desi and Lucy called one day quite upset. They had no heat in their home even though the day before they had their underground heating oil tank filled to the top. They had no way of quickly proving it, but they guessed their tank had sprung a leak and 150 gallons of heating oil had spilled into the ground. Being good citizens, they immediately reported it to the local pollution control people who, instead of expressing their gratitude for their good behavior and immediately beginning a cleanup, told them of their financial responsibility to pay all cleanup costs, which could become massive if the oil reached underground waters.

Homeowners policies almost universally exclude pollution liability. And my clients had declined umbrella coverage. Desi and Lucy were lucky this time. The oil never reached water. But they were out a few thousand dollars in legal fees and excavation and cleanup costs. Some umbrella policies would have paid all costs, subject to a small deductible.

The moral: If you have a fuel tank on-premises, especially underground, get an umbrella with pollution spill coverage. And if possible, reduce the risk significantly by not putting the tank underground. Keep it above ground where leaks and seepage can be noticed and fixed immediately.

It isn't just the wealthy, with their maids and gardeners, who have domestic help and need to buy Workers' Compensation and Employee Liability insurance. For example, lots of elderly or disabled people hire personal-care attendants. Or look at the explosion of nannies (people who care for your children in your own home as your employee).

What if you are sued, as a result of causing an employee's injury, for more than your Employee Liability coverage limit? You will want additional coverage from an umbrella policy. The majority of umbrella policies do not include additional Employee Liability coverage. A few, however, do.

If you have an employee or if you have a Workers' Comp policy for whatever reason, Employee Liability coverage should be in the umbrella you choose.

The pollution gap

Most liability policies these days exclude coverage for your liability for pollution. Two types of pollution can result in a lawsuit against you — immediate, accidental pollution, such as your underground fuel tank springing a leak and emptying into the surrounding soil, and gradual pollution, such as seepage from that tank over months or years.

The consequences of either can be severe — having to pay all cleanup costs, which can run into the tens of thousands of dollars, as well as potentially massive fines and penalties. So this is a pretty serious risk. See the sidebar, "The underground heating oil disappearing act," for an example of how this gap may affect you.

To the best of my knowledge, no umbrella covers the seepage kind of pollution. The good news is that some do cover pollution that's both sudden and accidental.

If you have pollutants stored on your premises, especially underground, add pollution coverage to your umbrella shopping list.

Creating Your Own Gap Checklist

Before you can go in search of the umbrella policy that best fills the gaps in your primary coverage, you need to be able to intelligently communicate your needs to an insurance agent or company.

To help you do that, I've created a gap checklist. I guarantee you that it does not include every conceivable gap in liability insurance coverage. But if you use the checklist, it will lead you to an umbrella policy that covers all or most of the gaps on the list. See the Appendix for this checklist.

Mandatory coverages

The mandatory section of the form includes exposures that are so common that each of them should be covered even in the most basic umbrella policy. Some insurance companies argue that coverage for *punitive damages* — extra damages awarded by a jury for gross negligence (like driving drunk even after your license has been suspended for drunk driving) — aren't important if you live in a state banning punitive damage awards. I disagree because people travel to other states. The state you're traveling in may allow punitive damages, so you need that coverage.

Optional coverages

Umbrella policies differ the most in the area of optional coverages. For example, many provide poor coverage on rented boats, extending coverage to only small boats and boats with small motors. In the land of 10,000 lakes, that's a very undesirable restriction. If you live in Minnesota, or any other state with a lot of boating, or if you occasionally rent boats no matter where you live, I recommend that unrestricted boat liability using non-owned or rental boats be a mandatory part of your umbrella coverage.

Another example: A lot of umbrella policies — and even boat policies themselves — exclude coverage for any liability incurred while racing a sailboat. If you race or even crew, you need your umbrella to cover this risk.

Yet another example: If you take some work home and have a home office, your Homeowners policy should include an *Incidental Office endorsement* (see Chapter 7 for the reasons why). Your umbrella must also be amended to include Incidental Office Liability coverage or you'll have a gap. "But what if I own my business and run it from home?" you ask. A Personal Umbrella won't help. See Chapter 9 on insuring a home business.

Finally, some companies offer excess Uninsured and Underinsured Motorist coverage. (See Chapter 3 for more detailed information on these two coverages.) These cover your serious injuries in a car accident caused by a driver with less liability coverage than your injury is worth according to a court of law. It's extra coverage that pays only if the value of your injuries exceeds the Uninsured and Underinsured Motorists coverage on your auto insurance policy. It is great coverage to have if you are seriously hurt. However, give it less priority than your uninsured lawsuit gaps. If you can cover all your uninsured gaps in an umbrella that also makes Uninsured and Underinsured Motorist coverage available — and if your budget can handle it — I recommend you take it.

Using the checklist

If you're going to buy an umbrella policy, you want one that covers the activities you actually engage in, right? You would never buy an auto policy that covered you Monday through Friday and excluded weekends. But that's exactly the type of umbrella policy that most consumers buy and agents sell — a policy that may leave you high and dry at claim time.

This chapter is all about getting those weekends covered. Here's how the umbrella checklist can help. Check off any of the optional coverage areas — gaps — that apply to you and begin the hunt for the right policy. Be forewarned — the insurance marketplace won't be prepared for you. When you hand out your checklist to prospective agents, most will be surprised. No one has ever bought an umbrella policy from them in this fashion before. All agents, including me, don't know off the top of their heads how their umbrella policies will fill those gaps you've checked, so you probably will need to leave a copy of the checklist with them. That's reasonable. This is a complex issue to be handled with care.

By the way, how your agent deals with your request is, in my opinion, one of the best tools to help you select a great agent. Pay attention to how knowledgeable prospective agents are in discussing your particular gaps. If an agent seems annoyed at the request, confused by it, or is clearly unknowledgeable about the gaps, find another agent. (See the Chapter 12 for tips on selecting a good agent.)

Buying the Policy

The three most common mistakes people make when buying a Personal Umbrella policy are:

- They buy their auto and home policies first and then buy the umbrella from the same insurance company. In short, the mistake is settling for whatever umbrella comes with the auto and home policies, no matter how poor it may be. *Note:* Buying your policies from the same *agent* is usually a good idea, but automatically buying them from the same *company* is a poor idea if you want the best umbrella policy (as the next bullet points out).

- They buy their umbrella policy from a different agent than the one who sold them auto and home insurance. The damage occurs because the two agents don't communicate, leaving you very vulnerable to gaps between your primary and umbrella coverages.

- They buy their umbrella on price and ignore coverage. Usually because they think all umbrellas are the same and because they don't realize the importance of gap coverage. They are unaware that they even have gaps.

Pick an agent, any agent

For the record, there are two types of insurance agents:

- Those who represent one insurance company only — often referred to as *exclusive agents, captive agents,* or *direct writer agents*

- Those who are free to represent more than one company — usually referred to as *independent agents*

Exclusive agents include those who represent insurance companies like State Farm, Farmers Insurance Group, or Liberty Mutual. Independent agent insurance companies include national insurers like Safeco, Hartford, and Chubb, and most regional insurance companies (Harleysville, AutoOwners, Cincinnati).

Which type of agent is better for you? The best insurance agent you can find is the one that can get you the coverage you need. Whether they are independent or exclusive makes no difference. The only real difference when trying to buy the right umbrella is convenience. If the exclusive agent you prefer offers only one umbrella choice that excludes coverage for a lot of activities you are exposed to, you will be forced to buy your Umbrella policy elsewhere. In contrast, the independent agent, by having more than one umbrella option, increases your chances that you won't have to seek another agent to get the coverage you want. But even the independent agent may not have in his portfolio the best Umbrella policy for your needs.

Great advice. Great coverage. That's all that matters.

The three antidotes to these mistakes are building your insurance program starting with the umbrella policy first, keeping your primary and umbrella coverages with the same agent, and considering price last rather than first. Here's more information on each one of these three.

Buying your umbrella policy first

If your only reason for having an umbrella policy is to get higher liability limits on your Automobile and Homeowners policies and if you don't have any concerns about gap coverage, taking the umbrella that comes from the insurer of your auto and home is fine. Taking that umbrella is also fine if it covers all the gaps in your umbrella checklist (unlikely but possible).

But if you want an umbrella that plugs as many of your liability insurance gaps as possible, the best way to build your insurance program is to start at the top with the umbrella policy and decide on that policy first, before you buy auto or home insurance. Here's why.

Due to the small premiums, many insurers don't even offer an umbrella policy unless they insure your home and auto, too. If your home and auto insurance is already set up with Company A but that company has an umbrella that doesn't suit your needs, and you discover that Companies B and C both have umbrella policies that cover all of your gaps but they require your car and home insurance, you'll have to cancel and move your auto and home insurance — a lot of unnecessary work to get the umbrella you need.

If, on the other hand, you compare umbrellas first, you will logically narrow down your choices to either Company B or C. You can then compare the prices of each company's auto and home policies and go with whichever of the two has the best total price. You may pay a little more for the whole program than you would have paid if you used Company A for the whole program, but when you are navigating across the ocean (of life), how much more will you pay for a boat that won't leak or sink?

Buying your insurance from the same agent or company

If you buy your primary and umbrella liability coverage from the same insurer, your insurance coverage fits together better with less chance of a gap (Legos and Legos versus Legos and Tinker Toys) than if you split your policies between two or more insurance companies.

If you do buy all your polices from different insurers but at least from the same professional agent, whatever gaps could exist between your polices can be reduced or prevented with the help of the agent. For example, suppose that you have auto and home insurance through Company A and your umbrella through Company G but all your policies are through the same agent. Now suppose you add an incidental office at home and add the appropriate Homeowners endorsement to cover injuries to delivery people. Your astute agent will know that your umbrella won't extend to that office without a special amendment. She will then add that amendment and thus avoid a potentially serious gap. If you had the umbrella with a different agent, the umbrella agent would never have been notified, and you'd have that gap.

To reduce the chance of gaps between policies, keep your auto, home, umbrella, and other personal liability policies together — ideally, with the same agent and the same insurance company.

Placing coverage and financial strength before price

Do not make your umbrella decision on the price of the umbrella alone. You could end up comparing a Yugo to a Lexus.

Start with selecting the umbrella policies that best cover the gaps you listed on your checklist. Then make sure the insurer is strong financially. (See the sidebar "Measuring insurer strength.") You don't want them going belly-up in the middle of a lawsuit against you. Then and only then look at the umbrella pricing. But only as a part of the pricing of the whole insurance program.

Measuring insurer strength

Why is insurer strength so important when purchasing a Personal Umbrella policy? Don't states have an insurance guarantee fund protecting consumers against insolvency? Yes, most states do have such a consumer protection fund. But few such funds protect as high as $1 million or more. Minnesota's limit, for example, is $300,000. But even if the fund limit was high enough, collecting from it is a long, drawn-out process — hardly the kind of stress you want in the middle of a lawsuit against you.

Several organizations rate insurance companies. The one with the longest track record —

and a great reputation — is the A. M. Best Company. They assign insurers a strength rating from A++ to C, much like school grades. (See www.ambest/ratings/definition. html for an explanation of the ratings.) If you would like more information on an insurer you're considering, go to www.ambest.com/ratings.html on the Internet, where you can get a wealth of information on any company. I don't recommend buying an umbrella from any insurance company with an A. M. Best rating below A (in other words, a B+ or worse) unless it's unavoidable.

Part V
Dealing with Insurance Companies

The 5th Wave   By Rich Tennant

"What do you mean, everyone on the bus has to sign the speeding ticket?"

In this part . . .

Knowing how insurance companies work can minimize the stresses that often accompany claim time. Very often, people learn how an insurance company processes claims at the point the insured is least able to provide documentation or other necessary proof. Being prepared to fortify your claim is as important as having the insurance policy in the first place. This chapter shows you how to be prepared for the demands your insurance company can make on you when you have suffered a loss.

Chapter 12

Buying Insurance the Right Way

. . . .

In This Chapter

▶ Understanding the dangers of buying insurance on price alone

▶ Discovering the right way to buy insurance

▶ Understanding the dangers of the usual agent selection process

▶ Finding, interviewing, and hiring your insurance advisor

. . . .

*I*n my second year in the insurance business, I was a claims adjuster for an insurance company. I was trained for, and specialized in, handling Automobile and Homeowners claims. I enjoyed the job a lot, especially because of the opportunity to help people with a claim and get their lives restored.

What I disliked about the job was having to deny claims made by perfectly nice people who did not have the right coverage — especially when I knew the right coverage was available, and that it would have cost them so little. Sadly, every day insurance adjusters have no choice but to deny or underpay claims because the right coverage wasn't purchased. Discover, in this chapter, how to keep your claims from being denied or underpaid. Discover the steps to getting the right coverage.

Buying Insurance the Wrong Way

Most people buy insurance the wrong way. First, they buy it like a commodity — on price alone. Then, they let whoever answered the phone and gave them the quote be their agent, without any knowledge of that person's skill level. What they end up with, usually, is a cheap price . . . for the wrong coverage. Not to mention a less-skilled agent than they could have had for the same price. What they end up with, ultimately, are claims that are either denied or underpaid because of wrong coverage. They end up with significant financial losses. They end up with an insurance program that didn't do the job they hired it to do.

Understanding the danger of price-only shopping

Why is the practice of calling around for the lowest price dangerous? Because insurance is *not* a commodity. It's a 20-page contract full of exclusions and limitations. To put it another way, people buy insurance like it's cheddar cheese when it's really more like swiss cheese — nutritious but *full* of holes!

In over 25 years, I have personally reviewed about 2,000 personal insurance portfolios. All but five have had at least one major coverage gap. More than half had five or more major gaps. Twenty percent had ten or more gaps. Many of these gaps were serious enough to have caused financial ruin if the uncovered claim occurred.

The tragedy is not that the holes exist. The tragedy is that over 90 percent of the holes in an insurance program can be plugged with inexpensive policy endorsements. Good coverage can't happen when insurance is bought on price alone. If you want to plug the holes in your insurance coverage, you must be willing to buy insurance carefully, and not just buy the cheapest available product.

Illustrating the danger

Telling you that dangers lurk in poorly constructed policies and giving you statistics doesn't make the point quite as strongly as real examples do. Here are some true stories, from my own files, about coverage gaps. All the examples of coverage gaps are real. Some of the claims are hypothetical. In each story, I've estimated the annual cost of the insurance coverage that would have eliminated the gap.

The roof leak

Imelda, condominium owner, suffered massive water, mold, and mildew damage to her unit from three heavy rains, due to some bad roof leaks. The value of the claim? $30,000. The amount of coverage? $1,000. The cost to fix the gap? $100 a year. She also suffered a $30,000 loss for damage to her furniture and clothing from water and mildew. The amount of coverage? $0. The cost to fix the gap? $40 a year.

The lawn care workers' compensation lawsuit

Caesar hired a lawn care service. One day, the owner of the service fell off a ladder while trimming a small tree branch, injuring his back. He sued for Workers' Compensation benefits to cover all his medical bills and lost wages —

about $75,000 — alleging that he should have been Caesar's employee. The cost to defend the suit? $40,000. The amount of coverage under Caesar's Homeowners or Umbrella policies? $0. The cost to fix the gap? $110 a year.

The older home fire

Donald and Ivana bought a beautiful, 80-year-old, two-story home in the lakes area of south Minneapolis. They paid $250,000. The lot was worth $50,000, so they insured their home for its full $200,000 value. A fire destroyed the kitchen and caused extensive smoke damage throughout the rest of the house. The total cost of cleanup and repairs? $180,000. The amount the insurance company paid? $110,000. The cost to have fixed this $70,000 gap? $500 a year.

The automobile injury lawsuit

Bill and Monica slid through a stop sign on some ice and struck another car, carrying George and Linda. Both George and Linda were injured — Linda more seriously. Two years later, the jury awarded Linda $250,000 and George $50,000. Bill and Monica had normal injury lawsuit limits of $100,000 each person and $300,000 each accident. The total value of the two injuries? $300,000. The amount the insurance company paid? $150,000. The cost to have fixed this problem before the accident? $40 a year.

The stolen sterling

Paul and Ringo inherited three heirloom sterling silver sets. They had them appraised and scheduled them for their appraised value of $35,000. Six months later, burglars broke in and stole all the silver. Only the silver had gone up in value to $50,000. The amount the policy paid? $35,000. The cost to have fixed this $15,000 gap? Almost nothing.

The stolen paintings

Laverne and Sherman appraised and scheduled five valuable paintings for $20,000. Two years later, when they were stolen, the paintings were worth $50,000. The amount the policy paid? $20,000. The cost to have fixed this coverage before the loss without having to get new appraisals? $0 — possibly even a $50 to $100 a year cost reduction.

The business package delivery

Boutros brings work home and had set up a small office area in which to work. His boss, needing Boutros's help on an urgent project, had the material delivered by courier. The courier fell on some loose front steps, was injured, sued Boutros for $200,000, and won. Boutros has $300,000 of home liability coverage. The amount the policy pays of the $200,000 judgement and Boutros's $75,000 defense cost? $0. The cost to have covered this $275,000 gap? $15 a year.

The stolen Mustang

Lee bought and restored the car of his dreams — a 1965 Ford Mustang. Then he had it appraised and insured it for $9,000 under the insurance company's special Stated Amount coverage for classic cars. Two years later, when the car was stolen, its value had climbed to $15,000. The amount of the claim check cheerfully given to Lee? $9,000. The additional cost to have the coverage that would have paid the entire $15,000? $0. In fact, Lee would have saved at least $50 a year.

The rental houseboat wind damage

Burt, Loni, and some friends rented a 75-foot, $300,000 houseboat for a ten-day vacation. One day it stormed, and gale-force winds seriously damaged the boat and drove it into some rocks. The total damage to the boat? $115,000. The amount Burt and Loni owed, as a result of the standard rental contract they signed? $115,000, plus three months lost rent in the amount of $9,000 while the boat was being repaired. The amount of personal insurance they had covering this $124,000 responsibility? $0. The cost of the policy that would have covered this entire loss? $125 a year.

These are just a few examples of the dangers of buying your insurance like a commodity — on price alone.

Bargain basement brain surgery

Suppose you've been told you need brain surgery. If you shopped for it like many shop for insurance, here's what you'd do:

You start by calling around town, getting quotes over the phone. You're not sure exactly what kind of brain surgery you need, so you decide to get a price for the type that you think you probably need. You get quotes from all over — from surgeons, clinics, hospitals, and even medical school interns. You're not concerned about skill — just price. After all, it's only brain surgery.

You find a clinic that will do the surgery you think you need for the lowest price. You sign up for the brain surgery. The intern who answered the phone when you called does the surgery, even though one of the top brain surgeons in the area works for the clinic and would do the surgery for the same price as the intern. The intern, lacking the expertise to diagnose the exact type of surgery you need, performs the surgery you asked for in the quote. The top brain surgeon would have known enough to recognize that what you requested was the wrong procedure for you and would put you at risk for serious brain damage. She would have recommended a different, more expensive, but much more helpful surgery instead.

Insurance isn't brain surgery. But it isn't a commodity either. The moral of the story is that if you shop for insurance like this, you'll probably end up with the wrong diagnosis, with possible serious side effects, and with a less skilled advisor than you need and could have had for the same price.

Buying Insurance the Right Way

Your goal in buying insurance should be to get a good price for a good policy. A good policy has the fewest possible major coverage gaps. The secret to eliminating gaps in coverage is to include, in your decision process, the findings of an agent or advisor who is highly knowledgeable in the particular type of insurance you need help with. The agent can identify gaps in your coverage and propose solutions that plug those gaps.

You can create a solid insurance portfolio without major coverage gaps and still get a good price using two different strategies:

- **Shop price first.** Shop for the company with the lowest price you can find for the coverage you need. Then, don't buy from whoever answers the phone. Find the most knowledgeable agent you can who represents that company. With her help, determine what coverage you need.

- **Shop expertise first.** Find the most knowledgeable expert you can. Then, buy the insurance from him at the best price he has available.

Shopping expertise first

The greater your assets and income, the more strongly I recommend this strategy of choosing expertise first as the most important element in your insurance-buying process. If you have a lot to lose, absolutely shop expertise first. Spend extra time to locate the most expertise you can find. Your up-front price won't be quite as low as with the other choices, but you'll have the least chance of a major uninsured loss. Which is far more important than any up-front premium savings, in your situation.

Shopping price first — a safe alternative

If you aren't very sueable and have a very simple lifestyle, I don't see a problem if you prefer to shop your price first by calling around or searching any of the insurance sites on the Internet. But before you buy, remember that you're probably shopping the wrong coverage, and get some professional advice!

Suppose you comparison-shop your Automobile and Homeowners coverage, and you discover that Safeco or State Farm blows away the competition. Locate the most knowledgeable State Farm or Safeco agent in your area. Remember, it won't cost you a penny more to have the best. You'll get good prices — and some good advice. Tips on finding a great agent are a bit later in the chapter.

1-800-cheap-insurance

Buying insurance directly from the company, without an agent, can usually result in savings of 10 to 15 percent. This type of insurance is available through 800 numbers, mail order, associations and organizations, and on the Internet.

Because not consulting with an agent increases the risk of having major uncovered claims, I recommend this strategy to no one other than the following types of buyers:

✔ Those with nothing to lose. For example, people with minimal income and assets who must buy mandatory car insurance to drive.

✔ Those who don't care if they have a major uncovered claim.

✔ Those who have their own insurance expertise through education and/or experience.

For example, I bought my insurance direct when I was a claims adjuster well trained in Automobile and Homeowners coverages.

✔ Those with access to someone who can provide them with the expertise they need to design the right coverage. For example, people sometimes hire me to design their insurance specifications and then they buy their insurance elsewhere.

✔ Those who get nothing but a quote from their agent — no real counsel on coverages and no coaching or advocacy for your right when you have a claim. In this case, your agent's not doing you any good, so why bother having an agent? (Although a better idea is to just get a better agent.)

The true cost of insurance is twofold: what you pay up front in premiums, and what you pay out-of-pocket at claim time for uninsured claims. People who buy insurance incorrectly focus only on the cost of the premiums. No one has ever gone bankrupt because of their insurance premiums, but many people have gone bankrupt because of uncovered claims.

Choosing Your Professional Advisor

Automobile, home, boat, umbrella, and other personal policies, as they are sold off the shelf, rarely, if ever, cover all your major property and liability risks. But they will cover most, if not all, of those major risks if they're customized to your needs with proper coverage limits and appropriate coverage endorsements. Customizing a policy requires a great deal of coverage expertise and care. And that's why, for most people, locating and hiring the best possible advisor has to be the very highest priority when it comes to buying insurance.

Common sense, smart cents, and percents

Almost all insurance buyers see an insurance premium as buying them one thing — an insurance policy. In reality, the premium pays for much more than that. The policy, the coverage, and the insurance company make up about 85 percent of the premium. Professional advice, policy service, and help from a professional agent when there is a problem make up the other 15 percent. Spend that 15 percent wisely! Get the best agent that you can get.

Understanding the good news and the bad news of agent compensation

In almost all the states, agents selling personal insurance get paid the same commission as every other agent representing the particular insurance company — usually about 10 to 15 percent. Regardless of experience, skill level, or the quality of the insurance plan they design. This payment structure is both good news and bad news for you.

The good news — getting an expert for the price of a novice

Although the flat commission compensation system is anticonsumer (rewarding quantity of sales rather than quality), you can really benefit from the system in one way — you can buy the very best talent for not a penny more than you would pay for the worst possible agent! Can you see how ridiculous it is to select your agent based on the warm body who gives you the quote? The vast majority of the time, the person you talk with the first time you call a company will not be one of that insurance company's most skilled agents.

The bad news — finding a needle in a haystack

The "everybody gets paid the same" rule for agent compensation has one big drawback. The marketplace pushes agents with greater skills away from smaller, personal insurance policies and their small commissions into business insurance, where the premiums and commissions more appropriately compensate the best agents' greater expertise. The current compensation arrangement makes finding agents with great skills a difficult task.

The more complex your lifestyle and the more of a lawsuit target you are, the more important it is to take the time to find an agent with the most expertise that you can. Under the current agent compensation system in most states, that better agent won't cost you a penny more.

Identifying what you want in an advisor

Okay, so you're sold on the idea of finding the best advisor that you can for the commission dollars that you're spending. Where do you look for candidates? And when you find two or more candidates, how can you select the one that's best for you? I suggest you build a checklist of what you want in your agent.

- ✔ **Do I want my life, health, disability, long-term care, and other coverages with the same agent?** If you do, then expertise in those coverages should be on your agent checklist.

- ✔ **Is a regular review (normally done annually) important?** If so, add this to your shopping list. I recommend reviews. A well-designed insurance plan starts to rust with coverage gaps if it's not polished up every year or two.

- ✔ **Do I have a home business?** If so, you must find someone with small business insurance expertise. Add that to your list.

- ✔ **Are top claim skills important to me?**

  - Do you want the best possible claims coaching, to maximize your claim when you file it?

  - Do you want an agent skilled enough to fight, successfully, for your rights if your claim is unjustly denied or underpaid?

Once you've determined the skills you require, you can begin the search.

Searching for candidates

You're seeking an agent to probe your needs, identify coverage gaps, solve problems, help you resolve claim disputes, do annual reviews, and in short, provide more quality. Here are some possible sources for candidates. Try to get at least two to three prospects.

Word of mouth

Word of mouth is always one of the best sources when seeking a professional of any kind. But be careful not to fall into the price trap. Since so many people buy their insurance solely on price, when you ask for a referral for a good agent, you might get: "Call Bob. He's a good guy. He saved me $200 a year. And he always remembers my birthday." So you call Bob, get his quote, save your $200 or more, and end up with a good price for the wrong coverage (and an annual birthday card). And you've done nothing about your uninsured coverage gaps.

To avoid the price trap, be specific when asking for a referral. You don't necessarily want the best salesman or the one you'd most like to go to a ball game with. You want the person who will give you the best professional advice.

Professional societies

An insurance agent can earn a number of advanced insurance designations by completing a series of courses and passing the exams. Here are just a few.

- ✔ Chartered Property Casualty Underwriter (CPCU)
- ✔ Certified Insurance Counselor (CIC)
- ✔ Certified Life Underwriter (CLU)
- ✔ Accredited Advisor in Insurance (AAI)
- ✔ Personal Risk Manager — a fairly new designation (PRM)

Many others designations exist as well. Anyone earning any insurance designation has to spend anywhere from 100 hours to 1,000 hours (for the CPCU) in classroom- and self-study, as well as pass national exams. These are people who have gained additional expertise in certain areas. But these are also people with a commitment to professionalism and ethical behavior. If you're seeking life-insurance expertise, you have three leads, and one has a CLU, chances are better than average that the CLU is the most knowledgeable and most professional. I wouldn't choose an agent based solely on her professional designations, but it would weigh heavily in my decision.

If you want some good leads to an agent prospect with expertise in personal property and liability policies — auto, home, umbrella, and so on — I'd contact both the CPCU Society and the CIC Society and get the names of agents in your area. Contact the Society of CIC by phone at 800-632-2165 and request that it sends you a list of CIC agents who share your zip code. Contact the Society of CPCU on the Web at www.cpcusociety.org. (See Chapter 21 for more information on this site.)

Neither organization makes this a simple process for you. Getting the names of agents will take a few minutes of your time, but I recommend putting up with the hassle.

Whatever names you get from these two societies will be good prospects for your agent search. (CPCU agents are more scarce, so you may need to request a state listing rather than asking for agents in your zip code.)

Insurance companies

Insurance companies are the best source of prospects if you have your mind made up to be insured with a particular insurance company. You can go directly to an insurer for agent prospects if you have a long insurance company relationship you wish to continue. You can also go to the insurer for agent leads if you have preshopped for a certain type of insurance and found one or two insurers that are the lowest priced (for the coverage you shopped but not the coverage you need!).

What you need to find out from the insurer is who the company's best, most knowledgeable agents are. The insurance company knows who these agents are, but is unlikely, for legal and other reasons, to give you their names. So here's what I recommend you do: Call the local company office and request they fax or e-mail you a list of all their agents in your state who have a CPCU or CIC designation. They may not have a list at their fingertips, but they can get it for you. Whichever method you use, it should yield a small supply of quality prospects.

Making the choice

At this point, you've lined up one or more candidates for your "job opening" for an agent/advisor. You're probably thinking, "How do I, with limited knowledge, make this choice? I don't even know what to ask." My suggestion is that you use a questionnaire to conduct an interview, check references, and most importantly, trust your instincts.

Interviewing your candidates

The job of protecting you from financial ruin caused by property or liability claims is an important one. I recommend that you approach it as seriously as you'd approach choosing a doctor, lawyer, or CPA. Do an interview — by phone or in person.

It is critical that you thoroughly interview your prospective insurance representative — they will be your best friend or worst enemy at claim time. A complete, professional interview makes sure that the agent is on your side when your need is the greatest. A list of questions is included in the Appendix.

When you've completed the interviews, you should have a pretty good feel for the agent's background, his educational and practical experience, and the kind of ongoing help you can expect — both as far as regular fine tuning of your program and the kind of assistance you'll get in a serious claim or dispute. I wouldn't consider any candidate who doesn't offer you the big three:

✔ The expertise to help you design a great protection plan with the least possible gaps

✔ Ongoing reviews and regular contact about new developments so your plan stays current

✔ Outstanding assistance at claim time, both coaching you and being a strong advocate for your rights in a dispute

The insurance audit

Suppose you're pretty content with your agent and even your insurance company. But you've got a lot to lose and you'd sure like a second opinion. You're a little nervous about whether all the bases are covered, especially considering that you have an older home, a lot of artwork and antiques, a vacation condo in the mountains, and a small business you run from home. The question is how can you get a second opinion from an expert? How much will it cost? And what results can you ask for?

If your state allows agents to charge fees for added services, approach an agent with good expertise and request an audit of your entire insurance program. Agree on an hourly rate or flat fee for the service. Here's the format I use that works very well.

✔ I meet with the clients for about 1½ to 2 hours and probe to identify the property and liability risks in their lives. At their option, I also include life and health risks. I particularly focus on the risks not covered by standard insurance policies.

✔ Next, I try to measure the size of the risks I've identified. I briefly review the prospective clients' income and assets to assess how sueable they are and help them determine an appropriate liability insurance limit.

I gather information on their home to double- and triple-check the adequacy of their home structural coverage. I help them determine how much life insurance to carry.

✔ I review their contracts and leases, such as town house association agreements or home business contracts to see what risks they have assumed in those agreements.

✔ Then, I gather and review all their personal insurance policies, including group insurance — life, health, disability — with the purpose of discovering where the holes are.

✔ Finally, I prepare a written report listing the problem areas and my recommended solution for each. The reports are usually 2 to 3 pages long and identify 8 to 20 problems.

The clients pay me for the report and can then use the information to buy insurance from any company or any agent. Or they can simply use the information to have their current agents make whatever policy changes are needed to plug their coverage gaps. I've done scores of insurance audits. I've never had a client not benefit immensely. Any advisor you select can do the same for you for a fair price, if your state permits it.

Checking references

Agents don't get asked for references. They should. Especially if you know nothing about them other than your interview. If you have any doubts or if you're having trouble choosing between two or more candidates, check references. I recommend at least three — all of them having to do with the agent's skills and performance. I recommend at least one be from a client whom the agent went to bat for at claim time.

Making the decision

You've completed your interviews. You've checked references. Now, make a provisional choice. Schedule a meeting for the purpose of designing your insurance specifications and identifying and plugging the coverage gaps in your current program. If you've narrowed your choice to two candidates, meet with them both and get advice from both. The better agent should really stand out.

Choosing Your Insurance Company

A good agent can advise you as to both the financial strength and the quality of claim service of any insurance company that you are considering. If, however, you are buying direct without advice or just want more information on a particular company, go to www.ambest.com/ratings.html.

A. M. Best Company analyzes and rates insurance companies based on their overall quality and strength. There are others, but A. M. Best has been doing it for about 100 years! It gives give insurers grades, much like school — A++, A+, A, A-, B+, B, and so on. For more details on each of the grades, go to its homepage or see the A. M. Best section in Chapter 21. The higher the rating, generally, the safer you are from the risk of the insurance company closing its doors and not being able to pay your claim.

Don't buy insurance from any insurance company with an A. M. Best policy-holder rating of less than "A" unless there's no other choice.

The larger your exposures and the greater your coverage limits, the stronger the insurance company rating you should seek. For example, if your income and/or assets make you a target for lawsuits, you will probably buy an umbrella policy. (See Chapter 10 for more on Umbrellas.) The A. M. Best rating for that Umbrella should, ideally, be an A+ or A++. Picking an insurance company can be a gamble. Fortunately, organizations like the A. M. Best Company help improve your odds.

Chapter 13

Getting What You Deserve for Automobile Claims

*I*nsurance is a 20-page promise to make you whole financially if certain events happen that threaten your financial well-being. It's not a promise to make you whole for *anything* that happens. If a circle represents every conceivable claim, a box within the circle represents claims covered by an insurance policy.

Many people assume that every possible claim is within the box. Nothing could be further from the truth! However, the box is expandable. If you have risks in your life that lie outside the box, use coverages and endorsements to expand the size of your box until it covers the areas you need it to.

The majority of claim disputes or unhappiness, in my years of experience, arise from claims or damage to your automobiles, your home, and your personal property. This chapter focuses on your automobile claims. The next chapter addresses home and personal property claims.

An automobile claim is underpaid or denied by an insurance company for three main reasons:

✔ The type of claim being submitted isn't covered by the particular policy — although it would have been covered by a more comprehensive policy (normally the case).

> ✔ The type of claim being submitted is never covered by any policy (rarely the case).
>
> ✔ The claim is mishandled by the insurance company (occurs enough that you need to be aware of the problem).

The majority of the other chapters in this book focus on the first bullet — protecting yourself by having coverages that are right for the unique risks in your life. This chapter's focus is on the last bullet. I show you what to do to make sure that your automobile claim will be paid in full.

Dealing with Insurance Adjusters

Insurance adjusters. Who are they? What do they do? An adjuster is the person empowered by an insurance company to investigate your claim, when you file one, and to determine how much you are entitled to receive. Adjusters not only have to determine whether you have coverage for your claim, but they also have to work to make sure that the repair or replacement costs are reasonable. Finally, they have to communicate to you — clearly — the settlement offer and how the offer was calculated.

Claims are usually pretty traumatic for the customer. Working with a knowledgeable and caring adjuster is a blessing.

Understanding claims problems

I find that most adjusters do a good job of knowing their coverages and knowing how to control costs. When they fall short, it's most often in one or more of these areas:

✔ **Poor communication.** Some adjusters don't explain how they arrive at the settlement, which is especially important if it's less than what the client had expected. Sometimes adjusters don't tell clients what to do if repair shops or contractors won't honor the adjuster's estimate, or if there's additional damage that the adjuster missed.

✔ **Failure to get an agreed price on an auto repair.** Some adjusters just mail a repair estimate and a check, putting the customer in the awkward position of having to find a body shop to do the work for that price.

✔ **Not being reachable.** Sometimes getting in contact with the adjuster is almost impossible, and the customer doesn't have an alternative way to reach someone familiar with the claim, such as the adjuster's supervisor.

Avoiding claims phone tag

The number one complaint I get from customers is the amount of phone tag they have to play to reach their adjuster, who's busy out in the field. Eliminate most of that frustration by getting the following information the first time you contact the adjuster. Be sure to write down the claim number, the date of the accident, the adjuster's name, the adjuster's phone numbers, and the name and phone number of the adjuster's supervisor. You can call the adjuster directly on his cell phone or call his voice mail. Call the adjuster's supervisor if you need to reach someone right away or if you're having a problem with the adjuster. See the Claim Contact Information Form in the appendix for a sheet you can fill in the first time you talk with the adjuster.

Managing claim communication problems

Here are some things you can do to make your claim go more smoothly:

- ✔ Request the claim number, and direct-dial phone numbers for the adjuster and her supervisor when the adjuster first contacts you.

- ✔ Never accept payment for any auto-repairs without the adjuster and your body shop agreeing to a price.

- ✔ If you can't reach the adjuster, or you are unhappy with her for any reason, call her supervisor.

- ✔ If you flat out don't think the adjuster is doing a good job, call the supervisor or even the claims manager and request that they reassign your file to another adjuster. You don't have to accept poor performance.

- ✔ If you have an agent, don't hesitate to ask for help with any kind of problem that you're having, especially if you feel the settlement offer is too low. A good agent has the skills to negotiate, on your behalf, to improve an unfair settlement offer.

Collecting from Your Collision Coverage

Collision coverage pays to fully repair your car or replace it if it's a total loss (minus your deductible, of course). If you are the primary cause of an accident and your car is damaged, there are only two places to get the money for repairs — Collision coverage or your grocery-money envelope.

Resolving problems with the insurance adjuster

You've just been involved in a collision and you have collision coverage on your auto policy. You report the claim either to your agent or directly to the insurer. A claims adjuster contacts you. If your car is drivable, you may be asked to get one or two estimates. Or, the adjuster may inspect the car herself and write her own estimate.

Here are a few of the common problems you may encounter and what you can do about them.

- ✔ **You don't like the shop that the insurer recommends.** Most insurance companies have relationships with body shops they have found to be easy to work with, who are reasonable in their estimates and in negotiating repair costs. In most states, though, you have the right to pick the shop of your choice, and you can insist that your insurance company work with that shop. Some shops are known to be price gougers. It benefits us all if you avoid those shops — keeping repair costs reasonable keeps premiums down.

- ✔ **The adjuster demands that you get two or three estimates.** Requesting one estimate is reasonable. Get it from your preferred body shop. If it's not inconvenient, getting a second estimate helps keep shops honest. If you prefer not to get a second estimate, you may have the right to refuse and request that the insurance company send an appraiser to work out a repair price with your shop, especially if your car is not drivable. As for a third estimate, refuse. Totally unreasonable.

- ✔ **Your preferred shop won't honor the adjuster's estimate.** This situation occurs often, unfortunately. When adjusters are busy, they will write an estimate and hand or mail you a check for that amount. At first, you may be happy to have such prompt service. Then you bring your car in, and the body shop refuses to repair it for the amount the adjuster gave you. The body shop often points out damage that the adjuster missed. Don't worry. You simply call the adjuster, and she works out a new repair price with your shop and issues you a second check.

  Never accept an estimate and payment before the body shop of your choice agrees to do the repairs for that amount.

- ✔ **The body shop wants additional money from you before it will release the car.** The shop may do this for one of two reasons. First, the adjuster may have approved additional damage, but the second claim check has not arrived. If so, the solution is to sign a form (available in every body shop) authorizing your insurer to bypass you and pay the shop directly for the additional cost. Then most shops will release your car without further problems. If the shop still won't release your car, the best bet is to charge the additional amount to your credit card.

A second possibility is that the shop may be trying to pull a fast one. All reputable shops know that any supplemental repairs must be approved by the adjuster. If they surprise you when you arrive with demands for more money, they did the repairs without an okay. The body shop is hoping that you'll be so desperate to get your car released that you will either pay the difference yourself or protest so loudly to your insurance company that it will pay just to appease you. If the shop did not get an approval, the shop is the bad guy. Don't pay them. Sign an authorization for your insurance company to pay additional amounts, if any, to the body shop. The shop then has to do what it should have done and attempt to work things out with your adjuster. But then it's the shop's problem, not yours.

✔ **The insurer won't pay for new parts.** You have a nice, clean, low-mileage, eight-year old car. It's banged up. The adjuster's estimate is for used parts, but you want new parts. The insurance company is within its rights to replace your used parts with used parts. You have the right to make sure that the parts are in good condition, and you can refuse to allow them to be used if they aren't. You also have the right to demand new parts, although you'll have to pay the difference between the cost of new parts and the cost of used parts. The insurance company is within its rights when it only pays for used parts because it only has to replace what you had — and your parts certainly had some wear and tear on them by the time you were in the accident.

✔ **Getting cash when you won't be making the repairs.** You need to know that the insurance company, not you, gets to choose whether to repair, replace, or pay cash. That being said, most insurers still let you choose cash if you prefer. Companies differ on the amount of cash they pay. Some pay you the full repair cost; others pay what they call an *appearance allowance* to compensate you for the loss in value of your damaged car. If you're not happy with the amount of an appearance allowance, go to a dealer. Show the used-car manager your car. Ask him to write on his letterhead both the preaccident and postaccident values of your car. You are entitled to receive the difference between these two values if you decide not to repair the car.

Deciding whether or not to file a small claim

You back into a post and cause $973 in damage to your car. You have a $500 Collision coverage deductible. You file the claim and collect the $473. Four months later, your auto insurance bill comes with an at-fault accident charge of $300 a year for three years. In short, you end up paying $900 to collect $473.

You aren't happy. Why didn't someone warn you so that you could have paid the claim yourself? And how unfair that the dollar amount of the rate increase for your minor accident could exceed what you collected in your claim! Here's why that happens and how you can protect yourself in the future.

Understanding insurance company pricing

Insurance is nothing more than a mechanism allowing people in similar circumstances to share their losses. In any given year, people who have accidents collect from those who don't. The insurance company is just the collection basket.

When you buy car insurance, you get grouped, and share losses with, people similar to you in age, location, use of car, and driving record (tickets and at-fault accidents). When any of these factors change, you move to, and share losses with, a different group of drivers. (Remember when you turned 25 and your rates dropped 30 percent? On that day, you weren't a better driver than the day before, but you transferred to a group of more experienced drivers who have fewer accidents and lower premiums.)

Similar changes in your insurance rate happen when you move from one city to another, or change the use of your cars, or when you get tickets or are in an at-fault accident. You simply change groups. When you hit a post and file a claim, you change groups — just like when you get a couple of speeding tickets.

Before you file a small claim with your insurance company, find out first how much more you'll pay over the next few years in insurance premiums. If it's greater than the claim value, you're probably better off paying the claim yourself.

Your agent, if you have one, should always warn you of this pitfall when you report a small claim. He or his staff can estimate for you the extra costs of reporting the claim and help you decide if it is in your best interest to do so.

Never file a small claim for an accident you cause without first knowing the total impact on your rates — unless there's even the smallest injury. If there's any kind of injury, *always* file the claim, no matter how small, or you could void your liability coverage for that injury.

A good agent will look at the entire family driving record when deciding to report a small claim. Maybe this minor accident, combined with a speeding ticket from two months ago, will jump your rates $1,500 over 3 years. Maybe the family driving record is so bad that one more accident will cancel your policy and force you into high risk insurance where the rates are double what you're paying now. Under these circumstances, you may not even report a $2,500 accident. It may be cheaper, in the long run, to pay for it yourself.

If you do have a poor driving history, it may make sense not to carry Collision coverage, and to have high deductibles. Why pay for coverage that you aren't going to use?

Considering Other Factors When It's the Other Guy's Fault

When you're in a collision caused by the other driver, you often have the choice between using your own Collision coverage, if you have it, or collecting from the other driver's liability insurance, if he had insurance. If you have no Collision coverage on your car, you only have one choice — to collect from his insurance (or from him, personally, if he has no insurance).

Proving your version of the accident

If you can remember, at the accident scene, to get the names of witnesses and/or a police report you'll have a much easier time proving your version of the accident. Write everything down, and take pictures if you have a camera. It not only helps your case, but also protects you from the other driver changing his story and blaming you. (Sadly, this happens a lot!) Call the police if anyone is injured, the property damage is serious, or there is any dispute over fault.

Expediting your claim

One of the biggest drawbacks to collecting from the other driver's insurance is the delay in getting paid. Before they can pay you, they have to interview their driver and investigate the accident. That can take two weeks. To expedite the process, you can:

- ✔ Call and report the claim directly to the other driver's insurance company or agent. When you aren't their customer, they often take a few days just to get the claim reported and set up.

- ✔ When reporting the accident, get the other driver's insurance company's okay to pay for a rental car. If it balks and you need a rental, get one anyway and let the insurer know about it. Why? Because when it's paying for a rental car, it speeds up your claim processing. Without a rental car, its slow processing hurts you; with a rental, delays hurt it. If the accident is the other guy's fault, his insurance owes you both for the cost to repair you car plus the cost of a replacement vehicle. Some insurance companies claim they don't cover your rental. That's baloney. If the company balks, send the bill directly to the other driver.

Gathering the facts you need at the accident scene

Standing at the scene of an accident is pretty traumatic if you were involved. Remembering to gather all the information that might be helpful is next to impossible. (Someone rear-ended me once, and darned if I didn't overlook getting the names of two witnesses standing 20 feet away!)

I've included a Claims Information Form in the Appendix. This form will help you remember what information you need to get at the scene of the accident. Make copies and always keep one in the glove box of each vehicle.

The list explains the importance of each section in the Claims Information Form. Hopefully, your claim will go smoothly and you won't need some of this information. But if anything goes wrong, you'll be glad that you've got it.

- **Accident location.** So your insurance company can investigate the accident scene

- **Police information.** So your insurance company can obtain a copy of the police report and speak with the right officer

- **The other vehicle's driver's information.** Who to go after, if it was his fault, and who to pay, if it was yours

- **Other vehicle's owner.** The owner's insurance is the insurance policy you would collect from first; the driver's is secondary

- **Injuries.** Who needs to be contacted about medical payments/personal injury coverage. If you're at fault, who may be a possible lawsuit threat so claims people can make a quick positive contact

- **Witnesses.** Important if it's not your fault to help you or your insurance company collect against the other driver or to support your version of the accident if you are sued but the accident wasn't your fault

- **Your passengers.** Possible witnesses and/or possible injuries

- **The other driver's passengers.** For possible injury claims

Deciding when it's best to use your Collision coverage

As a rule, if your damage is caused by the other driver and you have Collision coverage, collect from your own coverage, especially if your car is not drivable. You are their customer. Your company will almost always be faster and easier to deal with. And, unlike the other driver's insurance company, your claim won't be delayed for an investigation. Collision insurance pays to repair your car if it's damaged in an accident, regardless of who's at fault. Also, you will spend less in the long run, in spite of your Collision deductible, in states where *subrogation* (defined in the sidebar) and *comparative negligence* (defined in the following section) are allowed.

Subrogation (Sub-ro-what?)

You're in a wreck. Another driver caused the accident, but you choose to have your insurance, under Collision coverage, pay for the damage to your vehicle. Your legal rights to seek reimbursement from the other driver are transferred to your insurance company. This transfer of rights is known as *subrogation*. Your company gets compensated by the other driver's company.

When your insurance company subrogates against the other driver, it usually attempts to get your deductible reimbursed too, saving you a lot of hassle. For various reasons, it often collects less than 100 percent of the amount that it spent fixing your car. Whatever percentage it collects, you get the same percentage of your deductible back. The bad news is that the collection process often takes six months or more. So when you spend your deductible, don't look for the cash to come back to you any time soon.

Understanding comparative negligence

Most states use *comparative negligence* to apportion fault in an auto accident. It takes into account the fact that not all accidents are 100 percent the fault of only one driver. If you rear end someone who is sitting at a red light, you probably would be assessed 100 percent of the fault. If you pull from a stop sign into the side of a passing car, you might be assigned 85 percent of the fault. (Fifteen percent would go to the other driver.) The percentage of fault assessed the lesser at-fault driver depends on how much opportunity that driver had or should have had to avoid the accident. There's no hard and fast rule about fault. I only mention comparative negligence so that you're aware of it if it comes up in your claim discussions when attempting to collect from the other driver's insurance company.

If you live in a comparative negligence state, you're almost always better off to use your Collision coverage, pay your deductible, and let your insurance company subrogate against the other driver or insurance company.

If you have Collision coverage in a comparative negligence state, always use the coverage and pay your deductible unless the other driver is 100 percent at-fault. After subrogation, your net cost will always be less than collecting directly from the other driver's insurance. Plus, your claim will be handled much faster and smoother.

Of course, if you don't have Collision coverage or your damage is less than your deductible, you have no choice but to collect from the other driver's insurance company.

Navigating the Total-Loss Maze

One of the most difficult claims for an insurance adjuster to settle to a customer's complete satisfaction occurs in a *total-loss claim,* where the cost to repair the car exceeds the car's value. Here are some of the more common problems that occur in a total loss, with suggestions on how you can protect yourself or better your settlement. See the sidebar, "Determining if a car is totaled," for more information.

Getting more than the book value for your car

If your car is a total loss, the retail value of your car at the time of loss needs to be established. *Book value* is the average selling price of a car like yours, with similar features and mileage, in a cleaned up, dent-free condition. Various used car guides list these prices.

You should know three things about book value:

- ✔ It's the *average* selling price for a car like yours. Which means there were plenty of cars that sold for more — some even much more. Your mint car could be one of those. Of course, the reverse could also be true.

- ✔ It's a guide. It says so right on the cover. Not a bible.

- ✔ It doesn't always take into account the supply and demand factors in your particular area. A sports car in Alaska might not be worth as much as a sports car in Los Angeles.

For all these reasons, the book value will be different than your specific car's preaccident market value. (You can check out the blue book at www.kellybluebook.com.)

Understanding the fair and proper way to establish your car's value

The value of your car is what you would have to pay to replace it with a car almost exactly like yours. Therefore, your insurance company needs to check with used-car dealers to see what price your car, preaccident, would sell for. Push the insurance company to get at least three estimates from local dealers. (But be warned: The dealers may give the company a price that's *lower* than the book value.)

TECHNICAL STUFF

Determining if a car is totaled

Your insurance company must determine three values before concluding that your car is a total loss. They calculate the value of your car at the time of the accident, the total cost to repair your vehicle, and the amount a salvage yard would pay for your car.

Your car is a total loss if the repair cost exceeds the car's preaccident value minus any salvage value. For example, take your 1995 Taurus. Its preaccident value was $5,300 and the repair estimate is $4,800. (At this point, it seems like the insurer is $500 better-off repairing your car. But now factor in salvage value.) The salvage company bid is $ 850. The insurance company will

total out your car because their net cost to do so is $5,300 (paid to you) less $850 (from the salvage company). It ends up losing $4,450, which is $350 less than the $4,800 it would have had to pay to fix the car.

Now suppose the repair estimate was only $4,000. The insurance company would probably still total it, because of *hidden damage*. Most estimates to repair seriously damaged cars underestimate the final costs because all the damage can't be seen until repairs are started and the outer parts removed. What starts out looking like a $4,000 repair often ends up costing closer to $5,000 or $6,000.

Discovering how you can improve the insurance company's offer

Here is something you can do to assure you get the best settlement offer you can. Check with at least three dealers yourself. Clip out any newspaper used-car ads for cars similar to yours. When you call dealers, talk only to the used-car manager, whose opinion will carry more weight than a salesman's. Then write down the manager's name, the dealership's name, the manager's phone number, and his estimate of what hc would sell your car for. See Table 13-1 for an example. (If your car is really mint and you have good photos, I would recommend a personal visit to the dealership. The photos will help you get a higher estimate.)

Table 13-1	Determining the Preaccident Value of My 1996 Ford Taurus		
Dealer Name	*Used Car Manager*	*Value Range*	*Average Value*
Northern Ford	Cindy Peterson	$5,150–$5,450	$5,300
Central Ford	Marilyn Peterson	$5,425	$5,425
Gerald Ford	Buck Peterson	$5,350–$5,600	$5,475
Average preaccident value:			$5,400

Next, average those three estimates and any newspaper prices to come up with your own estimate of your car's preaccident value. Then sit on it. When the adjuster makes you an offer, if it's equal to or greater than your average estimate, smile at your good fortune. If the offer is less than yours, pull your information out and insist that either he accept your number or at the very least average your number with his. If he balks at that, enlist the aid of your agent if you have one.

When you buy a car, you also have to pay sales tax, title fees, and so on. Be sure that the insurance company pays you for all those added costs. And don't forget the prorated share of your license plate fee, based on the number of months until your plates would have renewed.

In a total loss situation where the accident was caused by the other driver and where your car won't be repaired, I recommend simultaneously filing a claim with the other driver's insurance and your own Collision coverage. By filing both claims, you will get two offers for the value of your car. Take the highest one.

Keeping your car after it's been totaled

Suppose you have a nice car. It's your baby. You've cared for it. Maintained it. Changed the oil every 3,000 miles. It's been a great car. Suddenly, it's in an accident. The front end is banged up and needs new parts — but it can be repaired and be as good as new. But your insurance company won't pay for repairs. They're calling it a total loss and offering you $5,300 for your baby. You protest, but the repair estimate is $5,800 — plus possible hidden damage. You're heartbroken. Is there anything you can do?

Yes, even though the insurance company won't generally volunteer this fact. You can accept the $5,300 (less your deductible) and keep the car by paying the insurance company what they would have received from the salvage yard, say $500. You now still own your banged-up car and have $4,800 you can use toward repairs. You then can either not repair all the damage, or do what most people do — find a quality, small shop who, with the aid of used parts, can probably repair the entire car for $4,800 or less. Remember this strategy. It really works.

Understanding the quirks of stolen car claims

A stolen car is deemed a total loss if it's not recovered. But the majority of stolen cars are recovered, usually with damage. If that happens to you, remember that, even though your car was in a collision, the initial cause of loss was theft. Therefore, you will owe your theft rather than your Collision deductible. It's usually lower.

Saving J. P.'s Honda

A few years ago, my 19-year-old son, J. P., stumbled across a treasure of a used car that he fell in love with — a 1982 Limited Edition Honda Accord. Very few were made. For a 1982 model, it was pretty neat — leather seats, power sunroof, and absolutely mint in condition. We paid $3,200 for the car.

Just a few months later, he drove the car into a post, pushing the front end of the car in and even damaging the radiator. The repair estimate was over $4,000 — with used parts. It had to be totaled. He was heartbroken. We knew we'd never find another car in that condition and with those features for that price.

So we kept the car and were paid, after subtracting the deductible and a $300 salvage value, about $2,500. We networked and located a small, family-owned shop in Excelsior, Minnesota, who had compassion for J. P. The owner located a front-end clip from a used Honda in a nearby salvage yard — bumper, headlights, radiator, hood, and both fenders — for only $600. He then cut off our damaged front end, welded on the replacement, and primed the hood and fenders, all for $2,500! J. P. was thrilled. (The shop agreed to paint the finish coat when J. P. raised another $400.)

Also, because the insurance company doesn't want to pay you for your car and then have it be recovered, it typically will wait to settle as long as three to four weeks. Even if you don't have loss of use coverage (car rental), because of this added wait, most policies will pay something (usually $15 a day) toward your cost of renting a car, starting 48 to 72 hours after you report the claim. Remember that in case the company forgets to offer it to you.

Resolving Claim Disputes

If your auto damage claim is unjustly denied, go to your agent for help. Many agents have the expertise and skills to be an effective advocate for your rights, and often succeed in getting your claim paid. But if that fails, you can mediate, arbitrate, or even sue your insurance company. (See Chapter 14 for more on those options.)

But what if the adjuster agrees that you are covered but disputes the amount of your claim? Fortunately, your policy has a simple, inexpensive solution built into the policy provisions — the *appraisal clause.*

Virtually every personal policy — auto, home, boat, and so on — contains an appraisal clause. Few people know of it. Fewer people use it. Discover here how to use it if you and your insurance company ever don't agree on how much your claim is worth. Use it *only* after the best attempts of you and your agent to settle the claim for a fair amount have failed.

Understanding how the appraisal clause works

Either you or your insurance company may request an appraisal if you fail to agree on the dollar value of a covered claim. If you're requesting one, you simply send the insurance company a letter with your request.

Each party picks an appraiser to represent their position. The two appraisers independently choose a disinterested umpire to resolve things if the two appraisers can't reach an agreement. Each party pays for their own appraiser and splits other appraisal expenses (including the umpire's cost, if needed).

The good news is that you aren't forced to accept the insurance company's offer. Also, the process is considerably cheaper and faster than lawsuits or arbitration.

A cheaper, simpler, and faster alternative

For *most* property valuation disputes, you don't need an elaborate group of three solemn judges. You just need a fair, unbiased, and disinterested person with excellent knowledge regarding the subject of the dispute — someone both parties are comfortable with. So my recommendation to you and your insurance company is to dispense with the two appraisers and just mutually agree on an umpire who will rule on the settlement amount. Both parties agree to abide by the umpire's decision.

Chapter 14

Getting What You Deserve at Property Claim Time

The most important event in a good Homeowners claim settlement occurs before the claim. I'm talking about setting up the right policy limits and the right policy endorsements. When people are unhappy with the way their claim is treated, it's almost always because they bought the wrong coverage. Choose the right agent, and choose the right coverages. Even the best insurance companies don't pay you for something you didn't have insured. (See Chapters 5, 6, and 7 on Homeowners coverage and Chapter 12 on choosing an agent.)

Understanding Structural Damage Claims

What you hope for when your home or garage is damaged or destroyed is that your insurance company will pay you enough to replace what you had. If you set up the right coverage, your policy will do exactly that. Here are some of the problems you may encounter, and tips on protecting yourself.

Contesting depreciation deductions

People think the Homeowners policy pays to rebuild structural damage, regardless of the age or condition of the damaged structural parts. This is a myth. Almost every Homeowners policy pays for the damage on a used or depreciated basis. If, and only if, you insure your home for approximately its replacement cost as a new home do you get paid the full replacement cost of the damage to your home. Essentially, the usual Homeowners policy says:

"We'll pay you in the same manner you insure your home. If you insure for the replacement cost, we'll pay replacement. If you insure based on its used value, we'll pay for the used value of the damage — the value after depreciation."

Homeowners policies allow you to underinsure your home by up to 20 percent, and they still pay the full replacement cost of the claim for partial damage to your structure. If you miss by more than 20 percent, you'll risk facing depreciation deductions. What about when you, in good faith, honestly attempt to insure for the replacement cost new and the adjuster at claim time argues you fall short and wants to deduct depreciation from your claim offer? What can you do?

Suppose your home is damaged by a fire, and the full replacement cost is $100,000. Suppose you had, in good faith, talked to a Realtor or a builder who estimated the cost to rebuild — when you bought the house — at $350,000. You insured it for that amount. Now, suppose that the claims adjuster estimates the actual cost to rebuild — at the time of loss — at $500,000. Because the difference between the amount for which you've insured the house and the amount to rebuild it is more than 20 percent, the adjuster is offering less than the $100,000 replacement cost of your claim. What can you do?

You can avoid the penalty in the following ways:

- ✔ Contest the adjuster's replacement estimate. Adjusters are human. They make mistakes. Request a copy of the computation and check it for accuracy. Sometimes all that's needed is to correct the data and thus lower the adjuster's replacement estimate to within the acceptable range. If the new estimate for the cost to replace the house is $420,000, you'll be within the 20 percent mark, and you'll have full payment on your $100,000 claim.

- ✔ If contesting the estimate fails, the next step is to put together a credible replacement cost estimate of your own. Your agent may do one for you. Or you could pay a credible builder to do one. (Or you can do one on the Web — see Chapter 20.)

✔ If you have a home loan, use the appraisal you paid for when you bought and financed the house. "But," you protest, "that was an appraisal for the market value, not the replacement cost." True. But almost every loan appraisal includes an estimate of the cost, new, as well. If the bank appraisal is older, adjust the value for inflation. Or simply call the appraiser who did the appraisal and pay for an updated value. The insurance company may even pick up the cost.

The bottom line? If you can't find fault with the adjuster's replacement cost worksheet measurements and home features, then you need to come up with a credible replacement cost of your own. If you do that, and if the source of the estimate is reliable, there aren't many adjusters who won't give you the benefit of the doubt and pay your claim in full. But if they don't, at least you have a leg to stand on to further contest the issue with the help of your agent in court.

Appraisals done for home loan purposes are always conservative. Never insure for less than the loan appraisal replacement estimate, adjusted for inflation.

Don't ever accept a depreciation penalty for underinsuring your home. Always contest.

Don't mess with Mom

Over the years, I've insured hundreds of homes. I've helped clients estimate the replacement cost of the home, new, for every house. I use three different replacement cost estimates to be as accurate as possible. My files contain lots of ammunition to help my clients avoid depreciation penalties at claim time.

As a result, every covered claim for over 25 years — storm, water damage, fire or smoke, and so on — has been paid with no deduction for depreciation. Every claim except one, that is. Guess who the claims adjuster was trying hit with a 30 percent depreciation penalty? My own

parents! The adjuster didn't even have the courtesy to call me first.

I requested a copy of his figures. They were so inaccurate I could hardly believe it. He had the wrong square footage. He had the house rated as a full two-story, when it was a tri-level (meaning it had three half-stories). He didn't deduct a built-in, unfinished garage. When I politely pointed out the errors and he still balked at revising his estimate, I went to his supervisor, showed her the accurate information, and the claim was paid in full. A year later, they fired him.

Coping with the matching problem

On May 15, 1998, the Minneapolis/St. Paul area was hit with the worst hail storm ever recorded here. In fact, it was the worst storm of any on record for the state of Minnesota. It lasted only 15 minutes, but it caused $500 million dollars in damage to cars and homes. There was a lot of unhappiness from that storm due to matching problems — especially with older homes.

The hail typically damaged half a roof, or two of the four walls of a house. But new shingles often didn't match an old, discontinued color. And siding from ten years ago wasn't made anymore, so the new, replacement siding didn't match the color or design of the siding on the undamaged walls.

Homeowners policies require the insurance company to repair or replace only the damaged area. Period. It's hardly their fault that a type of roof tile or siding isn't made anymore. And if they had to pay for an entire roof or re-side an entire house every time a few shingles blew off or a few siding panels were dented, Homeowners insurance rates would skyrocket. Most insurance companies didn't pay for replacing the undamaged areas just so it all matched. Lots of folks — especially those with older roofs or siding, for which the matching problem is worse — were pretty unhappy.

Insurance policies are supposed to make the customer whole. Having a hodge-podge of different roof tiles or two different sets of siding hardly restored the customer's home to what it had been before the loss. There was no joy in Mudville. If you ever have a structural damage claim where the repaired area won't match the rest of the house, here's how I suggest you proceed.

Using the Pair and Set clause

There is a little-known, seldom-used clause in the back pages of every Homeowners policy called the *Pair and Set* clause. It's used primarily to help settle personal property claims involving damage to one or more of a set of items (one shoe, one stereo speaker, one diamond earring, and so on) where the remaining item of the set is worth less because of the loss of one of the members. The clause recognizes the unfairness of paying for just one shoe or one earring. The other shoe or other earring loses value, too, without a mate.

The Pair and Set clause provides that if the damaged or lost item cannot be replaced exactly and the set, as a whole, is therefore lower in value, the insurance company must pay the difference. Assume you have a set of ten collectible dishes. The set is worth $6,000. You prominently display just one dish, and keep the other nine safely stored away. The dish you display is stolen. The exact dish can't be replaced and, without the dish, the set of nine is now worth only $3,000. Applying the Pair and Set clause, the insurance company owes you the $3,000 drop in the total value of the set, even though the lost plate itself may have been worth only $600 if you had tried to sell it.

Applying the Pair and Set clause to structural losses

It's obvious that roof shingles are part of a set and that siding panels are also. Using the Pair and Set clause, if some pieces of the set of roofing or siding panels are damaged and can't be matched, the insurance company would owe more than just replacing the damaged area with something that doesn't match the undamaged area. It would owe the difference in value, before and after the loss. It's not any more fair to put on mismatched shingles than it is to pay for a new plate that doesn't match the rest of the set.

So how do you determine the value of a set of roof shingles before and after a loss? You determine the replacement cost, new, of the shingles, less depreciation based on their life expectancy — an equitable system.

If you have math allergies, it's not important that you know the details of Pair and Set computations. But it is important to remember that a clause in your Homeowners policy may help you collect more than just the replacement cost of your damaged roof or siding if the new materials don't match the old materials.

Negotiating Hassle-Free Structural Claims Settlements

When damage is done to your home, a great insurance settlement would be where you close your eyes, turn around three times, and then open your eyes to a home without damages and with all the repairs paid for. That's the kind of service you expect after paying those insurance premiums, right? Unfortunately, the claims process doesn't involve magic. It's often slow and difficult. Here are some tips for keeping it moving smoothly.

Understanding how claims get mishandled

Here's how a typical Homeowners structure damage claim gets handled. The adjuster inspects the damage, writes a repair estimate, and sends the estimate and check, less the deductible, to the homeowner. The homeowner may be pleased to have the claim settled so quickly. Then she tries to find a contractor to do the work for the adjuster's price — especially difficult after a storm has pushed up the costs of labor and materials. She can't find anyone who will agree to do the repairs for the amount of money that her insurance has provided. Unfortunately, this problem occurs far too often.

What can you do if you're in a situation like this, where the adjuster's estimate and check are well below what a contractor wants for the job? How do you get the contractor to bend? How do you get the adjuster to pay more?

Understanding your rights

The "full cost to repair or replace the damage" — that's what your policy says the insurance company has to pay you. Not the amount an insurance adjuster *thinks* the repair should cost. Not what a contractor would like to charge. You're owed the actual repair or replacement cost. The insurance adjuster and the contractor who will be doing the repairs need to agree on what that price is. These two parties need to meet at the site and hammer out a price that they both can agree to.

When you settle a home structural damage claim, be sure that your preferred contractor agrees, beforehand, to do the repairs for the amount the insurance company is offering.

Following seven steps to a great settlement

Here are seven steps you can take to assure a fast and fair settlement, and to stay out of disputes on home structural claims:

1. **Get estimates.**

   If you don't already have a chosen contractor, get repair estimates from at least two contractors who have been recommended to you. Interview the contractors. You're not looking for the lowest bid. You want the best workmanship. (You can often tell a lot about the quality of the contractor by the quality and professionalism of the estimate.) I recommend using reputable, local contractors — watch out for out-of-town journeymen who flock to storms in hopes of a good payday. The locals are much more likely to be around to stand behind their work if a problem arises later.

2. **Choose your preferred contractor.**

   Check references. Get proof of liability insurance and Workers' Compensation insurance. (If they don't have both coverages, you're more vulnerable to claims brought against you for job-site injuries. Plus, if a repair fails and later causes injuries or property damage to your home or your family, you can go after the contractor's liability insurance company.) Then listen to your gut and pick the contractor who feels the most comfortable. It doesn't have to be the contractor with the lowest bid. After all, you have to live with the repairs. Most adjusters will work with the contractor you prefer, as long as the prices are reasonable.

3. **Don't allow solo inspections or estimates.**

   Don't agree to your insurance adjuster inspecting your home alone. Do not agree to the adjuster writing his own estimate. Without an agreed-on

price, the estimate is worthless, so don't allow him to waste his time —
or yours.

4. Connect the two parties.

Tell the adjuster the name and mobile phone number of your contractor.
Also share the adjuster's name and mobile phone number, and the claim
number, with the contractor. Then request — insist — that they call
each other to arrange a meeting at your home for the purpose of jointly
agreeing on the amount of damage and on an acceptable repair cost.

5. Don't sweat the dollar amount.

Don't worry if the agreed price is less — even significantly less — than
the contractor's initial bid. That's why adjusters have jobs — to make
sure that repair costs stay reasonable and to keep contractors from writing themselves blank checks.

6. Control additional damage problems up front.

Make sure that when the parties meet initially and agree on a price, they
also agree to work with each other directly if additional damage is discovered — and to keep you out of the middle. Then hold them to that
commitment. Don't let them suck you in. If your contractor calls needing
an okay for additional repairs, insist that he work out permission
directly with the adjuster.

7. Call on your agent.

If you encounter roadblocks or are in danger of pulling your hair out, call
on your agent for help. Part of your agent's job is to go to bat for you at
claim time to help you collect what you deserve.

Getting paid for your sweat

Whether a toilet overflows, a storm damages the roof, or a fire destroys the kitchen, you'll person-ally do some cleanup work — often extensive work. In these situations, most homeowners will spend personal time doing whatever they can to protect their property from further damage. In fact, the policy even requires homeowners to protect their property. If you don't do so, the insurance company doesn't owe you for the addi-tional damage you could have prevented.

Keep track of your time. The insurance company owes you fair compensation for it, up to the amount it would have had to pay a laborer to do the same work. I've hardly ever seen an adjuster tell a homeowner to keep track of the time he or she spends cleaning up after a minor incident or a disaster. A lot of homeowners unknowingly lose out on justifiable compensation.

Managing Additional Living Expense claims

One of the nice features of Homeowners insurance is that it pays not only for damage to your home and personal property but also for the added living expenses that you have to incur if you can't live in the house. You may, temporarily, not be able to live in your home because of the level of dangerous toxins (normally left over from a fire) or the sheer amount of repairs and cleanups that are needed. In the worst case, there is no home left. The additional costs of living and eating out can reach thousands of dollars.

Knowing how the coverage works

The key word is *additional*. The Additional Living Expense (ALE) clause pays reasonable costs for temporary living facilities, moving, furniture and appliance rentals, and meals out as needed. It can even pay for extra gasoline costs. It pays for almost any living expense that truly is additional — it pays for any expense that you wouldn't have had to pay if your home hadn't been damaged. It won't pay your house payment, because that's not an expense you've incurred because of the damage to your home. Any amounts paid are offset against living expenses that are lower, such as the heating and cooling bill being $75 less a month because the house is empty.

ALE pays the difference between your costs that go up and any costs that go down. The goal is to keep your bank account the same as it would have been if the claim had never occurred.

Bob and Bertha's kitchen fire

As I was penning this chapter, Bertha called from a local hotel. She and Bob had been up at their cabin for the weekend. Their 15-year-old daughter stayed home with a friend. Friday night, they went downstairs to play on the computer while dinner was cooking. A while later, the daughter returned upstairs to see smoke billowing from the kitchen and the wood cabinets above the stove on fire. The girls left the house (wisely) and immediately called 911. By the time the firemen got through punching holes in the roof so the smoke could escape and putting out the grease fire, the house was not only badly damaged but totally unlivable — the fumes and the toxic gases that remained after the fire made it impossible to sleep there.

So Bob and Bertha moved their family of five to a nearby residence motel and ate a lot of meals out. Because of Additional Living Expense coverage, Bob and Bertha will be reimbursed for all these expenses. They ended up being out of their home for three months. They collected nearly $40,000 in ALE payments, which made a huge difference for them.

One of the best things about ALE coverage is the impact it has on an adjuster. The adjuster wants to keep ALE expenses low. To do that, she has to get your house repaired and livable again. If she has two structural claims on her desk for the same amount, but one is also accruing $6,000 a month in ALE expenses, she'll take care of that one first.

Staying at Aunt Martha's

Many times, a close family member will put you up while your home is being repaired. You live with them. You eat meals with them. How does ALE coverage work in this situation?

Don't make the mistake that some clients have made of offering to pay Aunt Martha the $150 a day a hotel suite would cost. You won't be reimbursed. What's owed under the policy is all of Aunt Martha's added expenses to have you there — the costs for the extra phone line, the extra groceries, the extra utilities like power and water, even the extra dish and laundry soap. And ALE, no doubt, will pay for a thorough house cleaning when you all leave.

Getting the Most for Your Personal Property Claim

Again, I stress that the most important ingredient of a good claims settlement is getting the right advice and having the proper coverage. Assuming that your claim is, in fact, covered by your Homeowners policy, here are some tips to help you collect the most for your claim.

Understanding how Replacement Cost coverage works

Most Homeowners policies pay for the used or depreciated value of your damaged or stolen belongings. But they also offer an additional cost option called *Replacement Cost* that will pay for the cost — new — on all items you actually replace. The thing to know about this coverage is that to get a payment based on cost new, you must actually replace the item with something comparable (or better, if you want to pay the difference).

If you opted, wisely, to buy Replacement Cost coverage, you'll usually end up getting paid two or more times by the insurance company. The first check pays you for the used or depreciated value of your property. Then, as you replace what you lost, you get additional checks for the difference between the used and the replacement cost.

Don't let the adjuster forget to add sales tax to all payments in states that charge sales tax. It's easy to overlook, but you're definitely entitled to it.

Improving the settlement with your photographic inventory

If you've spent the half-hour it takes to photograph all your belongings and then stored the photos or videotape away from home, you'll have three major benefits at claim time, especially following a burglary or serious fire. (See Chapter 6 for tips on making a good photographic inventory.)

Jogging your memory

You don't get paid for something you don't remember to claim. Imagine returning to your home after a burglary. Rooms ransacked. Stuff missing. Some you remember. The TV. The stereo. Some you don't. The jewelry box. The guitar. The baseball card collection. Some clothing items. You're traumatized and not thinking clearly, and then the police and the insurance adjuster request that you list everything that was stolen. I guarantee you that you won't remember everything. Time to pull your photos out of the safe deposit box.

Documenting your loss

Sometimes a property claim can be a hassle if the adjuster starts asking for proof of purchase, like a receipt or a cancelled check. At best, the experience will be frustrating. At worst, you won't get paid for what you lost. Photos will, mostly, solve this problem too. Most adjusters accept a photo of the item in your home as proof of ownership. Imagine having to prove that you owned a $5,000 antique cherry desk. Having a picture of the desk in your home, covered with your papers, sure would help.

Getting fully paid for treasures

If your special treasure is destroyed or stolen, the burden of proof rests on you to prove what you lost. For example, you have to prove that the $20,000 painting that was stolen was indeed an original — not a $1,500 print. Imagine the potential fraud if adjusters paid these claims without proof. But pulling out the photos and the original receipt or appraisal enables the adjuster to easily pay you the full value. (In fact, by having the photos and bill of sale/ appraisal, the adjuster will even pay for a current value appraisal and pay you that value.) Documentation is everything at claim time!

Collecting faster and better

In sports, they say that the best defense is a good offense. That is certainly true for insurance claims.

If you want to collect top dollar from a busy adjuster for any type of personal property claim, provide solid documentation for the amount you want *before the adjuster prepares an offer to you.* You have a much better chance of getting what you want.

Losing on defense

Here's how a typical personal property claim goes: The adjuster asks you to list what you lost and provide photos, cancelled checks, or receipts. Then the adjuster shops around (which can take weeks) and comes back to you with an offer. It's your move to either accept the offer or contest it. You may want to contest if he's pricing the wrong model of television, computer, or camera. Or the clothing prices he uses are from a discount store. Or he's depreciating your clothing based on a five-year life, when your high-quality clothes had a much longer life.

Most people unhappily take the adjuster's offer, possibly getting him to bend in a few areas. The don't know they have further rights or how to contest the offer. But they do know that once an experienced, knowledgeable adjuster has done his homework, it's difficult to move him from his position. There's a better way.

Winning on offense

Here's how a claim goes when you're in charge. When you do the research. When you request the amount you want and have solid evidence to support it. You use your own inventory form. The one provided by most insurance companies, if they even provide one, is not at all user-friendly, nor is it complete. I include one in the appendix.

It's important you make up your own inventory and calculate what is due to you before the adjuster does any of his own research. Then he is less likely to contest your data. What any adjuster needs to justify paying you what you want for your claim is good documentation from you for his file. The adjuster needs documentation so that when his supervisor wants to know why he paid you those amounts, he has all the information in writing.

The adjuster, upon reviewing your data, will usually do one of two things — pay what you're asking or call you to dicker about a few items ("You've used a 15-year life for clothing. We don't ever allow more than 10 years.") There will be some give and take, but no matter how far he moves you from your position, it won't ever be as far as the offer he would have made to you if he had done the work.

Taking action when the adjuster won't budge

You've tried everything. So has your agent. But the adjuster just won't budge. She continues either to deny your claim or to pay you less than what you think it's worth. Your agent has even appealed to the insurance company claims manager without success. Here are some actions you can take to help resolve your differences:

✔ **The Appraisal clause:** Use this tool when the adjuster agrees that there is coverage but you disagree on the amount due to you — such as when you have a painting stolen and you disagree on the value, or when you can't find a contractor to repair your roof for the amount the adjuster is offering. The Appraisal clause is found in your Homeowners policy and is a relatively inexpensive way to get your dispute resolved fairly. See Chapter 13 for more on how the Appraisal process works.

✔ **Your state insurance department:** All state insurance departments have enforcement departments that help consumers resolve problems they are having with an insurance company, including claim disputes. The good news is that the cost to you is usually free, and the department is often successful. The bad news is that the process can be lengthy — usually requiring a month or more. You can access help either by calling the insurance department directly or by reaching them on the Web (at www.insure.com or www.naic.org). The Web site usually includes a complaint form you fill out and e-mail for faster service. See Chapter 21 for more information.

✔ **Arbitration:** Although they are not required to, most insurance companies will agree to binding arbitration to resolve differences. Contact the local office of the American Arbitration Association, who, upon receipt of your complaint and application fee, will appoint an arbiter. The arbiter will schedule a hearing, hear both sides, and then rule for, against, or somewhere in the middle — but usually only after first attempting to mediate your differences. You and the insurance company split the cost of the arbiter's time. Depending on the complexity and dollar amount involved, you may also have the added cost of hiring your own attorney. Arbitration's major advantages are that it's far cheaper and much faster than most lawsuits.

✔ **Small claims court:** For resolving smaller property claim disputes that qualify, I like small claims court. You generally don't need an attorney, and the cost is minimal. You present your side of things in an informal classroom-like environment. A decision is made in a week or so.

✔ **Litigation:** Anytime you have a dispute with an insurer, you can hire an attorney. Doing so is inexpensive if you just consult for an opinion or have the attorney send a letter to your insurance company on your behalf. But if you end up suing, an attorney can be an expensive option. Before you sue, you may want to consider some of the other less expensive options.

Part VI
Managing Life, Health, and Disability Risks

"Included with today's surgery, we're offering a manicure, pedicure, haircut, and ear wax flush for just $49.95."

In this part . . .

*W*hile sometimes it seems that there could be nothing more catastrophic than losing a home or a family heirloom, there is. Keeping ourselves and our loved ones safe and healthy is the most important thing in the world. If you suffer an injury for which you are unprepared, your financial health can be destroyed in an instant. This part shows you how to avoid suffering such catastrophic financial losses. It also covers life insurance, so that you can be sure to look after your loved ones, even when you're no longer with them.

Chapter 15

Understanding Group Health Insurance

. . . .

. . . .

Major medical costs are one of five types of losses that can cause you or your loved ones major financial hardship — the others being liability for personal injuries, destruction of your home, long-term disability, and premature death. Managing the risk of major medical expenses conscientiously is of great importance. The best way to reduce your chances of encountering ruinous medical costs is to combine good self-care (exercise, diet, stress management, rest, and personal safety) with a solid health insurance plan.

Sometimes, health insurance is provided to people by their employer. Sometimes it's not; you may have to buy coverage personally. And sometimes health insurance is provided through the government (Medicare).

Providing the tools to help you make good health insurance choices, no matter what your age or stage of life, is my objective in this chapter.

Say What? Defining Common Terms

To help you navigate through the pages that lie ahead, here are definitions for some of the insurance terms you meet.

✔ **Copayment:** The dollar amount your health insurance policy requires you to pay toward your bills. Examples of copayments include dollar copayment amounts ($15 for physician visits, $10 for prescription drugs) and percentage copayments (20 percent of your hospital bill).

✔ **Deductible:** The dollar amount of medical bills you personally pay before your health policy kicks in.

✔ **Excess Major Medical policy:** A major medical policy with a very high limit ($2 million, typically) and a high deductible ($5,000 or more) designed to dovetail with your other health insurance policy to cover most of what the other policy doesn't.

✔ **Health maintenance organization (HMO):** An organization set up to provide health care to its members at affordable costs and that puts an emphasis on preventive care. To encourage members to get preventive care, there are usually little or no deductibles or copayments. HMOs usually own their own clinics where the doctors and other medical staff are employees of the HMO. An HMO also sometimes forms a partnership with a local clinic as opposed to owning it outright. HMOs try to provide all the members' care in the clinic and referrals to outside specialists are given sparingly. HMOs operate under a managed care environment. Pure HMOs don't cover nonemergency care outside their own clinics without a referral. In recent years, many HMOs, to compete with insurance companies, now cover care outside the system subject to sizable deductibles and copayments.

✔ **Major medical:** Serious or catastrophic health problems.

✔ **Major medical policy:** A health insurance policy with a policy limit high enough to cover most serious health problems.

✔ **Managed care:** Health insurance coverage in which the decisions about your medical care are subject to your insurance provider's approval, including the type of medical procedures your doctor can use to treat you, what prescription drugs can be used to treat you, and how long you're allowed to remain in the hospital. Its primary purpose is to control costs and keep insurance premiums affordable.

✔ **Out-of-pocket maximum:** An important feature of health insurance policies that limits your annual responsibility for your health insurance policy copayments and deductibles.

✔ **Preferred provider organization (PPO):** Groups of doctors and hospitals that band together and agree to cost and managed-care controls. Formed in an attempt to compete with HMOs, they can be established and controlled either independently or by an insurance company such as Blue Cross. They operate a lot like HMOs except that doctors aren't employees. And they don't own their own clinics. To the average consumer, PPOs and HMOs are indistinguishable.

Discovering What Makes a Great Health Insurance Plan

Facing serious, life-threatening illness is traumatic. I know, I've been there. Everything else you're worrying about in life suddenly becomes unimportant. The only thing that could make it worse is fear about your health insurance coverage. Fear that the escalating bills will exhaust your coverage limit. Fear that the specialist you want to see for your illness isn't approved by your insurance company. Fear that holes in the coverage will leave you personally responsible for huge bills that could wipe out all your savings — and even put you in serious debt. That's why a solid health insurance plan is so important.

An excellent health insurance plan must include five key ingredients:

- ✔ A coverage limit high enough that it won't likely ever be exhausted, even for the most catastrophic medical expenses
- ✔ An annual dollar limit you can live with on your out-of-pocket responsibility
- ✔ No dollar limits on types of expenses, such as dollar limits on daily room charges or dollar limits for types of surgical procedures
- ✔ Freedom to see to specialists without a referral
- ✔ Worldwide coverage

Do most plans meet all five criteria? Nope. I estimate that less than half of the individual and group health plans sold in the United States include all five elements that a great health insurance plan must include.

Your plan should include all five of the crucial ingredients because you want a plan that won't, even in the worst case, cause you major financial hardship — and a plan that lets you choose the most skilled care provider, especially in serious or life-threatening situations, such as treating your 6-year-old's leukemia, surgically removing your spouse's brain tumor, or performing several skin grafting operations after you've been badly burned.

Determining a high coverage maximum

When I started selling insurance in the 1970s, health insurance policy limits were a whopping $10,000 per claim. Policies were available that provided up to an additional $25,000 in coverage. My clients could sleep well with $35,000 in total coverage. Today, that same peace of mind requires at least a $1 million coverage limit.

Policy limits come in two varieties:

- ✔ A dollar maximum *per claim*
- ✔ A dollar maximum *per lifetime*

The per-claim maximum is the most the insurance company will spend for any single illness or injury. If your limit is $1 million, for example, your policy will pay up to $1 million for your injuries in a recent car accident, and then up to another million for next year's cancer, and another million for the following year's Parkinson's.

Lifetime limits are more common, where every dollar spent this year reduces the limit available for future years. If your lifetime limit is $1 million, your $275,000 car accident bill reduces your lifetime limit to $775,000. Then your $150,000 cancer bill reduces the $775,000 lifetime limit to $625,000, and so on.

When buying health insurance, I strongly recommend a maximum policy limit of at least $1 million per claim or $2 million per lifetime. (Or a policy with no limits at all, if you can find one.)

If your coverage is provided by your employer and has only a $500,000 lifetime limit, I recommend a personal supplemental major medical policy (sometimes referred to as an *Excess Major Medical* policy) with the highest possible deductible to keep costs down. This supplement dovetails with your other insurance to plug gaps for more serious medical problems you might have.

Capping your out-of-pocket costs

Most health insurance plans contain some kind of copayment on your part. Perhaps you have a copay per visit, such as $15 for each office visit or $40 if you go to the emergency room. Perhaps you have a deductible of $500 a year before your coverage kicks in (meaning that you pay the first $500 of your medical expenses each year). Or perhaps your policy pays 80 percent of all covered medical bills, with you responsible for the other 20 percent.

Paying the per-visit copays or the deductible usually isn't a hardship. But paying 20 percent of all your major medical bills in one year, without any limit on the possible amount of your contribution, easily can be. If you have a baby who's born three months early and who needs pediatric intensive care for a long period of time, your bill could run $200,000; your 20 percent copay would be $40,000. If your baby needs surgeries, your bill could jump to $500,000, and your 20 percent copay would be $100,000! That's too big a risk for almost anyone to assume.

When buying health insurance that contains a percentage copayment, make sure that the policy includes an annual maximum that's reasonable for your out-of-pocket expenses. For example, a 20 percent copay on the first $5,000 in expenses you have for the year is a $1,000 cap — with the insurer paying 100 percent of the bills the rest of the year.

If you have group coverage from your employer that has no cap on the 20 percent copayment, you have a couple of options. If you work for a large employer, you often have more than one plan to choose from. See if another plan has a cap. Otherwise, buy a personal Excess Major Medical policy with a large deductible. This policy typically pays 80 percent of your 20 percent copayment responsibility. For example, if your medical bills are $100,000, your 20 percent copayment is $20,000. A personal excess policy paying 80 percent of your copayment would pay $16,000 of the $20,000. It may even share paying 100 percent of the bill with your group insurance company, with nothing owed on your part.

Avoiding internal policy limits

A good health insurance policy has only one policy limit — either a limit per claim or per lifetime. It contains no other dollar limitations. Many mediocre policies contain internal limits such as

- ✔ $100 a day for room and board
- ✔ $200 a day for intensive care
- ✔ Dollar limits on surgeries ($2,000 for an appendectomy, $16,000 for quadruple bypass surgery, and so on)

Even if the limits are adequate today (and most aren't), in four to five years, given the rapid pace of medical cost inflation, you may end up getting only half your bill paid.

Avoid like the plague any health insurance policy that contains internal policy limits on room and board, surgeries, or anything else.

If you have a group plan with internal limits from your employer, buy an Excess Major Medical policy with a large deductible that has no internal limits to pick up most of the shortcomings of the group plan.

Avoiding having to beg to see specialists

A lot of health care plans (such as many HMOs or PPOs) offer lower costs but take away your right to decide what kind of treatment you can get and whom you can get it from. Essentially, you agree to get all your primary care from a small list of approved clinics where costs can be controlled more easily. You agree to seeing a specialist only if your primary physician will refer you out (which means "referral begging" to you). Finally, you agree to give the insurance company the final say on what type of procedure or treatment you can have. That's a lot to give up for a savings of about 15 percent on your premiums.

See Table 15-1 for an example of how choice versus managed care works for your 6-year-old child who's ill with leukemia. The table does overstate the differences. Many times, the treatment and results will be the same. But sometimes they won't be. The question is who gets to make the care decisions — you and your doctor or someone else? When my loved ones or I have a serious or life-threatening illness, I want the best care and the latest technology. I don't want to beg for what's best.

Table 15-1	Managed Care versus Freedom-of-Choice	
	Managed Care	*Freedom-of-Choice*
Diagnosis	Primary care family doctor suspects leukemia. Runs diagnostic tests with objective of keeping treatment in-house as long as possible.	Your top pediatrician suspects leukemia.
Referral	You request a referral to a specific pediatric oncologist who was recommended to you. Referral denied. You are referred to a different oncologist who may be less skilled but has agreed to accept managed care's lower fee schedule.	Your doctor immediately refers you to a top pediatric oncologist who uses state-of-the-art testing methods.
Care	The leukemia is confirmed. The oncologist treats your son with traditional methods. You request a referral to the top oncologist at world famous Mayo Clinic, which is denied because Mayo isn't an approved provider.	The leukemia is confirmed. You call Mayo Clinic directly and arrange to have your son's ongoing treatment done there. No approval needed. Mayo uses the newest (and most expensive) procedures.
Results	?	Success. Your son is cured.

 If your employer-provided group plan doesn't offer choice, you can obtain an individual Major Medical policy with a moderately high deductible. If you don't like your choices under managed care, you go see whomever you want and pay just your deductible.

Avoiding having limited or no coverage when away from home

Many managed care plans don't cover outside your home territory, except for emergencies. Here are two stories from my own client files:

Managed care worth considering

In recent years, a managed care hybrid plan has emerged. It's a two-tiered system. Tier one is managed care. When I go to my chosen primary doctor, I get almost 100 percent coverage — even if I see a specialist, if it's a referral from my primary doctor. Tier two is freedom-of-choice.

I can go to almost anyone. Any specialist — no referrals needed. I just have to chip in on the extra cost (a $300 deductible, plus 20 percent of the bill). When something serious is going on, the extra out-of-pocket expenses for the freedom-of-choice are worth every penny.

✔ Lee just bought a winter vacation condo in Arizona. (Why anyone would want to flee Minnesota's winter wonderland of ice, snow, and below-zero temperatures is beyond me.) Checking the Medicare supplement policy he owned from a local HMO, he discovered that there was no coverage for anything but emergency care outside Minnesota — a real problem for someone living five months of each year outside the state. Luckily, we moved his coverage to another Medicare supplement policy that gave him greater freedom-of-choice before anything serious happened.

✔ Jim and Jane's daughter, Angela, was attending college out east. She fell and injured a knee. The emergency care was covered by their HMO policy, but follow-up care with physical therapists was not covered at all. It turns out that their truly excellent choice product has one major flaw: For anyone residing out-of-state part of the year, non-emergency care isn't covered!

Make sure that your policy covers you worldwide for nonemergency care. If it doesn't, either replace it or buy a supplemental policy that provides the coverage. Higher copayments for care given out-of-state are fine, as long as you have coverage.

Avoiding insurance plans that require you to file claims

Okay, this one's not important enough to have made the list of five crucial ingredients to a great health care program. But a sixth ingredient exists: paperless claims. Some choice plans are so independent of doctors and hospitals that all bills are sent to you rather than the insurance company, which can be a nightmare. Try to avoid plans that require you to do tons of paperwork every time you have a claim.

Freedom's just another word for . . .

A few years ago, I had a true freedom-of-choice plan. The plan had no networks of doctors or hospitals to go to. I could go anywhere in the world and get any care I wanted. Just one problem, as it turned out. I had to file every medical claim myself — and had to make copies, fill out claim forms, send duplicates when originals were lost, and call and haggle with the claims adjuster when they paid less than I expected. For my family of four, I was averaging three hours a month of stressful, hair-pulling time — every single month. I did this for two years until I couldn't stand another minute.

True freedom-of-choice was killing me. I surrendered and switched to a "near-freedom-of-choice" product, where 90 percent of doctors and hospitals countrywide file claims directly to the company for me, and I never see a bill. I can still go to the other 10 percent if I want to file my own claims, but I never do that. How much time do I spend on claims now? One hour a year! I can live with that.

Making Good Decisions Regarding Group Health Insurance

Having group health insurance can be difficult. There's no agent in your corner who can help you with problems. The insurance company can answer questions, but it can't give advice. Without good information and advice, it's easy to make a serious mistake. These are just a few of the kinds of questions I get from my clients about their group insurance programs:

- Should I cover my spouse under my group insurance even though she's covered on her own policy at her job?

- How can I, as a single parent, avoid paying for a nonexistent spouse under the group family rate?

- I'm between jobs. Should I exercise my COBRA rights or buy an individual policy now?

- Should I insure my college daughter on my group plan if she buys the school health insurance coverage?

- I have three different group plans to choose from at work. Which is best for me?

The following sections give you some tips on making good decisions on these and other issues.

Making the best choice when your employer offers two or more plans

I often get calls from clients who want help choosing among group insurance options offered to them at work. Having multiple options is especially common with large employers or the government. If your employer offers more than one group health insurance option, I recommend that you

- ✔ Consider price last (unless your finances are in poor condition).

- ✔ List the five ingredients of a good health insurance plan from the beginning of this chapter and see how the insurance options you have to choose from compare. Hopefully at least one of the available plans includes all five ingredients. If it does, take that one.

  If two or more include all five ingredients, choose the one that also has paperless claims (meaning the doctors and hospitals file the claims directly to the insurance company). If two or more plans also offer paperless claims, then, and only then, decide on price.

Suppose your employer offers these three choices for group health plans for your family of four:

- ✔ Option A is a true freedom-of-choice plan where you can go anywhere you want for care. The only drawback is that you have to file your own claims. Your monthly cost is $750.

- ✔ Option B is a limited choice managed care plan. It meets only one of the five key criteria of a good plan — it has a limit on annual out-of-pocket expenses. Its only advantage is low cost — $475 per month.

- ✔ Option C is a hybrid of A and B. You can get care anywhere without a referral. Its only drawback is that if you go outside the rather substantial primary care network (86 percent of the doctors in the state), you'll face a $300 deductible and probably will have to file your own claim. Your cost is $650 per month.

If these were your choices, you'd choose Option B only if, due to poor finances, price was all-important. It meets only one of the five criteria of a good plan.

You'd choose Option A if access to any doctor anywhere was worth the extra $1,200 a year and you could stand to file your own claims.

Personally, I would choose Option C. (In fact, these were my choices, and I did choose C.) It meets all five criteria of a good plan. And claims are paperless. I'm comfortable with the doctors who are available to me, and I can actually go to any other doctor if I'm okay with higher copays and filing my own claims.

To help you make a good decision, I put together a Health Insurance Comparison form, which you can find in the appendix. If, after completing the form, you're still unclear about what choice to make, consider consulting with a good insurance agent you know — perhaps the agent who helped you with your life insurance. If you bring the completed form, you won't need to buy a lot of the agent's time.

Deciding how best to cover your spouse and dependents

The following list includes some of the issues I get asked about regarding how best to cover family members — and my recommendations:

- **Double-covering a spouse.** The question of whether to cover a spouse under your plan as well as under your spouse's comes up most often when each spouse has coverage paid entirely by their own employer and one of the two employers also pays all or most of the spouse's and dependents' coverage.

  Do not double-cover your spouse. When two companies insure the same person, you can't collect twice, so claims are shared or fought over. It becomes a claims nightmare. So don't do it — unless you're a nightmare kind of person. Instead, choose the plan that best meets the five criteria of a good health insurance plan.

- **Covering children when both spouses have a group plan.** Where to cover the children — under your plan or your spouse's? In this situation, you weigh out-of-pocket costs in premiums, copayments, and deductibles against the coverage of each plan. These out-of-pocket costs can be dramatically different. But again, choose the plan that covers the five criteria best. Price should be the least important part of the decision. (Use the Health Insurance Comparison Form in the Forms Directory to compare your choices.)

  When choosing which plan is best, don't minimize how important the ability to choose top specialists will be if one of your precious ones is facing a serious illness or injury.

- **Avoiding the single parent penalty.** The most equitable group plans charge a price per head. So if you're a single parent, you don't pay for a nonexistent spouse. Or if you're childless, you don't pay for nonexistent children. But it doesn't always work that way. Sometimes group insurance offers only two choices — individual and family. Family includes husband, wife, and all children for one price. But family also includes single parent families and childless families. If your family is small, you pay the same amount as a person with a very large family.

Here's how you can avoid paying for nonexistent family members, assuming that your dependents are in good health:

- Accept the group coverage on yourself because the employer is footing at least part of the cost.

- Buy a quality individual policy on your dependents.

If even one of your dependents has a health problem that would make him or her ineligible for individual coverage, bite the bullet and pay the family rate at work to get your dependent covered.

Continuing Coverage When You Leave Your Job

Since 1985, the federal government has taken steps to allow employees and dependents to continue their health insurance when they would otherwise have lost it due to terminated employment, divorce, and other life events. The government's goal has been to try to make group health insurance portable, especially for those whose medical history would not allow them to qualify for individual health policies. Discover in this section two federal laws that may give you some insurance continuation rights when you lose your group health coverage, as well as advice as to when to exercise those rights.

Understanding COBRA

COBRA — the Consolidated Omnibus Budget Reduction Act of 1985 (a mouthful!) — gives employees of companies that employ 20 or more people the right to continue group medical coverage at their expense when an employer's plan ends, for a period of time — usually 18 months or 36 months — if the employee loses coverage because of certain triggering events:

- Your employment ends for any reason other than gross misconduct.

- You, as a covered spouse, and the covered employee get divorced or legally separated.

- Your hours are reduced below the minimum necessary to qualify for group coverage.

- You become eligible for Medicare.

- You become totally disabled.

- You cannot continue your children's coverage after their age disqualifies them from continuing under your group plan — the cutoff age is typically 19 (or up to 25 for a full-time student).

- The covered employee dies, if you are the spouse or child of the employee.

Some highlights of COBRA rules are in the list that follows. Be sure to check with your employer or a consumer Web site (for example, go to www.insure.com and enter "COBRA" in the site's search engine) for the most current information.

✔ **Employer size.** Generally, COBRA applies only to employers with 20 or more employees. But several states have enacted laws requiring COBRA to apply to smaller employers, too. Minnesota, for example, requires the law to apply to employers with as few as two employees. Check with your state insurance department or click on your state on the National Association of Insurance Commissioners Web site (www.naic.org). See Chapter 21 for more information on this Web site.

✔ **Required notices.** Your employer must notify you of your COBRA rights in writing when you are first hired and at the time of a triggering event. And when the triggering event happens, you have 60 days from the *later* of the day the notice was sent to you or the day your group health coverage ends to elect your COBRA continuation option.

✔ **Payment of premiums.** You have 45 days from the date you officially elect to continue your group coverage to pay the employer the first premium. You must pay retroactively back to the date your group coverage ended. So if your group coverage ended on June 30 and you elect to continue under COBRA on August 29, you have until approximately mid-October before the first premium is due. But if the premium is $700 a month for your family, you would need to remit $2,800 for July, August, September, and October, plus another $700 by October 31!

Once you have elected the coverage, all future monthly premiums for each month are due by the first of that month, although by law you can be up to 30 days late and not lose your coverage.

The employer is not required to, and generally will not, bill you. So if you forget to send a payment within 30 days of the due date, you are uninsured retroactively on the due date and you lose all further COBRA continuation rights.

If you know that you will need the coverage for only a short time (for example, you're eligible for coverage from your new employer in 120 days), eliminate the risk of accidentally missing a payment due date. Pay your ex-employer the full four months premium in advance.

✔ **Termination.** COBRA continuation coverage ends when

- You voluntary terminate it.

- Premiums aren't paid within 30 days of the monthly due date.

- A covered person becomes covered under another plan.

- A covered person becomes covered by Medicare.

- The employer discontinues offering group health insurance to all employees.

- The COBRA continuation maximum period has ended.

The triggering events, rules, eligibility, and so on for COBRA are current as of the publication date of this book. COBRA laws are regularly revised, so go to a reliable source for the latest information. I recommend going to www.insure.com and entering "COBRA" in the search engine.

Understanding HIPAA

The goal of the Health Insurance Portability and Accountability Act of 1996 (HIPAA) is to make it possible for you to move from one job to another when you or family members have health problems that otherwise would keep you trapped in your current job because either you would be turned down for health insurance at a new job or your preexisting medical problems would be excluded. (See the sidebar "Hip HIPAA Hooray!" for an example of how HIPAA makes it possible to change jobs. Also see the definition of *preexisting* just ahead.)

The HIPAA law makes it possible for you to change jobs even if you have a preexisting medical condition by

- ✔ Requiring that all insurers of groups of two or more employees cannot decline coverage on a new applicant for group insurance solely for health reasons.

- ✔ Limiting the length of time a preexisting condition can apply to a newly hired employee to 12 months (18 months for late entrants).

- ✔ Giving credit for any prior group or individual coverage during the 12 months prior to the effective date of the new group coverage (for example, if you had coverage for nine of the past 12 months, you would have only a three-month exclusion on preexisting conditions).

- ✔ Banning pregnancy and prenatal problems from being considered preexisting conditions.

Be sure to check for the most current information on HIPAA before acting. The information here is provided for illustrative purposes only.

Defining preexisting conditions

A *preexisting condition* generally means any physical or mental health problem diagnosed, cared for, or treated in the six months prior to the enrollment date on your new group plan.

Clarifying which health plans are affected by HIPAA

HIPAA rules apply to any application for group health insurance offered by a company that has two or more employees. It also applies to applications for individual health insurance plans but only if your prior coverage was group coverage.

HIPAA rules don't apply to changes from one individual health policy to another individual or group health policy. You can still be declined because of preexisting problems or have preexisting health problems excluded from the coverage. Therefore, don't ever drop an existing individual plan for another individual plan if you have preexisting conditions that won't be covered under the new plan.

Getting credit for prior coverage

Whenever individual or group health coverage you have is terminated (by you or by the employer), HIPAA rules require that the insurer provide you with a *certificate of credible coverage.* Give the certificate to your employer when you commence your new job and apply for the new company's group coverage. Likewise, give the certificate to your health insurer when you apply for additional coverage. As long as you've had health coverage for at least 12 months, with no lapse of 63 days or more, you can't be turned down for coverage or be subject to any unique limitations on account of preexisting conditions that you may have.

It's worth repeating: Don't make any decisions without checking on the most current HIPAA laws. HIPAA laws change often. Searching the Internet is probably the best way to find the latest changes; see Chapter 21 for great Internet sites.

Making good COBRA and HIPAA decisions

All right, enough with the boring details on COBRA and HIPAA law. How could all this affect you? Here are some possible scenarios.

- ✔ You're 55 years old and took early retirement. Should you elect the COBRA continuation option now for 18 months when you have ten years before you're eligible for Medicare?

- ✔ You're a 40-year-old homemaker with two children at home. You're covered by your husband's group health policy when he dies suddenly of a heart attack. The life insurance is sufficient to allow you to stay home with the kids for at least five more years. Should you take the 36-month COBRA option?

- ✔ You're age 65, retiring and starting Medicare. Your 55-year-old spouse, who has a home-based business, has been covered by your group policy. Should she take the three-year COBRA option that will cover her only to age 58?

- ✔ You're 36 years old and have been just laid off. You've decided to use the nice severance package to become self-employed. You have 29 years to retirement. Should you exercise your 18-month COBRA option?

Hip HIPAA Hooray!

Before HIPAA

Bill, a bright 43-year-old engineer, is stuck in a dead-end job doing work he loathes. He knows about some much better-paying jobs doing work he would be perfect for, but he can't take them. He's stuck. Why? Because he has an 8-year-old son with an enlarged heart condition that has already required two surgeries with at least two more scheduled in the next five years. If Bill takes a new job, either his son will be turned down for coverage or the heart condition will be excluded. So Bill's hands are tied. He can't make the job change he would love to make.

After HIPAA

Bill can take the best job he can find without any insurance concerns. Because he's had continuous coverage for more than the past 12 months, HIPAA guarantees that he can't be turned down, nor can there be a preexisting condition applied for his son's heart. Bill is a happy camper.

But suppose Bill wanted a break. He takes a six-month sabbatical between the old job and the new. How can he keep all the protection of HIPAA? Simple. He just has to elect to continue his prior group coverage, under COBRA, during the sabbatical.

These are just a few examples of the kinds of questions I get from clients. Even if you fully understand COBRA and HIPAA laws, rights, and pitfalls, applying them to your personal situation is a whole different ballgame.

A few general guidelines to help you with your decisions:

- ✔ Don't go even a day without major medical insurance. (Remember the rule from Chapter 1: Don't risk more than you can afford to lose.)

- ✔ Don't use temporary health insurance when you're between jobs, if you qualify for COBRA. Always exercise your COBRA continuation option instead. Yes, it's more costly. But unlike temporary policies, it covers preexisting conditions.

- ✔ Do exercise your COBRA continuation options anytime your maximum possible need for coverage won't exceed the maximum period of your COBRA option. The COBRA option is seamless, and it allows you to continue using the same doctors in the transition period.

- ✔ If the maximum possible need for coverage exceeds the length of your COBRA options:

- ✔ Do continue COBRA for the short term while applying for individual coverage. Then drop the COBRA option when the individual policy is approved and all preexisting conditions are fully covered. See Chapter 15 for your rights to an individual policy under HIPAA.

Chapter 16

Buying Individual Health Insurance

· ·

In This Chapter

▶ Discovering strategies to lower your individual health insurance costs

▶ Getting insurance when you're uninsurable

▶ Staying insured through life's transitions

▶ Avoiding the shortcomings of Medicare

▶ Making the Long-Term Care insurance decision

· ·

Most people are able to get the health insurance they need through their jobs. Lucky for them. But many people have to buy their own health insurance, for a variety of reasons: They are self-employed; they work for a small company; they retired before the age of 65; and so on. If you're in the market for individual health insurance, this chapter shows you what you need to know and what you need to do. *Note:* The prior chapter on group coverage contains lots of great information, even if you're shopping for individual coverage. You may want to take a quick glance through it.

Deciding between Individual and Group

Sometimes you have a choice between individually owned coverage and group coverage through your employer (such as where to insure your dependent children). Here's a brief comparison of advantages and disadvantages of both types of plans to help you make a good choice.

Pricing

Group policies are usually less expensive. Plus, the employer usually pays part of the group insurance bill. And whatever portion of the costs the employee has to pay is usually set up by the employer to be directly deducted from payroll using pretax dollars.

Underwriting

Group coverage wins again. When most people apply for group coverage, they're guaranteed to be accepted, no matter how poor their health. They could have diabetes, heart disease, or even terminal cancer. The only eligibility requirement is that they be employed. Sometimes, depending on the length of prior coverage, there may be a waiting period of up to a year for preexisting conditions, especially if the applicant had no insurance at the time he or she was hired. (See the section "Understanding HIPAA" in Chapter 15.)

Individual coverage, on the other hand, is strictly underwritten. (*Underwriting* is the process of reviewing an application to determine whether the applicant is acceptable for coverage.) Medical questions are part of the application. Your past medical records are often checked. The insurance company can do one of four things with your application: It can flat out turn you down. It can issue you a policy with no restrictions at preferred rates. It can issue you a policy with an extra charge for your condition. Or it can completely exclude coverage for a condition.

Benefit levels

Group coverage has the edge here, too, in most states. Many state legislatures have passed laws mandating benefits that must be included in health insurance plans. However, most of those laws apply only to group coverage (and, unfortunately, often exempt the largest employers, who partially self-insure their group claims). The benefits in a group policy that are required by law can be significant. Here are just a few examples, from Minnesota:

✔ Maternity expenses are fully covered and treated as any other medical bill.

✔ Only one spouse needs to be insured to have automatic coverage on newborns.

✔ Mental health expenses (for prescriptions or therapy) are fully covered and treated as any other illness.

✔ Copayments and deductibles are waived for children under 12 years old (so financially strapped parents don't delay getting their young children the care they need).

✔ Annual mammograms are fully covered.

✔ Chiropractic care is fully covered.

Renewability

Individual policies come out on top with regard to renewability. Most are guaranteed-renewable contracts that you can continue to hold up to age 65 regardless of your health. (Avoid buying individual policies that don't offer a renewability guarantee.)

Insurance companies offering group policies, on the other hand, can cancel a group policy anytime they feel like it. Your employer probably can replace it with another group plan, but coverages may be less, rates may be higher, and, in some cases, your existing health issues may not be immediately covered.

Another risk of group coverage is that your employer may discontinue it. Perhaps the company you work for has had some financial setbacks. Or perhaps employee claims have been so large that rates have skyrocketed 40 to percent 50 percent and are no longer affordable. Imagine if your employer stopped offering insurance and your child had leukemia. You would probably have to change jobs in order to get health insurance for your child.

Coverage flexibility

Another win for individual policies. With group coverage, you get what the employer offers. You can't cut costs by raising your deductible. You can't choose freedom-of-choice if your employer offers only managed care.

Nothing beats the flexibility of individual plans. You can choose to include or not include preventive coverage. If you're childless, you can strip out the expensive maternity coverage. You can choose all different levels of deductibles. And you can raise your deductible to help offset future rate increases. Best of all, you can choose as much freedom-of-choice of doctors and specialists as you want.

Saving Money on Individual Coverage

Two ways to control costs for individual coverage exist:

- ✔ **Direct:** You reduce coverage and the insurance company gives you a direct premium credit.

- ✔ **Indirect:** You select a higher deductible when your health and self-care are exceptional but for which the insurance company has no means to lower your premiums.

Saving directly

The best way to save money on an individual policy, without cutting back on coverage, is to become ten years younger. (Don't you wish?) Since that's not possible, the next best way to save money on your health insurance premium is not to smoke or use tobacco. Unlike group policies, almost all individual policies differentiate smokers from nonsmokers — significantly — because the claims costs for smokers are much higher. Blue Cross of Minnesota, for example, cuts 30 to 40 percent off its standard rates if you haven't used tobacco for three years.

You can also save by cutting out unneeded coverage (like maternity coverage if you're not expecting to need it), cutting back doctor choice (in other words, accepting managed care), or raising deductibles. The difference in cost, for example, between a $100 deductible and a $500 deductible with some insurers is 40 percent! As the size of your family or age increases, that 40 percent can save you a fortune — especially when you consider that you're assuming only $400 more risk per person each year. If you're paying $3,000 a year for just yourself, 40 percent would save you $1,200 in premiums! You're risking a "maybe" $400 for a "for sure" $1,200. Who wouldn't? Even if the savings were only 20 percent, that's still a $600 savings for a $400 risk.

The impact of higher deductibles on pricing

Table 16-1 illustrates what an insurance company rate card typically looks like for different deductibles and different ages. Notice how, as you increase the deductible, the amount of annual savings gets proportionally less. For example, a 25-year-old saves $750 a year to raise deductibles from $100 to $1,000, saves $150 to go from $1,000 to 2,000, and saves only another $150 to go from $2,000 to $5,000.

Table 16-1	ABC Health Insurance Company Annual Insurance Rate Card				
Deductible			**Age**		
	25	**35**	**45**	**55**	**Children**
$100	$1,500	$1,800	$2,400	$3,600	$1,200
$300	$1,200	$1,440	$1,920	$,2560	$960
$500	$900	$1,080	$1,440	$1,920	$720
$1,000	$750	$900	$1,200	$1,500	$600
$2,000	$600	$720	$960	$1,280	$480
$5,000	$450	$540	$720	$960	$360

Computing your ideal insurance deductible

Determining the best deductible for you (and your family, if you have one) means comparing the amount of annual premium savings to two things:

- **The maximum possible extra risk:** The difference in deductible times the number of family members.

- **The maximum probable risk:** Your best guess as to the additional amount you'll actually spend because of the higher deductible (based on your family's history, your judgment as to the overall fitness of your family, and what the tea leaves tell you).

When deciding between two deductibles, choose the lower deductible if you're in doubt. You can raise your deductible later, anytime you want to. But to lower it, the whole family must qualify medically — not likely if you've just incurred some big medical bills.

First, some definitions of items:

- The *Total* is the annual family cost for each deductible.

- The *Difference* is the annual family cost difference between the deductibles being considered. Assume that your family elected not to consider the $300 or $5,000 deductible.

- The *Maximum Possible Extra Risk* is the worst case scenario — all five members in the same year exceeding the higher deductible. (Highly unlikely, but you have to consider it in the decision. *Note:* Sometimes there is a family deductible maximum of three times the individual deductible maximum.)

- The *Maximum Probable Extra Risk* is your best guess as to a more realistic estimate of the worse case scenario. For example, at the $500 deductible, you may assume that you'll incur no more than two in a year for the whole family. There is a $400 spread between the deductibles times two uses = $800 annual maximum probable extra risk.

At the $1,000 deductible, again you may assume a maximum of two uses. Two times the $500 deductible difference = $1,000 probable maximum.

Finally, at the $2,000 deductible, you may assume that there will not be more than $1,500 of total family expenses that fall between the $1,000 and $2,000 deductible in a year.

Table 16-2	Choosing Your Health Insurance Deductible		
Deductible Increase	Maximum Possible Extra Risk	Maximum Probable Extra Risk	Annual Premium Difference
From $100 to $500	$2,000	$800	$2,880
From $500 to $1,000	$2,500	$1,000	$720
From $1,000 to $2,000	$5,000	$1,500	$740

To choose the best deductible for you, compare the annual savings in premium to the maximum probable number, while making sure that the maximum possible number is not more than you could ever afford to lose.

So what deductible would you choose? Clearly, at least $500. You'll save $2,880 and not likely risk more than $800. Even in the worst case, you'll save $880 ($2,880 versus $2,000).

The $1,000 deductible looks good, too. Your savings of $720 is almost as much as your $1,000 estimate of your maximum liability. If you can live with the $2,500 worst case, $1,000 is a good option.

Finally, the $2,000 deductible is a bit questionable. Your probable maximum of $1,500 would eat up two years of premium savings. And the $5,000 worst case is unappealing. Because of the ironclad rule to choose low if in doubt, be conservative and go with either the $1,000 or the $500 deductible.

Saving indirectly with self-care

Insurance companies offering individual health plans give substantial price discounts to nonsmokers. And they don't insure people who are high-risk medically. Everyone else, from the super-fit and super-healthy to the average or below-average health risk, pays the same rate and shares losses.

If you're healthy and practice good self-care (through exercise, diet, stress management, rest, and personal safety), how can you get credit if insurance companies don't offer any such credits for that? The answer: higher deductibles.

Remember, pricing for each level of deductible is based on average risk. If you're much fitter and healthier than average, you're paying more than your share, no matter what level of coverage you buy. But the more you self-insure through higher deductibles, the more you'll save. Being above average in terms of health, your chances of having to spend that higher deductible are much less — and a $1,000 deductible could save you 50 percent off your insurance costs.

Medical Savings Accounts

In 1997, Congress created a pilot program called *Medical Savings Accounts (MSAs)* and made the accounts available to self-employed individuals and their families. An MSA operates like an individual retirement account (IRA) coordinated with a high-deductible major medical health insurance plan.

✓ Like an IRA, contributions are income tax deductible.

✓ Earnings on the account are tax sheltered.

✓ The maximum contribution per year is 65 percent of your major medical plan deductible for individuals and 75 percent for families. The insurance plan must meet MSA standards.

✓ From the account, you can pay your deductibles and most other medical expenses not covered by your health plan. Because the MSA money has never been taxed, you're paying those bills with pretax dollars — a huge advantage.

✓ If you've stayed reasonably healthy, you can leave unused funds on deposit and either use them in future years or save them as supplemental retirement dollars. If not used for medical bills, withdrawals will be taxed much like traditional IRAs when you do retire.

If you're self-employed, I think an MSA is a wonderful benefit to set up for yourself. Unfortunately, health insurance companies aren't required to participate, and, much to my surprise, most do not. So you may have to change health insurance companies if you want an MSA. I'm disappointed that more insurers didn't jump on this bandwagon.

If you have interest in an MSA, check first with your agent or state insurance department. MSAs are not approved in all states. Also, because they are a federal pilot program, there's a good chance that they may not be available much longer. If MSAs are withdrawn by the government, those who have one set up will be grandfathered — meaning that you can continue contributions to yours as long as you want.

You can set up an MSA account wherever you can establish an IRA — banks, savings and loans, investment houses, insurance companies, and so on.

Out of $1 million of health coverage, half the premium pays the first $1,000 of annual claims. The other 50 percent pays the other hundreds of thousands of dollars. Discover what deductible makes good economic sense and go for it, especially if you're in good health.

Coping with Health Insurance Problems

There are times in your life when you face tough decisions regarding health insurance. Examples include the following:

✓ You or a family member can't get health insurance due to existing medical problems.

✓ You've fallen on hard times and can't afford health insurance.

✔ Your son or daughter has reached the age where he or she no longer qualifies for dependent coverage under your insurance.

✔ Your college student has coverage available through school.

✔ Your or a family member needs temporary coverage.

✔ Your coverage under your spouse's group coverage is being terminated due to a divorce.

✔ Your and your children's group coverage ends because of a spouse's death.

✔ You're between jobs and without insurance.

✔ You're traveling outside the country and are offered travel insurance.

✔ The school offers school accident insurance for your children.

Here's how I recommend that you manage each of those problems.

Insuring the uninsurable

If you or a family member for whom you are responsible has a health condition for which you can't get insurance (in other words, you've been rejected for individual coverage), I suggest that you broaden your way of looking at the problem. I don't believe that there are many people who can't get health insurance for a medically uninsurable condition if they're willing to make some life changes.

Over the years, I've read a number of horror stories about families who have suffered financial ruin because of one family member's medical expenses — often a child's. I remember one story in particular about a family who lost their insurance due to a job change. The new job did not offer group insurance, and their son was uninsurable. He had an ongoing condition that required years of treatment and thousands of dollars of expenses. According to the story, this family sat helplessly while their life savings dwindled to nothing. I believe that their financial ruin could have been prevented if they had considered some other choices. If you're willing to take one or more of the following actions, you can prevent a financial catastrophe from happening to you on account of an uninsured family member.

✔ If your employer doesn't offer group coverage, talk to your employer about starting to offer a group plan. Enlist the support of other coworkers. The Health Insurance Portability and Accountability Act of 1996 (HIPAA) requires insurance companies to accept all members of a group, regardless of health. The worst case scenario is that your son's condition won't be covered in the first 12 months. (See "Understanding HIPAA" in Chapter 15 for more information on preexisting conditions.)

✔ Change employers. Get a job with a company that offers group medical coverage to its employees and their families.

✔ If you're in a state that has a major medical insurance plan for uninsurable people, sign up immediately. Call your state insurance department to find out.

✔ Move to a state that offers catastrophic individual major medical coverage for uninsurable citizens. Minnesota, where I live, has such a plan, and so do many other states.

You may balk at the idea of doing something as seemingly drastic as changing jobs or moving to a different state in order to get health insurance for yourself or a sick family member. But from my perspective, those are far better alternatives than financial ruin.

Staying insured through hard times

If you're in a financial crisis — temporary or permanent — and you just don't have enough money available for health insurance, you can still protect yourself somewhat by managing your medical risks in advance. If you don't develop a game plan for handling medical costs before you're faced with them, you may end up being personally responsible for the entire cost of any emergency care that you need. I recommend that you look into various assistance programs for people in your circumstances, in which the medical care is provided either at no cost or at a nominal cost. In Minneapolis, for example, we have programs available through Lutheran Social Services or Catholic Charities. In exchange for a very small amount of money per month, all family members receive the medical care they need. Participants are limited to designated medical facilities, but they get medical care now without facing a huge debt later.

If you or a family member is in economic distress, research what's available in your community and know where you're going for care if and when you need it. A medical emergency isn't the right time to figure out what your options are.

Insuring your kids when your policy no longer covers them

Depending on your particular insurance policy terms, your children are only covered under your family plan to a certain age — usually age 19 or 25 for full-time students. Insurance polices are very inconsistent when it comes to the age at which children are no longer covered.

Managing the in-again, out-again school problem

If you have a daughter who can't seem to make up her mind about going to college (she's in for a semester, out for a semester, back in for a semester, and so on), I recommend that you do the following if you're covered by a group policy and are thus eligible for COBRA:

✔ When she drops out, notify your employer to exercise the 36-month COBRA continuation option. This way, she stays insured under your group insurance. The only difference is that you will foot 100 percent of her premium costs (if you weren't already) while she's out of school.

✔ When she returns to school (and is taking the required number of credits), cancel COBRA and add her back onto your coverage as a dependent.

✔ Each time she drops out and then returns, follow these same guidelines until she reaches the maximum age for students to be covered under your policy — usually 22 or 25.

✔ If she's still in school when she reaches the maximum age for students to be insured on your policy, or if she's without insurance for any other reason, exercise her COBRA option until she can arrange coverage on her own personal health policy.

If she's not eligible for COBRA (in other words, if you have an individual policy or your employer has too few employees to qualify for COBRA), set her up with her own individual policy the first time she drops out of school. The policy will stay in force during the revolving-door period.

Whether you have group or individual coverage, the bottom line is that when your son or daughter reaches age 18, check with your insurance company or agent and find out exactly what your insurance company's rules are for maintaining coverage for your child.

Find out how many credits your children must carry per school term to stay eligible. Will they be eligible in the summer if they haven't registered yet for the fall semester? What if they drop out of school for a while? Get clear on all this beforehand. Claim time is not the time to find out that your child isn't insured.

Evaluating the insurance available through the college

I've had many clients ask me if they should buy the optional student health insurance available from their child's college. If the insurance is provided automatically as part of tuition costs, my clients ask whether they should remove their son or daughter from the family health policy and rely exclusively on the school coverage. Before giving an opinion, I always have my clients send me a full copy of the college's student insurance policy. What I discover, in almost every case, is that the policy has

- ✔ Excellent preventive care — coverage for physicals, eye exams, and so on — at the student health center on campus
- ✔ Excellent coverage for other doctor care, if the care is provided at the student health center
- ✔ Hospitalization coverage at the university's hospital, but usually only for a limited time (such as 30 days)
- ✔ Poor medical coverage away from school — both hospital and doctor
- ✔ Poor coverage for substantial medical bills
- ✔ Often, no coverage during the summers

Keep your student insured on the family health plan. But if you can't afford it, consider buying student health coverage. The coverage is usually pretty inexpensive. Also, many family heath plans don't cover expenses incurred at your student's college health center. The student health insurance plans available from colleges always cover these expenses. If college students can just drop by the campus health center, they're a lot more likely to get the care they need than if they have to trek to the nearest hospital or doctor whom your plan covers. As a result, buying the student health plan can help keep your student healthier.

Never drop your college student from your family health insurance plan, even if you buy the student health insurance offered by the college. You'll need your family plan for any serious claims.

Understanding the role of temporary health insurance

Many states allow health insurance companies to offer the public *short-term* or *temporary* health coverage to meet short-term needs, such as covering a person who's between jobs or a college student who isn't covered by student health insurance during the summer. Coverage is usually available in increments of 30, 60, 90, 120, and sometimes 180 days. Coverage is usually quite good in many respects. Typically, temporary policies have a coverage limit of $1 million or more. They usually include freedom-of-choice and a maximum amount on out-of-pocket expenses.

The biggest advantage to a temporary policy is that you can qualify with almost no medical questions. Coverage can be immediate, if needed.

But temporary coverage has at least five disadvantages:

✔ Preexisting conditions aren't covered. If you've ever been treated for a condition in the past, you won't be covered if the condition flares up again.

✔ The insurance is usually not renewable.

✔ When the coverage period you've chosen ends, so does the coverage — often, even if you're lying seriously ill in the hospital.

✔ Claim payments are often delayed.

✔ Coverage outside the country is often excluded.

Because of these major limitations, you generally want to avoid buying temporary insurance unless you have no other option. If you're between jobs, continue your group coverage from your prior employer under COBRA if you can. And for summer coverage, keep college students continuously insured under your family plan.

In one situation, temporary coverage makes sense — when you're applying for individual coverage and you currently have no insurance. You complete an application and pay a premium to apply for individual coverage. If the insurance company approves you, it will generally issue your policy retroactively, if you desire, effective on the date you applied. If, while your application was pending, you were hospitalized or incurred other medical bills, they would be covered.

But suppose the company declined your application and returned your money due to your past health or medical problems? You would be uninsured for any bills that you'd accumulated since you applied, even if the medical conditions were new.

Even after you apply for individual coverage and pay the initial premium, you're not necessarily covered. Only if the company later approves you — a process that normally takes 30 to 60 days — will you have been covered since the date of your application. That's a long time to risk being uninsured.

Here's how you can use short-term coverage to protect yourself when you have no insurance and while your application for long-term coverage is being considered:

1. **Buy a 60-day short-term policy to be assured of insurance coverage for any new medical condition or injury that occurs while your long-term application is being considered.**

2. **Apply simultaneously for long-term coverage, requesting an effective date, if approved, for 60 days from now to coincide perfectly with the expiration of your short-term policy.**

Then, if your long-term policy application is rejected, you at least had coverage for new conditions while your application was being reviewed. Without the short-term coverage, the new medical problems would have been totally uninsured.

Continuing coverage following a divorce

Because about 50 percent of the marriages in the United States end in divorce, the problem of continuing health insurance after a divorce is significant.

Getting spousal coverage

If both spouses are employed full-time and have their own group health insurance coverage, health insurance isn't a problem. If one of the spouses is covered under the other's policy, all he or she needs to do is apply for coverage at his or her own place of work within 30 days of being dropped from the other policy to avoid having to qualify medically. If the spouse who's being dropped doesn't have group coverage available at work, he or she can, of course, obtain an individual policy through an agent. Coverage may be guaranteed under federal HIPAA laws — see Chapter 15.

Insuring the children after a divorce

If both parents are employed and each has coverage at work, the best thing to do is normally to continue the children's coverage through the parent whose coverage is best for the children. But what if one parent is required in the divorce decree to pay for the children's coverage and the children are currently not on that parent's policy? Here's an example:

Sue and Tom divorce. The court orders Tom to pay the children's health insurance costs to age 19. But Sue has them insured under her plan. Their options are as follows:

- ✔ Sue can continue having them on her plan with Tom reimbursing her — but getting that reimbursement sometimes can be a source of conflict.

- ✔ Tom can move them to his plan, usually without the children having to qualify medically if the move is done within 30 days of the divorce. But transferring coverage is a problem if Sue doesn't like Tom's policy or his plan won't cover the children's doctors.

- ✔ Sue can set up an individual policy covering just the children, with the bills sent to Tom (assuming that the children can qualify medically).

I like the option of setting up an individual policy, especially if Tom has the premiums paid electronically from his checking account and Sue's mailing address is on the policy. This way, the premiums are always paid on time, so the chance of a cancelled policy and a resulting uninsured claim is reduced. By having Sue's mailing address listed on the policy, Sue gets copies of the policies and changes and any late premium notices if the electronic payment isn't made for whatever reason.

The ideal divorce decree

If you're involved in a divorce, the court deems you responsible for paying the children's health insurance costs, and you prefer to set them up on an individual plan, it will cause both parties less friction later if the divorce decree does more than require which parent is responsible for the premiums. It should specify the type of coverage plan, the deductibles and copayments (and who's responsible for paying them), whether there must be freedom of choice for doctors and hospitals, and that the premium payments must be paid automatically and electronically from the responsible parent's checking account. Follow this tip, and you'll eliminate 90 percent of the conflict around your children's health insurance.

An individual plan gives the parents more flexibility to determine the coverage they want on the children. And the coverage won't end if Tom or Sue's job ends, which is safer for the children's welfare and much less stressful for their parents. See Chapter 15 for information on how the children's application for individual coverage might be guaranteed, regardless of any preexisting health problems.

Deciding on a conversion policy

Most state laws require people coming off of a group policy to be offered the right to convert their group coverage to a personally owned policy, regardless of their health, that they can keep indefinitely.

Requiring that conversion policies be offered is a good concept in theory, but the policies are seldom practical. Most states don't set limits on how much the company can charge, nor do they prohibit the company from watering down the coverage. As a result, most conversion policies are half the coverage of the prior group coverage at about twice the price. (Why? Because losses are so high. Usually, only those in poor health exercise the option.)

 If your state law requires the group insurance carrier to offer you a conversion policy with essentially the same broad coverage you had under the group without an increase in price, by all means consider it. Otherwise, avoid conversion policies unless you have absolutely no other health insurance available to you (in other words, if you can't qualify medically for a personal policy and your state does not have a health insurance pool for those who can't get insurance).

Evaluating options for survivors of a premature death

I've had clients die and leave their entire family uninsured, because the family had been covered through the deceased person's group insurance plan. Luckily, the family has a couple of options in this situation:

✔ If the surviving spouse is employed and has group coverage available, she can add herself and her kids to her group plan without proof of good health if she applies within 30 days of losing the other group coverage.

✔ If she chooses not to work outside the home indefinitely or is self-employed, I recommend the following:

- • Continue coverage through COBRA, if available, but only temporarily.

- • Buy an Individual policy if she and the kids are healthy enough to qualify — a policy that won't end in three years, like COBRA does. If you're in this situation, buy the policy *now*. Your health may change and disqualify you later.

- • Those family members that don't qualify will either need to go to a state pool for uninsurables or elect COBRA for the three years and then exercise a conversion option to an individual policy, if that option's available.

Evaluating options when becoming self-employed

If you're leaving your job to become self-employed, don't continue your COBRA option for the entire 18 months before applying for individual coverage. A lot of people make this mistake. The problem with the strategy is that it risks future insurability. During those 18 months, your health may go bad, and when the 18 months is over, you'll be stuck with less than desirable choices.

Here's a three-point plan I recommend that reduces the risks of coming up short on COBRA usage:

✔ Continue your group coverage under COBRA, if you are eligible, when leaving your job to have uninterrupted coverage.

✔ Stay with COBRA while you test the self-employment waters. If you don't like self-employment, just continue COBRA until you're back working for another company and are covered by its group plan.

✔ The moment you decide to stay self-employed, apply for a good individual health plan, keeping COBRA while your application is being evaluated. If you're approved, drop COBRA. If you're declined, keep COBRA until you've located replacement insurance.

Evaluating school accident insurance

Most elementary and secondary schools send information home with students about insurance for injuries that occur on school grounds or at school events. It's most commonly offered to student-athletes. Here's what I recommend you do:

- ✔ Assuming there aren't any exclusions to worry about and that it's reasonably priced, buy it if you have a high deductible on your health insurance plan.

- ✔ If you have minimal deductibles or copayments, don't buy it. It just duplicates coverage you already have.

Evaluating dread disease insurance

We all have fears of one kind or another. We universally fear cancer. Those of us close to other serious diseases probably fear those as well. Some parts of the insurance industry have responded to our fears with policies that cover only those things we fear. I'm totally against what I call Las Vegas insurance — policies that pay only on the first Tuesday after a full moon, like travel accident insurance, travel life insurance, accidental death insurance, rush hour auto liability insurance, and so on. Most of the time, these insurance programs are either wasteful because they duplicate other coverage or, if you're really tempted to buy them, are a warning to you that you may be underinsured in certain areas. Buying travel life insurance, for example, sends a red flag that you feel your current life insurance is inadequate. Skip the travel insurance and use the money you save toward increasing your life insurance coverage.

If a person has a high limit (like $2 million), quality major medical policy that covers cancer, buying another $1 million just for cancer coverage is throwing money out the window. However, if a person has a poor medical policy (such as one with a $250,000 lifetime limit), then buying an extra million dollars of coverage is a good idea — but not just for cancer.

If you're considering buying a dread disease insurance policy (a policy that covers only specific illnesses) because your health insurance isn't very good, don't. Save your money and use it instead to get a top health insurance policy or an excess major medical supplement to the policy you have that covers all illnesses and injuries — not just the ones you fear.

Evaluating travel insurance

I address two types of medically related travel insurance here. One pays medical bills you incur through travel, within a certain date range and up to a dollar limit (such as $5,000). The other covers the costs of airlifting you from a remote area, in a medically equipped and staffed aircraft, to a top hospital. The former usually duplicates your health insurance; the latter fills an important gap.

Travel medical insurance

Travel medical insurance is Las Vegas insurance. In other words, you're gambling that you'll get sick while you travel. Not a smart gamble — it violates almost all the rules for buying insurance that I introduce in Chapter 1. It often duplicates, unnecessarily, your health insurance. The only time the insurance may be of value is if you have a very large deductible on your health plan and you're buying travel medical insurance to cover the deductible while traveling.

Be very careful if you do buy travel medical insurance. Read the policy carefully. Many are *very* restricted; you may as well throw money down a rat hole.

If you're traveling abroad, call your health insurance company before you leave to discover its preferred method of handling claims incurred abroad. Is there a 24-hour toll-free phone number you can call? Are there any coverage restrictions abroad?

Medical evacuation insurance

If you travel much, especially if you travel abroad, and you get seriously ill, the hospital or treatment facility you end up in may not be state-of-the-art in terms of doctors, equipment, or both.

Medical evacuation insurance does not duplicate any other insurance you have. A good policy covers the cost (about $35,000) to bring an intensive-care jet to wherever you are in the world, fully staffed and medically equipped, and to fly you to your preferred treatment facility. Coverage is available from travel agents, tours, and credit card companies on a per-trip basis, and from travel assistance companies who sell the coverage on an annual basis for people who travel frequently.

If you buy medical evacuation insurance, try to obtain a policy that

- ✔ Pays for you to be transported to your home hospital or another hospital of your choice

- ✔ Has no dollar limits on costs (the cost to evacuate you from China may be $100,000)

- ✔ Transports you at your option, regardless of medical necessity

- ✔ Covers you within your home country — not just abroad

- ✔ Provides a full medical staff

The best company I've encountered is Med Jet Assistance (800-9MEDJET; www.medjetassistance.com). It meets all the criteria I just listed. The policy is underwritten by Lloyds of London, and it's reasonably priced — $175 a year for individuals and $275 for families — no matter how often you travel.

The benefits of medical evacuation insurance

A childhood friend and a current client, Connie M. vacationed annually with her mother in Mexico. During their last vacation, her mother collapsed on the bathroom floor. She was rushed to the closest hospital. Doctors told Connie that her mother would die if they didn't perform heart bypass surgery. Connie wasn't comfortable with the level of care available but reluctantly okayed the surgery — she had no other option. Her mother died. Connie had the task of bringing her mother's body home — a horrible experience.

If Connie's mother had had medical evacuation insurance, Connie may have been able to fly her home at no cost, where she could have received the best care. Her odds of survival would have gone up. But even if her mother had died in Mexico before she could have been flown to an American hospital, a good medical evacuation service would have flown to Mexico and brought the body home for burial.

If the coverage and the company are good, I think medical evacuation insurance is a good idea, especially if you travel a lot or have a health condition (like a heart problem) that places you more at risk for being in a medical emergency abroad.

Working with Medicare

In the month of your 65th birthday, you become eligible for our national insurance program for seniors: Medicare. Medicare is important and complex enough to have its own book. The Feds publish a book called *Medicare & You* that is available for free at 1-800-633-4227. You can also access a copy on the Web at www.medicare.gov. Look for publication HCFA-10050.

Understanding Medicare basics

Medicare has two components: Part A covers hospital bills, and Part B covers non-hospital bills (doctor and related bills). Part A is free to you if you've worked at least 10 years in covered employment. Part B has a modest monthly cost. Part A is mandatory; Part B is optional. Most seniors sign up for both parts right away upon becoming eligible. Some seniors who are still employed and have group coverage at work delay buying Part B until they retire — which is a good idea, by the way.

Both Part A and Part B have a deductible that you must pay before coverage kicks in. Neither part offers coverage outside the United States. Neither has prescription drug coverage.

In addition to the deductible, Part A has copayments, set up by Uncle Sam, for each day of hospitalization. Part A has a maximum of 90 days hospital coverage per illness, with an additional 60 days that you can use only once in your lifetime.

As far as Part B goes, after you pay a front-end deductible when you visit a doctor, have lab tests, or incur other medical bills, Medicare pays 80 percent of *approved* medical and doctor bills, without limit. You're responsible for the other 20 percent of approved bills, plus 100 percent of any charges beyond what Medicare allows for. If you have a $50,000 open-heart surgery bill, for example, Medicare may approve $30,000 and pay $24,000 (80 percent), leaving you owing $26,000!

Discovering the pitfalls

In Chapter 14, I lay out the five crucial components of a good health insurance plan. See Table 16-3 for how Medicare stacks up.

Table 16-3	Evaluating Medicare
Health Insurance Criteria	*Remarks*
High coverage limit	Room and board limited to 90 to150 days maximum.
Cap on out-of-pocket expenses	Your 20 percent doctor bill copay has no cap. And Medicare doesn't pay for any expenses that are unapproved by them.
No internal coverage limits	Medicare sets limits on doctor charges at its discretion and offers no prescription drug coverage.
Freedom-of-choice of doctors	No restrictions (unless you opt for managed care; I don't recommend that you do).
Worldwide coverage	Coverage in the United States and U.S. territories only.

Would you buy Medicare if it were sold in the marketplace? No way! It meets only one of the five criteria of a good plan. In fact, most states wouldn't even approve the product to be sold. Fortunately, the insurance industry has responded to the shortcomings of Medicare with Medicare supplement policies (known as *Medigap* policies) that plug many of Medicare's coverage gaps.

Don't have Medicare without a good Medicare supplement policy. Period!

Determining what makes a good Medicare supplement

A good supplement should

- ✔ Pay all of Part A hospital costs, for at least one year, when Medicare's coverage runs out after 90 or 150 days.

- ✔ Pay all of the 20 percent of Part B doctor's charges that Medicare allows but doesn't pay, plus at least 80 percent of the charges Medicare disallows.

- ✔ Include immediate medical coverage outside the United States — worldwide — with either no limit or a very high limit.

- ✔ Include coverage for nonemergency medical care, without penalty, when the care is provided in a state other than your home state.

- ✔ Include optional coverage for prescription drugs.

- ✔ Include the freedom to choose doctors and hospitals nationwide.

The majority of Medicare supplements fail to meet all the criteria I just listed. Federal law gives you an open enrollment period in the first six months after you turn 65 (or, if you're still employed and are covered by group insurance, six months after that ends). During this period, you can get any Medicare supplement you choose, guaranteed, with no medical questions. After that six-month period ends, you have to medically qualify to get a supplement. I encourage you to start shopping for a supplement about two months prior to your 65th birthday. Apply for a Medigap policy about one month prior to your 65th birthday so that coverage coincides with your Medicare start date. (Some new changes to Medicare laws also give you the opportunity to get any Medicare supplement, regardless of health, if your plan cancels or reduces your benefits.)

For the latest on Medicare rules and other information, go to www.medicare. gov on the Web. I intentionally left payment of the Part A and Part B deductibles off the list of criteria for a good supplement, because even the worst Medicare supplement usually pays those. Neither of the deductibles will cause you major hardship financially if you have to pay them yourself.

Never, under any circumstances, buy more than one Medicare supplement. If you currently have a poor one, don't buy another poor policy to supplement your first poor one; instead, replace the existing poor policy with a good one.

If you've been conned

A very small percentage of unscrupulous insurance salespeople have, over the years, sold seniors — worried that major medical costs could wipe out their savings — multiple policies. If you're one of those seniors, find someone to help you choose the best policy to keep, and cancel the rest. You can also lodge a complaint with your state insurance department — it may prosecute the insurance agent.

The two most common shortcomings of a poor supplement are that it doesn't provide extra days of hospital coverage and that it doesn't pay anything toward the portion of doctors' charges that Medicare disallows. Going back to the earlier example of the $50,000 open-heart surgery, for which Medicare allowed $30,000 and paid $24,000 (80 percent), see Table 16-4 for what your net costs would be under both a poor and a good supplement.

Table 16-4	Comparing Medigap Policies	
	Poor Supplement	*Good Supplement*
Total surgical bill	$50,000	$50,000
Medicare allows	$30,000	$30,000
Amount Medicare pays (80%)	$24,000	$24,000
Amount your supplement pays (the other 20%)	$6,000	$6,000
Amount disallowed by Medicare (A – B)	$20,000	$20,000
Supplement pays (80%)	$0	$16,000
Your out-of-pocket expenses	$20,000	$4,000

If you had saved a few dollars and bought the poor supplement, that would have cost $16,000!

Choosing your Medigap policy

Comparing Medigap policies used to be a horrendous job. Separating the handful of good policies from the scores of mediocre ones required an insurance expert. But not anymore. The job of comparing Medigap polices has become much easier. In fact, in every state except Minnesota, Wisconsin, and Massachusetts, Medigap policies must be one of ten flavors — Plans A through J.

Plans F, G, I, and J meet all the requirements of a good Medicare supplement if you don't need or want prescription drug coverage. Plans I and J do provide drug coverage as well as meeting all the other criteria. For more information, go to www.medicare.gov/mycompare/TenStandardPlans.asp.

Evaluating Your Need for Long-Term Care Insurance

Folks are living longer. That's the good news. The bad news is that 50 percent of the people who reach age 65 need assistance with daily living for at least two years at some point in their lives. Bathing. Dressing. Eating. Unless you get help from your family, you'll have to pay for it by draining your investments. Or you can buy *Long-Term Care insurance.* (Or you can rely on the federal Medicaid program if you're of minimal financial means.)

The cost to stay in a nursing home averages $40,000 to $70,000 a year — costs vary depending on the type of care and the region in which the care is provided. With costs increasing every year, what will the cost be in 20 years? $150,000 a year? $200,000 a year? Ask yourself if you have enough investments to cover those costs. If the answer is "yes," then you don't need to read further. You don't need Long-Term Care insurance. You may decide to buy it anyway to preserve your resources, but you don't *need* it.

Long-Term Care insurance basics

Long-Term Care insurance is one of the newest types of insurance in the marketplace. Policies weren't marketed in earnest until the mid-1980s. Then they were expensive and covered you only if you were confined to a nursing home. Today's policies are considerably better. Though nursing-home-only coverage is still offered, no one should buy it. It's way too restrictive. A good policy covers your care anywhere you receive it — even at home.

Here are a few of the criteria that make a Long-Term Care policy a good one:

✔ Lifetime coverage — not limited to a fixed number of years.

✔ Nursing home confinement is not required. Care can be received anywhere — assisted living apartments, hospices, even at home.

✔ Benefits are paid when you're unable to do either two or three self-care activities — bathing, dressing, eating, and so on, without assistance.

✔ Coverage for Alzheimer's and other nervous and mental disorders.

✔ Coverage increases at least 5 percent annually, so your coverage keeps up with rising care costs, with no requirement to qualify medically for the increase and with no increase in premium.

✔ Prices are guaranteed for at least the first five years, and the insurance company can demonstrate a history of little or no increased rates on existing policyholders — so you don't have the unpleasant experience of paying premiums for years and then having to drop the policy due to big rate increases right when you need it most.

✔ The policy is guaranteed renewable for your lifetime and can be canceled only for nonpayment of premium.

✔ A reputable, financially solid insurance company is offering the policy. The company should have several years' experience with Long-Term Care policies so that its rates are credible and more likely to be stable, and so that it's more likely to be in business when you finally have a claim.

An extremely good checklist to help you compare Long-Term Care policies is available on the Web at www.insure.com. Just enter "Long-Term Care" in the site's search engine, and you'll get a menu of helpful resource material. Select "A Long-Term Care insurance shopping checklist." A good Web site for information about long-term care is www.mrlongtermcare.com.

Buying the policy

Start with some resource information. Check with your state insurance department. It can send you information as well as any comparative studies it has done. Be sure to request a copy of the booklet put out by the National Association of Insurance Commissioners called *A Shopper's Guide to Buying Long-Term Care Insurance*.

Get leads on agents from friends. Try to find someone with lots of expertise. Don't shop price yet. Interview the agent. Have him or her explain the process he or she uses to determine your needs. Then, with the help of the agent or agents you've selected, design the coverage specifications you want:

✔ How many months will you self-insure before coverage kicks in? The longer you can wait, the lower the cost of the insurance.

✔ How many years do you want claim benefits to continue before they run out? Or do you want benefits paid for life? (I recommend the latter.)

✔ What's the going daily cost for nursing home care in your area? For home care? $150 per day? Do you have investment income you can use to pay part of that cost? Determine what your need may be beyond what your investment income can handle.

✔ Do you want an option to receive care at home? (I strongly recommend that you get this option in your policy — to keep all your care options open.)

✔ Do you want your coverage amount to increase each year to keep up with inflating care cost increases? Do you want the increase compounded or simple? (Always take compounded!)

✔ Do you want the price guaranteed for five years? Longer? Or do you want it guaranteed for the rest of your life? (I recommend that you get the longest price guarantee you can. With baby boomers retiring soon, demand for long-term care will probably push costs up significantly. More use equals higher insurance rates.)

Shop the coverage you want from at least three companies. Buy the policy that best meets your needs. If more than one fits your needs well, use price as the tie-breaker. Also, be sure to choose a solid insurance company, one rated A+ or A++ by the A. M. Best Company, and a company with a stable rate history. (See Chapter 21 for more information on the A. M. Best Web site.)

Chapter 17

Managing the Risk of Long-Term Disability

*W*e're told that, in order to eat healthy, we should have each of the four basic food groups in our daily diet — dairy, meat, fruits and vegetables, and breads and starch. Eating from each food group creates a balanced diet. A good insurance program also needs to be balanced.

You have to deal with five possible causes of a *major* financial loss through insurance: lawsuits, destruction of home and personal property, major medical bills, premature death with dependents, and long-term disability. Most consumers, in their insurance programs, carry protection for the first four threats. Good. But many consumers don't protect themselves from long-term loss of income from illness or injury unless their employer provides the insurance. Yet a person is three times more likely to become disabled for six months or more than to die prior to age 65.

The economic loss to disability survivors is worse than it is with death because the disabled person still needs a roof over her head, still has living expenses (such as groceries), and often needs additional care. Without this critical coverage in your insurance "diet," you unnecessarily risk a major financial crisis.

Keep one of the guiding principles from Chapter 1 in mind when thinking about long-term disability insurance: "Don't risk more than you can afford to lose." If you aren't financially independent and don't have income(s) protected by long-term disability insurance (either personally or through a group plan at work), in this chapter you discover how best to plug this serious gap in your protection.

Doing Your Homework Before You Buy

Before you buy insurance protection for lost income resulting from illness or injury, you need to determine whether you need such coverage and, if so, how much you need. Explore and decide on the best place to buy the coverage. And finally, before you buy, you need to learn the key components of a good long-term disability policy and select among several supplemental coverage options.

Disability is the inability to work due to illness or injury. *Long-term disability,* for my purposes, refers to a disability that lasts three months or longer. The longer the disability lasts, the more financial hardship it causes.

Assessing Your Disability Chances

To give you a better feel for your chances of being disabled for three months or longer prior to age 65, see Table 17-1. As you can see, the odds are tremendously high.

Table 17-1	Your Chances of Being Disabled for Three Months or Longer
Your Age	*Your Chances of a Disability*
25	44%
35	41%
45	36%
55	27%

You may be wondering what the chances are that the disability will last. Table 17-2 shows you the odds of a disability that has lasted one year continuing beyond that year.

Table 17-2	The Chances of a One-Year Disability Lasting Longer		
Age	*1 More Year*	*2 More Years*	*5 More Years*
25	67%	57%	47%
35	76%	67%	57%
45	79%	72%	62%
55	81%	73%	62%

If you're disabled for as long as one year, your chances of being disabled for a long time are staggeringly high — much higher than even I would have guessed.

Finally, look at Table 17-3. If you're disabled for just three months, here are your chances of being disabled for the rest of your life. If you're 25 years old and an injury or illness knocks you out of work for just three months, you have a one in four chance of having that disability last for life! At age 25, that could be 40 years or more.

Table 17-3	The Chances of a Three-Month-Long Disability Lasting for Life
Age	*Chances of a Lifetime Disability*
25	25%
35	28%
45	33%
55	40%

I share these three tables (source: 1985 CIDB Disability Tables) with no intent to frighten you. The risk of disability is real. It happens a lot more often than once in a blue moon. And when it does happen, it can last a long time.

Buying long-term disability insurance is essential unless you either are financially independent and your investment income will meet your monthly needs indefinitely, or you have adequate group disability coverage through your employer. The only thing worse than a long-term disability is a long-term disability with no income.

Determining Your Need

The goal of a good long-term disability strategy is that, if a disability happens, you have enough personal and insurance resources available to you that you won't have to make major life changes, such as selling your home. Being disabled is traumatic enough without having the added pain and stress of big changes in your lifestyle. Having the right amount of coverage is crucial. Too little coverage may mean that you still have to make major life changes in the aftermath of a disabling injury. Too much coverage and you're spending money unnecessarily.

Considering both incomes

If you're married, don't make the mistake of covering only one income if you need both incomes to make ends meet. Considering only one income is a common mistake. On the other hand, if you're a two-income family and can live quite comfortably on only one income, you may not need to protect yourself from the loss of the smaller of the two incomes. Also, don't overlook the economic impact of both incomes stopping simultaneously if you're both injured in the same accident.

Homemakers add value by the cost of the labor needed to replace their services (such as a full-time nanny). A disability to a homemaker creates a hardship and should have some disability protection. Unfortunately, most disability insurers won't insure homemakers.

Doing the math

Determine how much you will need monthly to pay the bills should your income stop. Do so even if you have coverage at work through your employer's group policy.

You have two ways to determine your monthly income need — the hard way and the easy way. The hard way is to make up a budget of your monthly expenses from memory. Not only is that method extremely time consuming — leading to such evils as procrastination — but I've found, through working with scores of clients over the years, that it's also very inaccurate. People tend to underestimate their actual needs by about 20 percent.

Including your spouse

Should you include your spouse's income when determining how much disability insurance you need? If your family needs $5,000 a month to meet living expenses and your spouse takes home, after taxes, $3,500 a month, do you, as a couple, need to cover you for only the $1,500 a month difference? Or should you ignore your spouse's income and cover your take-home pay?

Here are some reasons why you may *not* want to do that:

✔ Your spouse may lose her job while you're disabled. If she gets another job without disability coverage provided, her health conditions may not qualify her for a personal policy.

✔ You may divorce and thus have to rely exclusively on your coverage.

✔ She may die while you're disabled.

✔ She may have (or want) to quit her job to care for you (such as if you need help bathing, getting dressed, and eating).

✔ She may get disabled with you, stopping both incomes.

I recommend that you use the easy way (see the KISS principle in Chapter 1). The computation can be accomplished in about 20 minutes and is extremely accurate. Simply grab your last three months' check registers for all personal checking accounts. On the top of page one of each statement, you see a figure for the total amount of checks written for that month. Add the totals for each of the three months and divide by 3 to come up with a monthly average income need. If any particular month is extremely distorted — because you took an expensive vacation, for example, or were paying for holiday gifts — use a different month

I have provided a form in the appendix that walks you through the calculation. In short, you estimate your family financial need (the income it takes for you and your family to live now), deduct what your disability insurance would pay in the case of a loss, deduct any other income-producing assets, and deduct taxes. The amount that remains is what you need to survive if you and/or your spouse becomes disabled.

Understanding the Lingo

"Elimination period." "Own-occupation." "Residual." "Noncancelable." Disability insurance policies have their own unique terminology, using language you won't find in any other insurance policy. You need to understand these and other terms to make a good decision on those policy features that are important to you.

- **Total disability:** A person is considered totally disabled if he is unable to perform *all* the principal duties of his job, or any other job for which he's reasonably suited, considering his income, education, and experience. The pitfall to be wary of here is that if you can work only a few hours a week, you would have zero coverage under a policy covering only total disability.

- **Elimination period:** Disability lingo for *deductible.* The elimination period or waiting period represents the number of months you're willing to wait, while disabled, before coverage begins. Usually you have a choice of 30, 60, 90, or 180 days. Your choice will depend on how much money you have in the bank as a safety net combined with how long your employer will continue your salary or provide sick leave following a disability. Note that the longer you can wait, as with any deductible, the lower your premium will be. For example, waiting 60 days typically gives you about a 30 percent savings compared with a 30-day elimination period. Waiting 90 days saves you about another 10 percent. Premiums continue to go down as you increase the elimination period beyond three months, but by much smaller amounts. Your best bet is usually either a 60-day or 90-day elimination period.

If in doubt, choose the lesser waiting period due to the delayed claim check. For example, if you choose a 60-day elimination period, the payment for the next 30 days of disability comes to you only after you've been disabled for 30 days. So the first claim check you receive with a 60-day wait will come to you 90 days after your disability start date.

- **Benefit period:** This phrase refers to the duration for which you want a disability insurance paycheck — typically two years, five years, to age 65, or for your entire lifetime. Coverage to age 65 or lifetime coverage is obviously best if you can afford the cost — about 30 percent more than a five-year benefit. Because many disabled persons recover within five years, the five-year option is also a reasonable choice for those who couldn't otherwise afford the coverage they need. If you have to choose the five-year plan, be prepared to make a major lifestyle change should you face a disability that continues beyond five years. The good news is that at least you'll have five years to prepare for it. I don't recommend the two-year benefit period, because a large percentage of disabilities last beyond two years.

- **Noncancelable and guaranteed renewable:** You have two options regarding the renewability of your coverage — *noncancelable* and *guaranteed renewable* contracts. Both promise to renew coverage to age 65. Noncancelable contracts also guarantee never to raise the price up to age 65. Guaranteed renewable contracts can raise their overall rates anytime; they cannot single you out individually for an increase. How important is a price guarantee?

Disability insurance companies have experienced a worse-than-expected claims record over the past several years. Several companies have closed doors, and others have merged or been sold. The number of insurance companies offering individual disability policies has shrunken dramatically. Those insurers that are still active have taken some large rate increases on their guaranteed renewable contracts.

I would not let a price guarantee be the biggest issue in your selection. Buy all the coverage and features you need first. That's the highest priority. Then, if you can afford about another 20 percent to lock in the price, do so.

✓ **Cost of living adjustment (COLA) rider:** If you're disabled for several years, the monthly disability check you receive has diminishing spending power. The cost of living adjustment option annually increases your benefit while you're disabled by some predetermined percentage (usually from 3 to 6 percent).

If you're buying coverage to age 65, COLA is a pretty important option to include in your coverage. However, if you're buying only a five-year benefit or if you have a spouse whose projected future income will be rising dramatically, you may not need this rider.

✓ **Future purchase option:** This option guarantees, when you apply and qualify for your first policy, that, regardless of your future health, you can increase your coverage every one to three years, up to the option limit you've purchased.

If you think that you may need more disability coverage later, with increased expenses such as a bigger house, more children, or simple cost of living increases, I strongly recommend that you pay just a little more now for the privilege of being able to increase your benefit in the future regardless of health. A rather high percentage of people are declined for disability insurance due to back problems, diabetes, and so on. You may be such a person in the future. The future purchase option eliminates the possibility of your being turned down for additional coverage later. And it's usually quite inexpensive. Not only does the option guarantee you the opportunity to buy additional insurance regardless of your future health, but it also greatly simplifies the purchase of such additional insurance because no applications or physical exams are required.

The difference between future purchase options and COLA options is that the purchase option increases your coverage *before* you get disabled, and COLA increases your benefits *while* you're disabled. I recommend them both.

✔ **Residual disability:** Usually means proportionate coverage when you're unable to work full-time (from a back injury or a heart attack, for example) and usually resulting in an income loss of at least 20 percent. Under policies that cover only total disabilities, you would not receive a dime in benefits. But with residual coverage, if you work two days a week (40 percent of the workweek), you'll receive 60 percent of your monthly benefit.

I strongly recommend this coverage for absolutely everyone! Be sure to add a residual disability coverage option to any disability policy you buy. Without it, you won't get paid a disability insurance payment if you can still work even one or two days a week. Make sure that the residual benefit period isn't limited. If your disability coverage goes to age 65, so should the residual coverage. (Many benefits last only six months!)

✔ **Own-occupation protection:** *Own-occupation* coverage refers to the length of time you will be paid a full benefit when you can't do your specific occupation but could do another. In a disability policy, the period of occupation protection is found in the policy definition for *total disability.* The most restrictive definition is probably the one the Social Security Administration uses: complete inability to engage in *any* gainful occupation. The broadest definition is probably found in the expensive, deluxe policies offered to high-income professionals such as physicians and lawyers: the inability to perform the duties of your specific occupation. With the Social Security definition in your policy, you may not be eligible for benefits if you can sell pencils or wash dishes.

With the deluxe definition of own-occupation, if you were a radiologist making $300,000 a year and could no longer practice your specialty of radiology but could practice family medicine or teach radiology at the university and earn "only" $200,000, you would still be considered totally disabled. If you are that radiologist, you would get your full $300,000 benefit, plus your $200,000 teacher's salary for a total of $500,000. As you might guess, this coverage is expensive. I don't think it's necessary for most people.

Most disability policies use a definition of total disability that falls somewhere between the Social Security definition and the definition found in contracts that are sold to wealthy professionals. They pay full benefits if you can't perform your particular occupation for anywhere from two to five years, sometimes ten years; then, if you're still disabled after that period, your benefits are cut off only if you can't perform another occupation for which you're reasonably suited based on your education, training, and experience. The longer the period of protection for your specific occupation, the higher the premium. So make your decision to add an own-occupation clause based on how many years you've spent mastering your craft. A brain surgeon or a lawyer would probably want the broadest definition possible. Someone with two years of college employed as a sales representative would probably be satisfied with more limited protection on the occupation.

Always buy a disability policy that, if for whatever reason you work in another occupation that pays less than your original occupation, will still pay a proportionate/residual benefit for as long as that income difference persists.

In the example of the radiologist earning $300,000, now making $200,000 as a family doctor, his income was down one-third. A good disability policy will pay one-third of his policy benefit.

Creating Your Own Coverage Specifications

Here are my recommendations to help you customize your disability coverage:

✔ Start by determining the amount of coverage you (and your spouse) will need if you're disabled. Don't cut it too close to the bone. Allow something extra for continued contributions to a retirement plan of some sort.

✔ Determine how long you will need benefits paid to you. I recommend at least five years. Coverage to age 65 is best if you can afford the cost.

✔ Choose your elimination period. Calculate how many months you can live off your investments before you need coverage to start. I recommend at least a 60-day elimination period, but consider 90 days or 180 days if you have the cash reserves to afford it and the insurance price discount is worth the added risk. Also, consider a longer waiting period if you have some savings but are on a tight budget; it helps you afford a longer benefit period (a five-year benefit with a 30-day elimination period costs about the same as coverage to age 65 with a 90-day elimination period). Higher deductibles will hurt you far less than running out of coverage during a long disability.

✔ Look for a plan that includes full residual coverage that not only pays proportionate benefits when you can't work full-time in your regular occupation, but also pays proportionate benefits covering any income lost from changing to a lesser-paying occupation.

✔ Make sure that your policy is guaranteed renewable to age 65. Pay the increased premium to lock in the cost (in other words, buy a noncancelable contract) if you can afford it. But make the price guarantee a less important priority than obtaining the coverage you need.

✔ Don't spend a lot of money to get long-term, own-occupation coverage as long as your residual coverage will pay you a proportionate benefit for any income you lose in changing occupations.

✔ Definitely buy a future purchase option so that you can increase your benefits anytime, regardless of health — especially if you're young and your future income and living expenses grow. The best option has no dollar limit on it, so you can buy as much as your income qualifies you for.

✔ Definitely include a cost of living adjustment (COLA) rider that increases your benefits annually while you're disabled if you opt for benefits payable to age 65. COLA is less important if you choose a five-year benefit period.

Buying Disability Insurance

You've determined how much coverage you need. You've chosen the policy features that are most important to you. Your adrenaline is on high. You're primed! You're ready! The big moment you've been waiting for is finally here! Tell the truth. Is there anything more fun in life than shopping for insurance?

Even people who take great care of themselves and are very safe are stricken with disabilities, through heart attacks, falls, car accidents, illnesses, and many other things beyond their control. You've determined what amount of monthly income insurance to buy if a disability should occur. (If you haven't determined that amount, flip back to the beginning of the chapter.) Now you have to figure out where to buy your policy. In your lifetime, you'll receive many calls or fliers from insurance companies soliciting for life, auto, or home insurance. I doubt if more than 5 to 10 percent of Americans ever receive a single call soliciting for disability insurance. Definitely the most undersold (and underpurchased) major insurance coverage in America is long-term disability. With no one beating on your door, you have to start by searching out possible sources.

Evaluating possible sources

Start searching for a source of disability insurance the same way you would if you were buying any other type of insurance: Get referrals from trusted friends and interview the agent personally. Here are a few other sources to explore, with my thoughts on each:

✔ **Your employer.** If you can get group coverage through your employer for free or at little cost, taking advantage of the policy is often a good idea. Group coverage has some pitfalls, however. Benefits are taxable. You don't get to pick the features like residual or cost of living riders. If you change jobs, you lose the insurance. Its major advantage is that you can often get the insurance even if your health is poor.

✔ **Association plans.** Policies from an association that you belong to are often attractively priced. They usually have many of the same pitfalls as employer-paid insurance, however, and you usually have to qualify medically. You also lose it if you drop your association membership or if the plan is discontinued.

✔ **Your auto, home, or life insurance agent.** Many but not all agents have disability insurance available. Make sure that you interview them carefully to be sure they're knowledgeable in this area. If they aren't, ask for a referral to a disability specialist.

✔ **Disability-only agents.** A small percentage of insurance agents deal principally with disability insurance products. They tend to be quite knowledgeable about the subject. Unfortunately, they often tend to concentrate on the professional market (doctors, lawyers, CPAs, and so on). They also tend to deal in a more elite product that offers Cadillac coverage at a stiff price. Nonetheless, if you network, you'll be able to track down one of these specialists. The specialist should be able to help you find a quality product at a price you can afford, or know someone who can.

✔ **Creditors.** Often sold through lending institutions, insurance from creditors is designed to pay off loans (such as payments on a car, boat, home, or credit card balance) in the event of long-term disability. Avoid this type of insurance unless your health is such that you could not qualify for coverage in the standard market. No inquiries are made as to your medical condition when you apply for some of these policies, so the rates tend to be two, three, or more times higher than preferred rates for healthy individuals. These policies also have the added disadvantage of covering only that part of your monthly living expenses that has a loan tied to it and of expiring or running out when the loan is paid off. However, if your health is poor, buy all the coverage you can get your hands on.

Avoiding traps

When you're in the market to buy disability coverage, there are several types of policies to be wary of because of their severe coverage restrictions, their exorbitant pricing, or both. Here's a quick run-down of some of those to watch out for, including the reasons.

Short-term disability

The good news about this coverage is that it's usually offered, and paid for, by your employer. It usually starts paying you on the first day of disability caused by accidents and on the eighth day of disability caused by sickness.

Evaluating a credit card insurance offer

If you own a credit card (in other words, if you live and breathe), you receive offers all the time to buy credit insurance that will pay off the card balance if you become disabled. Unless you're medically uninsurable, these offers are usually a rip-off. Here's just one example.

A client was interested in buying disability insurance from a major national credit card company solicitation. It was a "special program for business owners," the ad proclaimed. He wisely ordered a sample policy and sent it to me for an opinion. Just how "special" was it? It only had a couple of limitations:

✔ Disability must be caused by an accident only (no coverage for heart attacks, cancer, or any other illness).

✔ After one year of disability payments, the coverage ends unless you are (and I quote) "unable to perform FOR THE REST OF YOUR LIFE any job for which you are or *can* become qualified." Any job? Selling pencils on the street corner?

Such consumer-friendly language gets me goose-bumpy all over! Needless to say, he passed on the offer.

The bad news is that it stops paying after either three or six months of disability. Then you're on your own. Unless you have a rich uncle you can live with after that, you'll need long-term protection.

The trap with this coverage is that a lot of people don't get around to buying the necessary long-term coverage. They get lulled to sleep by the mistaken belief that the odds of being disabled for more than six months are remote. Actually, the average person is three times more likely to be disabled six months or more than to die before age 65. Don't let that false sense of security given by short-term coverage distract you from buying the long-term coverage you need.

If you have short-term coverage from your employer, choose a longer elimination period when you buy your long-term policy — at least as long as the three-month or six-month short-term coverage.

Personally-paid-for group insurance

Whether you purchase it at work or from an association, personally-paid-for group disability insurance (as opposed to employer-paid-for) has a couple of traps:

✔ **Apparent lower cost.** Group insurance, especially if you're young, appears far less expensive than the private coverage you buy through insurance agents. And it is, for three reasons: The coverage is more restrictive, the renewal isn't guaranteed, and the price will increase about every four years — fairly dramatic increases, in fact, starting around age 40.

✔ **More restrictive coverage.** Group coverage often covers only total disability — when you can't work at all. Many policies don't include partial or residual coverage — a big shortcoming. Most don't contain cost of living adjustments, so once you're disabled, your benefit is frozen and the spending power of the dollar shrinks each year. Protection for your occupation is usually limited to only two or three years. Benefits under group insurance get offset by benefits from workers' compensation or Social Security; individual policy benefits usually do not. Your freedom to customize your coverage in a group plan is much more limited. Plus your coverage ends if you ever leave the group or association, or if it discontinues the plan.

I'm not saying not to buy a group plan. Some are very comprehensive. I'm saying to be careful.

Good rules regarding group insurance are the following:

✔ If it's paid for by your employer, take all of it and supplement any short-comings with a private policy. (See "Plugging Holes in Your Group Insurance Program" later in this chapter.)

✔ If you have to pay for it, get the help of a disability insurance expert to analyze it and compare costs and features to a personal or private plan. You're generally better off with a personally owned plan.

Accident-only disability insurance

Buying accident-only disability insurance is a trap that snares a lot of young people who see themselves as being quite healthy and see their disability occurring only from an accident. This is the same logic that would induce someone to buy extra car insurance to cover accidents during rush hour only, or buy extra life insurance out of a vending machine at the airport. Remember one of the guiding principles of Chapter 1: Don't buy Las Vegas insurance that only insures part of the risk.

First of all, a high percentage of young people *do* become disabled from illness (as well as accidents). Second, those mathematician actuaries at the insurance companies, when pricing comprehensive long-term disability insurance, price for the probability of both sickness and accident. Therefore, anything additional you pay to cover disabilities from sickness in a comprehensive policy is a fair reflection of the added likelihood of a sickness-caused disability.

Nonmedical disability insurance

Nonmedical disability insurance refers to any kind of disability insurance for which you simply have to pay a premium to have coverage. No medical questions are asked. You see this kind of insurance most often with credit companies covering loan balances. It can sometimes crop up in association or group plans. If no medical screening is going on, you share losses with a number of unhealthy risks, which equals much greater losses. And much greater losses lead to your paying much higher premiums.

If you're uninsurable

If your medical history prevents you from getting disability insurance, you still have choices. Buy the coverage from creditors that pays off your loans if you become disabled, including credit cards, perhaps. Also consider changing jobs to a larger employer that offers disability insurance to employees as a benefit, without medical underwriting. If you're totally dependent on your paycheck and you can't get disability for health reasons, you're probably a strong candidate for a career-ending disability. You may like your job a lot, but choosing to change jobs may be better than the financial ruin you would experience after becoming disabled while uninsured.

Instead of higher premiums, a lot of policies that don't ask health questions to qualify contain an often-hidden exclusion for preexisting conditions — so the very health problem you're trying to insure isn't covered. Almost every policy that doesn't ask health questions has this exclusion. Be careful.

If you're in good health, you'll almost always have lower premiums if you buy a policy for which medical history is screened.

Comparing policies

Comparing the price of one disability policy to another is almost impossible, even for agents, unless they make sure that they match up features as closely as possible. When comparing policies, insist that each agent quote apples to apples.

Once you know which two or three insurers have the best price for what you want, you're in a position to choose. Don't buy based on the lowest price. Other factors to consider include the agent's expertise, the insurance company's financial strength and reputation, or special coverage features not on my list that are really important to you.

Plugging Holes in Your Group Insurance Program

Suppose you're provided group disability coverage at work, entirely paid for by your employer. Coverage starts after 90 days of disability and is payable to age 65, covering total disability only — no partial or residual coverage.

Benefits are 60 percent of your salary with a maximum monthly benefit of $3,000. Further, suppose you're earning $90,000 a year.

Analyzing the problem

Here are the problems you'll have if this group policy is your only disability policy, assuming a 33 percent tax bracket:

- ✔ Zero coverage for partial disabilities. If you have a back injury that allows you to work only 20 hours per week for the rest of your career, the policy pays you nothing.

- ✔ You get only $2,000 a month, after taxes, if you have a total disability (the $3,000 maximum less 33 percent for taxes). Remember, group benefits are mostly taxable. Yet your current take-home pay, after taxes, is about $5,000 per month ($7,500 a month gross less 33 percent). Your group policy, after taxes, is paying only 40 percent of your current take-home pay!

- ✔ No additional group benefits if your income grows, due to the $3,000 per month cap.

- ✔ No ownership of the coverage, and no guarantee that it will continue. Coverage ends when the job ends. Even if the group policy guarantees the right to convert to an individual policy, most such conversion policies are overpriced with watered-down coverage, because the only people who convert are in poor health.

These are some serious shortcomings. Fortunately, the private insurance market has created a partial solution to at least three of the four gaps. Your group policy will be different from this hypothetical example, but it probably will have at least two of these holes.

Buying a supplement

Continuing on with the hypothetical example, here's what you ideally need in a supplemental policy to plug these four holes:

- ✔ Residual coverage for up to the first $3,000 per month. (My sources tell me that this may be impossible to obtain in today's disability insurance market.)

- ✔ Total *and* residual coverage beyond the $3,000 provided by the employer (the $2,000 after taxes) — as much as another $3,000 per month so that your after-tax income will be as high as $5,000 per month, your current take-home pay.

> ✔ The right to purchase additional coverage regardless of future health to cover increasing income (in other words, the future purchase option).
>
> ✔ The right to increase the total benefit regardless of health if the group insurance stops for whatever reason, such as changing jobs or the employer dropping the plan.

A few insurance companies offer the last three of these in a supplement (for example, Principal Financial Group). Take time to select a good agent who can help you identify the holes in your group plan and how to best plug them, and who is knowledgeable about supplemental policies.

In the 20-plus years that I've been in the insurance business, I've probably looked at insurance programs for about 2,000 people. Absolutely without question, the most common shortcoming is in the disability area. Amazingly, at least half of the people I talked to initially had no coverage whatsoever. The majority of the other half thought that they had coverage at work but were not sure how much. And just a handful had really taken it seriously and had arranged their own personal coverage. Please don't overlook this critical area in putting together a comprehensive insurance program for yourself.

Chapter 18

Buying Life Insurance

· ·

In This Chapter

▶ Determining how much life insurance you need

▶ Deciding between term and cash value insurance

▶ Buying life insurance smartly

▶ Debunking myths and avoiding mistakes

· ·

*W*e buy life insurance because we love. We love spouses and children and others who depend on us financially. We love them enough to face the cold reality of death (after all, none of us gets out of here alive). We love them enough to acknowledge the possibility that we could die young, leaving loved ones suffering without our income. We love them enough to plunk down our hard-earned dollars for insurance that will make sure that if we do die early, our death will not burden them financially — house payments will be made, groceries will be on the table, and college dreams can be realized.

Assessing the Need

Life insurance isn't for everyone. Neither is car insurance. Both are excellent ideas and provide good coverage. But if no one would be hurt financially by your death, you wouldn't buy life insurance, any more than you'd buy car insurance if you don't drive and don't own a car. Here's a look at some guidelines as to who does and who doesn't need life insurance.

Who doesn't need life insurance

Two groups of people do *not* need life insurance:

> ✔ **Anyone who's financially well off enough that survivors can meet all their financial needs and obligations using existing financial resources, without the possibility of depleting those resources.** For example, if you're married and have one teenage child, and you've managed to put

away $500,000 and have paid off your house, you may not need life insurance. Existing resources can support your child through college and also provide your spouse a cushion.

✔ **Anyone whose death won't cause a hardship to others.** For example, a married couple with no children who both earn a high enough income to easily support themselves if the other one dies. Another example is a single homeowner with a home mortgage and no dependents. If she has enough in savings to pay for final expenses and is okay with the home being taken over by the mortgage company if she dies, then she doesn't need insurance.

Who does need life insurance

Two groups of people *do* need life insurance:

✔ **People with someone who depends on their income.** The classic example is a wage-earning parent: If he or she dies prematurely, the surviving family members will need the financial help that only life insurance offers. Other examples include an adult son paying the bills for his elderly mother's assisted-living apartment. Life insurance will make sure that she's taken care of. Or the philanthropist with a favorite charity that relies on her generous annual gifts. Life insurance can keep those gifts coming indefinitely.

✔ **Those who provide services that would need to be hired out in the event of their death.** The classic example is a stay-at-home mom. If she dies when her children are young, her spouse will suffer a financial loss. He'll need, at the very least, money to pay for childcare. If he desires some sanity, he may want to hire household help as well. Over a ten-year span, childcare and occasional help around the house can cost $200,000 or more. Life insurance can make that outlay possible.

Also, the surviving spouse may not wish to work the same way when the stay-at-home spouse dies. It would be nice to take a different work schedule — fewer hours while your children are growing up. If you have more money, you can ask your employer for more flexible hours and less pay to be the present parent. Life insurance can make that possible.

Another example of a person in the second group is an adult who takes care of his elderly father's home — cuts the lawn, paints, and does all the handyman chores. Hiring a service to do that if the son dies may cost $500 a month. The interest on $120,000 of life insurance can make sure that those services are provided to Dad as long as Dad stays in the house. And when Dad needs additional help, the $120,000 from the insurance policy can help pay his nursing home costs. As I said earlier, buying life insurance is an act of love.

Determining How Much Coverage You Need

If you die early, exactly how much money will your loved ones need? How much will it take to pay off debt? How much to replace your income? Is providing funds to cover college costs for your children important, and if so, how much money will that take? How do you account for inflation?

Looking at a hypothetical family

So that you can get a better feel for evaluating how much coverage you need, look at a hypothetical family: Flip and Jennifer and their three children — Michael, age 11; Molly, age 10; and Flip Jr., age 7. Flip is a 38-year-old systems engineer earning $70,000 a year. Jennifer, age 37, is a high school math teacher earning $50,000 a year.

If either one of them dies prematurely, Flip and Jennifer's goal is to have enough life insurance and other resources to enable the survivors to maintain the current status of living, to pay off all final expenses, and to pay for the cost of four years of college at the state university, currently costing $30,000 per student ($7,500 a year). If their children want to attend a more expensive school, they can either get a scholarship or pay the difference themselves.

Flip and Jennifer chose not to consider retirement because each of them has an excellent retirement plan at work.

Assessing liquid assets

Any stocks, bonds, or other liquid assets that Flip and Jennifer have can be used at death to meet financial obligations and reduce the amount of life insurance needed. Flip and Jennifer have $10,000 in cash, another $20,000 in liquid investments, $80,000 combined in 401(k) retirement accounts, and $75,000 in home equity.

I don't recommend using retirement money to cover today's needs, even in a situation as dire as the premature death of a spouse. The survivor will still need those funds at retirement. I also don't usually recommend using home equity. Number one, it's not very liquid, and number two, the surviving spouse will probably want to keep the house. If the couple have no life insurance, $30,000 is available for the survivors to live on — the current assets in cash and liquid investments. (I have many clients who would prefer not to count the $30,000, keeping it instead for a family emergency fund — an excellent idea.) You never know what unexpected surprises lie ahead for your survivors. So it's good in your planning to err a little on the high side of what you think they will need.

Deducting "free" life insurance

Flip and Jennifer each have, through their jobs, employer-paid life insurance equal to one times their salary. That counts against any life insurance needs. They also buy supplemental group life insurance at work, which is not used for the calculation because, in most cases, you can buy it for less in the open market. Most often, personally acquired life insurance is both cheaper and better than supplemental group term. Group insurance costs are greater than individual because the group often insures anyone regardless of medical problems or smoking status.

Using the multiple of income method

Financial experts typically recommend that you have at least enough life insurance and liquid assets to equal a multiple of five times your annual income, ignoring inflation, and seven to eight times your income factoring in inflation. If you have children, be safe and err on the side of too much. I recommend that you use a multiple of 7.5, factoring in inflation. Why? Because life insurance is cheap — especially for young families, when the need for life insurance is greatest.

When buying life insurance, aim high. For the people you love who survive you, too much is far better than too little.

Using the Web to estimate needs

The Internet offers several life insurance sites that help you estimate your life insurance needs. One such site I consider quite good is Quicken (www. quicken.com/insurance — click on Family Needs Planner under the Life Insurance heading). Completing the questions takes about 20 minutes per person. I like the site because it's not only easy to use but also takes into account important factors such as estimated Social Security benefits to the survivors, estimated college costs, and even possible estate taxes. It also allows you to choose your own projected inflation rate and the assumed interest rate the life insurance proceeds will earn annually while they're invested.

Insuring homemakers

When you're estimating life insurance needs, overlooking or underestimating the economic value of a spouse who chooses to stay at home and care for the children is easy. After all, how *do* you determine the life insurance needs of a homemaker? You can't use the multiple of income method when the person doesn't have any income.

I have no ironclad rules for this. So much depends on the surviving spouse's preferences. How much cooking, cleaning, and laundry do you want to do when you get home from a hard day at work? Do you want to hire replacement care for your children in your own home, or do you prefer to haul them to a daycare provider? Do you want the freedom to work fewer hours and a more flexible schedule to be able to attend the special events in their lives?

When insuring a homemaker, buy enough insurance to give the surviving parent the option of paying for the nicest and least stressful "replacement" — a full-time, in-home nanny. To determine the amount of life insurance needed to make that possible, check the prices of an in-home nanny service, including cooking, cleaning, and so on, plus driving the kids wherever they need to go. Then multiply that cost over the number of years needed and round up for inflation. Your losing a loved spouse and your children losing a loved parent is tough enough without adding extra financial or workload stress to your lives.

And give the surviving spouse the economic freedom to choose if he so desires to soften his work schedule to be there more for the kids. One way to do that would be to buy enough life insurance to both hire a nanny and pay off the mortgage and all other debt.

When estimating those percentages for inflation and investment earnings, stay conservative. Don't use less than 6 percent for the assumed inflation rate — the percentage you expect the cost of living to rise each year. And don't use no more than 5 percent for the assumed interest rate — the percentage return you expect to earn on the life insurance proceeds being invested for your survivors' future needs.

Estimate your needs by using both the multiple of income method of this chapter and a credible, computerized estimate such as Quicken's, compare the results, and buy an insurance amount based on whichever method yields the higher recommended insurance amount.

Speaking the Language

Before looking at the different types of life insurance and the best places to buy them, here are a few definitions of insurance industry jargon. Some of the terms are used in the chapter, and some may be helpful when you buy your policy.

The *beneficiary* is the person or organization to whom the life insurance proceeds are payable at the death of the person insured. It could be a spouse, your children, a sibling, or a favorite charity. Every life insurance policy covering you — both those you buy and those at work — should name two beneficiaries: a primary beneficiary and a contingent beneficiary.

- ✔ A *primary beneficiary* is the person or organization to whom the life insurance proceeds are paid if that beneficiary is alive or in existence when you die.

- ✔ A *contingent beneficiary* is the person or organization to whom the life insurance proceeds are paid if the primary beneficiary is dead or no longer in existence. If no contingent beneficiary is named, the proceeds are paid to the estate of the primary beneficiary and possibly subject to delays and additional taxes.

The *face amount* (also known as the *death benefit*) of a life insurance policy is the amount of money payable at the time of death. The face amount usually can be found on the first page of the policy (the *face* page).

The *owner* of a life insurance policy may or may not be the person whose life is insured. The owner is the person or organization who controls the policy, pays the bills, chooses the beneficiary, and so on. Here are some examples of when the owner would be different from the person insured:

- ✔ A corporation owner insuring the life of a key scientist whose talents are vital to the company's survival

- ✔ A family trust owner insuring an aging parent in order to pay estate taxes due at death

- ✔ A parent insuring the life of a child to cover final expenses

Purchase options are options available with some policies that give the person insured the right to purchase additional coverage every few years, regardless of health. Coverage is guaranteed up to a certain amount per option. The options usually cease when the person is between ages 40 and 50.

For example, a couple, both 24, are engaged to be married and are planning to buy a home and have children in two to three years. They're both in good health. They don't want to spend a lot on life insurance that they don't need right now. They would like to guarantee, while they're still healthy, that they can buy coverage later even if their health sours. They may buy starter policies for $50,000 coverage on each and add a purchase option that every three years gives them the right to buy an additional $50,000 of coverage regardless of their health, their hobbies, or their increased size.

The *suicide clause* denies coverage for suicide during the first two years of the policy. After two years, suicide is fully covered.

Waiver of premium is an optional coverage that suspends your life insurance premium after you've been totally disabled for (usually) six months, until you are no longer disabled. It has two disadvantages: It's more expensive than personal disability coverage, and it won't normally pay if you can work part-time. You may not need it if you have plenty of disability coverage and you've included your life insurance premium in your estimated coverage needs.

Understanding the Types of Life Insurance

After you've determined how much coverage you need, you need to decide where to buy it and which type of policy is best suited to your needs.

There are really only two types of life insurance, although the two types come in many shapes, sizes, and colors. (The variations of each type are covered shortly.) The biggest difference between them is how long the coverage lasts.

- **Permanent life insurance** covers you for your entire life. Your death is certain. And when you die, it pays the death benefit.

- **Term life insurance** covers only a part of your lifetime. When that part or *term* ends, so does the coverage. It only pays a death benefit if you die within the designated term.

Here's a comparison of ideal use, pricing, and agent compensation for both types.

Ideal use

Permanent life insurance is ideally suited to permanent needs. Good examples are providing supplemental retirement dollars for surviving spouse, covering estate taxes due upon your death, or paying final expenses — burial, legal costs, and so on. Term life insurance is ideally suited for covering life insurance needs that are not permanent. Good examples include covering a 20-year mortgage, college costs for children, or family income needs while the kids are growing up.

Pricing

Every life insurance policy has two core parts to its price: the *mortality cost* — determined by your odds of dying at that moment — and the *policy expense cost* — your share of insurance company expenses (rent, staff, and agent commissions). The mortality charge increases each year as you age and your risk of dying increases. The expense charge stays relatively constant.

Most permanent life insurance policies have level premiums for life. How is that possible if the mortality charge increases each year? The insurance company averages the increasing mortality changes over your remaining expected life. In short, you overpay in the early years so that you can under-pay in the later years. That overpayment in the early years is set aside in a reserve for you, called *cash value*. If you cancel a permanent policy, by law you're entitled to the return much of those overpayments — that cash value. The cash value is minimal in the first couple of years because of heavy first-year costs — underwriting, medical exams, and agent commissions.

Term insurance costs, on the other hand, increase regularly as you age. Sometimes the increase is annual, and sometimes it's every five or ten years or more. Term insurance costs can be averaged over 10, 15, or 20 years, so the price is level for the entire term. Term insurance, however, does not have a cash value element. If you drop a term insurance policy in its early years, you receive no refund of any overpayment.

Agent commissions

Because term insurance has no cash value element, premiums in the first several years are considerably lower than permanent insurance premiums for the same death benefit. For example, a 30-year-old male nonsmoker may pay $200 the first year for $250,000 of term life insurance. He may pay $1,000 the first year for $250,000 of permanent life insurance. The agent selling the $200-per-year term life insurance policy typically makes $100 to $120 — often not enough to cover the costs of designing your plan and processing your application. The agent selling the $1,000 per year permanent policy generally earns $700 to $1,000 or more — good compensation for three to five hours of work.

The practice of paying agents, covering the same death benefit, five to ten times more for selling a permanent policy than for selling a term policy leads to heavy pressure on agents to sell permanent insurance, especially if they would lose money by selling you a term policy. See the sidebar "Changing agent compensation" for more information.

Changing agent compensation

The current system of paying agents five to ten times more to sell you permanent insurance instead of term for the same coverage amount is flawed. Taking the time to help a client determine the proper amount of coverage and then shop for the best deal, including completing and processing an application, is about a three- to five-hour proposition. Most term insurance commissions fall far short of paying for that effort. No one can succeed for long losing money on each sale.

One possible solution would be to pay the agent well for either type of policy but to pay about the same dollar amount regardless of which type of policy is sold. Then agents would have no incentive to recommend a permanent policy when term is better.

The biggest single negative consequence to consumers of the current system is that young families with tight budgets who need the most protection they can afford are often sold permanent instead of term insurance and are almost always far underinsured. I guarantee that if a premature death leaves a young family struggling financially because the deceased was grossly underinsured with permanent insurance, the family won't care a lick about cash value.

Of the over 300 young families I've had as clients over the years who had permanent life insurance in place when I met them, not a single one had enough death protection to meet all the family's needs. I don't recall even one that was close to adequate. That's a tragedy.

Insurance companies should pay agents the same dollar amount of compensation for the same death benefit (that is, an agent would get paid the same $600 for selling a $250,000 ten-year level term policy or a $250,000 permanent policy). Doing so would take away all incentives to do anything other than what's best for the customer.

The impact of equalizing the commissions would be as follows:

- Term insurance costs would increase a little to cover the increased commissions.

- Permanent insurance costs would come down a little to reflect the reduced commissions.

- More term insurance would be sold because agents could finally afford to sell it, and because agents wouldn't be influenced anymore to sell permanent when term is better.

- Young families would be much better protected — not only because term insurance costs less, but also because agents would get paid more only if they sold larger coverage amounts. The only negative to that system is that a family may have "too much" life insurance, and what a shame that would be. Instead of just getting by, the remaining parent and the kids may be able to live comfortably without fear of how they're going to make it. They can eat a little better, drive a little nicer car that doesn't break down quite as often, and thank God every day for that agent who sold them a little more than they "needed." And for the parent who loved them enough to pay for it.

Understanding the Variations of Permanent Life Insurance

All permanent policies have three components: mortality costs, expense charges, and cash value. Insurers offering permanent insurance compete in three ways: lowering mortality costs, lowering expense charges, and having better investment yield on the cash value.

Permanent policies vary by

✔ Whether they guarantee mortality and expense costs

✔ Whether they guarantee the yield on the cash value

Three types of permanent life insurance are on the market: whole life, universal life, and variable life. Every life insurance company offers hybrids of these three. See Table 18-1 for a quick overview of how they compare.

Table 18-1	Comparing Permanent Life Insurance Types		
	Whole Life	*Universal Life*	*Variable Life*
Mortality costs	Fixed	Variable	Fixed or variable
Expenses	Fixed	Variable	Fixed or variable
Cash value yield	Fixed	Variable	Variable
Investment risk to cash value	None	None	Yes
Option to vary the premium	No	Yes	Usually
Option to change the death benefit amount	No	Yes	Usually
Option to vary or suspend premiums	No	Yes	Yes

Whole life

People who choose whole life insurance want a lifetime policy with zero risk. They want the insurance company to guarantee, for life, the monthly cost. If an epidemic breaks out, significantly killing off a large part of the population and raising mortality costs to the insurance company, this policy cost isn't affected at all. Conversely, if science reduces heart disease rates and cures cancer, lowering deaths and mortality costs, the insurance company reaps more profits because it continues to receive the higher, guaranteed mortality charges of the whole life policy.

The same is true for expense costs. If the insurance company's expenses rise because it buys a new building or pays agents higher commissions, it can't pass on those higher costs to the whole life customers. Similarly, if it improves efficiency and cuts costs, only the insurance company reaps the benefits.

Finally, a whole life policy pays a minimal but guaranteed rate of return — usually from 3½ to 4½ percent for life. So guarantee, in fact, that the policy contains a page showing what the cash value will be for each year of the future. Today, 4½ percent guaranteed looks good. Ten years ago, when interest rates were in the double digits, it looked horrible.

With whole life, the insurance company takes all the risks. You take none. The insurance company bites the bullet when things sour and reaps extra profits when things improve. ***Note:*** If you buy a whole life policy that offers dividends, you share a little in good years and overpay in bad years. See the sidebar "Understanding life insurance dividends" for more information.

Understanding life insurance dividends

Several life insurance companies that sell permanent life insurance policies offer what they call *dividends* to their policyholders.

Unlike dividends paid on common stock holdings, life insurance dividends are essentially a refund of premiums paid. Because, in most cases, you've paid your premiums with after-tax dollars, these premium refunds (the dividends) are tax-free to you.

How can some insurers pay dividends and others not? Because those that do pay dividends charge a little more on the front end — your premium. Then if they have a good year — their investments do well — they refund some or all of that overpayment to you in the form of a dividend. Note that dividends are not guaranteed, although they are very likely. If the insurance company has a worse than expected year, it can choose not to pay a dividend at all.

If you choose a permanent policy that pays dividends, you have four choices as to how they are paid to you. You can leave them on deposit to earn interest, you can have them paid in cash and returned to you, you can apply them to reduce your premium, or you can buy *paid-up additions.* Paid-up additions are small increases in your life insurance coverage that are paid up for your lifetime. Your premiums don't increase, but when you die, your beneficiary will get your original death benefit, such as $100,000, plus the total of all paid-up additions paid for by the dividends, such as another $1,500 for a total of $101,500 paid to your beneficiary. For most people, using dividends to buy paid-up additions is the wisest of the four dividend options.

Universal life

In the 1980s, interest rates were rising to unexpectedly high levels, approaching 20 percent. Inflation was running rampant. Not only were the fixed rates of whole life eliminating most new sales, but existing customers were dropping their old policies in droves as, one by one, insurance companies began to offer a more flexible policy called *universal life insurance,* offering flexible rather than fixed interest rates on the cash value. At that time, a 13 to 14 percent return was common. Universal life later proved to be both good news and bad news for consumers.

The good news is that universal life is a flexible product. Everything that's fixed and guaranteed in a whole life policy is flexible and nonguaranteed. The risks of changes in mortality costs, expense costs, and interest rates are mostly passed on to the buyer. If costs decrease or interest rates rise, the customer reaps the benefit. If costs rise or interest rates plummet, primarily the customer takes the hit. The only risk the insurer takes is that the universal life policy has a ceiling on how high the mortality charges can go and a guaranteed minimum interest rate on the cash value — usually 4 to 4½ percent.

What I like about a universal policy is its flexibility — not only its adaptability to changing market conditions, but also its flexibility with the death benefit. With whole life, if you want to raise your coverage, you have to take out an additional policy. With universal life, you can lower the death benefit at any time and keep the same policy. You also can raise the benefit anytime, if you can prove good health, without having to buy additional policies.

Another thing I like about a universal policy is the ability to vary premium payments. To lower them or even temporarily suspend them, such as during hard times, or to pay in additional amounts when the rate of return is attractive — especially considering that the earnings are tax sheltered (free of income tax until withdrawal). With universal life, you have the option at any time to dump large additional sums into the cash value account, subject to federal maximums.

Be careful not to dump in additional amounts if any penalties for withdrawal exist. If there are penalties, usually it's best not to make the additional deposit.

Now the bad news. Universal life has one pitfall to be wary of, especially when interest rates are high. The sales illustration you receive estimates the amount of annual premium needed to be paid, assuming the current (high) interest rate remains constant, to fund the policy for life. When interest rates are high, that estimated premium is low because higher interest earnings will defray some of the policy costs. But when interest rates drop significantly, as they have in recent years, the original estimated premium will be inadequate to fund the costs, and you'll be required to significantly increase your contribution or cancel the policy. A nasty surprise.

If you want to be fairly safe from unexpected premium increases happening to you when you buy a universal life policy, choose a premium payment based on a very conservative interest rate. I recommend using the minimum guaranteed rate (that is, 4½ percent). If you do, you should never have to pay higher premiums later.

Variable life

When attached to life insurance, the term *variable* means that customers have a half a dozen or more investment options with their cash value — including investing in the stock market. The good news with variable policies is that you have the potential to outperform what you would have earned under a nonvariable contract. The bad news, like any stock market risk, is that you can lose part of your principal.

If you choose a variable policy, understand up front that if the cash value principal declines, you will have to make up the loss and pay increased premiums to fund the policy properly.

Understanding cash value options when dropping permanent insurance

If, for whatever reason, you decide to cancel a permanent policy that has accumulated cash value, you have three options (called *nonforfeiture values*) as to how that cash can be used to your benefit:

- ✔ You can receive the cash value in cash.
- ✔ You can receive prepaid permanent insurance for life for a reduced death benefit.
- ✔ You can receive term insurance for a certain length of time for the full death benefit.

Illustrating your choices

Assume the following scenario: You're a 43-year-old female. You own a $250,000 whole life policy that doesn't pay dividends. You've had the policy for ten years, for which you've paid $1,500 a year. You decide to drop the policy. Your cash value is $12,000. You can receive that sum in cash, but you have other options as well.

A fourth cash value option: Policy loans

A good way to access your cash value in a permanent insurance policy, especially when you need cash but want to continue the insurance, is to borrow against it with interest. "But it's my money," you protest. "Why can't I just pull it out? Why would I ever borrow it? And why would I have to pay interest for using my own money?"

Some permanent policies do allow you to access the cash by pulling it out. But in the first ten years or so, some surrender charges exist. If you've had the policy for a number of years, pulling out the cash value may cause some tax consequences. Borrowing from the funds has neither problem. A policy loan also has the psychological advantage of encouraging repayment, which is a good idea if you plan to keep the policy for life.

You do have to pay a modest interest charge — usually about 8 percent of the loan. But that is only done a) to cover the handling expenses and b) because while the money is in your hands, the insurance company still credits your policy with the policy guaranteed interest rate — usually 4½ percent. So the true cost of the loan to you is only about 3 to 4 percent.

If you do take a policy loan, your death benefit will be reduced by any unpaid balance. So if you have a $250,000 death benefit and have an outstanding policy loan for the $12,000 cash value at the time of your death, your beneficiary will receive $250,000 − $12,000 = $238,000. Whether to borrow your cash value or withdraw it outright is not an easy decision. Consult with your agent for the pros and cons of both options before deciding.

Given a $12,000 cash value and your age, your options might look like this:

✔ Prepaid permanent insurance of $35,000. You never pay another premium, and $35,000 is paid to your beneficiary whenever you die, now or 40 years from now.

✔ Extended term life insurance of $250,000 for 28 years and six months. Without every paying another premium, you can continue your full $250,000 of protection until you're in your early 70s.

Making the best choice

Continuing with the example, under what circumstances would you choose one option over the other? Here are a few pointers:

✔ Choose the $12,000 cash option when your need for life insurance has ended (that is, the kids are grown, the mortgage is paid, and you've become financially independent). Some people choose the cash option during hard times. If you're having financial difficulties but still need life insurance, here are two great options:

• If you temporarily can't make the premium payments, the cash value can pay them until you're back on your feet.

- If you simply need cash, you can borrow against the cash value via a policy loan at about a 3 to 4 percent net interest rate. (See the sidebar on policy loans in this chapter.)

✔ Choose the reduced, prepaid permanent insurance of $35,000 if your life insurance needs have diminished (the kids are grown, the mortgage is paid, and so on) but you still have life insurance needs such as covering final expenses.

✔ Choose the extended term insurance option if you still need the full death benefit of $250,000 and either can't afford or don't want to pay any more premiums. Term insurance is great option, especially if the need you're trying to cover with the insurance is going to end (for example, college costs and living expenses for your children) before the term insurance runs out.

Understanding the Variations of Term Life Insurance

Term life insurance contracts are differentiated based on the length of the coverage term, whether they can be renewed, the length of the price guarantee, and whether they can be converted to permanent insurance. Here are the three most common types of term life insurance.

Annual renewable term (ART)

Annual renewable term (ART) is pay-as-you-go life insurance. Each year, you pay for your mortality costs for that 12-month period, plus expenses. On each 12-month anniversary, you're a year older, your mortality costs have increased slightly, and your premium increases slightly as well.

You can renew ART policies every year simply by paying the premium. The ability to renew them could end, per the policy, in as few as ten years, but more typically it's guaranteed renewable until you're age 70 or even 100. Future prices are projected but normally not guaranteed for more than five or ten years. Premiums can increase; however, most policies do contain guaranteed maximum prices. If your health deteriorates, your future rates won't be affected, and normally you can *convert* (that is, exchange) the policy to a permanent policy anytime, without medical questions being asked.

Fixed-rate level term

Instead of annual price increases, as with annual renewal term, level term policies allow you to lock in pricing for anywhere from 5 to 30 years in 5-year increments. The most common options are 10, 15, and 20 years.

The process of setting up new life insurance policies (administering medical exams, ordering doctor reports, and so on) is expensive. The insurance company can spread these expenses over a longer period by selling level term insurance policies because people keep the policies longer than they keep annual term policies. As a result, insurers compete harder and offer more competitive prices for level term policies than they do for annual renewable term products.

Most level term policies can be converted to permanent policies anytime, regardless of health (although some policies limit the conversion period to 15 years or so). Also, most can be renewed beyond the first term. Where level term policies differ most dramatically is how that renewal happens and what happens to the price.

Never buy term life insurance that doesn't have an option to convert to permanent insurance, regardless of your health. You never know what the future may hold, so keep your options open.

Traditionally renewable level term

At the end of the first term, traditionally renewable level term policies renew for another period of the same length, without requiring you to requalify medically. The price changes on the renewal date, based on your age.

For example, assume that at age 30 you bought a ten-year traditional level term policy at preferred rates. On the renewal date ten years later, you receive a bill offering to renew for another ten years, only now at a preferred 40-year-old rate, without having to qualify medically and also at preferred rates.

Reentry renewable level term

Renewable level term works exactly like traditional level term in all respects except one. The renewal billing at the end of the original term is for your new attained age, but at sky-high rates that usually climb higher each year. Only if you're still healthy and can qualify medically (in other words, if you can reenter) can you reapply for the lowest preferred rates.

Because insurance companies aren't obligated to offer the lowest rates on renewal, reentry renewable level term policies are the lowest-priced term policies in the insurance market. The bad news is that their renewal price is the highest in the market if you're no longer in good health.

Mark's reentry story

Mark's $500,000, ten-year reentry term policy renews this month. Mark, who has exercised and eaten healthy all his life, was diagnosed with cancer two years ago. Instead of the $2,000 renewal bill he would have qualified for if he were in good health, the renewal offer came in at $14,000 a year for the first year and increased about $1,000 a year thereafter.

Fortunately, Mark's policy includes a conversion option. The cost to convert to a permanent policy with cash value is only $8,500 a year. I say

only because $8,500 is far less than $14,000, the premiums won't increase, and the permanent policy builds cash value. Mark pays $8,500 a year so that his daughter will get a $500,000 death benefit — given Mark's illness, that's a bargain. He couldn't find a new life insurance policy anywhere at any price. Even if he lives for ten more years, he'll pay $85,000 in premiums and his daughter's trust will receive $500,000. An easy decision!

If you decide to buy this type of product because of its great front-end price, give yourself a cushion. Buy it for a term of five to ten years longer than you think you'll need it to protect yourself (somewhat) from possible sky-high rates. And definitely don't use the product for a permanent need.

Decreasing term

Decreasing term policies have coverage that reduces annually, but the premium stays level for the duration — usually 15 to 30 years. Two types of decreasing term policies exist:

- ✔ **Level decreasing term coverage** reduces coverage a flat amount each year (for example, a 25-year level decreasing term policy reduces 4 percent a year).

- ✔ **Mortgage decreasing term coverage** reduces to match a mortgage payoff. Like a mortgage, coverage reduces very slowly in the first few years and picks up steam in the later years. The rate of reduction is tied to the mortgage interest rate and the length of the mortgage. So if you buy a 10-year, 7 percent mortgage decreasing term policy, like the mortgage balance, coverage declines much faster than a 30-year, 9 percent mortgage decreasing term policy. The 10-year, 7 percent policy is also far less expensive than the 30-year, 9 percent policy.

The good news about either type of decreasing term policy is that the rates usually won't change for the duration of the term you choose. The bad news is that your life insurance coverage is reducing at a time when your living expenses are rising. Not a good idea. The other bad news is that your life insurance normally ends when the term ends — the policies aren't renewable. But in all likelihood, your need for life insurance hasn't ended. And the rates for this type of coverage aren't nearly as good as level reentry term rates for the same coverage period.

If you're thinking of buying a decreasing term policy, don't. Unless decreasing term life insurance coverage is court ordered (covering the mortgage of an ex-spouse and children) or mandatory as part of a loan, buy reentry level term instead of decreasing term. You get coverage that doesn't decrease and a much lower cost.

Assessing insurance from your mortgage company

If you have a home mortgage, you probably receive offers in the mail for mortgage decreasing term insurance from the mortgage company. Buying the policy is tempting. You die; the mortgage gets paid. The price looks reasonable, and they can include the insurance premium with your house payment. What could be sweeter?

Buy it. Buy all that you can. But only if your health is bad, you're obese and a chain smoker, or you've been given six months to live. And only if coverage is automatic (no medical questions). In short, if you can't qualify for life insurance in the open market, buy all the mortgage decreasing term insurance you can get your hands on. If you're healthy, buy your insurance elsewhere. Here's why:

- Insurance from the mortgage company is almost always more expensive — often considerably more — than coverage you can buy privately.

- The coverage ends when you sell your home, whereas the same coverage purchased privately will not end. That's important, especially if your health has soured.

- The beneficiary is the mortgage company, not your family. Never a good idea. Your spouse may not want to pay off the mortgage with the money, such as if she could earn 10 percent in a money market account and the mortgage rate is only 7 percent. (Not to mention the tax write-off of the mortgage interest!) Or such as if something unexpected has happened and she desperately needs the money for something more important.

Be careful if the price from the mortgage company appears really attractive. A few years ago, an employee, Mary Jo, brought me an offer for mortgage insurance from her mortgage company. The rates were amazing and she was thinking of buying it. The nice brochure gave several examples of dying: car accidents, plane crashes, falling off a roof, and so on. The brochure lacked only one thing — it failed to mention that it was *accident coverage only!* No coverage for death from natural causes — which is, even for young people, the cause of the vast majority of deaths.

Making Your Choice

Clearly, a potpourri of different types of life insurance are out there. How do you choose among them? Here are a few pointers:

- If you have a permanent need, buy permanent life insurance if you can afford it. If you need it but can't afford it, buy cheap reentry level term that's convertible to permanent, regardless of your health. A permanent need is a need that, no matter how old you are today, will require cash for your survivors when you die — paying estate taxes, supporting an adult child with Down's Syndrome in a group home, continuing to support a favorite charity after your death, or providing supplemental lifetime income to a surviving spouse.

- If you have a nonpermanent need, buy term life insurance. Examples of nonpermanent needs include living expenses while the children are growing up, paying off a mortgage, or paying for the children's college education.

- Buy annual renewal term insurance if your need is pressing for only a year or two, but only if the price is less than that of a five-year reentry level term policy.

- Buy reentry level term if your need is great and your budget is small, such as if you're a parent with young children. However, make sure that you're clear on when the initial level term period ends. If you still need life insurance at that time, you may need to convert what you have into a much higher-priced permanent policy if you can't qualify medically for reentry. For that reason, I recommend that you buy reentry term insurance for a period of at least five to ten years longer than you think you need it. Also, because you want the company to be around when you convert, make sure that the quality of the insurance company is high. I suggest an A. M. Best rating of A or better. (See Chapter 12 for information on rating insurance companies.)

   For a small charge, some reentry term products offer a guarantee that, at the end of the first level term period, you can renew for another term at the low reentry rate regardless of your health. Unless you're 100 percent sure that you won't need coverage beyond the first term, buy this option if it's available.

- Buy only guaranteed renewable and convertible term products. You never know what the future may hold.

✔ Buy traditional non-reentry level term coverage anytime you find its pricing reasonably close to reentry term costs, or if you're willing to pay extra for the peace of mind of keeping preferred rates without ever having to requalify.

✔ Unless the price is significantly lower, always buy privately owned term life insurance rather than group insurance through employers, associations, or creditors and banks. Coverage from the latter sources can end (such as coverage from your employer ending when you leave your job).

✔ Be very wary about buying decreasing term life insurance. Prices usually aren't that competitive, and coverage is normally not renewable. Plus, people's coverage needs rarely decrease.

Evaluating Life Insurance Sources

As you get inundated with life insurance solicitations, do you ever feel that the first thing astronauts will encounter when landing on Mars will be a coin-operated machine selling accidental space-death insurance? There's certainly no shortage of places to buy life insurance out there.

After you have determined how much coverage you need and the type of policy — term or permanent — that best suits your needs, you can search out the best place to buy what you need.

Considering an agent

Permanent insurance is available almost exclusively from insurance agents. I recommend that you buy permanent insurance only from a top agent. Keep in mind that permanent insurance, due to its complexity and cash value element, requires added expertise in choosing among different products.

Buying term insurance is a completely different issue. Unlike almost any other kind of insurance, term insurance is close to a commodity. Term policies are the least complex policies you can buy. The policy boils down to one sentence: "If you die, we pay." Because, unlike most other policies, there aren't a lot of hidden exclusions, limitations, and other dangers, buying it direct, without an agent, is less risky than buying any other policy direct.

However, using an agent doesn't cost that much more (if anything). I recommend using one, but separate the wheat from the chaff and pick only a skilled agent. Hiring the best won't cost you a dime more, because all agents get paid about the same amount, determined by the premium you pay. A good agent can help you determine the right amount of coverage, determine the best type of term insurance product to use, set up the policy owner and beneficiary properly, and be an advocate for you if you're having problems with the insurance company. A top agent can also help you choose a financially solid company that will endure. And finally, if your application is rejected due to health, weight, or other problems, a good agent can help you search for a company that will insure you.

As to possible sources of agents, life insurance is available from career life insurance agents whose primary occupation is the sale of life insurance, from the agent who helps you with your auto and Homeowners insurance, and from many financial planners.

Career life insurance agents

The principal advantage of a career life insurance agent is that life insurance is their specialty. They tend to have a higher level of expertise, especially if they have more than five years in the business. Life insurance agents who have taken advanced classes and earned professional designations, such as the Certified Life Underwriter (CLU), are especially good bets.

Be careful of inexperienced agents, especially if you have complex needs. Many don't last. The washout rate for life insurance agents is one of the highest of any profession — close to 90 percent in the first two years! Most new agents also have less expertise than experienced agents (unlike the rest of us, who were geniuses the first day on the job!). In many states, a person can legally sell life insurance with just a week's schooling.

If you do work with a new agent and you have any concerns about what's being recommended to you, get a second opinion. If you decide to work with an agent, you may get a lot of pressure to buy permanent life insurance when you're asking for term life insurance. The dramatically higher commission that agents earn by selling permanent insurance compared to term insurance may be the reason. If the agent who's "helping" you insists that permanent insurance is your best option when your need isn't permanent, walking away from that agent may be your only option. But some real pros, who care about your welfare, may also believe that permanent insurance is the only way to go. After all, permanent insurance is always going to be there for you and your loved ones, as long as you pay the premiums.

I don't have a problem with buying permanent insurance, provided that you can afford the higher premiums for the coverage your survivors will need. What matters most isn't the type of policy you buy; it's that your survivors are well taken care of. The biggest problem I've seen, over and over, is that most young people who buy permanent instead of term end up underinsured.

Multiple policy agents

Many agents who sell auto and home insurance also have life insurance licenses. But less than half know much about life insurance or even actively sell it. And probably only 20 percent are quite knowledgeable about the subject.

If you like your current auto and Homeowners agent's skills in those areas but he is not an expert on life insurance, ask for a referral to a life insurance specialist. If your agent is good at his specialty, chances are excellent that the agent he refers you to will also be good. If your current agent is skilled with life insurance, working with him in that area, too, is to your advantage. Having one agent for everything simplifies your life. And the washout rate on these multiple policy agents is very small.

If you prefer one agent to help you with all your insurance needs, include life insurance expertise on your agent shopping list. (See Chapter 12 for tips on choosing an expert.)

Financial planners

Two types of people licensed to sell life insurance fit the broad *financial planner* category. The first is money managers who primarily dispense investment advice but also are licensed to sell life insurance. The second is career life agents who also offer investments. The primary difference between the two is that the former more often recommend buying term life insurance with your investments separate, whereas the latter often recommend permanent life insurance with its cash value as a part of your investment portfolio.

If you're considering buying life insurance from a financial planner, a pretty safe bet is that those who recommend term insurance for your nonpermanent needs are the better choice. Permanent insurance is not considered a good investment product. Buy permanent insurance if it's the best insurance for your needs, but don't buy it solely as an investment, for three reasons:

- ✔ Permanent life is non-portable — if something better comes along, it's hard to move without penalty.

- ✔ The mortality charges are usually higher than those for term insurance. To get a true reflection of the rate of return on the cash value of a permanent policy, you need to deduct the hidden costs of those extra mortality and expense charges. How? By shopping for the lowest term life policy, requesting that the agent disclose those same charges in the permanent, and then subtracting the difference between the two results from the cash value gain.

- ✔ The heavy front end cost of permanent due to the high sales commission significantly affects the cash value performances.

I'm not in the least advising you not to buy permanent life insurance. Just (as a rule) don't buy it as an investment.

A Christmas gift from my credit card company

I received an offer from my credit card company one December — apparently a Christmas present to its beloved cardholders. Here's what the form said: "Open Enrollment. My card balance paid in full if I die, up to $5,000; 5 percent of my card balance paid monthly if I'm disabled or unemployed more than 30 days. Cost: only $0.59 per month per $100 of balance." If by chance I was crazy enough to turn down this offer, it requested my refusal in writing. With a sentimental and grateful tear in my eye, I madly dashed to the phone to arrange for overnight express mail delivery when that dark Scroogy part of myself said, "Bah, humbug! How good a deal is $0.59? Cheeseburgers, maybe. But credit card insurance?"

Let's see — 59¢ per $100 per month is $70 per year per $1,000 of card balance. I know that life insurance costs between $1 and $5 per $1,000 for most age groups. That leaves about $65 for the disability and unemployment insurance, which pays only 5 percent of the balance monthly. So that's worth another $5 to $10 a year per $1,000 of balance. Expenses would run

another $5, which leaves $45. What's left? "Profit," you say? Oh, ye of little faith!

You're overlooking one important item: "Open Enrollment," which means that you qualify *regardless of health!* So this is really an offer for the "near-dead." It's the card company's way of saying thanks to you on your way out. Yes, Virginia, there is a Santa Claus! Suppose you have six months to live. The creditor apparently wants you to get ten of these cards, buy card insurance on each, and run each up to the $5,000 limit with cruises, vacations, cars, and the like. That's $50,000 of fun for $0.59 per $100 per month, or about $300 per month. Six months later, you're gone. The debt is wiped clean. $50,000 of fun for only $1,800! Can you think of a more generous offer? (And you were skeptical! Aren't you ashamed?)

You ask, "Wouldn't it have been easier to just say, 'Don't buy credit card insurance unless you're uninsurable or near death,' rather than tell this tongue-in-cheek tale?" Of course! But not nearly as much fun.

Buying without an agent

If you're considering buying term life insurance direct from an 800 number or on the job, first check with your favorite agent to see if she can match the price. The majority of the times she can — in which case, use an agent. If your agent can't match the quote or come close, consider paying the agent a fee (perhaps $100) to review your plans and make sure that you're not shooting yourself in the foot. All the following sources of term life insurance allow you to buy without an agent:

- ✔ **The Internet:** Several sites are set up to comparison-shop term life insurance.

- ✔ **Creditors:** Banks, mortgage companies, and credit card companies regularly solicit their customers to buy *credit life insurance* from them to pay off any balance if the customer dies. Look at what they get! If you buy the insurance from your mortgage company, for example, it makes a nice up-front commission on the sale, and later, if you die, it gets paid your outstanding balance. What a good deal (for them)!

But how good is the deal for you? Not very. Life insurance rates from creditors are usually much higher than on the open market. And the creditor — not your survivors — is the beneficiary. Unless your health makes you uninsurable through traditional life insurance sources, avoid obtaining insurance from your creditors.

✔ **Associations:** A lot of groups and associations offer term life insurance as a membership benefit. Sometimes the price is fantastic. Most of the time, the price is mediocre. The problem is that if you leave the association or the association quits offering the coverage, you lose your life insurance.

As a general rule, don't buy life insurance from an association; however, do buy as much as you can if you're uninsurable and the insurer asks no medical questions.

✔ **Group life:** First, let me say, "Take all the free life insurance your employer offers you." Second, if and only if your health is poor and you can't qualify for other types of life insurance, buy all the supplemental life insurance your employer offers on a nonmedical basis. (Sometimes that can be $50,000 or more.) Third, if you're healthy, don't buy any more than the free coverage paid for by your employer through work. Buy it privately. Why? Two reasons: You lose group insurance when you leave the job, and the rates are almost always higher than on the open market if you're in good health.

✔ **Direct mail and telemarketing phone solicitations:** Again, unless they offer guaranteed coverage and you're otherwise uninsurable, stay away from direct mail and 800 number sources. Most have a fly-by-night feel. Plus, they rarely offer prices that can compete with those you can get in the market if you're healthy.

✔ **Slot machines:** I mean those coin-operated flight insurance dispensers at airports and similar dispensers of "fear insurance." Unless you know ahead of time that the plane is going down, don't buy this stuff. (Or better yet, don't take the flight!) But *do* listen to your fear. It's telling you that you feel inadequately insured. Act on that fear and raise your life insurance coverage to a high enough level that you can comfortably walk by these machines (with a smile) the next time you fly.

Debunking Life Insurance Myths and Mistakes

All kinds of half-truths, myths, and common mistakes are associated with buying insurance. In this section, I show you the most common ones so that you can avoid falling into any traps.

Mistake: Trading cash value for death protection needs

Being underinsured with permanent life insurance may be the biggest single mistake that people make in buying life insurance. They get swayed by the lure of the investment portion or cash value of the policy but can't afford to have their cake and eat it, too. In other words, they can't afford to pay for all the death protection they need plus the investment, so they buy a cash value policy with less death protection than they need in order to have some investment — something to show for it in the end when they don't (unlike the rest of us) die. However, when they do die, their family doesn't have enough money to live on, creating a serious financial problem.

The most important thing about life insurance is the protection it offers. So first things first. Determine how much life insurance you need by using a credible method. Then buy as much of that protection as you can afford, using term insurance, even lower-cost reentry products if necessary. If your budget has something left over, only then is it okay to look at permanent life products for part of your coverage. Never trade critical protection for less-important investment opportunities.

Myth: Buying supplemental group life insurance is cheaper

Group insurance pools healthy and unhealthy people. Group insurance rates are, therefore, cheaper only if you're uninsurable or if the employer pays all or part of the premium.

Before buying optional coverage at work, compare the coverage with what the open market has to offer. Chances are you will do as well or better on your own, plus you can keep the policy when you leave the job.

Mistake: Buying your life insurance in pieces

Buying your life insurance in pieces is a lot more expensive than covering all your needs in one policy. Plus, buying in pieces leaves you vulnerable to a gap in your coverage. Examples of piecemeal buying are having mortgage insurance through your lending institution, credit card insurance through your credit card company, credit life insurance with your car loan, supplemental group life insurance at work, flight insurance at the airport, and so on. With some of these insurances, you don't have to qualify medically; therefore, if you're in poor health or near death, buy all you can. Otherwise, they're often three or four times the price of what you would pay if you're in good health.

Besides the higher prices, the other concern I have about buying life insurance in pieces is that you take care of only part of the risk, leaving a lot of needs unprotected. Using the piecemeal approach, you could buy a little grocery life insurance so that when you die, your family's groceries will be paid for. (The supermarket could offer it at the checkout.) Or insurance on your utility bills. If you die or become disabled, your survivors wouldn't have to pay utilities for a year or two.

When buying life insurance, figure out how much insurance you need to do the whole job and buy *one* policy.

Mistake: Buying accidental death/travel accident coverage

Both accidental death and travel accident policies are varieties of Las Vegas insurance, transferring only the accidental portion of your risk. In other words, you have no coverage for death from natural causes. Buying these policies is an especially bad move if you buy them in lieu of the full life insurance you really need. My belief about travel accident coverage is that anyone who buys it at the airport or from a travel agent is really saying, "I'm not comfortable with the amount of life insurance I have." The bottom line is that if you need insurance to cover a flight you're taking, you also need it for driving down the street, potential heart attacks, and the like.

When buying life insurance, buy only coverage that pays for any death — natural or accidental.

Mistake: Covering only one income

Covering only one income in a marriage is a serious mistake. If your household has two incomes and you depend on both of them, don't just cover one income (unless you have a crystal ball). One income may be larger than the other, but if the person with the lesser income dies and the surviving spouse can't make it on his or her income alone, you have a problem.

When buying life insurance in a marriage, always insure both incomes unless the person with the larger income brings home enough pay to completely support himself or herself and the second income is just gravy.

Mistake: Ignoring a homemaker's value

If one spouse stays home with the children and takes care of the home (cleaning, doing the shopping, and so on), that person has a real economic value to the household because a lot of those services would have to be hired out in the event of death. Many couples overlook insuring the home-maker because no outside income is being brought in. Big mistake.

Buy life insurance on a homemaker. Estimate the amount of coverage you need by determining the cost to hire someone to perform the same tasks that the homemaker does. Multiply that by the number of years you need help, and then add in money for an emergency fund, college fund, and so on. (Also consider funds for longer vacations and shortened workdays for the surviving spouse.)

Mistake: Covering the children in lieu of the parents

When Johnny or Susie is born, you try to be a responsible parent. You're deluged with a lot of solicitations about life insurance because of the birth announcement in the newspaper. You have hopes and dreams for your children, so you buy a nice cash value policy on your baby. It's understandable — you're so proud. But the economic effect on the family of a child's death is minimal compared to the major impact that one of the baby's parents dying would have.

When a child is born, seriously reevaluate and raise the amount of life insurance coverage that Mom and Dad have.

Mistake: Buying decreasing term insurance

Decreasing term life insurance generally gives you level premiums for a period of years with the protection amount decreasing each year. This type of policy is often used with mortgage insurance so that it decreases as the mortgage decreases. At first glance, going with a decreasing policy to cover a decreasing mortgage seems to make sense. And if that's the only life insurance need that you have, perhaps that would be a logical solution to the problem. But most people have many other life insurance needs. When some expenses are decreasing in a person's life, others are increasing due to inflation.

Don't buy decreasing term insurance. Instead, buy the cheapest reentry level term insurance you find. The coverage won't decrease. The cost will be significantly less than the cost of decreasing term. If you need less coverage down the road, you can always decrease your reentry level term life insurance coverage simply by exchanging it for a lesser policy.

Mistake: Being unrealistic about how much you can afford to pay for life insurance

In the 25-plus years that I've been an agent, I can't tell you how many times I've seen young people commit more money than they can actually afford to a large cash value life insurance policy and then two or three years later have to drop it and take a large financial loss — and perhaps even be exposed to the risk of a death without insurance. I recommend term insurance for young families. It provides the most coverage for the money spent. If you want a permanent policy later with more bells and whistles, you can always convert your term policy.

Mistake: Buying before you need it

Over the years, I've seen many single people with expensive cash value life insurance, years before anyone in their life would suffer financially by their death. Remember that you wouldn't buy car insurance if you didn't own a car. Don't buy life insurance unless someone depends on you financially.

Myth: Life insurance is cheaper when you're young

Life insurance really is cheaper when you're young. So are dentures, but you don't buy them until you need them, either. This myth started because the *annual* cost of life insurance is cheaper *per year* when you're young because your chances of dying are lower. But the *total* cost that you pay over the life of the policy is not cheaper! How could it be?

Suppose that you buy life insurance for $100 a year at age 25 and your friend waits until age 35 and has to pay $110 a year for the same coverage. Now you're both 35 and you pay $10 less per year — but how about the $1,000 that you paid for the ten years that you didn't need it? Plus interest? Don't buy life insurance until you need it.

Part VII
The Part of Tens

The 5th Wave   By Rich Tennant

SAFETY SEMINAR

In this part . . .

In this part, you find concise lists of ways to help yourself by insuring your life changes, by anticipating change, and by accessing useful insurance tools on the Internet.

Chapter 19

Ten Strategies for Managing Life's Changes

*W*hen you make a change in your life, you need to change your insurance coverage. The insurance plan you had before the change often won't cover some of the new risks you've taken on during and after the change. Under the standard Homeowners policy, you have no coverage for any of the following incidents:

- You're sued for $350,000 for injuries to three guests at a party your son hosted in his apartment — the apartment you helped him qualify for by cosigning the lease.

- You're remodeling your home. A carpenter is injured when his own scaffolding collapses. The accident is no fault of yours, whatsoever. But you're sued for Workers' Compensation benefits of $200,000 — $120,000 for medical bills and $80,000 for lost wages.

- In the same remodeling job, $25,000 of heating and air conditioning equipment, sitting in your yard and about to be installed, is stolen in the middle of the night.

- You're sued for $75,000 for damage to the furnishings of the condominium below your aging mother's, caused by water overflowing from a tub she was filling and forgot about. Your mother, on her attorney's advice, had just transferred ownership of her condominium to you.

These scenarios are just a few examples of possible serious, uninsured claims, all of which originate as the result of a significant change in your life. In this chapter, discover how to manage the insurance risks of ten of life's more common changes — from the cradle to the grave.

Marrying

From getting engaged up to the wedding ceremony, here are some of the special risks you face and some strategies to help you manage them.

Getting engaged

If a valuable ring is involved in the engagement and you want it insured in case it's lost or stolen, you should schedule it as an addendum to a Homeowners policy. A basic Homeowners policy provides little or no jewelry coverage, especially for the loss of a diamond or other gem, so the ring must be scheduled. If you already have the wedding rings and if they have any value, you may want to schedule them as well. See Chapter 6 on scheduling jewelry.

Generally, the ring should be insured under the policy of its owner. If the owner still lives with her parents, add the ring to the parents' Homeowners policy.

Cohabiting before the marriage

Engaged couples who choose to live together before the marriage are fairly common — usually sharing an apartment but occasionally co-owning a house. Here are my suggestions for handling the added risks associated with either arrangement.

Set up a Homeowners or renters policy in *both* names. If you buy the insurance under only your name, your partner has no personal liability coverage under your policy for activities — such as injuring someone while playing racquetball. Plus, your partner's personal belongings won't be covered.

Move both your car insurance polices to the same insurance company and buy the same liability limits on each policy. Why? Your Personal Auto policy won't cover you while driving your partner's car. (It excludes coverage on cars you have regular access to.) Being insured with the same company assures you that your policy terms will be identical, no matter which car you drive — which will also make for a far easier claim experience. Buying the same liability limits assures that the same amount of money will be available to each of you for lawsuits regardless of which car you're driving. If you buy $300,000 of coverage and your partner has $50,000 of coverage, when you drive your partner's car the only coverage you have is his $50,000. The only way you can get $300,000 coverage driving, when he lives with you, is for him to have the same $300,000 liability coverage as you. If your partner won't agree to the same coverage, don't *ever* drive his car.

Getting married

I recommend you set up Homeowners insurance in both names. Make sure the property limit is high enough to cover both your belongings as well as wedding gifts. Also, combine your vehicles into one car insurance policy. (See Chapters 3 and 5 for advice on buying both those policies.)

If you're both working, continue your group health coverage if it's provided to you by your employers. If one of you doesn't have health coverage through work, add the uninsured spouse to the insured spouse's group policy. You generally have 30 days from the wedding date to do so without having to *qualify medically,* meaning to prove that you're in good health. After 30 days, you can be declined due to poor health. (See Chapter 16 for advice on buying health insurance.)

Make sure you have enough life insurance to pay for a funeral and other final expenses. Most jobs include enough free life insurance to cover these costs. If one of you has life insurance through work and the other one doesn't, add the uninsured spouse onto the insured spouse's group policy. You can also buy an individual policy. (See Chapter 18 for tips on estimating your life insurance needs.)

Be sure to change the beneficiaries on all life insurance policies — individual or group — to each other. When the wedding announcement hits the papers, you'll be inundated with solicitations for life insurance. If you don't need it, don't buy it. Don't overlook long-term disability insurance, especially if you need two incomes to make ends meet.

Be careful of contracts you're asked to sign related to the wedding reception. Make sure the terms are reasonable. I had one client show me a restaurant rental contract where the wedding party had to agree to be responsible not only for injuries they caused, but also for injuries the restaurant caused — like food poisoning. Sign something like that, and you'll be in deep trouble — with the possibility of no insurance — if a guest is injured at the reception! Check with your agent to make sure that your personal liability coverage — home and/or umbrella — will protect you if you do get sued for injuries or property damage at the reception.

Building or Remodeling

Whether you're building your dream house or remodeling your current home, you've taken on a lot of additional risks, many of which are not automatically insured. Enjoy the excitement, but make sure that your insurance is adequate for the new risks in your life. Here's a list of some of those risks and how I recommend you handle them.

- ✔ **Risk:** Property damage to new construction from fire, wind, vandalism, and so on.

  Recommendation: If building a new home, have a clear understanding, in writing, with the builder as to who is responsible for the property insurance. Make it a requirement that the party who buys the insurance also names the other party as loss payee. Require that proof of the insurance be provided prior to the start of construction. If you, as the homeowner, are responsible for the insurance, buy a Homeowners policy rather than a Builders Risk policy. Homeowners coverage is much more comprehensive and includes, at no extra charge, liability coverage for job-site injuries.

  If you're remodeling, increase your Homeowners building-coverage limit, at the time the work starts, to the revised cost to replace your home with the improvements.

- ✔ **Risk:** Theft of building materials (normally materials aren't covered until they're installed in your home).

  Recommendation: Either contractually require the contractor to be responsible for all materials until they're installed or add a theft of building materials endorsement to your Homeowners policy and delete the endorsement when everything is installed.

- ✔ **Risk:** Lawsuits from job-site injuries (usually covered by your Homeowners policy).

  Recommendation: This is a good time to reevaluate your personal liability limits. Consider adding an umbrella policy if you don't already have one (see Chapter 10). Also, in your construction contract, require the contractor to defend you and pay any judgment against you for injuries or property damage he or his crew cause. Request proof of the contractor's General Liability insurance before work starts. If he doesn't have insurance, you're much more apt to be sued yourself if someone gets hurt.

- ✔ **Risk:** Workers' Compensation claims filed against you for medical bills and lost wages from any worker injured on the job (this risk is *not* covered by your Homeowners policy).

  Recommendation: Require written proof from your contractor that he has Workers' Compensation insurance covering all workers before any work starts. Run all labor costs — even if you're paying your friends to chip in — through the contractor, so that you're not at risk for anyone's injuries.

  Another option is to buy your own Workers' Compensation policy for the period of construction, especially if you are acting as your general contractor.

Don't start new construction without someone — you or the contractor — having Workers' Compensation insurance in place.

✔ **Risk:** Injuries and property damage that happen after the work is completed (examples: the furnace blows soot through the house, a defective fireplace causes a major building fire, or the roof leaks from a defective installation).

Recommendation: Require in your construction contract that the contractor provide you proof of General Liability insurance, including *Completed Operations Coverage,* which covers those kinds of claims. If there are injuries or damage later, you may have a source of insurance to collect from.

✔ **Risk:** The contractor skipping out and not paying subcontractors, who then file liens against your property.

Recommendation: Require the contractor to get lien waivers signed by all subcontractors prior to your paying for the work. Or, if he's not agreeable to that, pay the subcontractors directly.

✔ **Risk:** Misunderstandings between you and the contractor, causing significant frustration and financial loss.

Recommendation: Always work with a contract and a good attorney. Incorporate into the contract a lot of the issues addressed in this list!

Becoming a New Parent

Here are a few pointers for people expecting the birth of their first child:

✔ **Health insurance:** Under many health plans, newborns cease to be covered 30 days after birth unless you notify your health insurance company within that 30-day period requesting that your child be added to your coverage. So call the company. And don't wait 30 days. Call immediately. If you're married, you may have a choice between the mother's or father's policy. If you do, compare costs, features, and the freedom to choose doctors. (See Chapter 15 for the most important elements of a health insurance plan.)

✔ **Life insurance:** This may surprise you, but insuring your child isn't the most important issue. When a child is born, Mom and Dad must buy or significantly raise their life insurance protection to make sure that Junior won't be a "street baby." And don't forget to insure the homemaker if one of you will be staying home. This is also a good time to reassess life insurance beneficiaries and change your contingent beneficiary to "all surviving children" instead of "my brother Ralph." (See Chapter 18 on how to determine life insurance needs.)

> ✔ **Disability insurance:** If you've put off buying this coverage, now is a good time to rethink your decision. The loss of a paycheck would be a bigger hardship now that you have a new baby. (See Chapter 17 for more on disability insurance.)

Moving

Talk about great timing. As I was about to write this page, I received a call from clients Bill and Hillary. regarding a household move they're making. Their move is so typical that I'm sharing it, so that you can consider the added risks you'll have the next time you move.

Doing the moving yourself

On October 31st, Bill and Hillary will close on their current home. Their new home is still under construction and won't be completed and ready to close until mid-December. So for the six-week interim period, they will be storing most of their belongings in a rented warehouse space and also renting a fully furnished motel unit, complete with a kitchen. They're moving themselves and are going to rent a truck. They will need liability coverage to drive it. They also will be responsible, under the terms of the truck rental agreement, for *any* damage to the truck while they are using it — both when hauling their things to the storage facility and then, six weeks later, hauling the same items from storage to the new house.

Here's what I recommend you do if you find yourself in Bill and Hillary's shoes. To cover the floating personal property, don't cancel the Homeowners policy insuring the home you are selling.

> ✔ **Risk:** Property being moved while in transit. Basic Homeowners insurance covers only specific losses like collision and theft, but won't cover all losses, such as breakage of furniture and electronics from load shifting.
>
> **Recommendation:** Add Special Perils contents coverage to your Homeowners policy insuring the home you just sold. It covers almost any loss outside of a few exclusions such as breakage of fragiles (dishes, crystal, and so on). If you want fragile items covered for breakage, you'll need to schedule them.
>
> ✔ **Risk:** Property in storage. Basic Homeowners policies do cover, in full, all personal property in a locked storage facility up to the contents policy limit. But the types of losses covered are limited to fire, wind, vandalism, theft, and so on. No coverage exists, for example, for water damage from roof leaks or ground water damage of any kind.

Recommendation: Again, add the Special Perils contents coverage. It covers almost all losses. It covers water damage from roof leaks. And, although it excludes ground water damage at home, it covers it away from home, such as for items in storage.

✔ **Risk:** Property at the motel. Your Homeowners policy covers this property up to the contents policy limit for up to 30 days. Beyond 30 days, coverage drops to 10 percent of the policy limit on contents.

Recommendation: You don't need to make special insurance arrangements at the motel if you're okay with the 10 percent limit after 30 days. If you're not, ask your agent to negotiate on extension for the time you need. Or, if that fails, buy renter's insurance. (Since Bill and Hillary's motel was fully furnished, even with dishes, the 10 percent limit after 30 days was no problem for them — they had very little personal property at the motel.)

✔ **Risk:** Damage to the $40,000 rental truck. In the rental contract you sign, you're liable for anything — even storm damage. Coverage is available from the rental agency, but it's expensive.

Recommendation: Decline coverage from the rental agency, if you have both Collision and Comprehensive coverage on at least one of your cars. The coverage will transfer to the truck. If you don't have the coverage, either have your agent add the coverages to your car insurance policy or buy the coverage from the rental agency.

✔ **Risk:** Liability when operating the rental truck for injuries and property damage to the public.

Recommendation: No additional coverage is necessary. Personal Auto insurance fully covers this risk up to your policy limit. (It may be a good time, though, to reevaluate your auto liability limits. Should they be increased? Or is it time to buy a Personal Umbrella policy?)

Whenever you're between homes and having to make temporary living and storage arrangements, you need personal property and liability coverage at multiple locations. Do not cancel the Homeowners policy on the property you are moving from until coverage at the new, permanent location begins. That way, the contents and liability coverage from the Homeowners policy will continue to cover your needs while you're in transition.

Hiring a moving company

A fairly common twist to the previous moving example occurs when, instead of doing all the moving yourself, you hire a moving and storage company to move your stuff to their warehouse, store it for you, and then move it again to the new home. Aren't the movers liable for anything that happens? Including breakage, damage, and even water damage in storage?

It depends. (Don't you just love an answer like that?) If you don't make special arrangements, the fine print in your moving contract limits the moving company's liability for damage to your stuff to a fraction of its value, typically 50 cents per pound! (For your $2,000 large screen TV that weighs 80 pounds, they would owe you only 80 pounds x $.50 = $40.) The contract usually also exempts the movers from damage they didn't cause, such as flood damage to the property in storage.

Beware of moving contracts. They are usually very anticonsumer. Read them carefully, or have your agent read them, so that you know what you're responsible for before a claim happens. "But," you protest, "the moving company insures the full value of my property if I pay them a little extra." True — but still not for every kind of loss. Many still exclude acts of God or ground water. And they usually won't cover breakage unless you pay them to do the packing.

Before buying the optional insurance from the moving company, fax a copy of the coverage to your agent or attorney to make sure that there aren't any nasty surprises. I still prefer adding the Special Perils contents endorsement to your Homeowners policy. It's less expensive then the moving company's optional insurance and usually is far better coverage, except for excluding breakage of dishes, china, and the like. If you want these items covered, get the mover's insurance.

Adding a Teenage Driver

When your teenager is nearing driving age and is begging for a driver's license, remember the three people your decision will impact. If you consider all three, you should be fine:

✔ The life and health of your child. Inexperienced and immature drivers cause four times more accidents than the general population, which makes your child more vulnerable to serious injuries or death.

✔ The risk to your personal assets from your child's mistakes behind the wheel, leading to lawsuits against you.

✔ The life and health of others injured by your child's mistakes.

The bottom line is to take seriously your responsibility to make sure that your child is mature and responsible before cutting Junior loose. Reaching age 16 should not automatically entitle someone to a driver's license. Here's a three-point plan that helps you significantly reduce the risks associated with your new driver:

✔ In addition to the handful of hours your teen receives in drivers' training, require at least 40 hours of supervised practice with a learner's permit, under all different driving conditions.

✔ Implement a tier plan of driving privileges, like so many states have already mandated, such as allowing no more than one or two passengers, a 10 p.m. curfew, and no freeway driving until your son or daughter has one consecutive year with no tickets or accidents. Only then would your child have full driving privileges. (The tier system gives your child an incentive to drive more carefully.)

✔ Have a mutually signed agreement where you and your child agree not to drink and drive and where your child can call you anytime for a ride, hassle-free, if her driver has been drinking. I recommend the contract from SADD (Students Against Driving Drunk, a.k.a. Students Against Destructive Decisions). The contract is very loving and nonthreatening. You can get a copy online at www.saddonline.com. I also like the SADD contract because it forces you and your child into a dialogue about some important issues.

Sending a Child to College

Here's a quick list of tips to help manage the insurance risks of sending a son or daughter to college:

✔ **Health insurance:** Do buy the optional student health coverage if it's inexpensive. It enables your college student to access convenient care at the student health center. Let's face it: The more convenient care is, the more likely he'll get the care he needs right away. Don't rely on student health insurance exclusively. It's usually not that strong. Continue major medical coverage on your child as well, for the big stuff.

✔ **Car insurance:** Most insurance companies give a 10 to 25 percent discount for a B average or better, and another 30 to 40 percent (or more) discount if the student is attending college over 100 miles from home and has no car at school. Ask for the Good Student and Distant Student discounts. (*Note:* You can eliminate all charges for your student while at school if he surrenders his driver's license. Just get a receipt and send it to your agent. This idea is especially good if your child has recent tickets or accidents that are driving your insurance rates sky high.)

✔ **Personal property:** Most Homeowners policies do extend your Homeowners contents coverage to your child's belongings at school. Most policies stop coverage after 45 days of unoccupancy (meaning your son or daughter can't leave the stuff unattended for the summer and still have it covered by insurance.) If he isn't spending the summer at school, bring the stuff home or store it. *Note:* If your student has expensive valuables or an expensive laptop computer, those items can be scheduled on your Homeowners policy for the best possible insurance — covering everything from breakage to sodas spilled down the hard drive.

✔ **Your liability for their apartment:** Many college students, especially after a year or two, opt for an apartment off-campus rather than a dorm.

Do not cosign a lease to help your student qualify for the apartment. Sign a rent guarantee instead that guarantees you'll make the rent payment if your student doesn't. Being a cosigner makes you potentially sueable for everything that goes on in that apartment (like serious injuries at college parties).

If you've already made the mistake of cosigning the lease for your college student's apartment, buy some liability coverage for yourself. Adding the apartment to your Homeowners and umbrella liability policies should only cost about $20 a year.

Divorcing

Ending a marriage is tough enough without the additional stress of insurance disputes. Here's my advice to help you minimize problems.

Before the divorce

Because the divorce process takes a long time (sometimes a very long time), spouses often live separately while still being legally married.

Car insurance

As soon as you both agree to start divorce proceedings, separate your cars onto separate policies. Still list both names, but your name should be first and use your address so that the policy and bills are mailed to you. This strategy gives you the best possible coverage and it keeps you from being victimized if your spouse (intentionally or unintentionally) fails to pay the premium.

Home insurance

In a separation, usually one of the parties moves out of the home and rents an apartment. The primary Homeowners policy provides no theft coverage and no liability coverage at the apartment.

Rear-ended and blindsided

Cassandra called me one day to report that she was in a serious car accident. She was rear-ended. Her medical bills ended up totaling over $40,000, and she lost about a year from work. She had, much to her surprise and anger, no car insurance to cover the accident. Why? About a year earlier, she and her husband separated and filed for a divorce. Her husband insured only his car and never told her that she wasn't covered, even though he had verbally agreed to continue insuring both cars.

Cassandra was unnecessarily victimized. Had she followed the advice here and split up the insurance as soon as they separated, her own Personal Auto policy would have covered her injuries and lost wages. Luckily, her health insurance covered her medical bills. But the rest of her loss was out-of-pocket.

At the very least, get liability coverage for injuries and property damage at the apartment. The least expensive way to do that is by a policy endorsement added to the primary Homeowners policy (and umbrella policy if you have one), at a cost of about $15 a year. If theft is a concern, then buy a renter's Homeowners policy (normally referred to as just a *renters* policy) covering the apartment — in both names until the divorce is final. Costs for these policies start at $100 a year and up.

In a separation and pending the divorce, don't remove the person who moved out from the Homeowners insurance, even if the insurance company requests it. Both parties must remain as co-named insureds on the face sheet of the policy. Why? Because until the divorce is final, both parties still equally own the home. Both have an interest in the house if it is damaged or destroyed. And both need worldwide personal liability coverage.

When the divorce is final

If you haven't already split up the car insurance, do so now. Do not remove either spouse from the Homeowners policy until the deed has been changed and the other spouse has established their own Homeowners or renters policy.

Health insurance

If either spouse has been covered under the other's group policy, that spouse will lose his or her coverage when the divorce is final. If you're the one losing coverage, I recommend:

- ✔ If you have group coverage available on your job, request coverage from your employer right away, to start the date your coverage ends under your ex's policy. If you do so within 30 days of the divorce, you're usually guaranteed coverage without having to qualify medically.

- ✔ If you don't have coverage available through your job, exercise your COBRA right to continue coverage under your ex's group policy (if you're eligible) while applying for your own individual health policy. (See Chapter 15 for more information on COBRA and HIPAA rights.)

- ✔ If you're turned down for individual coverage, continue the COBRA coverage from your ex's employer for as long as COBRA allows (usually up to 36 months after the divorce).

Life insurance

Make sure that you're the owner of your policies. Have the billing address changed to your address. And change the beneficiaries from your ex-spouse to your children or another person. Reevaluate your life insurance needs. You may need less. Or, if you're a single parent, you may need substantially more. (See Chapter 18 for a guide to estimating your life insurance needs.)

Disability insurance

If you declined this coverage in the past because your spouse's income more than covered the bills, I recommend you now buy it. If your paycheck stops from a disability, you'll be hurting if you don't have this vital coverage. (See Chapter 17 for tips on buying long-term disability insurance.)

Retiring

When retiring, you need to address some specific and unique insurance issues. Changing the use of your car to pleasure use will save you about 15 to 20 percent on your car insurance. Make sure you're getting any senior discounts offered.

If you qualify under the federal COBRA law, exercise your right to continue your health insurance through your previous employer for up to 36 months. If you (or your spouse) are less than 62 years old (or if you are not eligible for COBRA), apply for guaranteed individual coverage under federal HIPAA laws for you and/or your spouse, and keep it until you're both 65 years old and qualify for Medicare. If you're between 62 and 65 years old and do qualify for COBRA, ride the COBRA continuation until you qualify for Medicare. If you're 65 or older, apply for both Part A and Part B of Medicare. Also apply for a good Medicare supplement policy to plug the many shortcomings of Medicare.

If you apply for a Medicare supplement policy within six months of turning 65 or losing your group coverage, whichever is later, there are no health questions. Coverage is guaranteed. See Chapter 16 for information on buying a good Medicare supplement and Chapter 15 for more on your COBRA and HIPAA rights.

Reassess your needs relative to life insurance. With less income, you may need less life insurance. If you still need life insurance and your health is poor, consider converting the group life insurance on the job to a permanent, personally-owned policy. Most group life insurance policies give you that option if you apply within 30 days of retirement.

Transferring Property Ownership to Trusts

Attorneys are increasingly recommending to their older clients that they transfer ownership of their home (and sometimes their personal property such as cars and boats) to a trust or to their adult children — usually for tax reasons. Although these transfers may save on taxes, they result in some serious insurance gaps if changes aren't made to the insurance program of the new owner to cover the ownership change.

For example, Betty, age 68, follows her attorney's advice and transfers ownership of her $400,000 home and all its contents to a trust, with a provision that gives Betty the right to continue to live in the house for as long as she wants. If Betty has a $400,000 Homeowners policy on the house and a tornado destroys it, how much will the policy pay Betty? Not much. She's no longer the owner. And the trust has lost a $400,000 asset because the trust had no insurance on the home. Betty's policy wouldn't pay the trust because the trust isn't named on the policy.

If you transfer ownership of your home to anyone else — to a trust or to one or more of your adult children — you no longer can collect under your policy as the owner. And the new owners cannot collect under your policy either. You must make some changes to your Homeowners insurance at the moment ownership is transferred, covering the new owner's ownership interest.

The former owner of the property should co-name the new owner — the trust or the adult children — on the coverage summary page of the policy. In insurance lingo, they need to be *co-named insureds*. The old and new owners are equally protected against damage if they're both named. And, as a bonus, the old and new owners are also equally protected for lawsuits. List any trust as a co-named insured on the umbrella liability policy as well.

If adult children, rather than a trust, receive the property, I recommend, in addition to being a co-named insured on the parent's policy, that the adult children extend their home and umbrella liability policies to the new location. This extension should cost about $20 a year.

Dying

One of the greatest acts of love is buying more life insurance than your survivors will need. And make sure they know about it, as well as where you keep the policies. One of the saddest things I see survivors go through after a loved one dies is the hunt for the life insurance policies. If they can't be found, they will never be collected on. Even if they eventually are found, searching for them is an unnecessary and traumatic experience for the survivors.

Make a list of every life insurance policy you have, make several copies of the list, and give the copies to two or more people. Include on the list the insurance company name and address, policy number, effective date, the death benefit amount, the beneficiary, and the agent's name and phone number. And include the location of the original policies.

Here's a checklist for the survivors:

✔ Gather the original life policies (or the inventory form, if you have one). Request the insurance companies to fax or mail you their claim form. Have certified copies of the death certificate and copies of the newspaper obituary to file with each claim form.

✔ Don't take the deceased off any insurance policy, including the Personal Umbrella policy, until the deceased's ownership interests have been properly transferred. Otherwise the estate is exposed, with no insurance.

✔ If a vehicle is involved, notify the auto insurance company of any new drivers.

✔ If you've been covered as a family member under the deceased's group health insurance policy, you may have the right to continue coverage for up to 36 months under COBRA. You also are guaranteed the right, under federal HIPAA law, to apply for and receive an individual policy. If you're in good health, apply for an individual health policy.

✔ If the deceased had disability insurance, cancel it. There may be a refund due you on prepaid premiums.

Chapter 20

Ten Ingredients for a Watertight Insurance Program

In This Chapter

▶ Avoiding inconsistencies in life and health insurance

▶ Plugging gaps in property and liability insurance

▶ Selecting the best agent and insurance company

I've audited over 2,000 insurance programs. Almost every one had at least one major coverage gap. The majority had from five to ten coverage gaps. The gaps generally fell into one of three areas:

✔ Inadequate coverage limits

✔ Inconsistent coverage

✔ Uninsured exposures

Inadequate coverage limits occur, for example, when a middle-class individual carries the most commonly sold auto liability limit in America — $100,000 per person. That's $100,000 you can use to pay for a human life you take in a car accident. It may have to cover unlimited medical bills, lost wages, and pain and suffering. Adequate automobile liability coverage today is $1 million or more — and the extra cost to have $1 million of coverage is often only about $200 a year. See Chapter 3 on car insurance and Chapter 10 on umbrella policies for more information.

Inconsistent coverage happens when one or more of the five major loss areas is out of balance. The five major loss areas are major lawsuits, destruction of home and personal property, premature death, long-term disability, and major medical bills. Common examples of inconsistent coverage include

✔ Inconsistent liability limits such as $100,000 for automobile, $300,000 for home and personal, and $50,000 for boat. Uneven coverage makes no sense because these limits are protecting the same income and the same assets. If you're going to get sued, you want the same amount of money available to protect you no matter where the lawsuit comes from.

> ✔ Three or four major areas are often well covered and one is either uncovered or minimally covered — such as having $1 million liability limits and no life insurance, or a superb life insurance plan but no disability insurance.

Uninsured exposures are almost always unintentional, arising out of either indifference when buying insurance or a belief that insurance policies are more comprehensive than they really are. Sometimes uninsured exposures are the result of picking an inexperienced or sloppy agent.

Sadly, virtually all these gaps can be plugged for a minimal amount of money. Here are ten general tips that, if you follow them, will go a long way toward helping you avoid major gaps in your insurance program.

Selecting the Best Agent You Can Find

A good agent is the main ingredient in a watertight insurance program. In fact, if you hire an expert, you'll barely have to worry about the other nine ingredients for a watertight program.

Insurance is bought and sold as if it were a commodity — a single page that says, "If you have a loss, we'll cover it." But pull out any insurance policy. What do you see? A 20-page legal contract packed with good coverage, but also packed with exclusions and limitations. Some of those exclusions and limitations exclude or limit coverage for risks in your own life — important risks that, if they happen, would hurt you financially, and sometimes seriously. Yet almost all the exclusions and limitations in a normal insurance policy can be deleted or minimized with available supplemental policy endorsements — most of which are inexpensive.

A top agent is a great bargain in at least five significant ways:

> ✔ She has the expertise and tools to help you choose adequate coverage limits in each major loss area.

> ✔ She helps you keep your coverage in those major loss areas balanced and helps you avoid inconsistent coverage.

> ✔ She takes the time to probe into your life deeply enough to identify those risks that your current insurance policies exclude. She then applies her expertise to help you properly plug your policies with the supplemental coverages you need to fill those gaps. A really great agent helps you change your coverages as the risks in your life change.

> ✔ When you have a claim, she does more than just file a report for you. She applies her coverage expertise to coach you on how to properly document your claim so you get paid all that you're owed with the least amount of delay or hassle.

✔ If your claim is unjustly denied or underpaid, she cares enough and has enough coverage expertise to get the claims department to reverse its position and pay you everything you rightfully deserve.

If your agent isn't as good as the agent I just described, you can and must do better. The consequences of having the wrong agent can be severe! Getting more talent generally doesn't cost you a dime. In most states, agents get paid the same commission, from the very best agent to the very worst agent. So spend your money wisely!

Don't buy insurance without the very best agent you can find! See Chapter 12 for more information on finding a top agent.

Covering All Your Natural Disaster Exposures

Floods. Earthquakes. Mudslides. Tornadoes. Hurricanes. In Minnesota, we worry about tornadoes and floods, but few of us lose sleep over a possible earthquake. Californians worry about earthquake and mudslides. Floridians sweat bullets about hurricanes. Paying attention to these weather risks is an important ingredient in a great insurance program. They have the potential to destroy your home and they're often excluded from Homeowners insurance coverage.

Virtually all Homeowners policies, for example, exclude coverage for any kind of water damage at or below ground level — flood, seepage, sewer backup. Almost all of them also exclude any kind of coverage for earth movement, including earthquakes and mudslides. And Homeowners policies on coastline properties exposed to hurricanes often exclude or limit hurricane coverage.

If you live in an area where you're exposed to a weather-related risk and you haven't addressed the issue in your insurance, your insurance program has a serious leak. Here's where you can find the patches to seal your leaks and make your program watertight:

✔ Earthquake, sump pump failure, and sewer backup coverages are usually available for an extra charge from your Homeowners insurance company as a Homeowners policy endorsement.

✔ Flood insurance from the federal government is available from almost any insurance agent. Good information on the coverage is available online at www.fema.gov/nfip.

> ✔ Hurricane coverage on coastal property is available from your state windstorm insurance pool. Your agent can help you arrange the coverage. To locate your state's pool, either call your state insurance department or access its Web site via a link on the National Association of Insurance Commissioners' Web site (www.naic.com).

You can find more information on insurance-related Web sites in Chapter 21.

Adding a Home Replacement Guarantee

One of the major losses you want to have well insured is the destruction of your home. The big risk when you buy Homeowners insurance is that you didn't buy enough structure coverage to rebuild your home if it's destroyed. You and your agent, in good faith, try to establish the replacement value of your home, but pinpointing that value is almost impossible. And you certainly don't want to grossly overinsure your home and pay way too much for your insurance. What's the solution?

The insurance industry offers a good solution for this dilemma. It's called the *Home Replacement Guarantee* (or something similar to that, depending on the company). If your home is destroyed, this optional coverage guarantees that the policy will pay the entire cost to rebuild, even if the cost far exceeds the amount for which the home was insured. The typical cost for this great coverage is only $5 to $10 a year.

This option has proven to be especially valuable for putting together a watertight insurance program for older homes, where estimating the cost new is so difficult. The Home Replacement Guarantee is also great for residents of hurricane-prone areas, where the demand for labor and materials far exceeds the supply after a storm has leveled the area and replacement costs go through the roof. After Hurricane Andrew, this endorsement resulted in insurance companies paying as much as twice the insured replacement cost of a home — something the insurance companies never anticipated. But what a godsend for those beleaguered homeowners who suffered so much.

You need to avoid two pitfalls when buying this guarantee:

> ✔ Avoid any insurer that offers only a watered-down version of this endorsement, where they put a ceiling on the coverage, such as 125 percent of your dwelling coverage. Especially if you live in a storm area or have an older home, the replacement cost may exceed the ceiling. Many insurers offer this coverage without a ceiling.

> ✔ If you have an older home, avoid insurance companies that don't offer this guarantee. Many insurance companies willingly make the Home Replacement Guarantee available to owners of older homes.

Always buy a Home Replacement Guarantee when insuring a dwelling.

Standardizing Your Liability Limits

When you buy automobile, Homeowners, boat, snowmobile, or any other liability policy, always buy the same liability insurance limit. No exceptions.

People make this mistake a lot, especially when they have their insurance coverage split between different agents and/or insurance companies. You can reduce the chances of this happening by having as much of your liability insurance as possible with the same agent.

Whenever you cause an injury or property damage, you want the same amount of money available to you for legal costs and judgments no matter what the cause of the accident. In the same way that you wouldn't buy more liability insurance for claims that occur on Monday, Tuesday, and Wednesday than the rest of the week, don't buy different liability limits for different policies.

If you have an umbrella policy, make sure that all the underlying liability insurance limits meet the minimum requirements of the umbrella policy. If they don't, you'll owe the difference.

Identifying and Plugging Liability Gaps

Plugging liability gaps is an area where having a highly-skilled agent pays big dividends. You want an agent who can identify risks you're exposed to that basic auto, home, and other personal policies don't cover. An agent who, for example, knows that the following lawsuits are not automatically covered but knows how to get them covered — usually very inexpensively:

- When making a delivery to your home office, a delivery person slips and falls on your icy sidewalk and is injured.
- The roofer you hire injures his back falling off a ladder and sues you for Workers' Compensation benefits.
- You injure a coworker when you drive the company car through a stop sign.
- A guest of yours is injured while vacationing with you at your timeshare condominium in Colorado.
- A person is injured in the boat you rented while on vacation in a northern Minnesota resort.

For more information and tips on plugging liability insurance gaps, see Chapter 3 on car insurance liability coverage and Chapter 5 on Homeowners liability coverage.

Choosing the Right Umbrella Policy

If you do buy an umbrella policy (and I strongly recommend that you do), don't just buy the policy that comes from the insurance company that provides your personal auto and Homeowners insurance. Umbrella policies are not standardized. For about the same money as a poor policy, you can get a top-of-the-line policy that covers most of the unique liability risks in your life.

Here are just a few examples of risks that would be covered by a good umbrella and not covered by a poor one:

- Renting a car outside the United States and Canada
- Renting a barn for a 50th birthday party
- Serving on the board of directors for your favorite charity
- Renting a boat on vacation

A top agent with expertise in the differences between umbrella policies can play a significant role in helping you buy the umbrella policy that best covers the unique liability exposures in your life. See Chapter 10 for general information on umbrella policies and Chapter 11 for tips on helping you buy the best umbrella for your needs.

Buying More Life Insurance than You Think You Need

This recommendation has two parts. The first is to buy life insurance. The second is to buy more than you think you'll need. Or, more appropriately, more than you think your survivors will need. A lot more — 25 to 50 percent more. Especially if you have a young family and/or especially if you're buying low-cost term life insurance. It's cheap stuff. You can afford to be extra generous.

For tips on how to determine how much life insurance you need, the best type of policy to meet your needs, and the best place to buy it, see Chapter 18.

Protecting Yourself from Long-Term Disability

By far, the most overlooked and undersold major loss coverage is long-term disability insurance. Almost everyone has some life insurance, but only a small percentage of people have long-term disability insurance unless it's provided by their employer. This, in spite of the fact that the odds of having a long-term disability are considerably greater than the odds of dying prior to age 65, and in spite of the fact that the family's living expenses during a disability are considerably higher than those following a death.

Unless you're one of the few people who have enough outside income to meet all your living expenses in the event of an illness or injury that would prevent you from working, buy long-term disability insurance. And don't necessarily rely on group disability insurance from your employer. Sometimes it's good, and sometimes it's not. For help determining your need for disability insurance, see Chapter 17 on long-term disability.

Buying Major Medical Insurance with a Stop/Loss

For a watertight insurance program, buy health insurance. Buy it with a limit of at least $1 million or $2 million. And if it contains copayment requirements, make sure that there's an annual out-of-pocket maximum on the copayments. If you're age 65 or over, don't rely exclusively on Medicare. Buy a quality Medicare supplement policy. For tips on what makes a great major medical health insurance policy and/or a great Medicare supplement policy, see Chapter 16 on health insurance.

Choosing a Strong Insurance Company

If you're working with a top insurance agent, you won't need to spend a lot of time checking out the insurance company or companies he recommends. But if you're buying insurance direct without an agent, have low confidence in your current agent, or simply want to be extra careful, go to www.ambest.com/ratings. The A. M. Best company is an independent organization that has been rating insurance companies for over 100 years and has an excellent reputation. Generally, stay with insurance companies rated A or better. Go to Chapter 21 for more information about this Web site and tips on using it.

An equally good Web site for evaluating insurance companies is www.insure. com. It's the best insurance Web site I have ever run across. See Chapter 21 for more information on this site as well. It offers access to Standard & Poor's ratings of insurance companies, as well as information on customer complaints for the states that keep those records.

If you take the time to locate an agent with great expertise and address the other issues presented here, you'll have such a watertight insurance program that you'll have to open some windows so you don't asphyxiate!

Chapter 21

Ten Online Insurance Resources

*B*eing that this is the 21st century, the publishers asked me to search the Internet and identify ten useful insurance Web sites.

What sounded like a lot of fun turned out to be a lot of work. Have you ever read an insurance policy? I think most of the Web sites that the insurance industry has developed were written by the same people who write insurance policies. The sites are very dry (in most cases) and definitely for insurance professionals — not consumers. But after much digging, I did find ten reasonably good sites. One of the sites is outstanding — as good as a Web site on insurance can possibly be. Almost everything you need to know regarding insurance is accessible on the site. Hats off and a gold star to the top insurance site on the Web — www.insure.com.

Discovering the Consumer Insurance Guide

The flat-out best insurance Web site out there is www.insure.com. Otherwise known as *The Consumer Insurance Guide,* this site is only a few years old but has a wealth of useful, consumer-friendly information. It's completely free to consumers, paid for solely by site advertising. Here are just some of the things that make this site exceptional:

✔ A glossary of insurance terms if you need help with any definitions.

✔ A newsletter that covers changes in the insurance industry and gives tips on buying different types of insurance. You can even have the newsletter e-mailed to you on a regular basis at no charge. The newsletters come to you as a list of headlines; you pick the topic you're interested in to get more information.

✔ An Insurance Company Guide that lists not only all the insurance companies doing business in your state, but also their Standard and Poor's financial strength rating. You even have the option of screening out companies whose financial ratings are less than you would be comfortable with. If you already know the company you prefer to do business with, simply enter the name of that company into the guide to get a full financial report.

✔ If you live in a state where the insurance department keeps track of complaints, this site has a Complaint Finder where you can find out how well the insurance company you're considering treats its current customers.

✔ The best links of any site to other helpful consumer sites of all kinds.

✔ An outstanding site search engine where you can get information and news on just about any insurance subject. (For example, enter "Long Term Care," and you get a list of articles, expert advice, and even a consumer shopping guide.)

Bookmark this site! And get on its e-mail newsletter list if you want to keep current with insurance developments and get great tips.

Finding Help from the Feds

You won't believe this, but the next three most useful Web sites for consumers are maintained by . . . the federal government! It must have brought in some new people, because the folks who write these pages are definitely not the same people who wrote the Internal Revenue Service tax code or tax forms that you laboriously fill out every year. Congratulations are in order for the people responsible for the sites for the Federal Flood program, the Federal Social Security program, and the Medicare program.

Discovering your Social Security benefits

The Web site from the Social Security folks is the first of three excellent Web sites from the feds. The site is clear and easy to use with great information.

At www.ssa.gov (click on Top 10 Services and then on Request a Social Security Statement), you can order a paper copy of your Social Security statement that pretty accurately tells the estimated survivor benefits to your children if you die, your disability benefits if you suffer a long-term disability, and your current retirement benefits.

If a rough estimate of your Social Security benefits is all you need, you can get pretty accurate estimates online without having to order a statement. From the Top 10 Services menu, choose Compute Your Benefit Estimate.

Another thing I like about this site is that you can access a lot of the consumer pamphlets published by the government. For example, I particularly like the brochure on Social Security disability coverage and how it works. To see this pamphlet for yourself, go to www.ssa.gov/pubs/10029.html, or, at the home page, choose Disability from the Electronic Publications menu, and then choose publication 05-10029. While this particular pamphlet's great, I recommend that you poke around and see what else interests you.

To make your poking a lot easier, this site also includes a useful search engine to help you locate almost any topic related to Social Security. As you can imagine, the search engine has to be able to access a ton of information.

The site even has something fun! Soon-to-be parents looking for a name for their baby can click on Top 10 Services and enter the database of the most popular names since 1880. (In the 1990s, Michael was tops for boys and Ashley was tops for girls.)

Comparing Medicare supplement policies

The Medicare site www.medicare.gov isn't quite as easy to use as the Social Security site, but it is a well-done site nonetheless. I chose this site because it includes a nice chart showing the coverage differences between Plans A through J — the ten Medicare supplement plans that must be offered in all states but Minnesota, Wisconsin, and Massachusetts. (Access directly at www.medicare.gov/mgcompare/TenStandardPlans.asp, or indirectly from the Medicare home page — click on Medigap Compare, then "standardized Medigap plans," and then "view standardized plans for [your state]."

Medicare coverage does have some good-sized shortcomings, so the chart showing coverage differences is especially helpful. Most Medicare recipients need a supplement. See Chapter 16 for the most important criteria of a good Medicare supplement policy.

The only plans that meet the criteria recommended in Chapter 16 are Plans I and J. If you don't feel that you need prescription drug coverage, Plans F and G are good choices as well. Finally, if you want to access a well-written summary of Medicare coverages A and B, select Medicare Basics on the home page, and then click on "What do Medicare Parts A and Part B cover?"

Accessing flood insurance information

Here's the third of Uncle Sam's three good Web sites for consumers — `www.fema.gov/nfip` — click on Information for Consumers from the menu on the left. This site was designed specifically for consumers by the National Flood Insurance Program. Considering that flood insurance is one of the most difficult policies to understand and to buy, the people who designed this site did a great job.

If you're in a community that participates in the National Flood Insurance Program, your home, apartment, or condominium is probably eligible for flood insurance.

Some of the better pages on this site are about

- Coverage information — what is and is not covered
- Cost of flood insurance, including examples
- Eligibility for the newer Preferred Risk flood policy, which has a low minimum premium of only $106 a year
- The different sources from which you can buy flood insurance (see Chapter 7 for details and recommendations regarding flood insurance)

Estimating Your Life Insurance Needs

From Quicken, designers of one of the better financial Web sites out there, comes an excellent insurance site. It helps you estimate your life insurance needs. The Web site's calculations consider things like interest rates, Social Security, inflation, college costs, and final expenses, even supplemental retirement dollars for the surviving spouse. I tried using the tool to estimate my own needs and thought it hit all the bases.

To access this life insurance estimator, go to `www.quicken.com`, click on the Insurance tab, and then click on Family Needs Planner. Input at the prompts your age, income, college preferences, mortgages and other debts, ages of your children, and so on.

I looked at several Web-based life insurance needs estimators and found this one to be the best. It's also one of the easiest to use. One of the things I like about this site that it doesn't just give you a total value for the life insurance that you need. It breaks the total down into components, such as final expenses, pre-retirement income, post-retirement income, and so on. Because it breaks down the total, you can see how the estimator arrived at its recommendation for how much life insurance you need. Also, if you made a mistake entering data, you can often catch your mistake by looking at the components. Seeing the components also helps you if you're on a tight budget: You can buy a certain amount of insurance now, enough to cover your pre-retirement needs, for example, and defer buying the rest of the insurance until later.

Estimating Your Home Replacement Cost

The site I recommend for estimating your home replacement cost, www. boeckhvalue.com, is not particularly consumer-friendly. And it costs $5 to use, which the Web site collects up front before you can enter the site. But it has two major advantages over its competitors.

- ✔ It's from the Boeckh Company, the provider of the home replacement cost estimator that the insurance industry uses to determine the replacement cost of your house at claim time.

- ✔ It's, hands down, the most thorough tool I've ever seen available for consumers to estimate home replacement cost. It takes a good hour to work your way through the site, but the resulting reports are outstanding.

Before you log in, have the exact ground-floor square footage of your home, as well as the square footage for decks, porches, finished basements, and so on. (You can measure the area or get the numbers from your Realtor, a real estate listing, or the bank appraisal done for your home loan.)

The site is not easy to use, but it has a "?" at the bottom of each screen that you can click on for more information. Use the "?" button liberally and go slowly. You want accurate results.

Determining the replacement cost of your home is very important. See Chapter 5 for more information.

If you use the Boeckh Web site to estimate the replacement cost of your home, you gain four advantages:

- ✔ You get an extremely thorough and accurate estimate — something that would cost you up to $300 if done by an appraiser.

- ✔ You have a tool to keep your insurance company from overcharging you by overinsuring your home.

- ✔ You avoid underinsuring your home, which helps you avoid severe penalties at claim time for both partial and total losses.

- ✔ You have a strong leg to stand on in the event of a serious structural loss from a fire, a windstorm, and so on if an adjuster tries to add depreciation penalties for underinsurance. You will have used a more thorough estimator than even the adjuster uses, and one from the same credible source.

Researching an Insurer's Quality

A handful of independent organizations out there analyze and rate insurance companies based on their strength and overall quality. I chose the A. M. Best site to recommend because A. M. Best has been rating insurance companies longer than anyone — over 100 years — and probably has the best reputation in the insurance industry.

Go to www.ambest.com and click on either Ratings Search or Company Reports. Enter the name of the company you want to investigate, and presto — up comes a list of companies with names similar to the one you're searching for. Just click on the name of the particular company you're interested in and up pops the Best rating. If you don't know the exact name of the company you're looking for, just type in what you do know and scroll through the list to track it down.

If you're checking one of the larger insurance companies, such as State Farm or Allstate, you'll usually see a list of anywhere from five to as many as 20 different companies with that name. I recommend that you look for the choice that includes the word *group* in the title (for example, "Allstate insurance group"). You'll get the A. M. Best rating given to the entire group of companies as a whole — that's the rating I use in evaluating companies.

The ratings go from A++ to F (just like in school). Click on Rating Definitions on the home page for more details. Check out Table 21-1 for a list of insurance company ratings.

Table 21-1	Insurance Company Ratings	
Rating	*Interpretation*	*Best's Opinion*
A++, A+	Superior	Secure
A, A-	Excellent	Secure
B++, B+	Very good	Secure
B and below	Fair or worse	Vulnerable

If you want more than just a company's rating, you can get an overview of the company by clicking on Best's Insurer Profile. You'll find the information very helpful.

Best's site has all insurance companies rated B+ or better as "secure" (as in safe to do business with) and lists all insurers rated B and below as "vulnerable" (or risky to do business with). I don't do business with a company that's rated B or below. To be safe, you shouldn't either. As much as possible, try to stay with companies rated A or better.

Getting Help from Your State Insurance Department

The insurance industry is regulated primarily by states rather than the federal government. As a result, all states have enforcement divisions whose purpose is to assist consumers in dealing with problems they're having with their insurance companies — anywhere from getting claims paid properly to reversing illegal coverage cancellations. Many state offices also offer supplemental services.

The site www.naic.org/1regulator/usamap.htm, from the National Association of Insurance Commissioners, presents you with a map of the United States and its territories. Simply click on your state or your state's name to access your state insurance department's Web site. Then locate from the menu the area devoted to consumers — which is usually packed with helpful information, including how to file a complaint. (If you can't access this site directly, go to www.naic.org; then click on Consumer Information and then The Insurance Regulator's Map.)

Insurance company employees are just as human as other professionals (surprise, surprise). They occasionally make mistakes, and they sometimes won't bend on an unreasonable or illegal position they've taken. Your tax dollars pay for the enforcement people in your state to help you resolve problems — to your satisfaction, in most cases.

When you're at the site for your state's insurance department, look for other helpful information, such as

- Tips on buying every type of insurance policy sold in the state

- *Complaint ratios* for every insurer (the number of complaints divided by the number of policies sold) to see whether the insurance company you're considering treats its customers well

- Information on state and federal insurance programs (Medicare, Flood, COBRA, State Assigned Risk Health Insurance Pools, and so on)

The NAIC site is not at all consumer friendly. But the locator is useful and easy to use. It does what it's supposed to do.

Accessing Insurance Tips

One of the functions of the Insurance Information Institute (III), created and supported by the insurance industry, is to help consumers. The III accomplishes its goal in two ways. First, it sponsors the National Insurance

Consumer Helpline (800-942-4242). About 50,000 people a year call the helpline with insurance problems.

Most of this information is accessible from the Web site www.iii.org/individuals. To access the information, just click on the icons for home, auto, business, or "all the other stuff." Then pick your title. This site is neither consumer friendly nor easy to use.

Finding a CPCU Agent

In Chapter 12, I recommend taking the time to find an agent with a lot of insurance expertise to help you properly design your insurance coverage. The experts get paid the same commission as the nonexperts, so you may as well have an expert. One of several ways to find such an agent is to find someone who has earned the most difficult of all insurance designations — the CPCU designation.

To locate a CPCU agent in your area, go to the CPCU Web site (www.cpcusociety.org/consumer) and click on Agent/Broker Locator on the left. The site allows you to search for a CPCU by city, state, or insurance company. I recommend that you search by state only. If you search by city, this site gives you agents only in the metropolitan area; it doesn't give you agents in nearby suburbs or other surrounding areas. And if you search by insurance company, such as State Farm, the site gives you all State Farm agents with CPCUs nationwide. It does not give you the opportunity to find a State Farm agent in your particular state who has a CPCU.

Appendix

. . . .

Personal Umbrella Gap Checklist

Gap Description	What Coverage You Need	Remarks
Territory of coverage	Worldwide	Make sure lawsuits outside the U.S. and Canada are covered
Personal injury liability	Libel, slander, false arrest, etc.	Underlying insurance may be required. Be careful.
Coverage of newly acquired vehicles, boats, etc.	Automatic, no notice required	Poor policies require notification in 30 days or no coverage. Dangerous!
Liability assumed in contracts	Weddings, parties, rentals of all kinds	Poor policies limit coverage to residential contracts only
Punitive damages	Allowed in some states that allows them	You could travel in a state
Damage to rented or borrowed property	Cars, boats, snowmobiles, rented residences, etc. insure the item	Coverage usually won't apply if you're required to

Estimating Your Own Payback Periods

	Collision Deductible			Comprehensive Deductible		
	$250	$500	$1,000	$100	$250	$500
Annual Premiums						
Extra risk (difference)		$250	$500		$150	$250
Annual savings						
Payback period (risk diff. / savings)		___ yrs.	___ yrs.		___ yrs.	___ yrs.

Optional Umbrella Coverages

Gap Description	What You Need	Remarks
Renting boats	No length or horsepower limitation	If there is a limit, it needs to be much larger than any boat you'd ever rent
Renting snowmobiles	No engine size limit	
Renting other motorized vehicles	ATVs, go-carts, trail bikes, golf carts, etc.	No restrictions
Renting cars outside the U.S. and Canada	Worldwide	No requirement that the suit be filed in U.S. or Canada only
Renting vacation property	Worldwide	
Service on nonprofit boards	Usually limited to bodily injury & property damage only	Usually no coverage if any compensation is paid to you
Employer-furnished car	Coverage for injured coworkers	Careful. Primary coverage may be required.
Coverage to drive other cars	Only needed if you have no Personal Auto policy	
Employer's Liability	Covering your domestic help (nannies, contractors)	Requires that you have a primary policy
Incidental office	Coverage for premises — injuries — usually an optional coverage	Will require primary coverage under your Homeowners policy
Pollution liability	For fuel storage leaks and other sudden spills	Covers only sudden and accidental — no coverage for seepage
Sailboat racing	A crew member	Often excluded in primary boat coverage
Aircraft liability	Including liability for damaging the aircraft, if rented	Owned — will require a primary coverage policy (Rented — may not require primary coverage)
Excess Uninsured and Underinsured Motorist	Additional coverage for your injuries in an accident — optional coverage under some umbrella policies	Caused by drivers with less injury liability coverage than you have. Buy if it's available and reasonably priced.

Health Insurance Comparison Form

Criteria	Option A	Option B	Option C
High policy limit (at least $1 million to $2 million per claim lifetime)			
A maximum for your out-of-pocket expenses			
No internal limits on surgery, room costs, etc.			
Freedom to see specialists without a referral			
Nonemergency coverage outside your home state			
Paperless claims? (Yes/No)			
Percent of doctors in your state who are covered			
My portion of the monthly premium			
Are my current doctors covered? (Yes/No)			
Annual deductible			

Disability Need Worksheet

	The Family's Need if You're Disabled	Your Family's Need if Your Spouse is Disabled
The family's average monthly need (both columns should be the same amount)	$	$
Add current income sources (after taxes)	$	$
Subtract spouse's monthly take-home pay*	$	$
Subtract investment income that you are willing to live off (conservatively)*(after taxes)	$	$
Subtract group disability insurance proceeds* (after taxes)	$	$
Net need after taxes	$	$

*These items are taxable. The numbers here should be the net amount you'll receive after paying state and federal taxes.

Claims Information Form

Date and time of accident:	Accident location:
Injuries (gather for each):	Witnesses (gather for each):
Name:	Name:
Address:	Address:
Phone (H):	Phone (H):
Phone (W):	Phone (W):
Police department responding:	Your passengers (gather for each):
Case #:	Name:
Officer's name:	Address:
Tickets issued:	
Phone:	Phone (H):
Other:	Phone (W):
Other vehicle — owner:	Other vehicle — driver:
Name:	Name:
Address:	Address:
Phone (H):	Phone (H):
Phone (W):	Phone (W):
Driver's license #:	Driver's license #:
Other vehicle:	Driver's passengers (Gather for each):
Year, make, & model:	Name:
	Address:
Vehicle ID:	Phone (H):
License plate #:	Phone (W):
Owner's insurance company:	Driver's insurance company:
Company:	Company:
Agent Name:	Agent Name:
Phone:	Phone:
Policy #:	Policy #:

Disability Insurance Comparison

Insurance Companies	A	B	C
Monthly benefit?			
Elimination period? (30, 60, 90, or 180 days)			
Benefit period? (5 years or age 65)			
Own-occupation? (2 years, 3 years, age 65)			
Price guaranteed to age 65? (yes or no)			
*Residual included?			
*Residual covers the entire term? (yes or no)			
*Residual covers income lost due to occupation change (yes or no)			
Future purchase option? (yes or no)			
*How often offered? (annually or every 3 years)			
*Maximum dollar amount per option?			
*Lifetime maximum option?			
Cost of living adjustment rider? (yes or no)			
*Annual % increase?			
Other? (describe)			
Annual premium	$	$	$

*Critical — should be in every policy you consider

Life Insurance Inventory Form

Insurance Company Name and Address	Policy No.	Death Benefit Amount	Beneficiary	Agent Name and Phone No.	Effective Date	Location of Original Policy

Personal Property Inventory Form

	Item 1	Item 2	Item 3	Item 4
1. Property description				
2. Quantity				
3. Store purchased from				
4. Original cost new				
5. Year of purchase				
6. Age (years)				
7. Replacement cost store name				
8. Store location				
9. Phone number				
10. Expected life (years)				
11. Today's replacement cost new (each)				
12. Depreciation $				
13. Today's actual cash value (ACV)				
14. Today's ACV total (#13 × #2)				

Insurance Professional Interview Checklist

- Tell me about your insurance background and experience.
- Tell me about any insurance designations you've earned.
- Tell me about the process you use with clients to help identify risks, plug insurance gaps, and design a solid protection plan.
- I am particularly concerned about __ (for example, my home business, my art collection, my liability limits, the adequacy of my home coverage, my heirloom jewelry and silver collections, etc.). Tell me about the steps you take to deal with this type of problem.
- Tell me about the advice you give your clients when their life changes (fill in a subject here — death, divorce, household moves, marriage, etc.)
- As part of your service, do you conduct annual reviews? Tell me about that process.
- Suppose I just had a __ claim (you choose — fire, collision, burglary, stolen car, injury lawsuit). Tell me about how you would coach me.
- Tell me about two or three times a client's claim was unfairly denied or underpaid and you went to bat for them.
- What insurance companies do you represent?

Index

IDG BOOKS WORLDWIDE
BOOK REGISTRATION

Register This Book and Win!

We want to hear from you!

Visit **http://my2cents.dummies.com** to register this book and tell us how you liked it!

- Get entered in our monthly prize giveaway.

- Give us feedback about this book — tell us what you like best, what you like least, or maybe what you'd like to ask the author and us to change!

- Let us know any other *For Dummies*® topics that interest you.

Your feedback helps us determine what books to publish, tells us what coverage to add as we revise our books, and lets us know whether we're meeting your needs as a *For Dummies* reader. You're our most valuable resource, and what you have to say is important to us!

Not on the Web yet? It's easy to get started with *Dummies 101*®: *The Internet For Windows*® *98* or *The Internet For Dummies*® at local retailers everywhere.

Or let us know what you think by sending us a letter at the following address:

For Dummies Book Registration
Dummies Press
10475 Crosspoint Blvd.
Indianapolis, IN 46256

BESTSELLING
BOOK SERIES